Lecture Notes in Artificial Intelligence 12241

Subseries of Lecture Notes in Computer Science

More information about this series at http://www.springer.com/series/1244

Mufti Mahmud · Stefano Vassanelli ·
M. Shamim Kaiser · Ning Zhong (Eds.)

Brain Informatics

13th International Conference, BI 2020
Padua, Italy, September 19, 2020
Proceedings

 Springer

Editors
Mufti Mahmud (ID)
Nottingham Trent University
Nottingham, UK

Stefano Vassanelli (ID)
University of Padua
Padua, Italy

M. Shamim Kaiser (ID)
Jahangirnagar University
Dhaka, Bangladesh

Ning Zhong (ID)
Maebashi Institute of Technology
Maebashi, Japan

ISSN 0302-9743   ISSN 1611-3349   (electronic)
Lecture Notes in Artificial Intelligence
ISBN 978-3-030-59276-9   ISBN 978-3-030-59277-6   (eBook)
https://doi.org/10.1007/978-3-030-59277-6

LNCS Sublibrary: SL7 – Artificial Intelligence

This Springer imprint is published by the registered company Springer Nature Switzerland AG
The registered company address is: Gewerbestrasse 11, 6330 Cham, Switzerland

Preface

Brain Informatics (BI) is an emerging interdisciplinary research field which aims to apply informatics when studying the brain. This combines efforts from diverse related disciplines such as computing and cognitive sciences, psychology, neuroscience, artificial intelligence, etc., to study the brain and its information processing capability. From the informatics perspective, the efforts concentrate on the development of new software tools, platforms, and systems to improve our understanding of the brain, its functionality, disorders, and their possible treatments. The BI conference is a unique avenue which attracts interdisciplinary researchers, practitioners, scientists, experts, and industry representatives who are using informatics to address questions pertaining to brain and cognitive sciences including psychology and neuroscience. Therefore, BI is more than just a research field, it is rather a global research community aiming to build improved, inspiring, intelligent and transformative technologies through the use of machine learning, data science, artificial intelligence (AI), and information and communication technology (ICT) to facilitate fundamental research and innovative applications of these technologies on brain-related research. The BI conference series started with the WICI International Workshop on Web Intelligence Meets Brain Informatics, held in Beijing, China, in 2006. It was one of the early conferences which aimed at focusing informatics application to brain sciences. The subsequent editions of the conference were held in Beijing, China (2009), Toronto, Canada (2010), Lanzhou, China (2011), and Macau, China (2012). But in 2013, the conference title was changed to Brain Informatics and Health (BIH) with an emphasis on real-world applications of brain research in human health and wellbeing. BIH 2013, BIH 2014, BIH 2015, and BIH 2016 were held in Maebashi, Japan; Warsaw, Poland; London, UK; and Omaha, USA; respectively. In 2017, the conference went back to its original design and vision to investigate the brain from an informatics perspective and to promote a brain-inspired information technology revolution. Thus, the conference name was changed back to Brain Informatics (BI) in Beijing, China, in 2017. The last two editions, in 2018 and 2019 were held in Texas, USA, and Haikou, China. The 2020 edition was supposed to be held at Padova, Italy, which was not possible due to the unexpected circumstances created by the COVID-19 pandemic. This led to the organization of the 13th edition of the BI conference to be virtual.

Due to the COVID-19 pandemic, the conference was reduced to one day from the usual three days which has been practiced over the last few editions. The BI 2020 conference solicited high-quality papers and talks with panel discussions, special sessions, and workshops. However, considering the reduced conference duration, the workshops, special sessions, panel discussions, and the networking events were postponed to the future edition of the conference in 2021. Therefore, the BI 2020 online conference and was supported by the Web Intelligence Consortium (WIC), the University of Padova, the Padua Neuroscience Centre, Chinese Association for

Artificial Intelligence, the CAAI Technical Committee on Brain Science and Artificial Intelligence (CAAI-TCBSAI), and the Nottingham Trent University.

The theme of BI 2020 was "Brain Informatics in the Virtual World." The goal was to see how the world-leading BI researchers are coping with this current pandemic and still continuing to contribute to the knowledge base and disseminate their amazing work. BI 2020 addressed broad perspectives of BI research that bridges scales that span from atoms to thoughts and behavior. These papers provide a good sample of state-of-the-art research advances on BI from methodologies, frameworks, and techniques to applications and case studies. The selected papers cover five major tracks of BI including: (1) Cognitive and Computational Foundations of Brain Science, (2) Human Information Processing Systems, (3) Brain Big Data Analytics, Curation, and Management, (4) Informatics Paradigms for Brain and Mental Health Research, (5) Brain–Machine Intelligence and Brain-Inspired Computing.

This edition of the BI 2020 conference attracted 52 submissions including 5 abstracts and 47 full papers from 20 countries belonging to all 5 BI 2020 tracks. The submitted papers underwent a single-blind review process, soliciting expert opinion from at least three experts: at least two independent reviewers and the respective track chair. After the rigorous review reports from the reviewers and the track chairs, 33 high-quality full papers and 4 abstracts from 18 countries were accepted for presentation at the conference. Therefore, this volume of the BI 2020 conference proceedings contains those 33 full papers which were presented virtually on September 19, 2020. Despite the COVID-19 pandemic, it was an amazing response from the BI community during this challenging time.

We would like to express our gratitude to all BI 2020 Conference Committee members for their instrumental and unwavering support. BI 2020 had a very exciting program which would not have been possible without the generous dedication of the Program Committee members in reviewing the conference papers and abstracts. BI 2020 could not have taken place without the great team efforts and the generous support from our sponsors. We would especially like to express our sincere appreciation to our kind sponsors, including Springer Nature and Springer LNCS/LNAI. Our gratitude to Springer for sponsoring 12 student first-author registrations, selected based on the quality of submitted papers and their need for financial support. We are grateful to Aliaksandr Birukou, Anna Kramer, Celine Chang, Nick Zhu, Alfred Hofmann, and the LNCS/LNAI team from Springer Nature for their continuous support in coordinating the publication of this volume. Also, special thanks to Hongzhi Kuai, Vicky Yamamoto, and Yang Yang for their great assistance and support. Last but not least, we thank all our contributors and volunteers for their support during this challenging time to make BI 2020 a success.

September 2020

Mufti Mahmud
Stefano Vassanelli
M. Shamim Kaiser
Ning Zhong

Organization

Conference Chairs

Mufti Mahmud	Nottingham Trent University, UK
Stefano Vassanelli	University of Padova, Italy
M. Shamim Kaiser	Jahangirnagar University, Bangladesh
Ning Zhong	Maebashi Institute of Technology, Japan

Advisors

Amir Hussain	Edinburgh Napier University, UK
Hanchuan Peng	SEU-Allen Joint Center - Institute for Brain and Intelligence, China
Maurizio Corbetta	Padua Neuroscience Centre, Italy
Qionghai Dai	Tsinghua University, China

Organizing Committee

Alessandra Bertoldo	University of Padova, Italy
Michele Giugliano	SISSA, Italy
Michela Chiappalone	IIT, Italy
Xiaohui Tao	University of Southern Queensland, Australia
Alberto Testolin	University of Padova, Italy
Marzia Hoque Tania	Oxford University, UK
Yang Yang	Beijing Forestry University, China
Peipeng Liang	Capital Normal University, China
Marco Dal Maschio	University of Padova, Italy
Marco Zorzi	University of Padova, Italy
Samir Suweis	University of Padova, Italy
Claudia Cecchetto	Okinawa Institute of Science and Technology, Japan
Saiful Azad	University of Malaysia Pahang, Malaysia
Shouyi Wang	The University of Texas at Arlington, USA
Vicky Yamamoto	Keck School of Medicine of USC, USA
Zhiqi Mao	Chinese PLA General Hospital, China
Hongzhi Kuai	Maebashi Institute of Technology, Japan
Shuvashish Paul	Jahangirnagar University, Bangladesh
Md Asif-Ur- Rahman	PropertyPRO Technology Pty Ltd, Australia

Technical Program Committee

Alessandra Pedrocchi	Politechnico di Milano, Italy
Alessandro Gozzi	IIT, Italy

Bernd Kuhn	OIST, Japan
Bo Song	University of Southern Queensland, Australia
Daniel Marcus	University of Washington, USA
Davide Zoccolan	SISSA, Italy
Dimeter Prodonov	Imac, Belgium
Egidio D'Angelo	University of Pavia, Italy
Eleni Vasilaki	The University of Sheffield, UK
Francesco Papaleo	University of Padova and IIT, Italy
Gabriella Panuccio	IIT, Italy
Gaute Einevoll	Norwegian University of Life Sciences, Norway
Giacomo Indiveri	University of Zurich, Switzerland
Giancarlo Ferregno	Politechnico di Milano, Italy
Giorgio A. Ascoli	George Mason University, USA
Guenther Zeck	NMI, Germany
Gustavo Deco	Pompeu Fabra University, Spain
Jonathan Mappelli	University of Modena, Italy
Laura Ballerini	SISSA, Italy
Luca Benini	ETH, Switzerland
Luca Berdondini	IIT, Italy
Luciano Gamberini	University of Padova, Italy
M. Arifur Rahman	Jahangirnagar University, Bangladesh
M. Mostafizur Rahman	AIUB, Bangladesh
Manisha Chawla	IIT Gandhinagar, India
Marco Mongillo	University of Padova, Italy
Martin McGinnity	Ulster University, UK
Mathew Diamond	SISSA, Italy
Mathias Prigge	Weizmann Institute of Science, Israel
Md. Atiqur Rahman Ahad	Osaka University, Japan
Michele Magno	ETH, Switzerland
Mohammad Shahadat Hossain	University of Chittagong, Bangladesh
Mohammad Shorif Uddin	Jahangirnagar University, Bangladesh
Muhammad Golam Kibria	University of Liberal Arts, Bangladesh
Muhammad Nazrul Islam	MIST, Bangladesh
Ofer Yizhar	Weizmann Institute of Science, Israel
Paolo Del Giudice	National Institute of Health, Italy
Paolo Massobrio	University of Genova, Italy
Patrick Ruther	University of Freiburg, Germany
Ralf Zeitler	Venneos GmbH, Germany
Roland Thewes	Technical University of Berlin, Germany
Sergio Martinoia	University of Genova, Italy
Shamim Al Mamun	Jahangirnagar University, Bangladesh
Silvestro Micera	Scuola Superiore Sant'Anna, Italy
Stefano Ferraina	University of Rome, Italy

Contents

Informatics Paradigms for Brain and Mental Health Research

Brain-Machine Intelligence and Brain-Inspired Computing

Cognitive and Computational
Foundations of Brain Science

An Adaptive Computational Fear-Avoidance Model Applied to Genito-Pelvic Pain/Penetration Disorder

Sophie van't Hof[1], Arja Rydin[1], Jan Treur[2(✉)], and Paul Enzlin[3,4]

[1] University of Amsterdam, Brain and Cognitive Sciences/Computational Science, Amsterdam, The Netherlands
sophievanhethof@gmail.com, arja.rydin@gmail.com
[2] VU Amsterdam, Social AI Group, Amsterdam, The Netherlands
j.treur@vu.nl
[3] Department of Neurosciences, Institute For Family And Sexuality Studies, KU Leuven, Leuven, Belgium
paul.enzlin@kuleuven.be
[4] Centre for Clinical Sexology and Sex Therapy, UPC KU Leuven, Leuven, Belgium

Abstract. This paper presents a first study to apply a computational approach to Genito-Pelvic Pain/Penetration Disorder (GPPPD) using a Fear Avoidance Model. An adaptive temporal-causal network model for fear avoidance was designed and therapeutic interventions were incorporated targeting one or two emotional states. Validation with empirical data shows that for one type of individual therapeutic intervention targeting two states can reduce pain and other complaints. For three other types of individuals, targeting two emotional states was not sufficient to reduce pain and other complaints. The computational model can address large individual differences and supports the claim that interventions for GPPPD should be multidisciplinary.

Keywords: Genito-pelvic pain/penetration disorder · Pain disorder · Fear avoidance model · Computational modelling · Adaptive temporal-causal network

1 Introduction

Genito-Pelvic Pain/Penetration Disorder (GPPPD) is a prevalent sexual dysfunction affecting approximately 20% of heterosexual women [18], but underlying mechanisms are still poorly understood. Studies suggest that treatment should be based on multi-disciplinary interventions that take into account individual differences [8, 10, 21]. Thomtén and Linton [27] approached GPPPD as a pain disorder by applying the Fear Avoidance Model of Vlaeyen and Linton [30] to the disorder. This approach might be helpful to better understand how sexual pain starts and what interventions could be useful. This is the first study to apply a computational approach to GPPPD using the Fear Avoidance Model. An adaptive temporal-causal network model was designed and therapeutic interventions were incorporated targeting one or two emotional states.

© Springer Nature Switzerland AG 2020
M. Mahmud et al. (Eds.): BI 2020, LNAI 12241, pp. 3–15, 2020.
https://doi.org/10.1007/978-3-030-59277-6_1

Validation with empirical data of Pazmany et al. [20] shows that only for one type of individual a therapeutic intervention targeting two emotional states reduces pain and other complaints, although recovery does not go back to baseline. For three other types of individuals, targeting two states was not sufficient to reduce pain and other complaints. This computational model can address large individual differences and supports the claim that interventions for GPPPD should be multidisciplinary. The model has the potential to be expanded to see how many states should be targeted for a specific individual. First, some background information is presented, after which the computational model is described. Next, simulation outcomes are reported followed by a description of how the model was verified and validated.

2 Background

In this section, some background information on GPPPD and the Fear-Avoidance model is given in order to facilitate a better understanding and interpretation of the computational model.

Genito-Pelvic Pain/Penetration Disorder and Vulvodynia. GPPPD is a relatively new diagnostic category of female sexual dysfunction, introduced in the DSM-5 [2]. It reflects the combination of two previous categories, dyspareunia and vaginismus, in one entity [10]. One of the following criteria have to be met for diagnosis, with at least six months duration and presence of clinically significant distress: difficulties during vaginal penetration during intercourse, marked culcovaginal or pelvic pain during vaginal intercourse or penetration attempts, marked fear or anxiety about vulvovaginal or pelvic pain in anticipation of, during, or as a result of vaginal penetration, and marked tensing or tightening of pelvic floor muscles during attempted vaginal penetration [2].

Implications. Sexual pain disorders have co-morbidity with other disorders and diseases, both physical [14, 21, 24], and mental [1, 5, 17, 20]. In addition, repeated pain during coitus has a substantial negative impact on quality of life [3, 12, 15, 28], and altered sexual functioning [6, 19, 20, 22, 23].

Interventions. The etiology of GPPPD is multi-factorial and complex, which means that biological, psychological and relational factors interact to perpetuate and maintain a women's pain response [10]. GPPPD should thus never be viewed as a purely medical or psychogenic problem but always be evaluated and treated from a biopsychosocial perspective [14, 21]. GPPPD often also impacts the partner relationship and therapy may benefit from also including the partner [9]. Cognitive and behavioral interventions – either with the women, with the partners or in group – can be useful in treating sexual pain disorders, although with varying results [4, 9, 11, 13, 25, 26]. In sum, there are different therapies but there currently is not one therapy effective for all individuals. People with sexual pain disorders generally try many different treatment modalities, often over the course of many years, before experiencing any significant relief [7].

Multidisciplinary treatment in chronic pain has held strong support but is relatively new for sexual pain specifically. In order to create specific multidisciplinary treatment programs that fit for individual cases, the underlying mechanisms of vaginal pain should be better understood. There still is a lack of theoretical models that describe the psycho-social mechanisms involved in the development of GPPPD.

The Fear Avoidance Model. GPPPD is classified as a sexual dysfunction and is thereby the only pain disorder outside the category of 'pain disorders'. Vlaeyen and Linton [30] introduced the fear-avoidance (FA) model to understand musculo-skeletal pain disorders in the transition from acute to chronic pain. Thomtén and Linton [27] have reviewed, adapted and extended the Fear Avoidance Model in the light of pain during vaginal penetration.

This adapted FA model could thus be helpful in understanding GPPPD as a multifaceted sexual disorder but also as a pain disorder. Thomtén and Linton [27] state that the model needs to be further examined by evaluating interventions targeting the specific concepts (e.g., fear, catastrophizing). Figure 1 shows the adapted version of the Fear Avoidance Model presented by Thomtén and Linton [27]. This informal model will be used as a basis for our computational model in order to get more insight in the mechanisms underlying GPPPD and the possibilities for intervention.

The computational model is similar, though adjusted in a few ways. The nodes representing a verb have been changed to an emotional state of being. The arrows represent the actions, and the nodes represent a state of (emotional) being. Furthermore, the branch 'exiting' the fear-avoidance loop (recovering from GPPPD) has been removed, because in the computational model this occurrence will be represented by low values of pain, fear et cetera.

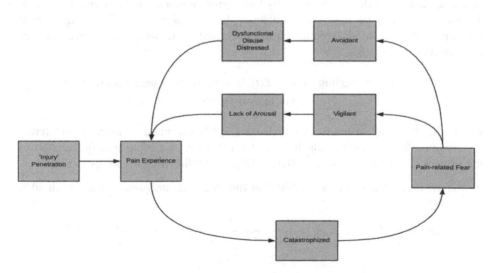

Fig. 1. Adjustment of the fear avoidance model to GPPPD. Adapted from [27].

3   The Designed Computational Network Model

In this section the adaptive temporal-causal network model is presented; see Fig. 2.

The Modeling Approach Used. The adaptive computational model is based on the Network-Oriented Modelling approach based on reified temporal-causal networks [29]. The *network structure characteristics* used are as follows. A full specification of a network model provides a complete overview of their values in so-called role matrix format.

- **Connectivity:** The strength of a connection from state X to Y is represented by weight $\omega_{X,Y}$
- **Aggregation:** The aggregation of multiple impacts on state Y by combination function $c_Y(..)$.
- **Timing:** The timing of the effect of the impact on state Y by speed factor η_Y

Given initial values for the states, these network characteristics fully define the dynamics of the network. For each state Y, its (real number) value at time point t is denoted by $Y(t)$. Each of the network structure characteristics can be made adaptive by adding extra states for them to the network, called *reification states* [29]: states $\mathbf{W}_{X,Y}$ for $\omega_{X,Y}$, states $\mathbf{C}_Y$ for $c_Y(..)$, and states $\mathbf{H}_Y$ for η_Y. Such reification states get their own network structure characteristics to define their (adaptive) dynamics and are depicted in a higher level plane, as shown in Fig. 2. For example, using this, the adaptation principle called Hebbian learning, considered as a form of plasticity of the brain in cognitive neuroscience ("neurons that fire together, wire together") can be modeled; e.g., see [29], Ch 3, Sect. 3.6.1.

A dedicated software environment is available by which the conceptual design of an adaptive network model is automatically transformed into a numerical representation of the model that can be used for simulation; this is based on the following type of (hidden) difference of differential equation defined in terms of the above network characteristics:

$$Y(t+\Delta t) = Y(t) + \eta_Y[\mathbf{aggimpact}_Y(t) - Y(t)]\Delta t \text{ or } dY(t)/dt = [\mathbf{aggimpact}_Y(t) - Y(t)]$$
$$\text{with } \mathbf{aggimpact}_Y(t) = c_Y(\omega_{X_1,Y}X_1(t),\ldots,\omega_{X_k,Y}X_k(t)) \tag{1}$$

where the X_i are all states from which state Y has incoming connections. Different combination functions are available in a library that can be used to specify the effect of the impact on a state (see Treur, 2016, 2020). The following two are used here:

- the *advanced logistic sum* combination function with steepness σ and threshold τ

$$\mathbf{alogistic}_{\sigma,\tau}(V_1, \ldots, V_k) = \left(\frac{1}{1+e^{-\sigma(V_1+\cdots+V_k-\tau)}} - \frac{1}{1+e^{\sigma\tau}}\right)(1+e^{-\sigma\tau}) \tag{2}$$

- the *Hebbian learning combination function* **hebb$_\mu$(..)**

$$\textbf{hebb}_\mu(V_1, V_2, W) = V_1 V_2 (1 - W) + \mu W \qquad (3)$$

with μ the persistence parameter, where V_1 stands for $X(t)$, V_2 for $Y(t)$ and W for $\mathbf{W}_{X,Y}(t)$, where X and Y are the two connected states

The Introduced Adaptive Network Model. The specific adaptive network model introduced here consists of 13 nodes or states and 22 connections; see Fig. 2. The 13 states of the adaptive network model are explained in Table 1. Each node stands for a physical or emotional (re)action or experience and the connections represent causal relations. For example, an occurring injury will cause a pain experience, so an arrow points from the node injury to the node pain experience. In simulations by this model, a spiral can be found of how an experience of pain can cause a closed loop resulting in a continuing non-descending pain experience. Note that the dysfunction, disuse and distress state were simplified. In addition, the link between disuse and increased levels of pain has been theorized, but not supported with empirical data [27]. The full specification of the network characteristics of the introduced network model (connection weights $\omega_{X,Y}$, speed factors η_Y, and combination functions $c_Y(..)$) and their parameters σ, τ, and μ) and the initial values can be found in the role matrices in the Appendix at https://www.researchgate.net/publication/338410102. The states X_1 to X_8 are also displayed in Fig. 1. The other states X_9 to X_{12} shown in Fig. 2 in addition address emotion regulation by control states, strengthening of emotion regulation by learning, and therapy to support that. In this model, there are control states for both the catastrophized state and the dysfunction/distress state. The graphical representation shown in Fig. 2 displays the overall *connectivity* of this network model, also shown in role matrix **mb** in the abovementioned Appendix.

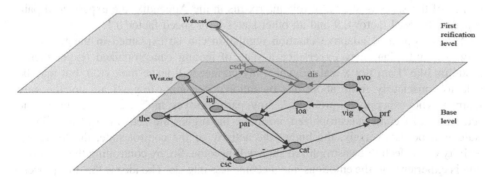

Fig. 2. Overview *of the reified network architecture for plasticity and meta*-plasticity with base level (lower plane, pink) and first reification level (upper plane, blue) and upward causal connections (blue) and downward causal connections (red) defining inter-level relations. (Color figure online)

As can be seen in role matrix **mcw** in the Appendix, most connection weights are positive, the only exceptions being the weights of the connections from control states X_{10} and X_{12} to emotion states X_3 (catastrophized) and X_8 used for emotion regulation.

Table 1. Representation of all states used in the adaptive temporal-causal network

State number	State name	Description	Level
X_1	inj	injury	
X_2	pai	experienced pain	
X_3	cat	catastrophized	
X_4	prf	pain-related fear	
X_5	vig	vigilant	
X_6	loa	lack of arousal	Base level
X_7	avo	avoidance	
X_8	dis	distressed	
X_9	the	therapy	
X_{10}	csc	control state for catastrophizing	
X_{12}	csd	control state for distress	
X_{11}	$\mathbf{W}_{cat,csc}$	reified representation state for connection weight $\omega_{cat,csc}$	First reification
X_{13}	$\mathbf{W}_{dis,csd}$	reified representation state for connection weight $\omega_{dis,csd}$	level

If one node negatively affects another node, in the picture also an arrow points to the affected node, but labeled with a negative sign (-). For *aggregation*, the combination function **hebb$_\mu$**(..) is used for the two **W**-states X_{11} and X_{13} in the upper plane and **alogistic$_{\sigma,\tau}$**(..) for all other states in the base plane (role matrix **mcfw** in the Appendix). The values for parameters σ, τ and μ for these combination functions can be found in role matrix **mcfp**; for example, $\mu = 0.99$ and steepness σ mostly varies from 5 to 7. The *timing* of the states is shown in role matrix **ms** in the Appendix: the experienced pain has a high speed factor 0.9 and all other states have speed factor 0.1.

The incorporated adaptive emotion regulation can be explained in the following way. An individual may experience a state of feeling catastrophized (experiencing thoughts like 'I am not a real woman', 'my partner will leave me', etc.), but may be able to consciously think about this by rational reasoning (e.g., 'I am not the only woman who experiences problems', 'my partner loves me', etc.). The higher the activation of feeling catastrophized, normally the higher the activation of the control state will be. Conversely, the higher the activity of the control state, the lower the activity of the feeling catastrophized state will become. So, by controlling the emotions one is experiencing, the emotions may become less intense. The idea is that this process is adaptive in the sense that the strength of the connection from the catastrophized state to the control state can be 'trained' by interventions such as therapies.

Different types of therapies may target one or more states. However, it is unclear which specific therapy targets which specific state(s), and we shall thus continue using the general term 'therapy' that targets some specific state(s), instead of e.g., cognitive behavior therapy that is said to target the catastrophized state. The model is adaptive in the sense that the weights of the incoming connections for the control states supporting emotion regulation can be adapted by learning. For example, if a healthy individual starts to catastrophize, normally spoken she will learn to control this state. The adaptive W-states for these incoming connections are the states portrayed on a higher level in the model (the upper plane) in Fig. 2. Therapy will positively affect one or more of the control states. In turn, the activation values of the catastrophized state and control state together can strengthen (or weaken) the connection from the catastrophizing state to the control state: i.e., Hebbian learning to control the catastrophizing level. This happens by the Hebbian combination function (2) applied to the W-states (X_{11} and X_{13}) in the upper plane. The Hebbian learning function takes in the values of the two connected states from the base level and of the connection weight itself, and uses a certain persistence factor as parameter μ: if $\mu = 1$, the connection weight keeps its strength for 100%, and if it is, for example, $\mu = 0.99$, every time unit the connection loses one percent of its strength.

4   Simulation Results

Using the computational model, simulations have been performed for different scenarios. The first scenario includes no therapy and therefore should show that the pain experience increases and finally becomes high. In the second scenario, therapy targeting the control state of the catastrophized state, was included. The third scenario also makes use of a therapy, targeting both the control states catastrophized and distress; thus two states in the cycle. Both therapies strengthen the control state of the state, with the idea that therapy helps people control these states, to break to cycle. The simulations were run until an equilibrium is reached to see what the end state will be.

Scenario 1: No Therapy. In Fig. 3 left it is shown that the injury triggers the experienced pain. This in turns creates a wave of catastrophisation, followed by a pain-related fear. The pain-related fear triggers both vigilance and avoidance behavior. These states in turn increase the lack of arousal and the state of distress. The lack of arousal, combined with dysfunction/distress, feed back into the pain experience, finishing off the loop. There is no way in this loop to break the cycle.

Scenario 2: Therapy Targeting One State. The model has a control state embedded for the state of being catastrophized. The idea is that the individual can consciously think about her emotions and feelings and control these to some extent. The activation of the control state thus negatively affects the state of being catastrophized.

In the model, the strength by which this happens, is typically variable per person and situation, and it can be positively affected by therapy. A therapy was incorporated that targets the strength of the control state, and thus weakens the catastrophized state, hopefully breaking the cycle. Simulation results of therapy targeting one state is presented in Fig. 3 middle. What is seen, however, is indeed a dip in the cycle, but the therapy is not strong enough to actually break the cycle, and eventually the pain and all other states again get higher values. This suggests that it concerns a system problem, where the problem cannot be solved by solving only one particle in the system, but the system as a whole needs to be revised. Therefore, in a following scenario two parts in the cycle are targeted.

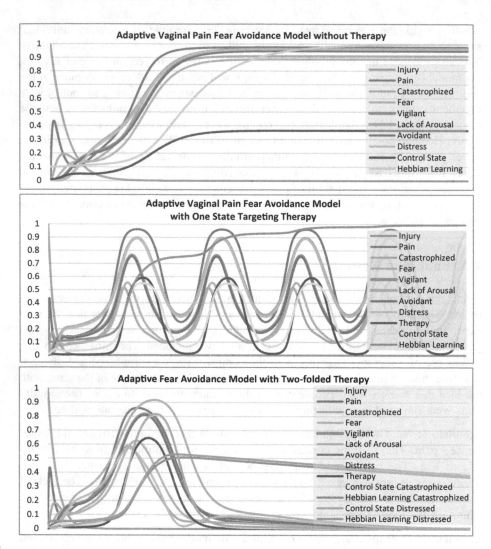

Fig. 3. Results from running the Fear Avoidance model for an individual with GPPPD (a) Left: without a therapeutic intervention. After the injury, we see how a cycle is increasingly elicited by an initial increase in pain experience, resulting in high values for all states in the GPPPD cycle. (b) Middle: with a therapy targeting the control state for the catastrophized state. After the injury, we now also see therapy becoming active, which lowers the cycle states. However, the therapy alone is not enough to break the cycle, and when the experienced pain goes down, and therefore also the therapy, the cycle repeats itself. Even though there is an increase in the connection between the control state and the emotion, the therapy in this form is not strong enough to keep the GPPPD under control. (c) with a therapy targeting both the control state for the catastrophizing state and for the distress state. The therapy is effective: the cycle is stopped and the pain and other parts of the cycle are controlled after the therapy is discontinued.

Scenario 3: Therapy Targeting Two States. Another control state was incorporated for being distressed, and the therapy was targeting both control states in the cycle. The result of the simulation can be seen in Fig. 3 right. The therapy successfully alters the nature of the system, suppressing the activity of the reoccurring pain experience, and thus breaking the cycle of GPPPD.

5 Verification by Mathematical Analysis

The model can be verified per state, by taking a state value at a time point that the system is in equilibrium, considering the incoming connections, and calculating the aggregated impact on the state. The difference between the simulation result and the aggregated impact shows a certain measure of accuracy of the model, as theoretically they are equal in an equilibrium. The states that have been chosen to verify, are X_2, X_{11}, and X_{13}. Time point $t = 498.2$ was used as a reference time point. State X_2 has three incoming connections: X_1, X_6 and X_8. The aggregated impact for this state X_2 is the logistic function, as defined above in (1). The values found for the incoming connections of X_2 are: $X_1 = 1.42 \cdot 10^{-18}$, $X_6 = 0.0049$, $X_8 = 0.0037$. The steepness and threshold of the logistic function are $\sigma = 5$, $\tau = 0.6$. This results in the outcomes shown in Table 2. States X_{11} and X_{13} use the Hebbian learning function (2) for aggregation. Their incoming connections and their values are, respectively: $X_3 = 0.0013$, $X_{10} = 0.29481$, $X_{11} = 0.3673$ and $X_8 = 0.0037$, $X_{12} = 0.71057$, $X_{13} = 0.3822$. Both persistence parameter values are $\mu = 0.99$. The aggregated impacts for these two states were calculated by:

$$\mathbf{aggimpact}_{X_{11}}(t) = X_3 X_{10}(1 - X_{11}) + \mu X_{11}$$
$$\mathbf{aggimpact}_{X_{13}}(t) = X_8 X_{12}(1 - X_{13}) + \mu X_{13}$$

Table 2. The values for three states in an equilibrium time point have been extracted from simulation data and compared with the aggregated impact of the incoming states. These states have been chosen because they have the highest number of incoming connections (three), and thus the highest probability of deviating strongly from the theoretical equilibrium point. The highest deviation is the 0.04 found in X_2, but still small enough not to suggest an error in the model.

State X_i	X_2	X_{11}	X_{13}
Time point t	498.2	498.2	498.2
$X_i(t)$	0.0015	0.3673	0.3822
$\mathbf{aggimpact}_{X_i}(t)$	0.0417	0.364	0.380
deviation	0.0403	−0.00343	−0.00220

The highest deviation that we found was for stat X_2, being 0.0417671, which is not considered to indicate a problem for our model as it is close enough to 0.

6   Validation of the Model

The simulations in Sect. 3 were run without using numerical empirical data. In order to validate the model, data from [20] were used. In this study, data for levels of pain, sexual arousal and distress were acquired with validated questionnaires in women with GPPPD. From this data set, data of four different individuals with GPPPD with different levels of pain, arousal, and distress were used. The model will therefore be validated for four different types of individuals. The numbers are based on the different questionnaires that the women filled out, giving a score regarding several aspects in their sexual life. The numbers were scaled to a [0, 1] range for the optimization program by dividing the score on the questionnaire by the maximum score. The Female Sexual Function Index questionnaire is used to determine sexual pain and sexual arousal, with higher scores being more positive. Both scores were subtracted from 1, since higher scores on pain and lack of arousal indicate higher levels of pain and lower levels of arousal. Simulated Annealing was used as optimization method, which makes use of a cooling schedule to find the best fitting parameter values [16]. The empirical values of the three states for the four individuals can be found in Table 3, including the indication whether the value is low, medium or high.

The four individuals all experience medium to high levels of pain, but varying levels of (lack of) arousal and distress. The values have been added to the optimization program at a time point where the therapy (targeting both catastrophizing and distress) has not been activated yet, but the symptoms of GPPPD are significantly prevalent ($t = 50$). The model was tuned for all connection weights, except for the connection weight going from pain to therapy. The model was also tuned for all the function parameter values (threshold and steepness), except for parameter values that belonged to the therapy. Values for the remaining RMSE (Root Mean Square Error) found were around 0.04, 0.04, 0.05, 0.25, respectively, for persons 1 to 4.

Table 3. Empirical data of the four individuals are shown in this table. For each individual, three levels have been used in the parameter tuning optimization procedure: experienced pain, lack of arousal, and distress.

State	Explanation	Individual			
Number		1	2	3	4
X_2	**Experienced pain** level	0.667 *high*	0.400 *medium*	0.467 *medium*	1.000 *high*
X_6	**Lack of arousal** level	0.750 *high*	0.050 *low*	0 *low*	1.000 *high*
X_8	**Distress** level	0.125 *low*	0.750 *high*	0.0417 *low*	1 *high*

7 Conclusion and Discussion

In this paper, a computational model for GPPPD has been introduced. This was done by building a temporal-causal network based on the Network-Oriented Modelling Approach from [29]. In this model, GPPPD is classified as a sexual disorder and characteristics of the Fear Avoidance Model are incorporated by adding the cyclic component. The Fear Avoidance model suggests that GPPPD can also be modelled as a pain disorder. Perceiving GPPPD not only as a sexual disorder, but also as a pain disorder opens the doors for new types of interventions. For example, acceptance and commitment therapy has recently been developed for chronic pain disorders [11]. It could be useful to apply this type of therapy for GPPPD as well.

Characteristics of GPPPD and interventions targeting one or two states have been captured, by creating an adaptive temporal-causal network. Different therapeutic interventions can target different states of the model. For example, catastrophizing is the primary target of CBT [11]. However, when modeling a therapy that only targets catastrophizing, the therapy does not seem to be effective. CBT for GPPPD is described as the reframing and restructuring of basic (irrational) beliefs that interfere with sexual function [9]. It could thus be hypothesized that CBT does not only target catastrophizing, but also distress (e.g., feelings shame and guilt) and maybe even more states. Which states are targeted, could even differ per psychiatrist, individual and/or couple.

It would be interesting to research which states exactly are being targeted with different therapies and whether this indeed does differ between psychiatrist, individual and/or couple. In addition, it would be interesting to collect data of different states during a therapy over time. This model could be easily extended to incorporate control states for other states in the model. In this way, a model can be created to see which states could and should be targeted in different individuals. The obtained results show that for an individual with low distress and high sexual arousal levels, targeting two states lowers the values of the states, but do not get the individual back to baseline. For women with either high distress, low arousal or both therapy that targets two states does not lower the state levels at all. These results thus show that for most individuals, targeting two states is not enough to break the cycle. This supports claims that there are large individual differences between GPPPD patients and that interventions for GPPPD should be multidisciplinary and tailored to individuals specifically.

This study is the first to apply a computational approach to GPPPD. The parameter tuning suggests that therapy targeting two states is not sufficient for most individuals with GPPPD to lower the pain and other complaints. Future research could collect more empirical data of different states before and after therapy. Adding more control states, to more states of the model would also create a more elaborate model that would be able to characterize more kinds of therapies, and thus increasing the effectiveness of the therapies, specialized for different kinds of individuals. Another future extension of the model may incorporate metaplasticity by making the learning speeds and the persistence factors adaptive, for example, following [29], Ch. 4, so that a second-order adaptive network is obtained taking into account the effect that circumstances may have on a person's learning capabilities and that even may block learning.

References

1. Aikens, J.E., Reed, B.D., Gorenflo, D.W., Haefner, H.K.: Depressive symptoms among women with vulvar dysesthesia. Am. J. Obstet. Gynecol. **189**(2), 462–466 (2003). https://doi.org/10.1067/S0002-9378(03)00521-0
2. American Psychiatric Association: Genito-pelvic pain/penetration disorder. In: Diagnostic and Statistical Manual of Mental Disorders, 5th edn. pp. 437–440. American Psychiatric Association, Arlington (2013)
3. Arnold, L.D., Bachmann, G.A., Kelly, S., Rosen, R., Rhoads, G.G.: Vulvodynia: characteristics and associations with co-morbidities and quality of life. Obst. Gynecol. **107**(3), 617–624 (2006)
4. Bergeron, S., Khalif'e, S., Dupuis, M.J., McDuff, P.: A randomized clinical trial comparing group cognitive-behavioral therapy and a topical steroid for women with dyspareunia. J. Consult. Clin. Psychol. **84**(3), 259–268 (2016)
5. Brauer, M., Ter Kuile, M.M., Laan, E.: Effects of appraisal of sexual stimuli on sexual arousal in women with and without superficial dyspareunia. Archiv. Sex. Behav. **38**(4), 476–485 (2009). https://doi.org/10.1007/s10508-008-9371-8
6. Brauer, M., Ter Kuile, M.M., Laan, E., Trimbos, B.: Cognitive-affective correlates and predictors of superficial dyspareunia. J. Sex Marital Ther. **35**(1), 1–24 (2009). https://doi.org/10.1080/00926230802525604
7. Brotto, L.A., et al.: A comparison of demographic and psychosexual characteristics of women with primary versus secondary provoked vestibulodynia. Clin. J. Pain **30**(5), 428–435 (2014)
8. Brotto, L.A., Yong, P., Smith, K.B., Sadownik, L.A.: Impact of a multidisciplinary vulvodynia program on sexual functioning and dyspareunia. J. Sex. Med. **12**(1), 238–247 (2015). https://doi.org/10.1111/jsm.12718
9. Carlson, J., Dermer, S.B.: The SAGE Encyclopedia of Marriage, Family, and Couples Counseling (2016). https://doi.org/10.4135/9781483369532
10. Conforti, C.: Genito-pelvic pain/penetration disorder (GPPPD): an overview of current terminology, etiology, and treatment. Univ. Ottawa J. Med. **7**(2), 48–53 (2017). https://doi.org/10.18192/uojm.v7i2.2198
11. De Boer, M.J., Steinhagen, H.E., Versteegen, G.J., Struys, M.M.R.F., Sanderman, R.: Mindfulness, acceptance and catastrophizing in chronic pain. PLoS ONE **9**(1), 1–6 (2014). https://doi.org/10.1371/journal.pone.0087445
12. Desrosiers, M., Bergeron, S., Meana, M., Leclerc, B., Binik, Y.M., Khalife, S.: Psychosexual characteristics of vestibulodynia couples: Partner solicitousness and hostility are associated with pain. J. Sex. Med. **5**(2), 418–427 (2008). https://doi.org/10.1111/j.1743-6109.2007.00705.x
13. El-Sayed Saboula, N., Shahin, M.A.: Effect of cognitive behavioral therapy on women with dyspareunia: a nursing intervention. IOSR J. Nurs. Health Sci. Ver. I **4**(2), 2320–1940 (2015). https://doi.org/10.9790/0837-04218191
14. Graziottin, A., Gambini, D.: Evaluation of genito-pelvic pain/penetration disorder. In: The Textbook of Clinical Sexual Medicine (2017). https://doi.org/10.1007/978-3-319-52539-620
15. Kaler, A.: Unreal women: sex, gender, identity and the lived experience of vulvar pain. Feminist Rev. **82**(1), 50–75 (2006)
16. Kirkpatrick, S., Gelatt, C.D., Vecchi, M.P.: Optimization by simulated annealing. Science **220**(4598), 671–680 (1983)

17. Masheb, R.M., Wang, E., Lozano, C., Kerns, R.D.: Prevalence and correlates of depression in treatment-seeking women with vulvodynia. J. Obstet. Gynaecol. 25(8), 786–791 (2005). https://doi.org/10.1080/01443610500328199
18. McCool, M.E., Zuelke, A., Theurich, M.A., Knuettefcci, C., Apfelbacher, C.: Prevalence of female sexual dysfunction among premenopausal women: a systematic review and meta-analysis of observational studies. Sex. Med. Rev. 4(3), 197–212 (2016). https://doi.org/10.1016/j.sxmr.2016.03.002
19. Pazmany, E., Bergeron, S., Van Oudenhove, L., Verhaeghe, J., Enzlin, P.: Body image and genital self-image in pre-menopausal women with dyspareu- nia. Archiv. Sex. Behav. 42(6), 999–1010 (2013). https://doi.org/10.1007/s10508-013-0102-4
20. Pazmany, E., Bergeron, S., Verhaeghe, J., Van Oudenhove, L., Enzlin, P.: Sexual communication, dyadic adjustment, and psychosexual well-being in premenopausal women with self-reported dyspareunia and their partners: a controlled study. J. Sex. Med. 11(7), 1786–1797 (2014). https://doi.org/10.1111/jsm.12518
21. Pukall, C.F., et al.: Vulvodynia: definition, prevalence, impact, and pathophysiological factors. J. Sex. Med. 13(3), 291–304 (2016). https://doi.org/10.1016/j.jsxm.2015.12.021
22. Reissing, E.D., Binik, Y.M., Khalifé, S., Cohen, D., Amsel, R.: Etiological correlates of vaginismus: sexual and physical abuse, sexual knowledge, sexual self-schema, and relationship adjustment. J. Sex Marit. Ther. 29(1), 47–59 (2003). https://doi.org/10.1080/713847095
23. Smith, K.B., Pukall, C.F.: A systematic review of relationship adjustment and sexual satisfaction among women with provoked vestibulodynia. J. Sex Res. 48(2–3), 166–191 (2011). https://doi.org/10.1080/00224499.2011.555016
24. Sobhgol, S.S., Alizadeli Charndabee, S.M.: Rate and related factors of dyspareunia in reproductive age women: a cross-sectional study. Int. J. Importence Res. 19(1), 88–94 (2007). https://doi.org/10.1038/sj.ijir.3901495
25. Ter Kuile, M.M., Melles, R., De Groot, H.E., Tuijnman-Raasveld, C.C., Van Lankveld, J.J. D.M.: Therapist-aided exposure for women with lifelong vaginismus: a randomized waiting-list control trial of efficacy. J. Consult. Clin. Psychol. 81(6), 1127–1136 (2013). https://doi.org/10.1037/a0034292
26. Ter Kuile, M.M., van Lankveld, J.J.D.M., de Groot, E., Melles, R., Neffs, J., Zandbergen, M.: Cognitive-behavioral therapy for women with lifelong vaginismus: process and prognostic factors. Behav. Res. Ther. 45(2), 359–373 (2007)
27. Thomtén, J., Linton, S.J.: A psychological view of sexual pain among women: applying the fear-avoidance model. Women's Health 9(3), 251–263 (2013)
28. Törnävä, M., Koivula, M., Helminen, M., Suominen, T.: Women with vulvodynia: awareness and knowledge of its care among student healthcare staff. Scand. J. Caring Sci. 32 (1), 241–252 (2018). https://doi.org/10.1111/scs.12455
29. Treur, J.: Network-oriented modeling for adaptive networks: designing higher-order adaptive biological, mental and social network models. Springer, Heidelberg (2020). https://doi.org/10.1007/978-3-030-31445-3
30. Vlaeyen, J.W.S., Linton, S.J.: Fear-avoidance and its consequences in chronic musculoskeletal pain: a state of the art. Pain 85(3), 317–332 (2000). https://doi.org/10.1016/S0304-3959(99)00242-0

Are We Producing Narci-nials? An Adaptive Agent Model for Parental Influence

Fakhra Jabeen[✉], Charlotte Gerritsen, and Jan Treur

Vrije Universiteit Amsterdam, Amsterdam, The Netherlands
fakhraikram@yahoo.com, {cs.gerritsen, j.treur}@vu.nl

Abstract. Parental influence plays an important role in the mental development of a child. In the early years of childhood, a parent acts as a role model to a child, so most of the children try to mimic their parents. In our work, we address a complex network model of a child who is influenced by a narcissistic parent from his/her childhood to his/her adolescence. This concept of mimicking in childhood is represented by social contagion. Later on, he/she can learn to develop his/her own personality based on experience and learning. This model can be used to predict the influence of a parent over the personality of a child.

Keywords: Narcissism · Parental influence · Reified architecture · Social contagion

1 Introduction

Parents' behavior contributes significantly to the development of their children's mental and psychological health, as they act as a role model to them [1]. During their childhood, copying is considered to be an important part of learning and, thus depicts the behaviors and personality of a child [1, 2]. Parental narcissism can also be responsible for narcissism in a child, as (s)he unconsciously internalizes it [3].

Literature indicates that the self-esteem of a child is positively correlated with approval/disapproval from parents [4]. However, overvaluation and following a narcissistic parent often result in narcissism, where a child develops a feeling of superiority over others [5]. In the field of computational modeling narcissism has been addressed along with possible reactions to positive/negative feedbacks [6]. However, it would be interesting to see how a narcissistic parent influences his/her child, while being happy.

Causal modeling is a field of artificial intelligence, which is used to address many biological, cognitive and social phenomena [7, 8]. It is used to study the real-world processes, and entails how an event can influence the behavior of a process. For example, how a parent feeling happy or sad can influence behavior of a child, and how his/her behavior can vary if a parent is narcissistic. Here, we aim to answer a) which processes can be responsible to develop a narcissistic personality in children and, b) how maturity can change this behavior, while using social media. The obtained computational model can be used to predict narcissism and its progression in a child, especially when this child is interacting over social media. Prediction of such behaviors

© Springer Nature Switzerland AG 2020
M. Mahmud et al. (Eds.): BI 2020, LNAI 12241, pp. 16–28, 2020.
https://doi.org/10.1007/978-3-030-59277-6_2

can be helpful to detect narcissistic traits in a child [5], and can be used as a basis to cope with narcissism.

This paper is organized in five sections. Section 2 discusses the related work, Sect. 3 discusses the designed network model of the child based on the approach described in [8]. Section 4 addresses the simulation experiments and Sect. 5 concludes the paper.

2 Related Work

Much literature is available to address the mental and social development of children and adolescents under parental influence [2, 9, 10]. This section covers the development of a child of a narcissistic parent using three types of input: psychological, social and neurological sciences.

Psychologically and socially, a clear distinction is to be made between narcissism and self-esteem. The former is related to self-love/self-rewarding behavior, while the latter is related to the sense of self-worth [11] without feeling superiority. An outcome of parental warmth results in high esteem, however overvaluation can result a narcissistic child [9]. The self-inflation hypothesis states that when a child is overly admired, this leads him or her to be a narcissist, as children use this kind of feedback to form a view of themselves, like they believe others look at them [5]. Using social media at childhood is not a new thing, and can be used for entertainment or for self-expression [12]. A reason to use social media can be novelty, which can be related to: technology, remaining active over social media/trend setting, or the content itself [13]. Through literature, it has been shown that children use copying behavior from their surrounding people [1]. Another study indicates, that children mimic the grandiosity of their mothers by internalizing experiences based on mutual interactions. This internalization helps to form the image of oneself, which in this way is an unconscious projection of early care-givers (e.g., parents) [3]. Another study indicates that narcissism may get less with maturity of a child [14].

From a neurological perspective, parental influence is addressed from early age of a child [15]. Variations in the brain have been explored in different studies, which indicate changes in the brain volume or the grey matter that are a result of parent-child interactions [15, 16]. Another study showed that the child and mother have greater perceptual similarity for a situation [17]. For narcissism and self-exhibition different brain regions like Prefrontal Cortex (PFC), Anterior Cingulate Cortex (ACC), insula and temporal lobe are enhanced along with striatum during self-rewarding behavior [18–20].

Temporal-causal modelling is a branch of causal modeling is used to address different biological, social, behavioral, cognitive, affective and many other types of processes in an integrative manner. For example, while being in a social environment, one person can influence another person. From a social science view, this is called 'social contagion', through which behavior of a person influences another person's behavior. However multiple inputs can affect this behavior [21], along with the social contagion. Previously, a narcissist's vulnerability was modeled, through a reified network architecture. This indicates how different brain parts are causally related to each other to dynamically generate a reaction over a positive or negative online feedback [6]. However, the parental influence of a narcissist parent, was not addressed, but should be addressed to detect and to provide support to a narcissistic child [9].

3   The Designed Complex Network Model

This section presents a multilevel mental network model of a child who is influenced by his/her parent based on the literature discussed in Sect. 2. The architecture is based on the reified architecture approach and consists of three levels, each of which signifies a special role related to the behavior of the model [8]. For instance, level I indicates the base model, level II and III address the adaptive behavior of the model. Here Fig. 1, depicts the graphical representation of one of the agents, i.e. a child and, Table 1 and 2 provide the information of each level. For the second agent (on left), i.e. the model of a narcissistic parent, who influences his/her child, please see here [6].

3.1   Level I: Base Level

The designed network model is a conceptual representation of a real-world scenario. For example, consider a scenario "*He likes ice-cream, so he buys ice-cream*", this can be represented by a causal relationship between two states X ('*like ice-cream*') and Y ('*buy ice-cream*'), i.e., $X{\rightarrow}Y$. The *activation level* of Y is determined by the *impact* of X on Y at a certain *time*. A temporal-causal network model is identified by three types of characteristics of a network:

Connectivity:
Connection weights $\omega_{X,Y}$ indicate how strong state X influences state Y.
Aggregation of Multiple Impacts:
Combination functions $c_Y(..)$determine the aggregated causal impact from the single impacts $\omega_{Xi,Y}X_i(t)$ of all incoming states $(X_i : i = 1$ to $N)$ on state Y.
Timing:
Speed factors η_Y indicate the speed of causal influence over state Y.

Level I shows the base level of the model of a child, which consist of 26 states. Here, three types of arrows can be observed. Black arrows indicate a positive connection between two states with connection weights between [0,1]. Purple arrows indicate suppression (negative $\omega_{X,Y}$) from one state to another, which is indicated by a negative sign with magnitude of connection weight in $[-1, 0]$. Green arrows represent adaptive connections between two states, which can change/learn over the time and will be discussed in detail in Sect. 3.2.

According to the literature addressed in Sect. 2, parents influence a child's behavior. Here, we address that how a narcissist influences his/her child when he is happy. The parent is shown on the left with only one state es$_{happy}$ without complex details of the model, for details of that part we refer to [6]. So es$_{happy}$ (narcissistic parent is happy) acts the only input received from the parent. Upon getting the stimulus, the sensory (ss$_h$) and representation (srs$_h$) states get activated and, the child tries to act in the same way as his/her parent. An example can be '*being in a crowd and feel good to be noticed*'. This makes him believe positive (child belief state cbs) about him/herself and (s)he self exhibits. Moreover, he/she realize that the parent is factual. Thus, (s)he learns to replicate the parent's reward seeking behavior (cfs_{love}; $c_{striatutm}$; c_{insula}; cfs_{reward}) in a conscious way (cPFC). This process models social contagion behavior.

However, it is quite possible that he/she doesn't agree with his/her parent with the passage of time. An example, can be that he/she may realizes with age ($eval_h$) that the parent is an attention-seeker or a narcissist, so (s)he may react in another way. Here, learning is shown by the adaptive link (green). An example can be '*he can sit at a calm place* (cps_{act}; ces_{act}) *where he remains unnoticed*', this action will give him or her inner satisfaction (fs_{sat}). This kind of behavior can be learned from experiences (hipp). This also reflects that with age/maturity, narcissism might fade away.

Table 1. Categorical explanation of states of the base model (Level I).

Categories		References
Stimulus states:		*Stimulus is sensed and leads to representation:* [21]
es_{happy}	Input from a narcissistic parent	
ws_s	Using social media	
Social contagion related states:		*"yet familiarity.. infants copy more actions of a familiar, compared to an unfamiliar model"*[1] *"mothers show high self– child overlap in perceptual similarity in the FFA regardless of their relationship quality with their child"* [17]
cbs	Belief state of child	
	cstriatum	
	Striatum: Brain part of child	
cPFC	Prefrontal Cortex: Brain part	
$csfs_{love}$	Feeling of self-love (Amygdala)	
cfs_{reward}	Feeling of self-reward (Amygdala)	
ces_{happy}	Execution state of happiness	
Non-narcissistic related states:		*"adolescents was associated with neural activation in social brain regions required to put oneself in another's shoes"* [17]
$eval_h$	Evaluation state for analyzing behaviors	
cps_{act}	Preparation state	
ces_{act}	Execution state	
hipp	Hippocampus: Brain part for memories	
fs_{sat}	Feeling of satisfaction	

(*continued*)

Table 1. (*continued*)

Categories		References
Social media related states:		*"Emotion then facilitates behavior that is in*
ws_s	Input from social media (e.g. a post)	*line with our concerns"* [22]
ss_s	Sensory state	
srs_s	Representation state	
$eval_s$	Evaluation of the input, based on belief	
os	Ownership state	
ps_{share}	Preparation state	
es_{share}	Execution state	
exp	Experience	
fs_i	Feeling states i = novelty (nov)/emotion (em) / urge	

Another stimulus to the child is when (s)he starts using the social media. This is represented by the world state (ws_s), respective sensory (ss_s) and representation state (srs_s). A child can share the content after evaluating ($eval_s$) it, based on three attributes: novelty (fs_{nov}), some emotional value attached to it (fs_{em}), and the urge to share (fs_{urge}) it. This can be earned by experience (exp) and learning. Moreover, his action is self-attributed (ownership state: os). Here the control state (ccs) controls the sharing phenomena based upon beliefs influenced by his/her parent. Similar to his/her parent, when the child starts using social media, he/she might get pleasure by exhibiting himself.

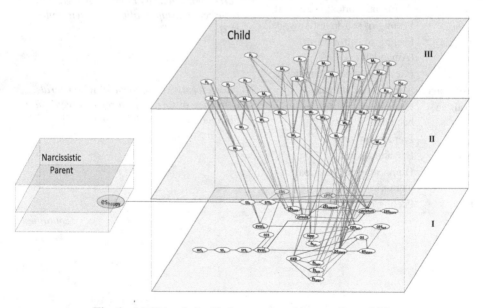

Fig. 1. Multi-leveled reified network architecture for a child.

3.2   Level II: First-Order Adaptation

This level addresses the adaptation principle related to 'Hebbian Learning', which is represented at Level II, by twelve W-states W_i (where $i = 1$ to 12 representing the weights of the twelve green colored connections at Level I). The dynamics of these W-states shows the learning of these connections in terms of persistence and time addressed in Sect. 3.3. The involved states at level I act as presynaptic and postsynaptic states for a W-state. For illustration, consider W_{10} (or $W_{fs_{nov}, ps_{share}}$), for fs_{nov} and ps_{share} as presynaptic and postsynaptic states for connection $fs_{nov} \rightarrow ps_{share}$. This indicates that the strength of a connection $fs_{nov} \rightarrow ps_{share}$ can change over time according to W_{10}. Table 2 enlist the W-states for the twelve adaptive connections. See [8] for more details about modeling the hebbian learning principle.

3.3   Level III: Second-Order Adaptation

The adaptation principles can themselves change over time as well, which is represented by the notion of meta-plasticity exhibited at this level III [8]. Here, 24 meta-plasticity-related states are represented by M_i and H_i (Table 2). The former is related to the persistence while the latter is related to the speed of learning of the states W_i (where $i = 1$ to 12). These states have upward (blue) arrows from the presynaptic, postsynaptic and relevant W-states. The downward causal connections (red) from H- and M-states influence the related W-states. To illustrate it further, consider M_{10} and H_{10}, they have upward arrows from the state fs_{nov} (presynaptic), ps_{share} (postsynaptic) and W_{10} state ($W_{fs_{nov}, ps_{share}}$) for connection $fs_{nov} \rightarrow ps_{share}$. For the downward connection, states M_{10} and H_{10} have downward arrows to W_{10}, to control its persistence and speed, respectively. A low value of H_{10} makes a low speed of learning of W_{10} and can be used (together with M_{10}) to control the learning and persistence of the concerning base level connection ([8], p. 110).

Table 2. Explanation of states in level II and III.

States per Level		References
Level II (Plasticity/Hebbian learning for Omega states):		*First-order adaptation level for plasticity by Hebbian learning [8,*
W_1: $W_{srs_h}, eval_h$	for $srs_h \rightarrow eval_h$	*21]*
W_2: W_{bs}, fs_{love}	for $cbs \rightarrow cfs_{love}$	
W_3: $W_{fs_{love}}, bs$	for $cfs_{love} \rightarrow cbs$	
W_4: $W_{striatum,insula}$	for $cstraitum \rightarrow cinsula$	
W_5: $W_{fs_{reward}}, striatum$	for $cfs_{reward} \rightarrow striatum$	
W_6: $W_{fs_{love}}, striatum$	for $cfs_{love} \rightarrow striatum$	
W_7: $W_{ps_{sat}}, hipp$	for $ps_{sat} \rightarrow hipp$	
W_8: $W_{fs_{sat}}, ps_{act}$	for $fs_{sat} \rightarrow cps_{act}$	
W_9: $W_{ps_{share}}, exp$	for $ps_{share} \rightarrow exp$	
W_{10}: $W_{fs_{nov}}, ps_{share}$	for $fs_{nov} \rightarrow ps_{share}$	

(continued)

Table 2. (*continued*)

States per Level		References
W_{11}: $W_{fs_{em}}, ps_{share}$	for $fs_{em} \rightarrow ps_{share}$	
W_{12}: W_{urge}, ps_{share}	for $urge \rightarrow ps_{share}$	
Level III (Meta-Plasticity/Learning rate and persistence): M_i: Persistence for $i = W_j$: $j = 1,...,12$ H_i: Learning rate for $i = W_j$: $j = 1,...,12$		*Second-order adaptation level for meta-plasticity to control the Hebbian learning* [8]

We used two type of inputs for the model of a child. One is received from the parent: es_{happy} is equal to the value obtained from his/her parent. As we address here the influence of a happy parent, the value ranges between 0.8–1. The second input is when the child uses social media, which is indicated by $ws_s = 1$ and 0 otherwise. Three combination functions were used to aggregate causal impact:

a) States ss_h, srs_h, ces_{happy}, fs_{sat}, ss_s, srs_s used the Euclidian function.

$$\mathbf{eucl}_{n,\lambda}(V_1,\ldots,V_k) = \sqrt[n]{(V_1^n + \ldots + V_k^n)/\lambda}$$

b) For 43 states (cbs; $cPFC$; cfs_{love}; cfs_{reward}; $cinsula$; $cstiatum$; $eval_h$; ps_{act}; es_{act}; $hipp$; ccs; $eval_s$; exp; fs_{novel}; fs_{em}; fs_{urge}; os; ps_{share}; e_{share}; H_i; M_i $i = 1$–12), the function **alogistic** (with positive steepness σ and threshold $\tau < 1$) was used:

$$\mathbf{alogistic}_{\sigma,\tau}(V_1,\ldots,V_k) = \left[\frac{1}{1+e^{-\sigma(V_1+\ldots+V_k-\tau)}} - \frac{1}{1+e^{\sigma\tau}}\right](1+e^{-\sigma\tau})$$

where each V_i is the single impact computed by the product of weight and state value: $\omega_{X,Y}X(t)$.

c) Lastly, for the 12 adaptation states (W_i: $i = 1$–12) we used Hebbian learning principle defined by the following combination function:

$$\mathbf{hebb}_\mu(V_1, V_2, W) = V_1 V_2(1 - W) + \mu W$$

Numerically, a reified-network-architecture-based model is represented as follows [8]:

1. At every time point t, the activation level of state Y at time t is represented by $Y(t)$, with the values between [0, 1].
2. The single impact of state X on state Y at time t is represented by $\mathbf{impact}_{X,Y}(t) = \omega_{X,Y} X(t)$; where $\omega_{X,Y}$ is the weight of connection $X \rightarrow Y$.

3. Special states are used to model network adaptation based on the notion of network reification, which means that network characteristic are represented by network states. For example, state $\mathbf{W}_{X,Y}$ represents an adaptive connection weight $\omega_{X,Y}(t)$ for the connection $X \to Y$, while $\mathbf{H}_Y$ represents an adaptive speed factor $\eta_Y(t)$ of state Y. Similarly, $\mathbf{C}_{i,Y}$ and $\mathbf{P}_{i,j,Y}$ represent adaptive combination functions $c_Y(.., t)$ over time and its parameters respectively. Combination functions are built as a weighted average from a number of basic combination functions $bcf_i(..)$, which take parameters $P_{i,j,Y}$ and values V_i as arguments. The universal combination function $\mathbf{c}^*_Y(..)$ for any state Y is defined as:

$$\mathbf{c}*_Y(S, C_1, \ldots, C_m, P_{1,1}, P_{2,1}, \ldots, P_{1,m}, P_{2,m}, V_1, \ldots, V_k, W_1, \ldots, W_k, W) = W + S[C_1 bcf_1(P_{1,1}, P_{2,1}, W_1 V_1, \ldots, W_k V_k) + \ldots + C_m bcf_m(P_{1,m}, P_{2,m}, W_1 V_1, \ldots, W_k V_k)]/(C_1 + \ldots + C_m) - W]$$

where at time t:

- variable S is used for the speed factor reification $\mathbf{H}_Y(t)$
- variable C_i for the combination function weight reification $\mathbf{C}_{i,Y}(t)$
- variable $P_{i,j}$ for the combination function parameter reification $\mathbf{P}_{i,j,Y}(t)$
- variable V_i for the state value $X_i(t)$ of base state X_i
- variable W_i for the connection weight reification $\mathbf{W}_{X_i,Y}(t)$
- variable W for the state value $Y(t)$ of base state Y.

4. Based on the above universal combination function, the effect on any state Y after time Δt is computed by the following *universal difference equation* as:

$$Y(t + \Delta t) = Y(t) + [\mathbf{c}*_Y(\mathbf{H}_Y(t), \mathbf{C}_{1,Y}(t), \ldots, \mathbf{C}_{m,Y}(t), \mathbf{P}_{1,1}(t), \mathbf{P}_{2,1}(t), \ldots, \mathbf{P}_{1,m}(t), \mathbf{P}_{2,m}(t), X_1(t), \ldots, X_k(t), \mathbf{W}_{X_1,Y}(t), \ldots, \mathbf{W}_{X_k,Y}(t), Y(t)) - Y(t)]\Delta t$$

which also can be written as a *universal differential equation*:

$$d Y(t)/dt = \mathbf{c}*_Y(\mathbf{H}_Y(t), \mathbf{C}_{1,Y}(t), \ldots, \mathbf{C}_{m,Y}(t), \mathbf{P}_{1,1}(t), \mathbf{P}_{2,1}(t), \ldots, \mathbf{P}_{1,m}(t), \mathbf{P}_{2,m}(t), X_1(t), \ldots, X_k(t), \mathbf{W}_{X_1,Y}(t), \ldots, \mathbf{W}_{X_k,Y}(t), Y(t)) - Y(t)$$

The dedicated software environment used was implemented in MATLAB, which takes input of the network characteristics represented by role matrices. A role matrix is a specification indicating the role played by each state. This involves the states of the base models and the states related to plasticity and meta-plasticity and their roles along with the related parameters. Detailed information for the model can be found online [23].

4   Simulation Experiments

Simulation experiments offer insights in the model dynamics reflecting the human behavior. In this section we present how a narcissistic parent influences his/her child. Here, we have discussed only the scenarios, when a parent is happy, thus es_{happy} is high for the parent [6]. The simulation scenarios related to a child are when he/she is a) exhibiting narcissism under parental influence, b) when he/she is learning not to be a narcissist, and c) exhibition of narcissism while using the social media.

4.1 A Child Displaying Influence of a Parent's Narcissism

This first scenario addresses a child which is not using social media, but gets parental influence. An simple example scenario can be: A parent is an actor on a TV-show; when a child is along his/her parent then he will also like to react in a duplicate/ instructed manner, to make the parent happy.

Figure 2 shows the results of such a scenario, here es_{happy} (blue) acts as input to the child (gains value = 0.95 at time point $t = 25$) [6], and $ws_s = 0$, as the child is not using the social media. The respective sensory (ss_h) and representation (srs_h: mustard) activates after es_{happy}. This activates the belief state (cbs: purple dots) and cortex (cPFC: green) of the child at the same time $t \approx 11$. Reward related states (cstriatum: brown - bold and ces_{happy}: mustard - bold) starts to activate around $t = 15$ but stays till value = 0.55. At this moment the child's feeling related to self-reward are not active indicating that the child is just mimicking his/her parent without being influenced by his/her own feelings. However, at time point $t > 280$, feelings of self-love (cfs_{love}: red) and self-rewarding (cfs_{reward}: brightgreen) start to increase due to activation in the insula (cinsula: magenta) at time point $t = 250$. This leads to reflect the narcissistic behavior (through social contagion), by increasing cstriatum and ces_{happy} to value = 1 at time point $t = 300$. This is also reflected by an increase in cbs at $t \approx 280$, indicating the learning of self-view or belief (cbs).

Here, the dotted lines show the dynamics of the involved W-states (i.e.: W_2, W_3, W_4, W_5 and W_6), indicating the hebbian learning effect through the involved states of the base model. It can be seen that learning for the self-rewarding states starts at time point $t > 50$ shown by W_4, which leads W_5 and W_6 to learn around time point $t \approx 280$ and the child is able to learn this contagion behavior around time point $t > 300$. Here it can be noted that W_2 and W_3 also reflect this at $t \approx 280$ thus reflecting learning of connections cbs $\rightarrow$ cfs_{love} and $cfs_{love} \rightarrow$ cbs (at Level I). This behavior indicate that the child has learnt how to act in a social environment.

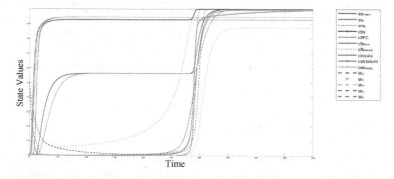

Fig. 2. Child replicating his parent's narcissism ($es_{happy} = 1$)

4.2   Influence of Age Over Narcissism

In this second scenario, with the passage of time (age) the child notices that his parent is a narcissist and he chooses for him/herself not to be a narcissist. An example can be that the child is in a social gathering along with his/her parent but prefers to sit at a calm/unnoticed place, rather than replicating the parent's behavior. So, while the parent is exhibiting his grandiosity, the child prefers to remain unnoticed.

Figure 3 shows such a scenario, the child gets the stimulus (es_{happy} = 0.95 at time point < 25) while not using the social media ws_s = 0. He/she starts to learn through hebbian learning that (s)he should not replicate his/her parent. This evaluation is shown by the corresponding evaluation state ($eval_h$: purple), which is activated around time point t = 20, after the sensory (ss_s: brown) and representation state (srs_s: mustard). It further activates the states of action with personal satisfaction in the duration of t = 50–150 (cps_{act}: green, fs_{sat}: blue, hipp: brown and ces_{act} : light blue).

Here, dotted states show the W-states of the model. It can be seen that the learning starts at time point t $\approx$ 25 with his/her age (W_1) and helps W_7 and W_8 to learn by t = 100. This indicates that the child is able to learn by his experience till time point t = 200 which is also reflected in his behavior/action (ces_{act}). Here, it is interesting to notice the behavior of W_1 and W_8, at first he/she un-learns the feeling of satisfaction and evaluation regarding the grandiosity of parent, by using his memories (hipp), which doesn't drop over the time and, the experiences are earned by the action (W_1 and W_8).

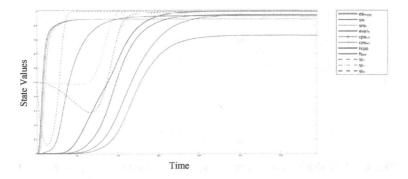

Fig. 3.   Child learns to be non-narcissistic (es_{happy} = 1)

4.3   Child Using Social Media

In this section, we address the dynamics of the adaptive network model, when a child uses social media (like WhatsApp/Twitter). This is shown in episodes a) when a child is not using the social media and b) when child is using the social media (Fig. 4). Initially, when a child doesn't use social media at all and, (s)he is under the influence of a parent (es_{happy} = 1), the self-rewarding states are already active (bold curves - cstriautm: purple; ces_{happy}: green; cinsula: cyan) before time point t = 60.

The new episode starts at t = 60, when (s)he starts using social media i.e. ws_s = 1 (shaded region). This activates the corresponding sensory (ss_s) and representation (srs_s) states. After some time, the control state (ccs: purple) and evaluation state ($eval_s$:green) activate and increases the preparation (ps_{share}: magenta) and execution states (es_{share}: red). The three associated feelings: novelty (fs_{nov}: brown dotted), urge (fs_{urge}: blue dotted) and emotion (fs_{em}: light blue) associated to the content, tends to grow by every episode along with the experience (exp). An example of experience can be, the number of likes or comments obtained from others over certain content. Here, the self-rewarding states are alleviated during sharing of the content, indicating that sharing gives him/her narcissistic pleasure. The suppression of self-rewarding states between $t = 120–180$, indicate that the child enjoys self-exhibiting on social media with parental influence. However, once narcissistic pleasure reaches a maximum (value = 1), the self-rewarding states stay high, indicating that (s)he is always looking for reward and attention or love.

In Fig. 5, it can be seen that W-states related to self-rewarding behavior (W_i: $i = 2–6$) continue to learn with each episode of sharing the content over the social media till $t = 250$. This shows that the narcissistic instinct of the child is fulfilled by sharing any content over social media. The W-states related to sharing the content over social media (W_i: $i = 9–12$) slowly increase with time, and after $t > 450$, they reach their maximum values. This indicates that the child has learnt about sharing from his/her experiences in each episode. It would be interesting to see behavior of $W_{12}(W_{urge,psshare})$, as it shows that the urge of sharing content is almost new at the start of each episode (/exposure to social media) till he is a regular user of social media.

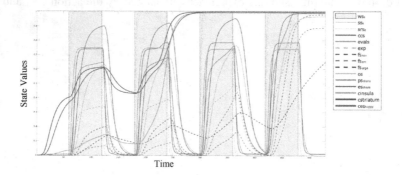

Fig. 4.   Child sharing and self-rewarding states are active ($es_{happy} = ws_s = 1$)

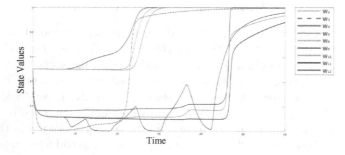

Fig. 5.   W states while child is sharing and self-rewarding states are active ($es_{happy} = 1$; $ws_s = 1$)

5　Conclusion

Our work aims to explore computationally how a child can be influenced by her or his parent's narcissism through a second-order adaptive network model. The model was designed based upon social, cognitive and psychological literature. Three simulations were presented. First we showed a) how a child mimics his/her parent grandiosity, then we showed b) how she or he learns to act in a non-narcissist way based upon experience. We also explored c) how a child decides what she or he should share over social media and how this influences his behavior.

As a future work, we would like to collect and use empirical data related to our model, to verify the behavior of the model with real-world data.

References

1. Wood, L.A., Kendal, R.L., Flynn, E.G.: Whom do children copy? Model-based biases in social learning. Dev. Rev. **33**(4), 341–356 (2013). https://doi.org/10.1016/j.dr.2013.08.002
2. Paley, B., Conger, R.D., Harold, G.T.: Parents' affect, adolescent cognitive representations, and adolescent social development. J. Marriage Fam. **62**(3), 761–776 (2000). https://doi.org/10.1111/j.1741-3737.2000.00761.x
3. Mahler, M.S., Pine, F., Bergman, A.: The Psychological Birth of the Human Infant. Symbiosis and Individuation. Basic Books, New York (1975)
4. Wickstrom, D.L., Fleck, J.R.: Missionary children: correlates of self-esteem and dependency. J. Psychol. Theol. **11**(3), 221–230 (1983). https://doi.org/10.1177/009164718301100308
5. Brummelman, E., Nelemans, S.A., Thomaes, S., Orobio de Castro, B.: When parents praise inflates, children's self-esteem deflates'. Child Dev. **88**(6), 1799–1809 (2017). https://doi.org/10.1111/cdev.12936
6. Jabeen, F., Gerritsen, C., Treur, J.: 'I ain't like you' a complex network model of digital narcissism. In: Cherifi, H., Gaito, S., Mendes, J.F., Moro, E., Rocha, L.M. (eds.) COMPLEX NETWORKS 2019. SCI, vol. 882, pp. 337–349. Springer, Cham (2020). https://doi.org/10.1007/978-3-030-36683-4_28
7. Kuipers, B.: Commonsense reasoning about causality: deriving behavior from structure - ScienceDirect. Artif. Intell. **24**(1–3), 169–203 (1984). https://doi.org/10.1016/0004-3702(84)90039-0
8. Treur, J.: Network-Oriented Modeling for Adaptive Networks: Designing Higher-Order Adaptive Biological Mental and Social Network Models. Springer, Heidelberg (2020). https://doi.org/10.1007/978-3-030-31445-3
9. Brummelman, E., Thomaes, S., Nelemans, S.A., Orobio de Castro, B., Overbeek, G., Bushman, B.J.: Origins of narcissism in children. Proc. Natl. Acad. Sci. **112**(12), 3659–3662 (2015). https://doi.org/10.1073/pnas.1420870112
10. Dwairy, M.: Parental acceptance–rejection: a fourth cross-cultural research on parenting and psychological adjustment of children. J. Child Fam. Stud. **19**(1), 30–35 (2010). https://doi.org/10.1007/s10826-009-9338-y
11. Brummelman, E., Thomaes, S., Sedikides, C.: Separating narcissism from self-esteem. Curr. Dir. Psychol. Sci. **25**(1), 8–13 (2016). https://doi.org/10.1177/0963721415619737
12. Gross, D.: Social networks and kids: how young is too young? CNN Tech (2009)

13. Jadin, T., Gnambs, T., Batinic, B.: Personality traits and knowledge sharing in online communities. Comput. Hum. Behav. **29**(1), 210–216 (2013)
14. Foster, J.D., Keith Campbell, W., Twenge, J.M.: Individual differences in narcissism: inflated self-views across the lifespan and around the world. J. Res. Pers. **37**(6), 469–486 (2003). https://doi.org/10.1016/S0092-6566(03)00026-6
15. Sethna, V., et al.: Mother–infant interactions and regional brain volumes in infancy: an MRI study. Brain Struct. Funct. **222**(5), 2379–2388 (2016). https://doi.org/10.1007/s00429-016-1347-1
16. Kok, R., et al.: Normal variation in early parental sensitivity predicts child structural brain development. J. Am. Acad. Child Adolesc. Psychiatry **54**(10), 824–831.e1 (2015). https://doi.org/10.1016/j.jaac.2015.07.009
17. Lee, T.-H., Qu, Y., Telzer, E.H.: Love flows downstream: mothers' and children's neural representation similarity in perceiving distress of self and family. Soc. Cogn. Affect. Neurosci. **12**(12), 1916–1927 (2017). https://doi.org/10.1093/scan/nsx125
18. Daniel, R., Pollmann, S.: A universal role of the ventral striatum in reward-based learning: evidence from human studies. Neurobiol. Learn. Mem. **114**, 90–100 (2014). https://doi.org/10.1016/j.nlm.2014.05.002
19. Fan, Y., et al.: The narcissistic self and its psychological and neural correlates: an exploratory fMRI study. Psychol. Med. **41**(8), 1641–1650 (2011). https://doi.org/10.1017/S003329171000228X
20. Olsson, J., Berglund, S., Annett, J.: Narcissism – Brain and Behavior: Self-views and Empathy in the Narcissistic Brain, p. 45. School of Bioscience (2014)
21. Treur, J.: Network-Oriented Modeling. Springer, Cham (2016). https://doi.org/10.1007/978-3-319-45213-5_18
22. Zeelenberg, M., Nelissen, R.M.A., Breugelmans, S.M., Pieters, R.: On emotion specificity in decision making: why feeling is for doing. Judgm. Decis. Mak. **3**(1), 18–27 (2008)
23. Jabeen, F.: N_Child Specifications, MsFakhra Specs, 04 February 2020. https://github.com/MsFakhra/ParentalInfluence_NarcissticInfluence

A Systematic Assessment of Feature Extraction Methods for Robust Prediction of Neuropsychological Scores from Functional Connectivity Data

Federico Calesella[1] , Alberto Testolin[1,2] ,
Michele De Filippo De Grazia[3] , and Marco Zorzi[1,3(✉)]

[1] Department of General Psychology, University of Padova, 35141 Padua, Italy
{alberto.testolin,marco.zorzi}@unipd.it
[2] Department of Information Engineering, University of Padova,
35141 Padua, Italy
[3] IRCCS San Camillo Hospital, 30126 Venice, Italy

Abstract. Multivariate prediction of human behavior from resting state data is gaining increasing popularity in the neuroimaging community, with far-reaching translational implications in neurology and psychiatry. However, the high dimensionality of neuroimaging data increases the risk of overfitting, calling for the use of dimensionality reduction methods to build robust predictive models. In this work, we assess the ability of four dimensionality reduction techniques to extract relevant features from resting state functional connectivity matrices of stroke patients, which are then used to build a predictive model of the associated language deficits based on cross-validated regularized regression. Features extracted by Principal Component Analysis (PCA) were found to be the best predictors, followed by Independent Component Analysis (ICA), Dictionary Learning (DL) and Non-Negative Matrix Factorization. However, ICA and DL led to more parsimonious models. Overall, our findings suggest that the choice of the dimensionality reduction technique should not only be based on prediction/regression accuracy, but also on considerations about model complexity and interpretability.

Keywords: Resting state networks · Functional connectivity · Machine learning · Feature extraction · Dimensionality reduction · Predictive modeling

1 Introduction

Resting State Functional Connectivity (RSFC) represents the correlation in the spontaneous fluctuations of the blood oxygen level-dependent signal between brain regions, measured at rest [1]. In stroke patients, RSFC has been successfully employed to predict individual deficits in several cognitive domains, such as attention, visuo-spatial memory, verbal memory and language [2, 3]. Machine learning has been a key enabling technology in this field, since the analysis of neuroimaging data requires the adoption of multivariate approaches that can efficiently operate over high-dimensional

M. Mahmud et al. (Eds.): BI 2020, LNAI 12241, pp. 29–40, 2020.
https://doi.org/10.1007/978-3-030-59277-6_3

feature spaces [4–6]. At the same time, neuroimaging datasets typically have a much greater number of features than observations [5, 7], which raises the risk of overfitting, that is, extracting rules or statistical patterns that specifically describe the training data but cannot be generalized to new observations [8, 9]. One possible way to mitigate the overfitting issue is to adopt regularization methods. For example, regularized regression methods such as ridge regression [3], elastic-net regression [10] and least absolute shrinkage and selection operator (LASSO) [11] include a penalty term that pushes the estimated coefficients of irrelevant features toward zero [12]. Besides limiting multi-collinearity and overfitting, this often also improves model interpretability [10, 13, 14], making regularized algorithms particularly suitable for the analysis of neuroimaging data (for a recent review, see [15]). Another useful approach to tackle the "curse of dimensionality" in neuroimaging data is to first apply unsupervised dimensionality reduction techniques [5, 7, 16], in order to extract a limited number of features that can compactly describe the data distribution.

However, both regularized regression methods and feature extraction techniques can vary in performance, depending on the type of data and the task [7, 15], calling for a systematic assessment of the differences between these methods on neuroimaging data. Some recent works have compared the performance of several machine learning algorithms [15], and their interaction with dimensionality reduction methods [17]. Nonetheless, to the best of our knowledge a similar approach has not yet been applied to multiple unsupervised feature extraction techniques.

The goal of this work is thus to systematically explore the impact of regularization in combination with different dimensionality reduction techniques, in order to establish which method can be more effective to build predictive models of neuropsychological deficits. In particular, we used RSFC data from stroke patients to predict neuropsychological scores in the language domain using a machine learning framework. In a first step, the RSFC matrices underwent a feature extraction analysis, implemented through different dimensionality reduction methods: Principal Component Analysis, Independent Component Analysis, Dictionary Learning and Non-Negative Matrix Factorization. In a second step, the extracted features were entered as predictors into a regularized regression model, which was estimated using different cross validation schemes.

2   Materials and Methods

2.1   Participants and Data Acquisition

RSFC data was taken from a previously published study [3], in which 132 symptomatic stroke patients underwent a 30 min long RS-fMRI acquisition, 1–2 weeks after the stroke occurred. 32 subjects were excluded either for hemodynamic lags or excessive head motion. For each patient, a symmetric RSFC matrix (324 × 324) was calculated across 324 cortical parcels [18] (Fig. 1). The matrices were then vectorized, resulting in 52,326 FC values per subject. After fMRI acquisition, all participants underwent a behavioral assessment spanning several cognitive domains. In the present work we focus on the language scores, which are available for a subset of the participants ($n = 95$). We used an overall "language factor" score [2] which captures the shared variance of several sub-tests (first principal component accounting for 77.3% of variance). The score was normalized to represent impaired performance with negative values.

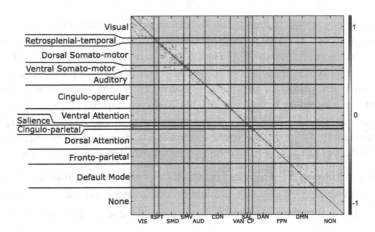

Fig. 1. Mean RSFC matrix (324 × 324) across all patients. Parcels in the matrix are sorted in relation to 12 large-scale intrinsic brain networks.

2.2 Unsupervised Feature Extraction

Since the feature extraction process was unsupervised, in this phase the entire dataset was used (here $n = 100$ and $p = 52{,}326$), regardless of the availability of the language score. All the employed feature extraction methods aim to find a weight matrix W that can linearly transform the original $n \times p$ data matrix X in a new set of k features, with $k < p$ and usually $k < n$, such that:

$$F = XW \qquad (1)$$

where F is the new feature space, and the parameter k is the number of features to be extracted. Since choosing the value of k is non-trivial, we systematically varied k from 10 to 95, with step size = 5, which resulted in 18 feature sets for each employed technique.

The original data can be reconstructed by back-projecting the new feature set in the original space:

$$X_R = FW^T \qquad (2)$$

where X_R is the reconstructed data. In order to compare the compression ability of the feature extraction methods, the reconstruction error was calculated as the mean squared error (MSE) between X and X_R, for each value of k.

Principal Component Analysis (PCA). PCA linearly transforms the original data into a smaller set of uncorrelated features called principal components, sorted by the data variance they explain [19]. First, X must be centered [20], so that it has zero-mean.

PCA then searches for the eigenvalues and eigenvectors of the $p \times p$ covariance matrix $X^T X$. Hence, matrix factorization via singular value decomposition is applied, such that:

$$X = UDW^T \tag{3}$$

where U is an $n \times n$ matrix containing the eigenvectors of XX^T, D is an $n \times p$ matrix with the square root of the eigenvalues on the diagonal, and W is a $p \times p$ matrix containing the eigenvectors of $X^T X$. However, if $p > n$, there are only $n-1$ non-zero eigenvalues, so only the first $n - 1$ columns of D and W are kept [20]. Eigenvectors are sorted in descending order of explained variance. Hence, W contains $n - 1$ principal components, expressed as a set of p weights that can map the original variables in a new compressed space. Since PCA is the only deterministic method we explored, it was performed only once and the first k features were then iteratively selected. For the other methods, the procedure had to be run repeatedly for each value of k.

Independent Component Analysis (ICA). ICA assumes that a p-dimensional signal vector $X_{i,*}^T$ is generated by a linear combination of k sources (with $k \leq p$), contained in vector $F_{i,*}^T$. The sources are assumed to be latent, independent and non-Gaussian [21]. Therefore:

$$X_{i,*}^T = AF_{i,*}^T \tag{4}$$

where A is a $p \times k$ unmixing matrix, which maps the signal in the sources. Hence, the sources are obtained by:

$$F_{i,*}^T = WX_{i,*}^T \tag{5}$$

where W is the inverse of the unmixing matrix A. Then, $F_{i,*}^T$ represents k latent independent features [21, 22]. In order to simplify the ICA problem, the data distribution is first centered, and then pre-processed through whitening so that a new vector $X_{i,*}^T$ with uncorrelated components and unit variance is obtained. In this case, PCA was used for data whitening [22]. The *FastICA* function of the scikit-learn library was used.

Dictionary Learning (DL). The DL algorithm, sometimes known as *sparse coding*, jointly solves for a $p \times k$ dictionary W and the new set of features F that best represent the data. However, an L_1 penalty term is included in the cost function, in order to obtain only few non-zero entrances. Hence, the cost function becomes:

$$(W, F) = \min_{(W,F)} \frac{1}{2} \left\| X - FW^T \right\|_2^2 + \lambda \|F\|_1$$

$$subject\ to\ \left\| W_j \right\|_2 \leq 1,\ \forall j = 1, \ldots, k \tag{6}$$

where λ is the L_1 penalty coefficient, controlling for the sparsity of the compressed representation [23]. The *DicitonaryLearning* function of the scikit-learn library was used.

Non-negative Matrix Factorization (NNMF). NNMF is a form of matrix factorization into non-negative factors W and H [24, 25], such that the linear combination of each column of W weighted by the columns of H can approximate the original data X:

$$X \approx WH \tag{7}$$

In order to do that, the NNMF aims to minimize the following loss function:

$$\|A - WH_F^2\|$$

$$subject\ to\ W, H \geq 0 \tag{8}$$

The *nnmf* MATLAB function with the "multiplicative update algorithm" was used.

2.3   Regularized Regression

The feature sets extracted by each method were then used as regressors for the prediction of the language scores. Note that only the subjects with available language score were kept in this phase ($n = 95$). The regressors were first standardized, and then entered into the elastic-net penalized regression [10, 14, 26] (the MATLAB *lasso* function was used). The elastic-net regression solves for:

$$\min_{\beta} \left(\frac{1}{2n} \sum_{i=1}^{n} \left(y_i - x_i^T \beta \right)^2 + \lambda P_\alpha(\beta) \right) \tag{9}$$

where n is the number of observations, y_i is the prediction target at observation i, x_i is the data observation i with p variables, λ is the non-negative regularization coefficient, β are the p regression coefficients and P_α is defined as:

$$P_\alpha(\beta) = \sum_{j=1}^{p} \left(\frac{1}{2}(1 - \alpha)\beta_j^2 + \alpha|\beta_j| \right) \tag{10}$$

Therefore, the elastic-net loss function requires two free parameters to be set, namely the λ and α parameters. The λ parameter regulates the penalization strength, so the larger the λ, the more coefficients are shrunk toward zero. The α parameter sets the regularization type: with $\alpha = 1$ an L_1 penalization (LASSO) is obtained, whereas with $\alpha \approx 0$ the L_2 penalty (ridge regression) is approached [27]. The main difference is that LASSO forces the coefficient estimates to have exactly-zero values, whereas the ridge regularization shrinks the coefficients to near-zero values [13]. Lastly, the elastic-net regression combines both the penalization terms [27]. The λ was tuned over 100 possible values, logarithmically spaced between 10^{-5} and 10^5. The α value ranged between 0.1 and 1 with step size $= 0.1$ (10 possible values).

2.4   Cross Validation Setup and Model Estimation

In order to find optimal hyper-parameters, it is common practice to employ a grid-search with cross-validation (CV). The complete dataset is split into a *training* set and a *test* set: the training set is used for hyper-parameters tuning, and the resulting model is then evaluated on the test set. In the "nested" CV setup the training set is further split into training and *validation* sets using random permutations: the hyper-parameters are optimized on each validation set, and the best model is finally evaluated on a completely left-out test set [5, 16, 26]. A major issue in nested CV is that a different model is estimated for each test set, and there is no standard practice for choosing the hyper-parameters of the final model.

Here, combinations for the possible values of all hyper-parameters (k, λ and α) were tested using both a Leave-One-Out (LOO) and a nested LOO (n-LOO) CV. In order to produce the final model of the n-LOO, three measures of central tendency were used for choosing the optimal hyperparameters, namely *mean* (n-average condition), *median* (n-median condition) and *mode* (n-mode condition).

2.5   Model Comparison

In order to compare the models generated by the different feature extraction methods, both the R^2 and the Bayesian information criterion (BIC) [28] were calculated (note that only the non-zero coefficients were used for BIC calculation). Furthermore, potential differences in the distributions of the quadratic residuals were statistically tested through the Wilcoxon signed rank test [29].

3   Results

The feature extraction methods were first assessed based on their reconstruction error. For all methods, the reconstruction error decreased when increasing the number of features (Fig. 2, top-left panel), and NNMF showed generally higher reconstruction error. The regression model using the PCA features reached the best R^2 in all CV setups (Fig. 2). The ICA-based model performed slightly worse, except for the n-average CV. For the DL-based model the results further decreased in all the CV variants. The NNMF features led to the worst R^2; however, they also resulted in a smaller decrease in the n-average condition, approaching the DL performance.

Results can be interpreted differently when considering the BIC score (Fig. 2), which penalizes models with more parameters (i.e., features). The ICA- and DL-based models obtained a lower BIC compared to the PCA-based model, while the NNMF-based model still obtained the worst results.

Interestingly, it turns out that the measure of central tendency used for choosing the final model in the n-LOO can have a relatively large effect on both the R^2 and the BIC. The predictive model is poor when averaging the parameters across subjects, whereas choosing the median and the mode allows to achieve the same performance of the LOO. This might be caused by the high susceptibility of the mean to outliers, so that major departures from the distribution of the selected parameters could drive the choice

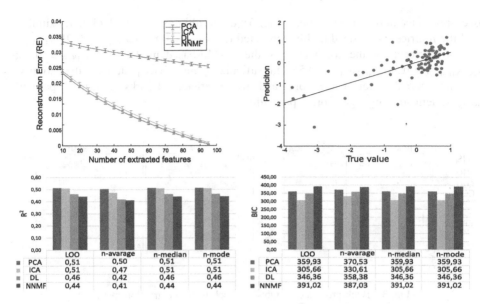

Fig. 2. Top left: Reconstruction error as a function of the number of extracted features. Top right: PCA-model predictions with LOO CV. Bottom: R^2 and BIC of the models for each feature extraction method and CV scheme.

toward the outlier values. In this case, median and mode might represent more stable measures of central tendency. In light of these results, we only considered LOO models (which achieved a performance comparable to that of n-median and n-mode n-LOO models) for further analyses.

Interestingly, different feature extraction methods led to slightly different optimal hyper-parameters (Table 1). The ICA- and DL-based models were chosen with fewer features than the PCA- and NNMF-based models. Regarding the regularization type, both PCA and DL led to the smallest α value, thus approaching the ridge regression, whereas ICA and NNMF led to an intermediate elastic-net solution, approaching LASSO in the NNMF case. Despite such variability in model performance and selected hyper-parameters, Wilcoxon signed rank tests did not highlight any significant difference across the models' squared residuals (all $p > 0.05$).

Table 1. Selected hyper-parameters (λ, α and k) for each feature extraction method.

	λ	α	Features
PCA	0.1385	0.1	35
ICA	0.087	0.3	23
DL	0.1385	0.1	30
NNMF	0.0343	0.7	39

In the Appendix we report the weights of 6 features ordered by the absolute value of the associated coefficient. The estimated coefficients of each method were also back-projected in the original space (Fig. 3): the resulting structures look fairly similar, and the matrices are indeed highly correlated ($r_{PCA-ICA} = 0.89$; $r_{PCA-DL} = 0.91$; $r_{ICA-DL} = 0.88$), except for the coefficients of the NNMF-based model ($r_{NNMF-PCA} = 0.58$; $r_{NNMF-ICA} = 0.58$; $r_{NNMF-DL} = 0.54$). In particular, connectivity patterns in the auditory, cingulo-opercular, dorsal attentional and fronto-parietal networks seem to be particularly salient for language scores' prediction.

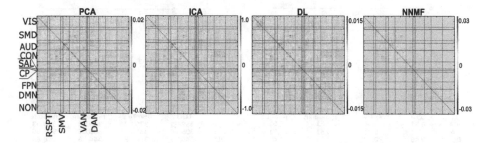

Fig. 3. Back-projected weights for each feature extraction method.

4   Discussion

In this work we systematically compared four unsupervised dimensionality reduction methods in their ability to extract relevant features from RSFC matrices. In particular, we assessed how different methods influenced a regularized regression model trained on the RSFC features to predict the cognitive performance of stroke patients.

Overall, in relation to the accuracy of the regression, PCA appeared to be the best method for extracting robust predictors, followed by ICA, DL and NNMF features. However, when considering the BIC score for model evaluation and comparison, ICA and DL obtained the best result, suggesting that these methods can guarantee acceptable predictive accuracy even relying on a more limited number of features. One possible interpretation is that ICA and DL extract features that can individually retain more information, so that fewer features are required to explain the data. A reduced number of descriptors might also allow to better generalize to out-of-sample predictions; in conclusion, balancing model accuracy and parsimony, the ICA-based seems to be the preferable method.

Future studies should further extend our results to the prediction of a broader range of behavioral scores, in order to better assess whether some feature extraction methods could be more general than others. For example, in our case PCA could have obtained the best regression performance because it extracts features that are particularly useful to predict the language scores. Based on model parsimony, one could thus speculate that ICA and DL might be able to extract more general features, which are less specifically tuned for language prediction and could thus be used to build predictive models in other cognitive domains. Note that the impact of the feature extraction method might also be evaluated for other types of neuroimaging data available for stroke patients, such as EEG connectivity measures or 3D images of brain lesions [30].

Despite the differences across methods, we also observed high correlations between the back-projected coefficient matrices, which suggest that these methods extract similar structure from the RSFC matrices. Specifically, all methods highlighted key structures in the intra- and inter-network connectivity in the auditory, cingulo-opercular, dorsal attentional and fronto-parietal networks. NNMF was less aligned with the other methods, probably due to the non-negativity constraint applied on the transformation matrix.

Acknowledgments. This work was supported by grants from the Italian Ministry of Health (RF-2013-02359306 to MZ, Ricerca Corrente to IRCCS Ospedale San Camillo) and by MIUR (Dipartimenti di Eccellenza DM 11/05/2017 n. 262 to the Department of General Psychology). We are grateful to Prof. Maurizio Corbetta for providing the stroke dataset, which was collected in a study funded by grants R01 HD061117-05 and R01 NS095741.

Appendix

The extracted features are sorted in descending order based on the absolute coefficient value. Regression coefficients and the first 6 features are displayed for each dimensionality reduction method (Fig. 4, 5, 6, 7 and 8).

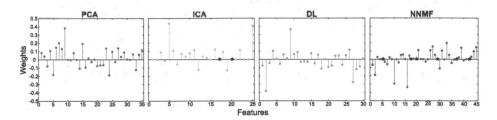

Fig. 4. Regression coefficients for each model. Black stars represent coefficients = 0.

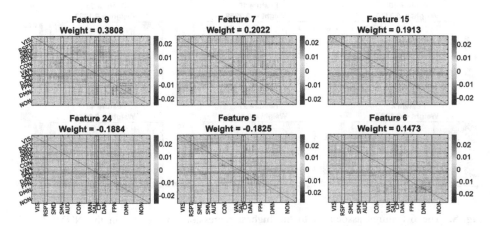

Fig. 5. The 6 features associated to the highest regression coefficients in the PCA-based model.

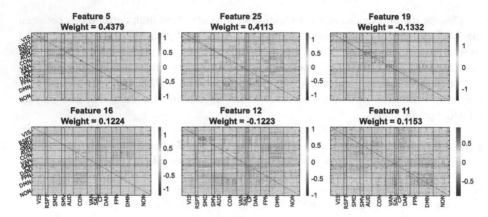

Fig. 6. The 6 features associated to the highest regression coefficients in the ICA-based model.

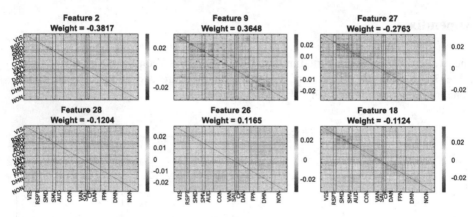

Fig. 7. The 6 features associated to the highest regression coefficients in the DL-based model.

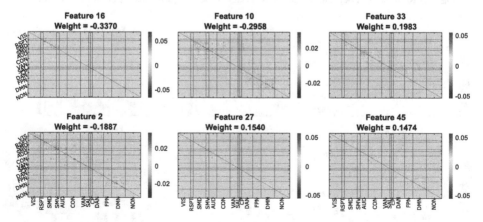

Fig. 8. The 6 features associated to the highest regression coefficients in the NNMF-based model.

References

1. Biswal, B., Zerrin Yetkin, F., Haughton, V.M., Hyde, J.S.: Functional connectivity in the motor cortex of resting human brain using echo-planar MRI. Magn. Reson. Med. **34**, 537–541 (1995)
2. Salvalaggio, A., de Filippo De Grazia, M., Zorzi, M., de Schotten, M.T., Corbetta, M.: Post-stroke deficit prediction from lesion and indirect structural and functional disconnection. Brain **143**(7), 2173–2188 (2020). awaa156
3. Siegel, J.S., et al.: Disruptions of network connectivity predict impairment in multiple behavioral domains after stroke. Proc. Nat. Acad. Sci. US Am. **113**, E4367–E4376 (2016)
4. Norman, K.A., Polyn, S.M., Detre, G.J., Haxby, J.V.: Beyond mind-reading: multi-voxel pattern analysis of fMRI data. Trends in Cognitive Sciences. 10, 424–430 (2006)
5. Pereira, F., Mitchell, T., Botvinick, M.: Machine learning classifiers and fMRI: a tutorial overview. NeuroImage **45**, S199–S209 (2009)
6. Dosenbach, N.U.F., et al.: Prediction of individual brain maturity using fMRI. Science **329**, 1358–1361 (2010)
7. Mwangi, B., Tian, T.S., Soares, J.C.: A review of feature reduction techniques in neuroimaging. Neuroinformatics **12**(2), 229–244 (2013)
8. Guyon, I., Elisseeff, A.: An introduction to variable and feature selection. J. Mach. Learn. Res. **3**, 1157–1182 (2003)
9. Hua, J., Tembe, W.D., Dougherty, E.R.: Performance of feature-selection methods in the classification of high-dimension data. Pattern Recogn. **42**, 409–424 (2009)
10. Carroll, M.K., Cecchi, G.A., Rish, I., Garg, R., Rao, A.R.: Prediction and interpretation of distributed neural activity with sparse models. NeuroImage **44**, 112–122 (2009)
11. Wager, T.D., Atlas, L.Y., Lindquist, M.A., Roy, M., Woo, C.W., Kross, E.: An fMRI-based neurologic signature of physical pain. N. Engl. J. Med. **368**, 1388–1397 (2013)
12. Teipel, S.J., Kurth, J., Krause, B., Grothe, M.J.: The relative importance of imaging markers for the prediction of Alzheimer's disease dementia in mild cognitive impairment - beyond classical regression. NeuroImage Clin. **8**, 583–593 (2015)
13. Tibshirani, R.: Regression shrinkage and selection via the lasso. J. Roy. Stat. Soc.: Ser. B (Methodol.) **58**, 267–288 (1996)
14. Zou, H., Zhang, H.H.: On the adaptive elastic-net with a diverging number of parameters. Ann. Stat. **37**, 1733–1751 (2009)
15. Cui, Z., Gong, G.: The effect of machine learning regression algorithms and sample size on individualized behavioral prediction with functional connectivity features. NeuroImage **178**, 622–637 (2018)
16. Haynes, J.D.: A primer on pattern-based approaches to fMRI: principles, pitfalls, and perspectives. Neuron **87**, 257–270 (2015)
17. Jollans, L., et al.: Quantifying performance of machine learning methods for neuroimaging data. NeuroImage **199**, 351–365 (2019)
18. Glasser, M.F., et al.: A multi-modal parcellation of human cerebral cortex. Nature **536**, 171–178 (2016)
19. Jolliffe, I.T.: Principal Component Analysis. Encyclopedia of Statistics in Behavioral Science (2002)
20. Mourão-Miranda, J., Bokde, A.L.W., Born, C., Hampel, H., Stetter, M.: Classifying brain states and determining the discriminating activation patterns: support vector machine on functional MRI data. NeuroImage **40**, 1533–1541 (2005)
21. Calhoun, V.D., Adali, T.: Unmixing fMRI with independent component analysis. IEEE Eng. Med. Biol. Mag. **25**, 79–90 (2006)

22. Hyvärinen, A., Oja, E.: Independent component analysis: algorithms and applications. Neural Netw. **13**, 411–430 (2000)
23. Mairal, J., Bach, F., Ponce, J., Sapiro, G.: Online dictionary learning for sparse coding. In: ACM International Conference Proceeding Series, pp. 689–696 (2009)
24. Lee, D.D., Seung, H.S.: Algorithms for non-negative matrix factorization. In: Advances in Neural Information Processing Systems, pp. 556–562 (2001)
25. Berry, M.W., Browne, M., Langville, A.N., Pauca, V.P., Plemmons, R.J.: Algorithms and applications for approximate nonnegative matrix factorization. Comput. Stat. Data Anal. **52**, 155–173 (2007)
26. Hastie, T., Tibshirani, R., Friedman, J.: The Elements of Statistical Learning. Springer Series in Statistics (2009)
27. Friedman, J., Hastie, T., Tibshirani, R.: Regularization paths for generalized linear models via coordinate descent. J. Stat. Softw. **33**, 1–22 (2010)
28. Schwarz, G.: Estimating the dimension of a model. Ann. Stat. **6**, 461–464 (1978)
29. Demšar, J.: Statistical comparisons of classifiers over multiple data sets. J. Mach. Learn. Res. **7**, 1–30 (2006)
30. Chauhan, S., Vig, L., de Filippo De Grazia, M., Corbetta, M., Ahmad, S., Zorzi, M.: A comparison of shallow and deep learning methods for predicting cognitive performance of stroke patients from MRI lesion images. Front. Neuroinform. **13**, 53 (2019)

The Effect of Loss-Aversion on Strategic Behaviour of Players in Divergent Interest Tacit Coordination Games

Dor Mizrahi$^{(\boxtimes)}$, Ilan Laufer , and Inon Zuckerman

Department of Industrial Engineering and Management, Ariel University,
Ariel, Israel
Dor.mizrahil@msmail.ariel.ac.il,
{ilanl, inonzu}@ariel.ac.il

Abstract. Previous Experiments in the field of human behavior and game theory has shown that loss aversion has a major effect on players' decisions in coordination problems. The overarching aim of our study was to model the effect of loss aversion on individual player behavior in divergent interest tacit coordination games. Based on a large-scale behavioral data we have designed a model predicting the total number of points players allocate to themselves as a result of increased penalty values in cases of non-coordination. Understanding the effect of loss aversion in case of divergent interest coordination problems on players' behavior will allow us to better predict the human decision-making process and as a result, create more realistic algorithms for human-machine cooperation's. Understanding the effect of loss aversion in the context of divergent interest tacit coordination games may enable the construction of better algorithms for human-machine interaction that could more accurately predict human decision behavior under uncertainty.

Keywords: Tacit coordination games · Decision making · Divergent interest · Loss aversion · Cognitive modeling

1 Introduction

The overarching aim of our study was to model the effect of loss aversion on individual players' behavior in divergent interest tacit coordination games. Divergent interest tacit coordination games constitute a sub-group of tacit coordination games, in which an agreed-upon solution might yield a different payoff for each player, while communication between the players is not allowed.

Previous research has demonstrated that loss aversion is a key factor in decision making in the context of coordination games [1, 2]. Loss aversion is a psychological phenomenon that describes the tendency of people to prefer avoiding possible losses to acquiring equivalent gains (e.g. [3, 4]). Research on decision making in the context of risk and uncertainty has shown that loss aversion is a key factor in deciding between alternatives [5, 6].

© Springer Nature Switzerland AG 2020
M. Mahmud et al. (Eds.): BI 2020, LNAI 12241, pp. 41–49, 2020.
https://doi.org/10.1007/978-3-030-59277-6_4

In this behavioral study, we have conducted a large-scale tacit coordination experiment in order to model the players' behavior under different penalty values charged for non-coordination. We then sought the best fitting polynomial regression model for the observed data in order to model the relationship between loss aversion and the absolute individual payoff.

2   Materials and Methods

2.1   "Bargaining Table" Game

In order to explore the effect of loss aversion on strategic behavior of individual players in the context of diverge interest tacit coordination games we have utilized the "Bargaining Table" Task [7, 8]. The "Bargaining Table" tacit coordination game consists of a 9×9 square board. Discs are scattered around the board, each assigned with a numeric value. Alongside the discs, there are two squares with two different colors (see Fig. 1). The blue square denotes player 1 and is located at board position (2, 5); The orange square denotes player 2 and is located at board position (8, 5). The task of each player is to assign each of the discs to one of the squares (either blue or orange). The payoff for each player is the total sum of the numeric values of the discs that are assigned to their own square. For example, in Fig. 1 the blue player attained a payoff of [4 + 5] points, while the orange player attained a payoff of [1] point.

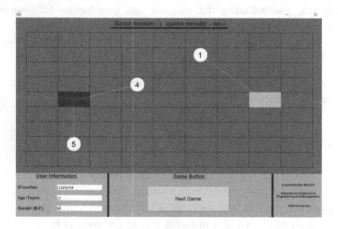

Fig. 1. "Bargaining Table" board game (Color figure online)

The "Bargaining Table" poses a tacit coordination task since the two players must assign each of the discs to one of the squares tacitly, without knowing what assignments were performed by the other player. In this setting, the value of each disc is given as payoff only if both players assign it to the same specific player (blue or orange square). If a given disc was assigned differently by the players (i.e. each player assigned the disc to a different square), both players received a penalty computed on the basis of disc value. The "Bargaining Table" game is a divergent interest version of the "Assign Circles" (e.g. [9–13]) pure tacit coordination games. Previous studies conducted on the latter [9–11, 13] have shown that the most prominent strategy players utilize to select a focal point is the rule of closeness. By implementing the rule of closeness the player assigns each disc to the closest available square.

There was a penalty for non-coordination. This penalty value was randomized by the computer at the beginning of the session and remained constant for all ten games. The value of the penalty ranged from 0.1 to 0.9 with a resolution of 0.1 for each step. The penalty value was randomized using a uniform distribution (i.e. with a probability of 1/9 per each penalty option). The penalty values (e.g. 80%) appeared at the start of each game on the opening slide as well as during game progression in each slide's header (Fig. 1).

The varying penalty values for non-coordination enabled the modeling of the players' behavior in different levels of loss aversion.

Specifically, we have examined the effect of loss aversion on the tradeoff between selecting a prominent focal point solution and a more self-maximizing one, while taking into account the penalty value which in turn affects the amount of potential gains and losses.

2.2 "Bargaining Tables" Game Boards Design

To examine players' loss aversion behavior across different scenarios associated with different penalty values we have created a set of ten game boards (see Fig. 2), each presented to all of the players. To avoid a situation where a player might be systematically biased by a specific strategic position, we have designed a balanced set of games. Specifically, each player played the following games: four games in which they were defined as the dominant player (the dominant player is expected to gain over 50% of the total game points should a focal point is chosen); four games in which the player was defined as the weak player (the weak player is expected to gain less than 50% of the total game points should a focal point solution is chosen); and two games were considered to be 'equal division' games, i.e. in these games the focal point solution entailed an equal division of the points between the players. In addition, if the player chose a focal point solution by implementing the closeness rule in all ten games, each of the two players received an equal payoff of 52 points. Importantly, in all of the ten games each player was always assigned the role of the 'blue' player so that all the participants will be assigned the same strategic positions across the different games (either weak, dominant or 'equal payoff').

Looking at Fig. 2 it can be observed that from the perspective of the 'blue' player, the dominant-position games are [3, 5, 7, and 9],the weak-position games are [2, 4, 6, and 8] whereas the equal division games are [1, and 2].

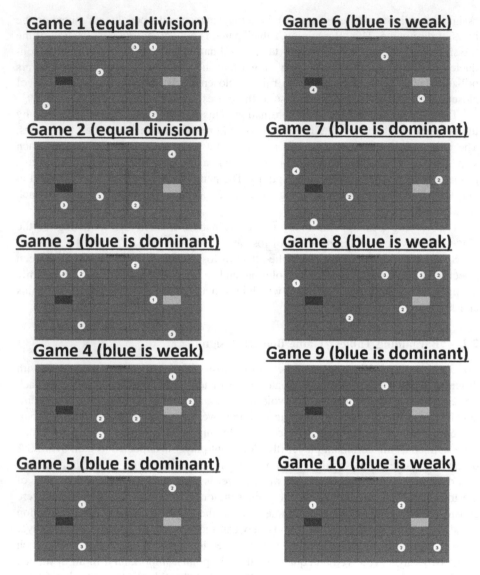

Fig. 2. Diagrams presenting "Bargaining Table" games (1–10). Note the strategic position of the 'blue' player in each of the games with no equal division. (Color figure online)

2.3 Experimental Design

The experiment involved 70 university students that were enrolled in one of the courses on campus (34 females; mean age = ~23.5, SD = 2.74). The study was approved by the IRB committee of Ariel University. All participants provided written informed consent for the experiment.

The study comprised the following stages. First, participants received an explanation regarding the overarching aim of the study and were given instructions regarding the experimental procedure and the interface of the study application. Participants were offered a reward incentive according to their level of coordination with their unknown counterpart that was chosen at random from the entire pool of participants. Next, each participant performed the ten games that were included in the "Bargaining Table" application. Finally, the output file comprising the logs was uploaded onto a shared location for offline analysis. The games were presented for each of the players in a random sequence to eliminate order effects bias.

3 Results and Discussion

3.1 Characterizing the Distribution of the Total Amount of Points

The main measure of our study was the total number of points gained by each player before deducting the amount of penalty from the total payoff. This measure was calculated by summing up the values of the discs, which each player has allocated to him- or herself, across the ten games.

Figure 3 displays the payoff distribution and Table 1 presents five percentile values. The average payoff was 58.45 with a standard deviation of 10.9 points.

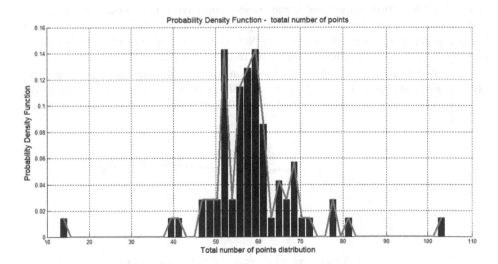

Fig. 3. Probability density function - total numer of points

Table 1. Main percentiles values - total number of points distribution

Percentile	5-th	25-th	50-th	75-th	95-th
Number of points	47	53	58	61	78

For example, between the 5th percentile player and the 75th percentile player there is a 14 points gap, which is a 30% increase in the number of points. We have examined whether this variability in player's behavior might be linked to the amount of penalty charged for trials with no coordination.

3.2 Modeling the Effect of Loss Aversion on Players Behavior

To identify the effect of loss-aversion on players' behavior, we grouped the players by the amount of penalty charged for non-coordination and averaged the cumulative individual payoff by the number of players in each of the groups (see Table 2). To account for the variability in the different group sizes, in Table 2 the standard error of the mean (SEM) is displayed instead of the standard deviation for each of the groups.

Table 2. Statistics - number of points as a function of loss-aversion

Non coordination penalty	0.1	0.2	0.3	0.4	0.5	0.6	0.7	0.8	0.9
Mean number of points	61.11	61.85	60	60.5	59.42	59.3	55.87	52.66	49.37
Standard error	2.27	1.94	7.63	1.19	4.34	1.96	2.37	0.33	1.90
Sample size (n)	9	14	7	4	7	10	8	3	8

Table 2 demonstrates a negative relationship between the amount of penalty charged for non-coordination and the average group payoff: the higher the penalty for non-coordination, the lower is the average group payoff. The data was modeled using linear regression with a polynomial model. Several polynomials models have been used ranging from first-order polynomials to 7th-order polynomials.

The model selection criteria were based on two parameters, R-squared (e.g. [14–16], an F-statistic (e.g. [17, 18]). The optimal value of the polynomial degree was determined by using the elbow method (e.g. [19–21]) which is often used in clustering

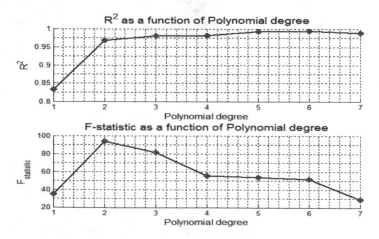

Fig. 4. Model selection process using R-squared and F-statistic

problems. Figure 4 displays the R-squared and F-statistic values, respectively, as a function of polynomial degree.

It is evident from Fig. 4 that according to the elbow method the second-order polynomial modeling is the optimal choice to be used among the other tested degrees. As can be seen, higher degrees than 2 resulted in a negligible increase in the R-squared, and in addition the F-statistic has a local maximum at that point. Nevertheless, we have also tested the third-order polynomial model, which displays similar values for the F-statistic and the R-squared (Fig. 4). The two models of the second and third degree turned out to be statistically significant ($p < 0.01$). Figure 5 shows the two models fitted on the same data set together with the standard error bars corresponding to each of the groups associated with a specific amount of penalty (Table 2).

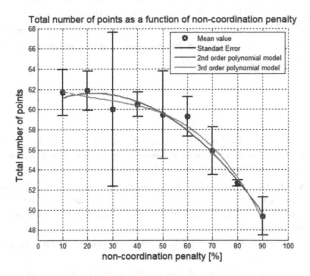

Fig. 5. Total number of points as a function of non-coordination penalty

These models clearly demonstrate that a significant relationship exists between loss aversion (manipulated by the penalty value) and the individual absolute payoff. In addition, the use of polynomial models has demonstrated that the relationship between loss aversion and the amount of penalty can be optimally described by using a quadratic model.

4   Conclusions and Future Work

A quadratic relationship (see Fig. 5) exists between the penalty value and the payoff that players have accumulated in the divergent interest tacit coordination game. This relationship demonstrates that the higher the payoff, the fewer points the player has gained. This result is in accordance with previous research showing that people tend to sacrifice gains in order to avoid losses [22] and resembles the section of the "S-shaped" function which is concave for gains [23].

Our findings open new avenues of research as follows. Future studies should examine the impact of personality traits such as the social value orientation (SVO) of the player on penalty value perception, as the SVO has been shown to affect strategic decision making ([9, 12, 24, 25]). Thus, it is worthwhile examining, for example, whether a player with an individualistic orientation (who aims at maximizing their own profits), would behave differently from a cooperative player (who aims at maximize the profits of both players). Additionally, it will be interesting to explore the electro-physiological correlates of loss aversion in the context of divergent interest games as a function of different penalty values charged for non-coordination. Another interesting extension of the current study would be to model the effect of loss aversion in the context of common-interest tacit coordination games, in which the players' profits are evenly divided (e.g. [10, 13]). Finally, understanding the effect of loss aversion in the context of divergent interest tacit coordination games may enable the construction of better algorithms for human-machine interaction that could more accurately predict human decision behavior under uncertainty.

References

1. Feltovich, N.: The effect of subtracting a constant from all payoffs in a Hawk-Dove game: experimental evidence of loss aversion in strategic behavior. South. Econ. J. **77**, 814–826 (2011). https://doi.org/10.4284/0038-4038-77.4.814
2. Sabater-Grande, G., Georgantzis, N.: Accounting for risk aversion in repeated prisoners' dilemma games: an experimental test. J. Econ. Behav. Organ. **48**, 37–50 (2002)
3. Tversky, A., Kahneman, D.: Loss aversion in riskless choice: a reference-dependent model. Q. J. Econ. **106**, 1039–1061 (1991)
4. Köbberling, V., Wakker, P.P.: An index of loss aversion. J. Econ. Theory **122**, 119–131 (2005)
5. Liu, W., Song, S., Wu, C.: Impact of loss aversion on the newsvendor game with product substitution. Int. J. Prod. Econ. **141**, 352–359 (2013)
6. Wang, C.X.: The loss-averse newsvendor game. Int. J. Prod. Econ. **124**, 448–452 (2010)
7. Isoni, A., Poulsen, A., Sugden, R., Tsutsui, K.: Focal points and payoff information in tacit bargaining. Games Econ. Behav. **114**, 193–214 (2019)
8. Isoni, A., Poulsen, A., Sugden, R., Tsutsui, K.: Focal points in tacit bargaining problems: experimental evidence. Eur. Econ. Rev. **59**, 167–188 (2013)
9. Mizrahi, D., Laufer, I., Zuckerman, I., Zhang, T.: The effect of culture and social orientation on player's performances in tacit coordination games. In: Wang, S., et al. (eds.) BI 2018. LNCS (LNAI), vol. 11309, pp. 437–447. Springer, Cham (2018). https://doi.org/10.1007/978-3-030-05587-5_41
10. Mehta, J., Starmer, C., Sugden, R.: Focal points in pure coordination games: an experimental investigation. Theory Decis. **36**, 163–185 (1994)
11. Mizrahi, D., Laufer, I., Zuckerman, I.: Individual strategic profiles in tacit coordination games. J. Exp. Theor. Artif. Intell. 1–16 (2020)
12. Mizrahi, D., Laufer, I., Zuckerman, I.: Collectivism-individualism: strategic behavior in tacit coordination games. PLoS ONE **15**, e0226929 (2020)

13. Mehta, J., Starmer, C., Sugden, R.: The nature of salience: an experimental investigation of pure coordination games. Am. Econ. Rev. **84**, 658–673 (1994)
14. McQuarrie, A.D., Tsai, C.-L.: Regression and Time Series Model Selection. World Scientific, Singapore (1998)
15. West, S.G., Taylor, A.B., Wu, W.: Model fit and model selection in structural equation modeling. Handb. Struct. Equ. Model. **1**, 209–231 (2012)
16. Gayawan, E., Ipinyomi, R.A.: A comparison of Akaike, Schwarz and R square criteria for model selection using some fertility models. Aust. J. Basic Appl. Sci. **3**, 3524–3530 (2009)
17. Habbema, J.D.F., Habbema, J.D.F., Hermans, J.: Selection of variables in discriminant analysis by F-statistic and error rate. Technometrics **19**, 487–493 (1977)
18. Geisser, S., Eddy, W.F.: A predictive approach to model selection. J. Am. Stat. Assoc. **74**, 153–160 (1979)
19. Bholowalia, P., Kumar, A.: EBK-means: a clustering technique based on elbow method and k-means in WSN. Int. J. Comput. Appl. **105**, 17–24 (2014)
20. Syakur, M.A., Khotimah, B.K., Rochman, E.M.S., Satoto, B.D.: Integration k-means clustering method and elbow method for identification of the best customer profile cluster. In: IOP Conference Series: Materials Science and Engineering, vol. 336 (2018)
21. Kodinariya, T.M.: Review on determining number of cluster in k-means clustering. Int. J. Adv. Res. Comput. Sci. Manag. Stud. **1**, 90–95 (2013)
22. Dickert, A.: Essays on bargaining and coordination games: the role of social preferences and focal points (2016)
23. Tversky, A., Kahneman, D.: Prospect theory: an analysis of decision under risk. Econometrica **47**, 263–291 (1979)
24. Balliet, D., Parks, C., Joireman, J.: Social value orientation and cooperation in social dilemmas: a meta-analysis. Group Process. Intergr. Relations **12**, 533–547 (2009)
25. Zuckerman, I., Cheng, K.L., Nau, D.S.: Modeling agent's preferences by its designer's social value orientation. J. Exp. Theor. Artif. Intell. **30**, 257–277 (2018)

Effect of the Gamma Entrainment Frequency in Pertinence to Mood, Memory and Cognition

Ryan Sharpe and Mufti Mahmud(⊠)

Department of Computing and Technology, Nottingham Trent University, Clifton, Nottingham NG11 8NS, UK
ryansharpe118@gmail.com, mufti.mahmud@ntu.ac.uk, muftimahmud@gmail.com

Abstract. This research provides evidence highlighting that through the use of a gamma 40 Hz entrainment frequency, mood, memory and cognition can be improved with respect to a 10 participant cohort. Participants constituted towards three binaural entrainment frequency groups; the 40 Hz, 25 Hz and 100 Hz respectively. Additionally, we asked participants to attend entrainment frequency sessions twice a week for a duration of four weeks. Sessions involved the assessment of a participants cognitive abilities, mood as well as memory; where the cognitive and memory assessments occurred before and after a 5 min binaural beat stimulation. The mood assessment scores were collected from sessions 1, 4 and 8 respectively. Within the gamma 40 Hz entrainment frequency group, we observed a weak statistical significance (alpha = 0.10, p = 0.076) mean improvement in cognitive scores; elevating from 75% average to 85% average upon conclusion of the experimentation. Additionally, we observed memory score improvements at a greater significance (alpha = 0.05, p = 0.0027); elevating from an average of 87% to 95%. Moreover, we observed a similar trend across the average of all of the frequency groups for the mood results. Finally, correlation analysis revealed a stronger correlation value (0.9838) within the 40 Hz group between sessions as well as mood score compared across the entire frequency group cohort.

Keywords: Gamma frequency · Brain entrainment · 40 Hz · Cognition improvements · Memory improvements · Mood improvements

1 Introduction

It is suggested that theta as well as gamma oscillations contribute to episodic memory regulation [26]. As a result, interest in binaural beat entrainment has been noted within the recent decades. Moreover, an additional study notes that binaural beat entrainment has been able to demonstrate the regulation of psychomotor skills as well as mood [16]. Binaural beat entrainment works by utilising two distinct and coherent tones running at different frequencies to an individual. This results in a phenomenon, where an additional phantom frequency is

© Springer Nature Switzerland AG 2020
M. Mahmud et al. (Eds.): BI 2020, LNAI 12241, pp. 50–61, 2020.
https://doi.org/10.1007/978-3-030-59277-6_5

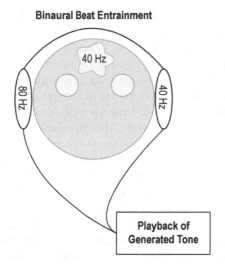

Fig. 1. Example of binaural beat entrainment at 40 Hz

interpreted by the cerebral cortex. The third frequency can be observed as the difference between the two coherent tones; hence, a left ear stimulation of 40 Hz and a right ear stimulation of 80 Hz would propagate the entrainment of a 40 Hz oscillation in the form of a binaural beat [1,28]. The concept of the experimentation is shown in Fig. 1.

Literature has examined the use of binaural beat entrainment in relation to human creativity [29]. A study reveals that creativity is highly dependent on the neurotransmitter dopamine; specifically the interactions between striatal and frontal dopaminergic neuronal pathways [34]. Meta analyses reveal that striatal D2 and D3 receptor density is, on average, 10–20% higher in those with Schizophrenia; it is also noted that, this is independent of the anti-psychotic drug implications [13,17,35]. Additionally, observations highlight that those with Schizophrenia demonstrate an exaggerated creative ability in comparison to those without Schizophrenia [25].

The ways in which the brain perceives as well as processes binaural beats is still not fully understood. It is noted that evidence does suggest that the inferior colliculus and the reticular activation system aid in this perception [15,20,33]. Moreover, EEG analysis has demonstrated detection of neuronal phase locking upon exposure to binaural beat entrainment; where the observed neuronal action potentials are in synchronisation with stimulus frequency [6]. This may then allow the identification of particular oscillations that contribute to a particular cognitive function; especially with regards to memory [14].

A more recent meta-analysis has measured the efficacy of binaural beats in relation to anxiety, cognition as well as pain perception [7]. The analysis considered multiple factors, including the number of exposures, the frequency of exposure as well as the duration. It was highlighted that the effectiveness of a binaural beat cannot be masked out either by utilising pink or white noise. Moreover, the findings suggest that the exposure of a binaural beat before a task vs before and during a task may implicate lower binaural beat entrainment effectiveness. Additionally, the meta-analysis also highlights that a longer exposure to a binaural beat often results in an increased effect; with this said, it is advisable to increase the duration of time an individual is exposed to a binaural beat when carrying out an experiment. Moreover, a further study has analysed emotion and working memory in pertinence to a gamma 40 Hz binaural beat stimulation [12]. The study notes that binaural beat stimulation for an average of 20 min can enhance memory function within a recall task. Beta and gamma oscillations were induced by a gamma 40 Hz binaural beat and as a result, mood improvements were observed. Criticism highlights that the measurements performed only occurred once throughout the two experiments, and therefore did not consider long term results. Moreover, it still remains unclear what the benefits, if any, of psychoacoustic stimulation through the means of 40 Hz binaural beat entrainment provides.

2   Methods and Experiments

2.1   Entrainment Frequency Generation

To provide the full range of the gamma frequency band, an internal software was developed to not only generate, but also customise the frequencies being delivered on separate channels. To prevent any loss of data, frequencies were generated in a lossless format such as .wav. The idea was to utilise a stereo headset to deliver independent frequencies to each ear. Additionally, the internal software allowed the tracking of each participant over the course of the 4 weeks, including the ability to log each session and its constituent results; moreover allowing an analysis at a later date.

2.2   Participants

Participants were constituent of individuals who were in a position to lend their time for a duration of 4 weeks in which the experimentation would take place. The volunteers were gathered independent of race, gender, or background. Individuals had no underlying health conditions; particularly any involving the auditory system. Additionally, participants were 18 years or older in age and were gathered through the means social media advertisement. This allowed individuals to request the joining of the commencing study. The experimentation phase was comprised of 10 participants and as a result, three separate frequency groups; groups of 3, 3 as well as 4; 25 Hz, 100Hz and 40 Hz respectively. The final individual was included within the 40 Hz cohort due to the interest in the entrainment at the 40 Hz frequency band. Privacy was protected through the adherence to confidentiality guidelines; participants were additionally allocated unique identifiers to prevent the usage of any personal information. Moreover, there were requirements of consent form signing to allow data acquisition, processing and further analysis before the study was to commence. Participants were gathered through the permission of the Non-Invasive Human Ethics Committee and the protection of participant data was regulated by the BCS Code of Conduct guidelines. To further elaborate, the data collected was only stored for duration of the experimentation phase of the research; participant data collected was also stored in a physical document format. Once processed, these documents were then permanently destroyed via shredding. Moreover, stored data through the participant tracking application contained no personal information. A SmarterASP.NET server was temporarily leveraged to store information regarding the experiment; additionally utilising firewalls, anti-virus protection and following SSAE 18 SOC 2 Type 2 Compliance. Withdrawal of participants as well as all constituent data was able occur at any point during the experimentation phase; given that the participant formally requested to do so. Participants were not required to perform any particular activities between sessions and instead it was requested that they carry on with their daily routines regardless of the undergoing research.

2.3 Experiment

The experimental phase of the research ran from the 12th of February 2020 up until a concluding session occurring on the 8th of March 2020. Participants would attend scheduled sessions between 10am and 10pm every Wednesday as well as Sunday. Upon participant arrival, they were asked to complete an initial cognitive test within a timed routine. The timing of all tests were performed via a stopwatch. Additionally, once a participant had completed their task, a one second time unit was removed from their finishing time. This was to minimise human error implicated by halting and resetting the stopwatch. A custom model was utilised in order to evaluate cognition; aiming to assess participant using eight distinct questions; each emphasising an ability to problem solve. This would involve questions where participants would have to find the next value within a set of numbers. Additionally, mathematical problems that aimed to assess a participants understanding mathematical operator precedence. Upon completing the first cognitive test for that particular session, a completion time was recorded and the stopwatch was reset. The participant would then be requested to return the paper; where a memory test would commence. A custom memory evaluation, would be performed and emphasised memory recall abilities. Additionally, it is noted that the participants would never see these evaluations beforehand. Participants would be asked to remember a sentence, a word and to solve a mathematical problem; without aid or the ability to solve the problem. Performances were scored from 1 to 5; where 1 would mean no questions were answered correctly, and 5 would mean all were answered correctly. Completing the task would result in the exposure to the corresponding binaural beat for the participants group. This would be delivered through a Sennheiser HD 400S headset with a frequency response 18–20,000 Hz (-10 dB), sound pressure level (SPL) 120 dB (1 kHz/1 Vrms), total harmonic distortion (THD) $<0.5\%$ (1 kHz/100 dB) with an acoustics closed sensitivity of 120 dB SPL @ 1 kHz, 1 V RMS (power). Given the recommendation from scientific literature, noting that a longer exposure to a binaural beat can contribute to a higher probability of positive results [7], participants were exposed to the corresponding binaural beat entrainment for 5 min. No distractions were to implicate the entrainment, this included the usage of mobile devices as well as exposure to any external noise sources. Upon listening to the binaural beat, participants would be asked to repeat an additional cognitive test for that session; again, under timed conditions. Moreover, the same was true for a new memory test; performed in regards to the method already outlined. Finally, sessions would conclude upon completion of the final two cognitive and mood tasks.

Additionally, once every 2 weeks, a mood assessment would occur before listening to the binaural beat. The mood evaluation was comprised of an already established Mood and Feelings Questionnaire (MFQ) [11,18]. These evaluations took place from the initial session, at the halfway point and at the end session; sessions 1, 4 and 8 respectively. With regards to mood scores, a lower score generally infers an improvement in mood for that particular individual.

2.4   Data Processing

Data collected was converted in a percentage, with the intention of allowing for a more accurate comparison between the entrainment frequency groups. Additionally, MFQ scores remained in integer format due to a lower score correlating with a lower mood and the converse being true for higher scores; this would infer that further processing would be required for accurate comparisons to be established. Upon the completion of result marking, the data was inputted into a Microsoft Excel work booklet. The data columns went as followed: session number, participant unique identifier, cognitive score before, cognitive before time, memory before score, cognitive after score, cognitive after time, memory score after and finally the MFQ score if applicable to the session. Finally, all of the inputted data were statistically analysed using Microsoft Excels statistical analysis tools. All Cognitive, memory and mood scores were calculated as means over the duration of the 4 week experimentation phase. Additionally, cognitive and memory scores were statistically analysed utilising homoscedastic T-Tests. Product Moment Correlation Coefficient (PMCC) provided the mood score analysis and aimed to show how strongly mood score changes correlated with exposure to binaural beat entrainment over the duration of experimentation.

3   Results and Discussion

3.1   Cognition

The intention of the cognitive assessment was to establish whether any significant changes would be observed with regards to the experimental condition (pre and post) for the duration of the experimentation phase. All values were given as

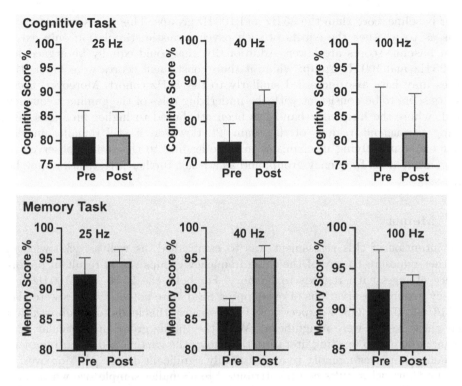

Fig. 2. Above, the cognitive task contextualises each frequency cohort (25 Hz, 40 Hz and 100 Hz) in relation to their respective cognitive scores (y-axis) with respect to the experimental condition both pre and post exposure to a 5 min long binaural beat. Below, the memory task contextualises each frequency cohort (25 Hz, 40 Hz and 100 Hz) in relation to their respective memory scores (y-axis) with respect to the same experimental condition. Additionally, both cognitive scores and memory scores are given in percentages for ease of comparison. Bar graphs are constituent of the means for the duration of the 8 sessions over the course of the 4 weeks; error bars are given as mean ± SEM. Moreover, cognitive and memory scores were statistically analysed using homoscedastic T-Tests.

means ± SEM from week one until week four; due to literature suggesting that an increased duration of exposure would potentially correlate with improved entrainment results [7].

Overall, no significant changes in cognition were observed within the frequency groups 25 Hz and 100 Hz; shown in Fig. 2. Interestingly, statistical analysis using a homoscedastic T-Test revealed a weak significance (p = 0.076188387, alpha = 0.10) between the mean before and after cognitive scores within the 40 Hz frequency band group; elevating from 75% to 85%. Additionally, it could be criticised that the results were constituent of a small sample size and therefore any uncertainties could be eliminated through increasing the size of the sample population. Further criticism also highlights that the gamma 40 Hz group had a lower baseline score than the 25 Hz and 100 Hz groups. This raises further questions as to whether the effects of such psychoacoustic stimulation only exists when baseline scores are lower. Additionally, this could equally be argued for the 25 Hz and 100 Hz group; where if their constituent scores were lower, the scores may have also increased similarly to the 40 Hz cohort. Moreover, these results seem to be consistent with the underlying roles of the gamma frequency band; where the frequency band has been attributed to higher functions persisting throughout regions of the brain [2]. However, it still remains unclear what exact underlying mechanisms may be leading to the results observed in the gamma 40 Hz frequency group; and as a result further investigation may be necessary.

3.2 Memory

The intention of this assessment was to established, as well as acknowledge, whether exposure to any of the three frequency groups would result in performance changes with regards to memory. For both the 25 Hz and 100 Hz frequency groups, observations of overlapping SEM were noted, p values were also 0.1616 and 0.855131824 respectively. Furthermore, this leads to an observation that these results were insignificant. With the 100 Hz group in particular, this is contradictory to existing literature that notes the gamma 100 Hz entrainment frequency improves memory to a statistically significant degree [1]. Moreover, it may be that such results can be attributed to a smaller sample size when compared to the entire participant contribution towards the overall gamma 100 Hz frequency mean; which may explain the higher p value observed.

The 40 Hz frequency cohort demonstrated a statistically significant increase from pre to post scores over the duration of the experimentation (alpha = 0.05, p = 0.0027). Additionally, this is in line with existing evidence provided by a 2015 meta-analysis [4] as well as other literature on the topic of entrainment and memory improvements associated with both the gamma and theta frequencies [26]. It is therefore noted that the results observed add to the ever-growing research demonstrating memory improvements through exposure to binaural beat entrainment.

3.3 Mood

With regards to the mood portion of the experimentation, the general trend across all cohorts was a strong negative correlation between the MFQ score and the experimental condition (sessions); where a lower MFQ score indicated an improvement in overall mood. This, when regarded with literature suggesting gamma frequency band attributes to mood improvements during entrainment [4], would highlight that the results observed are indeed consistent. Interestingly, referring to Fig. 3, the data suggests that the coefficient observed within the gamma 40 Hz group (R-squared = 0.9838) is stronger than the one observed in the gamma 100 Hz (R-squared = 0.8369) as well as the gamma 25 Hz

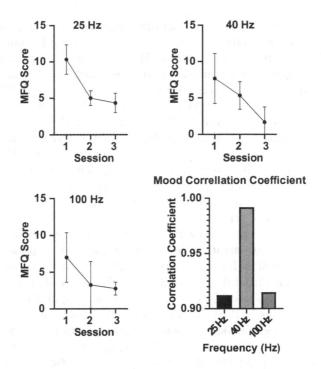

Fig. 3. The first three graphs depict the MFQ score (y-axis) changes over the sessions (x-axis) where mood questionnaires took place. In this instance, sessions 1, 2, 3 refer to the study sessions 1, 4 and 8 respectively; where sampling occurred every two weeks during the 4 weeks, including the start and end points of the study. Additionally, the final graph contextualises the correlation coefficient in pertinence to each frequency group; where the correlation efficient value is depicted by the y-axis and the frequency group is depicted by the x-axis.

(R-squared = 0.8322). This is consistent with the suggested evidence attributing improvements in mood with respect to the gamma 40 Hz entrainment frequency in particular [4,12]. This also highlights a potential that the gamma 40 Hz entrainment frequency has a greater implication on overall mood when compared to the other frequency bands. Similarly, when the initial and final mean results are compared within the MFQ graphs that constitute to Fig. 3, there is observed overlapping between the SEM values within the gamma 100 Hz group. With this said, it could be inferred that the gamma 100 Hz cohort mood improvements observed are likely to be statistically insignificant; even more so when considering the small sample size.

3.4   Potential Application to Chronic Traumatic Encephalopathy

Chronic Traumatic Encephalopathy (CTE) is a neurodegenerative disease which has been attributed to prolonged exposure of head injuries. It has therefore become highly regarded within the scientific consensus. This is especially true when considering a case study of a retired National Football League player [27]. CTE was first noted in 1928 by Harrison Martland. He described, what in the early 1920's was regarded as a condition known as punch drunk syndrome; a disease that was implicated by numerous repetitive head injuries (RHI's) in those that boxed [19]. The term dementia pugilistica was then eventually attributed to these neuropathological changes [23]. The name of Progressive Traumatic Encephalopathy and later, CTE were preferred when activities other than boxing were attributed to the neuropathological changes consistent with the disease pathology [5]. Moreover, it is noted that the diagnosis of CTE in-vivo within a living individual cannot be achieved. Furthermore, making the neuropathological symptoms difficult to diagnose and distinguish between other existing neurodegenerative disease [21].

CTE symptoms are present in a variety of ways such as executive dysfunction, memory impairment, concentration difficulties, explosivity, depression, impulse control problems as well as language impairments [3]. The same literature also identifies the top differential diagnoses of CTE. This is constituent of dementia with Lewy Bodies, Alzheimer's Disease (AD), frontotemporal dementia, corticobasal degeneration as well as vascular dementia. This highlights how often CTE symptoms may be mistaken for other neurodegenerative diseases; which in turn, may highlight the difficulty of conducting epidemiological studies. Moreover, it has been further identified that the prodromal stage of CTE may not begin with any particular symptom. As a result, two varieties of CTE have been noted; one which implicates a higher degree of mood changes, and the other which implicates a higher degree of cognitive changes [31]. Of 36 subjects, 3 were asymptomatic at the time of death, 22 subjects presented mood as well as behavioural issues that correlated with earlier RHI exposure, and 11 subjects presented cognitive impairment which correlated with an older age of RHI exposure. This may suggest that behavioural issues are more common in those with early RHI exposure. A 2012 evaluation of 85 brains implicated by repetitive mild traumatic brain injury was performed. With regards to the evaluation, RHI's are thought to be a contributing factor to CTE pathogenesis. This is thought to trigger the development of progressive neuropathological changes characterised by the widespread deposition of p-tau in the form of neurofibrillary tangles [22]. To elaborate, the widespread accumulation of p-tau in neurons and astrocytes is what defines CTE. Additionally, p-tau aggregates throughout the cortical layers 2 and 3 allow CTE to be distinguished between AD and other neurodegenerative diseases [8, 9, 32].

It is still misunderstood whether CTE exhibits any changes in wave power within regions of the brain; this is mostly due to a low amount of research regarding the topic. This is highly likely to be a result of the poor ability to accurately diagnose living individuals with the disease. However, there is some existing literature to suggest that deficits exist in pertinence to TBI's; an established precursor to CTE pathogenesis. A 2017 analysis noted deficits with regards to overall brain wave power implicated by individuals with mTBI's [24].

The analysis was constituent of 40 athletes; comprised of 20 control individuals as well as 20 concussed individuals. Moreover, all individuals were analysed using an electroencephalogram (EEG). With regards to the results, evidence was presented that suggested that the concussed athletes demonstrated increased theta, delta and alpha power. It was also noted that there was a lowered beta power. Differences within the gamma frequency band were not noted. However, further hidden frequency analysis revealed that from 1–40 Hz, major deficits at particular frequencies occurred. These hidden deficits were identified at the 1–2 Hz, 6–7 Hz, 8–10 Hz, 16–18 Hz, 24–29 Hz and finally the 34–36 Hz band. Interestingly, this highlights that although deficits were not noted within full bands, hidden deficits may still occur upon further analysis. This is then consistent with additional research on those with TBI's; finding disturbances and delays within the gamma 40 Hz range [30].

Given the symptoms of CTE and that TBI's are a potential precursor to the disease pathology, along with a lacking amount of research associated with this disease in relation to entrainment. There may be a need to investigate the further implications of particular frequencies in mice models and those with TBI's; even more so in pertinence to the gamma 40 Hz frequency entrainment.

4   Conclusion and Future Work

Given the limited amount of time for the research to be conducted, a much more robust methodology would have been more favourable. Issues pertaining to the use of a custom model for measuring cognition and memory were also noted. Increasing the difficulty of the questionnaires during the course of the study aimed to reduce the natural increase in performance due to the ability of an individuals natural learning capabilities. Moreover, adjusting per questionnaire is difficult due to the need to estimate the difficulty of one questionnaire to another.

A mitigation to these issues could be achieved by using existing peer reviewed as well as established cognitive, memory and mood models; a suggested example would have been the Cambridge Neuropsychological Test Automated Battery (CANTAB) [10]. An EEG (Electro-Encephalogram) analysis could have also been performed in parallel with the assessment; which may have also verified the expected responses from regions of the brain.

In addition to the highlighted limitations, a greater sample size would have reduced the effects of various factors such as baseline scores observed in the 25 Hz and 100 Hz cohorts. Additionally, this may highlight the need to perform similar tests with those with naturally lower baseline scores such as those suffering from Mild Cognitive Impairment (MCI) to observe if improvements may also be noted.

References

1. Beauchene, C., Abaid, N., Moran, R., Diana, R.A., Leonessa, A.: The effect of binaural beats on visuospatial working memory and cortical connectivity. PLoS ONE 11(11), e0166630 (2016)

2. Bosman, C.A., Lansink, C.S., Pennartz, C.M.: Functions of gamma-band synchronization in cognition: from single circuits to functional diversity across cortical and subcortical systems. Eur. J. Neurosci. **39**(11), 1982–1999 (2014)
3. Budson, A.E., McKee, A.C., Cantu, R.C., Stern, R.A.: Chronic Traumatic Encephalopathy: Proceedings of the Boston University Alzheimer's Disease Center Conference. Elsevier Health Sciences, Amsterdam (2017)
4. Chaieb, L., Wilpert, E.C., Reber, T.P., Fell, J.: Auditory beat stimulation and its effects on cognition and mood states. Front. Psychiatry **6**, 70 (2015)
5. Critchley, M.: Medical aspects of boxing, particularly from a neurological standpoint. Br. Med. J. **1**(5015), 357 (1957)
6. Gao, X., et al.: Analysis of EEG activity in response to binaural beats with different frequencies. Int. J. Psychophysiol. **94**(3), 399–406 (2014)
7. Garcia-Argibay, M., Santed, M.A., Reales, J.M.: Efficacy of binaural auditory beats in cognition, anxiety, and pain perception: a meta-analysis. Psychol. Res. **83**(2), 357–372 (2019). https://doi.org/10.1007/s00426-018-1066-8
8. Hof, P.R., Bouras, C., Buee, L., Delacourte, A., Perl, D., Morrison, J.: Differential distribution of neurofibrillary tangles in the cerebral cortex of dementia pugilistica and alzheimer's disease cases. Acta Neuropathologica **85**(1), 23–30 (1992)
9. Hof, P., Knabe, R., Bovier, P., Bouras, C.: Neuropathological observations in a case of autism presenting with self-injury behavior. Acta Neuropathologica **82**(4), 321–326 (1991)
10. Fray, P.J., Robbins, T.W., Sahakian, B.J.: Neuorpsychiatyric applications of CANTAB. Int. J. Geriatr. Psychiatry **11**(4), 329–336 (1996)
11. Jeffreys, M., et al.: Factor structure of the parent-report mood and feelings questionnaire (MFQ) in an outpatient mental health sample. J. Abnorm. Child Psychol. **44**(6), 1111–1120 (2016)
12. Jirakittayakorn, N., Wongsawat, Y.: Brain responses to 40-Hz binaural beat and effects on emotion and memory. Int. J. Psychophysiol. **120**, 96–107 (2017)
13. Kestler, L., Walker, E., Vega, E.: Dopamine receptors in the brains of schizophrenia patients: a meta-analysis of the findings. Behav. Pharmacol. **12**(5), 355–371 (2001)
14. Kraus, J., Porubanová, M.: The effect of binaural beats on working memory capacity. Studia Psychologica **57**(2), 135 (2015)
15. Kuwada, S., Yin, T.C., Wickesberg, R.E.: Response of cat inferior colliculus neurons to binaural beat stimuli: possible mechanisms for sound localization. Science **206**(4418), 586–588 (1979)
16. Lane, J.D., Kasian, S.J., Owens, J.E., Marsh, G.R.: Binaural auditory beats affect vigilance performance and mood. Physiol. Behav. **63**(2), 249–252 (1998)
17. Laruelle, M.: Imaging dopamine transmission in schizophrenia: a review and meta-analysis. Q. J. Nucl. Med. Mol. Imaging **42**(3), 211 (1998)
18. Lundervold, A.J., Breivik, K., Posserud, M.B., Stormark, K.M., Hysing, M.: Symptoms of depression as reported by Norwegian adolescents on the short mood and feelings questionnaire. Front. Psychol. **4**, 613 (2013)
19. Martland, H.S.: Punch drunk. J. Am. Med. Assoc. **91**(15), 1103–1107 (1928)
20. McAlpine, D., Jiang, D., Palmer, A.R.: Interaural delay sensitivity and the classification of low best-frequency binaural responses in the inferior colliculus of the guinea pig. Hear. Res. **97**(1–2), 136–152 (1996)
21. McKee, A.C., et al.: Chronic traumatic encephalopathy in athletes: progressive tauopathy after repetitive head injury. J. Neuropathol. Exp. Neurol. **68**(7), 709–735 (2009)
22. McKee, A.C., et al.: The spectrum of disease in chronic traumatic encephalopathy. Brain **136**(1), 43–64 (2013)

23. Millspaugh, J.: Dementia pugilistica. U. S. Nav. Med. Bull. **35**(297), 297–303 (1937)
24. Munia, T.T.K., Haider, A., Fazel-Rezai, R.: Evidence of brain functional deficits following sport-related mild traumatic brain injury. In: 2017 39th Annual International Conference of the IEEE Engineering in Medicine and Biology Society (EMBC), pp. 3212–3215. IEEE (2017)
25. Nelson, B., Rawlings, D.: Relating schizotypy and personality to the phenomenology of creativity. Schizophr. Bull. **36**(2), 388–399 (2010)
26. Nyhus, E., Curran, T.: Functional role of gamma and theta oscillations in episodic memory. Neurosci. Biobehav. Rev. **34**(7), 1023–1035 (2010)
27. Omalu, B.I., DeKosky, S.T., Minster, R.L., Kamboh, M.I., Hamilton, R.L., Wecht, C.H.: Chronic traumatic encephalopathy in a national football league player. Neurosurgery **57**(1), 128–134 (2005)
28. Oster, G.: Auditory beats in the brain. Sci. Am. **229**(4), 94–103 (1973)
29. Reedijk, S.A., Bolders, A., Hommel, B.: The impact of binaural beats on creativity. Front. Hum. Neurosci. **7**, 786 (2013)
30. Slewa-Younan, S., Green, A.M., Baguley, I.J., Felmingham, K.L., Haig, A.R., Gordon, E.: Is 'gamma' (40 Hz) synchronous activity disturbed in patients with traumatic brain injury? Clin. Neurophysiol. **113**(10), 1640–1646 (2002)
31. Stern, R.A., et al.: Clinical presentation of chronic traumatic encephalopathy. Neurology **81**(13), 1122–1129 (2013)
32. Tokuda, T., Ikeda, S., Yanagisawa, N., Ihara, Y., Glenner, G.: Re-examination of ex-boxers' brains using immunohistochemistry with antibodies to amyloid β-protein and tau protein. Acta Neuropathologica **82**(4), 280–285 (1991)
33. Turow, G., Lane, J.D.: Binaural beat stimulation: altering vigilance and mood states. Music. Sci. Rhythm. Brain Cult. Clin. Implic., 122–136 (2011)
34. Zabelina, D.L., Colzato, L., Beeman, M., Hommel, B.: Dopamine and the creative mind: Individual differences in creativity are predicted by interactions between dopamine genes DAT and COMT. PLoS ONE **11**(1), e0146768 (2016)
35. Zakzanis, K.K., Hansen, K.T.: Dopamine D2 densities and the schizophrenic brain. Schizophr. Res. **32**(3), 201–206 (1998)

Investigations of Human Information Processing Systems

Temporal-Spatial-Spectral Investigation of Brain Network Dynamics in Human Speech Perception

Bin Zhao[1,2] (iD), Gaoyan Zhang[2](✉) (iD), and Jianwu Dang[1,2](✉) (iD)

[1] Japan Advanced Institute of Science and Technology, Nomi, Japan
jdang@jaist.ac.jp
[2] College of Intelligence and Computing, Tianjin University, Tianjin, China
{zhaobeiyi,zhanggaoyan}@tju.edu.cn

Abstract. Human speech function, as an incredible manifestation of human intelligence, entails intricate spatiotemporal coordination of brain networks transiently and accurately. Current investigation using neuroimaging and electrophysiological techniques laid the foundation of our understanding regarding the brain activities in the spatial, temporal, and spectral domains. However, a comprehensive view integrating these three aspects yet to be achieved by not only adopting multi- modalities of the data acquisition system but also employing algorithms to integrate them into a systematic framework. Thus, this study conducted a passive listening task using words and white noises as acoustic stimuli and utilized high-density electroencephalography (EEG) system with effective connectivity analysis to reconstruct the brain network dynamics with high temporal and spectral resolution. Besides, we introduced the high-spatial-resolution functional magnetic resonance imaging- (fMRI-) constraints into a representational similarity analysis to examine the functional performance of spatially distributed networks over time. Our results revealed that during speech perception, networks for auditory and higher cognition functioned along the ventral stream via theta and gamma oscillations and exhibited hierarchical responsive differences between word and noise conditions. Speech motor programming networks participated along the dorsal stream mainly in the beta band during a later period of speech perception. Alpha band activity served as a mediation for the dual pathway through oscillatory suppression. These functional networks progressed parallelly for the completion of the complex speech perception.

Keywords: Brain network dynamics · Temporal-spatial-spectral analysis · Representational similarity analysis · Effective connectivity · Speech perception

1 Introduction

How brain networks develop, function, and support cognition is a large and growing topic in many branches of neuroscience [1,2]. Current theories on brain

© Springer Nature Switzerland AG 2020
M. Mahmud et al. (Eds.): BI 2020, LNAI 12241, pp. 65–74, 2020.
https://doi.org/10.1007/978-3-030-59277-6_6

organization suggest that cognitive functions such as language are organized in widespread, segregated, and overlapping networks [3], and that oscillatory synchronization over multiple frequency bands is likely the underlying neural mechanism for the interaction and integration of local and large-scale networks [4]. Though theoretically reasonable and physically plausible, to practically demonstrate these assumptions, we need to not only combine different modalities of brain imaging and electrophysical techniques that emphasize spatial and temporospectral aspects, respectively but also computational algorithms to relate these different modalities of brain-activity measurements into a systematic framework [5,6]. This motivated the current study to reveal from a temporal-spatial-spectral view for the illustration of the speech perception mechanism.

Our current understanding of the cortical distribution of speech functions largely comes from a functional anatomy framework based on functional magnetic resonance imaging (fMRI) and positron emission tomography (PET) studies [7,8]. The representative dual-stream model [9] proposed that early stages of speech processing occur bilaterally in auditory regions on the superior temporal gyrus and sulcus (STG and STS), and then diverges into two broad streams: where a ventral stream (over the superior and middle portions of the temporal lobe) is involved in linking acoustic input to the conceptual-semantic representations via hierarchical processing (e.g. acoustic, phonetic and semantic), and a dorsal stream (over the posterior planum temporal region and posterior frontal lobe) is involved in translating acoustic speech signals into articulatory representations. The involvement of the dorsal stream was also largely documented in speech perception tasks [10,11], implying a critical role of articulatory simulation in the facilitation of speech perception [12–14].

Meanwhile, speech as a quasi-rhythmic acoustic signal, though aperiodic, involve complex spectrotemporal modulations at a millisecond time scale [15]. Such instantaneous activities require temporally precise interactions of neuron populations, which is presumably via oscillatory synchronization [13]. Also, accumulating acoustic, neurophysiological, and psycholinguistic analyses of speech demonstrated that there exist organizational principles and perceptual units of analysis at very different time scales [16]. Generally, slow modulations, typically peaking in the theta range around 4–8 Hz, correspond roughly to the syllable structure of speech. High modulations, typically in the gamma range around 30–50 Hz, correlate with attributes of the speech fine structure at the phonetic scale [13]. Alpha rhythms (8–15 Hz) once associated with working memory and speech comprehension [17], is now gaining attention in its role of top-down, inhibitory control processes through selective suppression [18–20]. Beta (15–30 Hz) activities in speech processing were mainly attributed to the articulatory planning and execution with a power decrease in the (primary) motor areas, also known as mu rhythms [21].

To integrate the accumulated knowledge as above mentioned and provide a comprehensive view, this study was designed to combine EEG acquisition and network analysis methods with fMRI functional network template for a systematic spatial-spectral-temporal investigation. To be more specific, we utilized a high-density (128-channel) EEG equipment to capture the transient brain oscillation of subjects when they are performing a passive word listening task. Then, the scalp-recorded EEG signals went through: (i) preprocessing for noise and artifact reduction; (ii) independent component analysis (ICA) and boundary element modeling (BEM) for cortical source localization; (iii) multivariant auto-regressive (MVAR) modeling for effective connectivity estimation between cortical regions; (iv) fMRI-constraint representational analysis for network analysis of temporal significance; and (v) frequency decomposition for the detailed revealing of the frequency-specific network properties.

2   Experiment and Methods

2.1   Experimental Paradigm

The experiment performed a speech perception task. The auditory stimuli consist-ed of (i) 160 Chinese disyllable words (two-character words); (ii) 160 white noise, balanced with words in duration and loudness. The duration of each auditory item lasted for 900 ms. The auditory task started with a fixation on the screen for 400 ms, followed by the auditory stimuli pseudo-randomly presented with E-prime 2.0 soft-ware (PST, USA). After a 500-ms blank interval, the subject was asked to make a button press between word and white noise based on what he/she has heard in this trial. Then after a 1000-ms inter-trial interval comes another trial (320 in total). During the whole process, EEG signals were recorded from the scalp of the subjects with a 128-channel Quik-Cap (Neuroscan, USA) at a sampling rate of 1000 Hz. The elec-trode configuration conformed to the extended 10–5 system [22], and the channel impedance was maintained below 5 kΩ throughout the acquisition.

Twenty-two subjects (12 males, 10 females) with the mean age of 22.30 years (SD = 1.14) participated in this experiment. They were all right-handed with normal hearing and reported no history of neurological deficits. Ethical approval for this experiment was obtained from the Local Research Ethics Committee.

2.2   EEG Preprocessing and Source Localization

To reduce the noises and artifacts, the scalp-recorded EEG data was firstly preprocessed with EEGLAB toolbox [23], in which the raw EEG data were band-passed filtered at the range of 1–50 Hz and down-sampled to 250 Hz. Non-stationary high variance signals were removed with the artifact subspace reconstruction (ASR) method [24]. Then, the continuous EEG data were segmented into epochs of −1000–2000 ms around the stimuli onset. Next, we applied the adaptive mixture independent component analysis algorithm (AMICA) to transform the scalp-EEG data from a channel basis to a component basis [25] and separated those maximally independent cortical sources from biological (eyes, muscles and heart) artifacts and line noises. After that, equivalent current dipole (ECD) models of the components were computed using the boundary element model (BEM) to find out the component cortical sources. Based on the source locations, the components were further mapped to 76 cerebral cortical areas, conforming with the standard fMRI template for later connectivity and representational similarity analyses.

2.3   EEG Effective Connectivity Analysis

To estimate the effective connectivity between the component time-series. Effective connectivity methods represented by the granger causality (GC) were implied. GC is based on the assumption that causes precede their effects in time. If a signal can be predicted by the past information from a second signal better than the past information from its own signal then the second signal can be considered causal to the first signal [26]. GC is a time-domain bivariant approach, but has been applied to the frequency domain which enabled the analysis of coupling between EEG frequency bands that have a well-known biomedical significance. GC has also been generalized from bivariate to multivariate signals, as recently Partial Directed Coherence (PDC) method [27], which is able to detect not only direct but also indirect pathways linking interacting brain regions. In this study, we followed a routine from the source information flow toolbox (SIFT), and adopted a linear vector adaptive multivariate autoregressive (AMVAR) model of order 10 to fit the multi-trial ensemble with a 500-ms sliding window and a step size of 25 ms, using the Vieira-Morf lattice algorithm. The PDC was estimated from the AMVAR coefficients to quantify time-varying connectivity for the brain network analysis. After these steps, a group-level effective connectivity patterns were generated at each time point of the speech perception process, forming a series of 76 * 76 matrices representing the average interregional connectivity strengths.

2.4   FMRI-Constraint Network Dynamic Analysis

As one can imagine, at each time point of the continuous speech processing, there are probably more than one network involved. In most cases, a number of functional networks are interlaced and paralleled with each other. Facing such a complex situation, disentangling each line of different functional processes is needed for deciphering the language system. For this purpose, we introduced fMRI-based templates into a representational similarity analysis [5]. Each fMRI template corresponds to a network distribution for a specific function. By calculating the similarity between the fMRI network distribution and each frame of the previously constructed EEG-based connectivity by means of correlation coefficient, we could estimate the activity strengths of that fMRI-defined functional network that actually presented in our real-time EEG signal at that time point. And with the point-by-point time series of such activity strengths, we could also compare the temporal significance of a specific functional network along the whole speech perception procedure. The graphical illustration for this algorithm is shown in Fig. 1. Five fMRI functional networks were tested, including nonverbal sound processing, categorization, speech attention, word memory retrieval and speech motor programming.

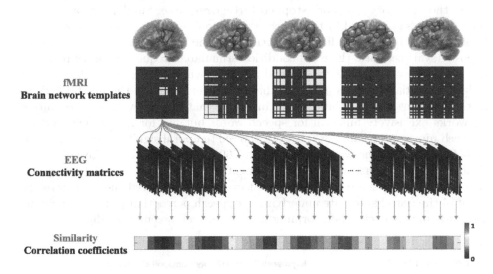

Fig. 1. Graphical illustration of the fMRI-constraint representational similarity analysis. The bottom left plot shows one functional network distribution on an fMRI template and its matrix representation (76 * 76 ROIs). The similarity between the fMRI functional network templates and the connectivity matrices of EEG network dynamics were calculated as correlation coefficients frame-by-frame, ranging from 0 (low similarity) to 1 (high similarity) as shown in the color bar at the bottom. (Color figure online)

3   Results

3.1   Brain Network Dynamics

Figure 2 illustrated the temporal dynamics of the five functional networks during the auditory stimuli range (0–900 ms) for both word and white noise (shortened as noise) conditions. In the first panel for the "nonverbal sound processing", the fMRI network was distributed over the superior temporal gyrus (STG), the primary auditory processing area, as well as the parietal lobe (PL), the sensory integration area. From the color bar, it can be noticed that high similarity values (shown in red) appeared in both word and white noise conditions recurrently after onset (0–100 ms, 400–700 ms, and 800–900 ms for the word condition), indicating frequent and active involvement of primary auditory processing regardless of noise or speech. In the second "categorization" network, cortical areas of the STG, the middle (MTG) and inferior temporal (ITG) gyrus as well as the

PL showed lengthy involvement in two periods (0–400 ms, 600–900 ms) that are basically consistent with the two-character ranges in the auditory stimuli for the word condition. While in the noise condition, activation only occurred at the initial start (0–100 ms), which suggests that after categorizing the stimuli as white noise, the "category" network stopped further response. Similar activation pattern could also be found in the "speech attention" network, showing a response bias towards different auditory conditions. In the frontal-parietal "word memory retrieval" network, the word condition stimulated frequent network response for exploratory search (200, 400 and 700 ms), while the noise condition once failed the initial screening (100 ms), has no longer access to the mental lexicon in the following period. These results indicated that higher level speech cognitive networks exclusively function for speech words but not for noises. The bottom "speech motor programming" network showed temporal significance in the range of 550–650 ms for the word condition and 600–750 ms for the white noise condition, which demonstrated the recruitment of the motor system in perception tasks. This makes sense considering that evolution facilitated the joint development of the neural substrate underlying the speech perception-production circuit so as to support each other, forming inseparable cell assemblies [13].

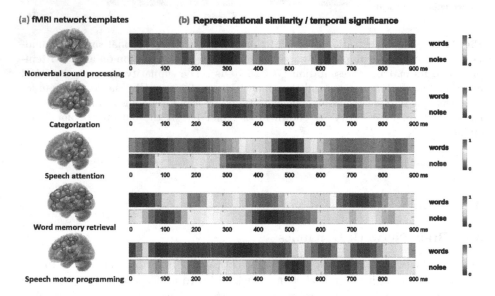

Fig. 2. Functional network dynamics. (a) fMRI network templates. (b) correlation coefficients between the fMRI network templates and the EEG network sequences (high value in red ranges indicates high similarity and thus high temporal significance, in contrast, blue ranges indicate low similarity and thus little activation during this period). (Color figure online)

3.2   Frequency-Specific Network Dynamics

Considering that the EEG contains oscillatory activity in distinct frequency bands that are associated with different brain states, we further examined the frequency-specific network activities in the theta (4–8 Hz), alpha (8–15 Hz), beta (15–30 Hz) and gamma (30–45 Hz) bands. For each frequency band, the average connectivity strength differences between word and noise conditions (word-noise) were depicted in Fig. 3. As shown, network connections in the high gamma band were mainly distributed in the temporal lobe along the ventral path, which is conventionally correlated with the processing of the speech fine structure at the phonetic scale [13,28]. Theta rhythms, closely correlates with the acoustic envelope of naturalistic speech at the syllabic rate [28,29] was also found with dominant network activity in the ventral path. This theta-gamma coupling is also in line with its spatial function in the temporal lobe for the transformation from phonetic to syllable and lexical perception. Beta band, in close relation with sensorimotor behavior [30], appeared with stronger connectivity along the dorsal stream. Alpha oscillation showed up with a wide connection along both ventral and dorsal streams, consistent with its mediation function for pathway direction and selective attention.

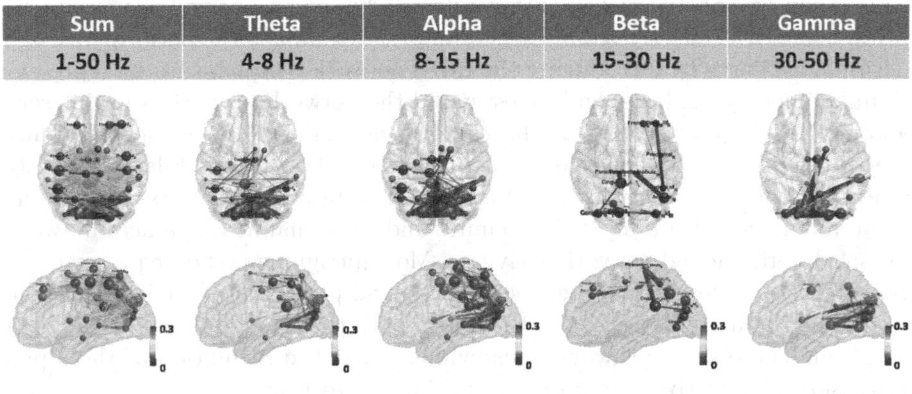

Fig. 3. Brain connectives in the Theta, Alpha, Beta, and Gamma bands.

Figure 4 unfolded the brain network dynamics onto a time-frequency grid. Notice that functional network along the ventral stream showed up early in the gamma the theta bands for the primary auditory processing. Alpha oscillation also showed an early involvement for pathway direction. Over time, network connection in the gamma and theta bands flowed from STG to MTG and ITG in the posterior parts for higher cognition. Whereas dorsal connections in the beta band appeared much later near the end of the auditory stimuli as articulatory simulation for speech confirmation.

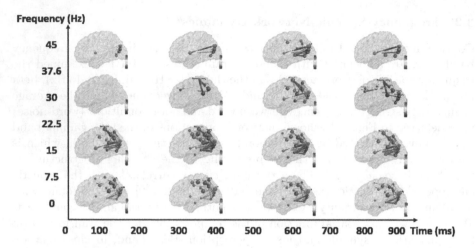

Fig. 4. Temporal-spatial-spectral brain network dynamics.

4   Discussion

In this study, we constructed the brain network dynamics involved in speech perception using EEG effective connectivity analysis, examined the performance of 5 functional networks by introducing the fMRI network templates in the representational similarity analysis, and investigated the network properties in different frequency bands. Our results of the time-varying and frequency-specific functional network dynamics revealed that brain networks were modulates not only temporally, but also spectrally and spatially. In addition, our results detailed the dual steam model with temporal dynamics and the dynamic differences between noise- and word-elicited network activities. Most intriguing is the frequency characteristics that differentiated between the ventral path that is mediated by the gamma and theta oscillations, and the dorsal path that is modulated by the beta oscillation. These two pathways, meanwhile, under the regulation of the alpha suppression for selective attention and pathway direction.

5   Conclusion

This study explored the temporal-spatial-spectral brain network dynamics for speech perception by applying dynamic network reconstruction methods on the EEG signals and spatial similarity analysis method with fMRI network constraint in different frequency bands. The results extended the dual stream model of speech processing with details of the temporal dynamics and frequency characteristics for different functional networks. A functional hierarchy along the ventral stream between words and white noise conditions was revealed in the theta and gamma bands, and a perception-production circuit along the dorsal stream was also found with neural substrate and oscillatory activity in the beta band. Pathway direction and selective attention is supposed to be mediated via alpha suppression. Further investigation extending to other speech tasks such as sentence processing and oral reading will be continued to push forward our systematic understanding of the speech functions as well as cognitive mechanisms in general.

Acknowledgements. This study is supported in part by JSPS KAKENHI Grant (20K11883), and in part by National Natural Science Foundation of China (No. 61876126).

References

1. Sporns, O.: Networks of the Brain. MIT Press, Cambridge (2011)
2. O'Neill, G.C., Tewarie, P., Vidaurre, D., Liuzzi, L., Woolrich, M.W., Brookes, M.J.: Dynamics of large-scale electrophysiological networks: a technical review. Neuroimage **180**(Part B), 559–576 (2018). ISSN 1053-8119
3. Saur, D., Kreher, B.W., Schnell, S., et al.: Ventral and dorsal pathways for language. Proceeding Natl. Acad. Sci. **105**, 18035–18040 (2008)
4. Schoffelen, J.-M., Hultén, A., Lam, N., et al.: Frequency-specific directed interactions in the human brain network for language. Proc. Natl. Acad. Sci. **114**, 8083–8088 (2017)
5. Kriegeskorte, N., Mur, M., Bandettini, P.: Representational similarity analysis – connecting the branches of systems neuroscience. Front. Syst. Neurosci. **2**, 4 (2008)
6. Mahmud, M., Kaiser, M.S., Hussain, A., Vassanelli, S.: Applications of deep learning and reinforcement learning to biological data. IEEE Trans. Neural Netw. Learn. Syst. **29**(6), 2063–2079 (2018). https://doi.org/10.1109/TNNLS.2018.2790388
7. Price, C.: A review and synthesis of the first 20 years of PET and fMRI studies of heard speech, spoken language and reading. Neuroimage **65**, 816–847 (2012)
8. Vigneau, M., Beaucousin, V., Hervé, P.Y., et al.: Meta-analyzing left hemisphere language areas: phonology, semantics, and sentence processing. Neuroimage **30**, 1414–1432 (2016)
9. Hickok, G.: The cortical organization of speech processing: feedback control and predictive coding the context of a dual-stream model. J. Commun. Disord. **45**, 393 (2012)
10. Zhao, B., Dang, J., Zhang, G.: A neuro-experimental evidence for the motor theory of speech perception. In: INTERSPEECH, pp. 2441–2445 (2017)
11. Hickok, G., Costanzo, M., Capasso, R., Miceli, G.: The role of Broca's area in speech perception: evidence from aphasia revisited. Brain Lang. **119**, 214–220 (2011)
12. Liberman, A., Mattingly, G.: The motor theory of speech perception revised. Cognition **21**, 1–36 (1985)
13. Anne-Lise, G., David, P.: Cortical oscillations and speech processing: emerging computational principles and operations. Nat. Neurosci. **15**, 511–517 (2012)
14. Liu, L., Zhang, Y., Zhou, Q., et al.: Auditory-articulatory neural alignment between listener and speaker during verbal communication. Cereb. Cortex **30**, 942–951 (2019)
15. Giraud, A.L., Poeppel, D.: Speech perception from a neurophysiological perspective. In: Poeppel, D., Overath, T., Popper, A., Fay, R. (eds.) The Human Auditory Cortex. Springer Handbook of Auditory Research, vol. 43, pp. 225–260. Springer, New York (2012). https://doi.org/10.1007/978-1-4614-2314-0_9

16. Poeppel, D., Emmorey, K., Hickok, G., Pylkkänen, L.: Towards a new neurobiology of language. J. Neurosci. **32**(2), 14125–14131 (2012)
17. Weisz, N., Hartmann, T., Müller, N., Lorenz, I., Obleser, J.: Alpha rhythms in audition: cognitive and clinical perspectives. Front. Psychol. **2**, 73 (2011)
18. Mayer, A., Schwiedrzik, C.M., Wibral, M., Singer, W., Melloni, L.: Expecting to see a letter: alpha oscillations as carriers of top-down sensory predictions. Cereb. Cortex **26**, 3146–3160 (2015)
19. Klimesch, W., Sauseng, P., Hanslmayr, S.: EEG alpha oscillations: the inhibition–timing hypothesis. Brain Res. Rev. **53**, 63–88 (2007)
20. Foxe, J.J., Snyder, A.C.: The role of alpha-band brain oscillations as a sensory suppression mechanism during selective attention. Front. Psychol. **2**, 154 (2011). https://doi.org/10.3389/fpsyg.2011.00154
21. Mcfarland, D.J., Miner, L.A., Vaughan, T.M., Wolpaw, J.R.: Mu and beta rhythm topographies during motor imagery and actual movements. Brain Topogr. **12**, 177–186 (2000)
22. Oostenveld, R., Praamstra, P.: The five percent electrode system for high-resolution EEG and ERP measurements. Clin. Neurophysiol. **112**, 713–719 (2001)
23. Delorme, A., Makeig, S.: EEGLAB: an open source toolbox for analysis of single-trial EEG dynamics including independent component analysis. J. Neurosci. Methods **134**, 9 (2004)
24. Mullen, T.R., Kothe, C.A.E., Chi, Y.M., et al.: Real-time neuroimaging and cognitive monitoring using wearable Dry EEG. IEEE Trans. Biomed. Eng. **62**, 2553–2567 (2015)
25. Sheng-Hsiou, H., Luca, P.T., Jason, P., et al.: Modeling brain dynamic state changes with adaptive mixture independent component analysis. NeuroImage **183**, 47–61 (2018)
26. Seth, A.K., Barrett, A.B., Barnett, L.: Granger causality analysis in neuroscience and neuroimaging. J. Neurosci. Off. J. Soc. Neurosci. **35**, 3293–3297 (2015)
27. Sameshima, K., Baccalá, L.A.: Using partial directed coherence to describe neuronal ensemble interactions. J. Neurosci. Methods **94**, 93–103 (1999)
28. von Stein, A., Sarnthein, J.: Different frequencies for different scales of cortical integration: from local gamma to long range alpha/theta synchronization. Int. J. Psychophysiol. **38**, 301–313 (2000)
29. Morillon, B., Liégeois-Chauvel, C., Arnal, L.H., et al.: Asymmetric function of theta and gamma activity in syllable processing: an intra-cortical study. Front. Psychol. **3**, 248 (2012)
30. Thornton, D., Harkrider, A.W., Jenson, D., Saltuklaroglu, T.: Sensorimotor activity measured via oscillations of EEG mu rhythms in speech and non-speech discrimination tasks with and without segmentation demands. Brain Lang. **187**, 62–73 (2018). ISSN 0093-934X. S0093934X16301274

Precise Estimation of Resting State Functional Connectivity Using Empirical Mode Decomposition

Sukesh Das[1]($\boxtimes$)(iD), Anil K. Sao[1](iD), and Bharat Biswal[2](iD)

[1] Indian Institute of Technology Mandi, Mandi, HP 175005, India
d17025@students.iitmandi.ac.in, anil@iitmandi.ac.in
[2] New Jersey Institute of Technology, Newark, NJ 07102, USA
bharat.biswal@njit.edu

Abstract. The estimation of functional connectivity from the observed Blood Oxygen Level-Dependent (BOLD) signal may not be accurate because it is an indirect measure of neuronal activity or the existing deconvolution approaches assume that hemodynamic response function (HRF), which modulates the neuronal activities, is uniform across the brain regions or across the time course. We propose a novel approach using empirical mode decomposition (EMD), to reduce the effect of HRF from estimated neuronal activity signal (NAS) obtained after blind deconvolution for a BOLD time course. The first two intrinsic mode functions (IMFs), obtained during EMD of the neuronal activity signal represent its highest oscillating modes and hence have characteristic of impulses. The sum of the first two IMFs is computed as a refined representation of neuronal activity signal to estimate resting state connectome using the framework of dictionary learning. Usefulness of the proposed method has been demonstrated using two resting state datasets (healthy control and attention deficit hyperactivity disorder) taken from '1000 Functional Connectomes'. For quantitative analysis, Jaccard distances are computed between spatial maps obtained using BOLD signals and refined activity signals. Results show that maps obtained using NAS are a subset of that obtained using BOLD signal and hence avoid false acceptance of active voxels, which illustrates the importance of refined NAS.

Keywords: Dictionary learning · EMD · fMRI · HRF · Neuronal activity signal

1 Introduction

Functional connectivity (FC) using blood oxygen level-dependent (BOLD) signal represents significant temporal correlation between physically distant regions of the brain at rest [2]. It plays an instrumental role in predicting human behavior and its alteration with a number of clinical cases including neuro-degenerative

© Springer Nature Switzerland AG 2020
M. Mahmud et al. (Eds.): BI 2020, LNAI 12241, pp. 75–84, 2020.
https://doi.org/10.1007/978-3-030-59277-6_7

and psychiatric diseases [1,2]. The sparse behavior of BOLD signal over a dictionary is exploited very well in the framework of dictionary learning (DL) to effectively estimate the resting state networks (RSNs) [5,11,14]. However, DL based approaches mostly use the BOLD signal, which is an indirect measure and may not represent the neuronal information and contaminated by physiological factors like-cardiac and respiratory cycles [2]. These issues can be addressed by either suppressing the noise from observed BOLD signal or using the estimated neuronal activity signal (NAS), which produces reliable FC [13,18]. Several approaches have been reported in the literature to estimate NAS from the measured BOLD signal as a source separation problem [8,9,18]. These approaches could be based on either parametric [3,8,9,18] or non-parametric [16,17] assumption on HRF as well as HRF variability [8,18] or its uniformity across brain [13]. For example, Wu and colleagues [18] proposed a methodology to estimate NAS from resting-state functional magnetic resonance imaging (rs-fMRI) with a parametric blind deconvolution approach by using spontaneous pseudo-events. Here, the estimated neuronal information is still not completely separated from the hemodynamic response function (HRF) because the assumption of the predefined basis of HRF and its uniformity across time do not hold true in practice [7].

In this study, a novel approach based on empirical mode decomposition (EMD) is proposed to minimize the effect of HRF from the NAS estimated using the method described in [18]. We decompose the NAS obtained from [18] where HRF with minimum noise variance over different lags, is estimated, followed by its blind deconvolution. Here, the observation is exploited that neuronal activity has the highly varying characteristic [8,18]. So, precise neuronal information can be estimated from the high-frequency region of the spectrum of the NAS and hence can be represented well using first few intrinsic mode functions (IMFs) obtained while EMD of the NAS. It has been observed that the HRF, due to slow in nature, is eliminated in sum of first two IMFs and hence used as refined NAS for estimation of FC.

The efficacy of the estimated neuronal information, computed using the proposed method, is evaluated in the framework of the DL to estimate RSNs. The RSNs obtained using the proposed method are tested with two different resting state datasets taken from '1000 Functional Connectomes' project - healthy control and attention deficit hyperactivity disorder (ADHD) data. For a quantitative comparison, we computed Jaccard distances between functional connectivity map obtained by using preprocessed BOLD and refined NAS. It shows that maps obtained using NAS are a subset of that using BOLD signal. It should be noted that fMRI analysis using EMD, in temporal and both spatial and temporal domain have been reported in [4,15] to study energy/period content of IMFs and to compute voxel specific global signal respectively. Both the approaches use the preprocessed BOLD signal and estimated information is not directly associated with NAS. On the other hand, the proposed work performs the EMD on deconvolved signal to remove further the effect of HRF so that the resultant signal is reliable representation of neuronal information.

The organization of the paper is as follows: Sect. 2 explains the proposed pipeline, including estimation of neuronal information and DL based approach for estimation of RSNs. Experimental results are explained in Sect. 3. The summary is provided in Sect. 4.

2 Proposed Approach

We have proposed an approach to minimize the remaining effect of HRF from NAS, obtained using blind de-convolution [18] and use the refined NAS in the framework of DL to estimate the RSNs. The reasons for using the refined neuronal activity is that it encodes the transient behavior of the BOLD signal which is less susceptible to noise and relates the underlying neuronal activity by reducing the effect of HRF present in NAS obtained using the blind deconvolution method. Hence, we hypothesize that the estimation of functional connectivity will be advantageous with the obtained activity signals compared to the raw BOLD signals. The block diagram of the proposed method is shown in the Fig. 1. Deconvolved signal is decomposed using EMD and the sum of the first two IMFs representing the refined NAS is used to form a time-voxel matrix which is again decomposed using DL to estimate the RSNs.

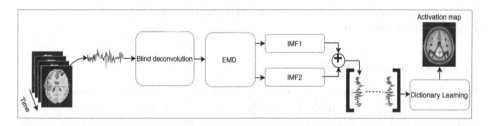

Fig. 1. Block diagram of the estimation of the RSNs using neuronal activity signal obtained by the EMD

The BOLD signal denoted as $m(t)$, assume to be resulted from the convolution of the neuronal activity signal with the HRF, can be written as

$$m(t) = s(t) * h(t) + \epsilon(t), \tag{1}$$

where $s(t)$ is the NAS, $h(t)$ is the HRF and $\epsilon(t)$ is the noise. Here "$*$" denotes the convolution operator. The estimation $\hat{s}(t)$ of the NAS ($s(t)$) is carried out using Wiener filter based blind deconvolution approach as explained in [18], as

$$\hat{s}(t) = FT^{-1}\{\frac{H^*(\omega)M(\omega)}{|H(\omega)|^2 + |\epsilon(\omega)|^2}\} \tag{2}$$

where $H(\omega)$, $M(\omega)$ and $\epsilon(\omega)$ be the Fourier transforms of the $h(t)$, $m(t)$ and $\epsilon(t)$ respectively and $'*'$ denotes the complex conjugate. $h(t)$ is estimated by fitting general linear model (GLM) at optimal lag of onset where variance of noise ($Var[\epsilon(t)]$) is minimum. However, the estimation of neuronal activity $\hat{s}(t)$ may not be fully deconvolved from HRF due to the following two reasons: 1) HRF is assumed to be the canonical HRF, 2) It is assumed that the HRF is a stationary signal for a time course. The remaining effect of HRF from $\hat{s}(t)$ can be reduced using EMD [10] of NAS. The EMD of NAS is as follows

$$\hat{s}(t) = \sum_{k=1}^{K} I_k(t) + r(t), \tag{3}$$

where, $\hat{s}(t)$ is the estimated NAS, $I_k(t)$ is the kth IMF, $r(t)$ is the residual signal and K is the total number of IMF.

It has been observed that $I_1(t)$ and $I_2(t)$ contain more oscillations (high frequency) of $\hat{s}(t)$ in comparison to the other IMFs. Hence, the sum of the first two IMFs, $s_e(t) = I_1(t) + I_2(t)$ is considered as a good representation of neuronal activities as it consists of higher oscillating modes leading to a slightly wide band signal by capturing the transient behavior of the underlying neuronal information. Figures 2 (e), (d), and (c) illustrate the first three IMFs computed from NAS, $\hat{s}(t)$ (Fig. 2 (b)) estimated from $m(t)$ of a given active voxel taken from the left lateral parietal cortex of default mode network (DMN). Figure 2 (f) represents the refined NAS ($s_e(t)$). It can be observed that first two IMFs give the high varying components of NAS and can be used as a refined representation of neuronal information.

2.1 Estimation of RSN

Data driven based approaches, such as principle component analysis (PCA), independent component analysis (ICA), DL have been demonstrated to provide a good estimate of RSNs in rs-fMRI analysis. Moreover, among the data driven based approaches, DL exploits the inherent sparse behavior of the BOLD time course over an over-complete dictionary and here used in this work to demonstrate the effectiveness of refined NAS for precise estimation of RSNs. In DL based approaches [5,6,11,14], the multi-subject functional connectivity of different brain regions can be estimated by decomposing rs-fMRI data $\mathbf{S} \in \mathbb{R}^{nm \times v}$ as

$$\mathbf{S} \approx \mathbf{DA} \quad with \quad \mathbf{D} \in \mathbb{R}^{nm \times d} \quad and \quad \mathbf{A} \in \mathbb{R}^{d \times v}. \tag{4}$$

The data matrix $\mathbf{S}$ (refined NAS) is formed by temporally concatenating n number of consecutive scans (refined NAS) obtained from m number of subjects each with v number of voxels. Here, dictionary $\mathbf{D}$ is learned such that the rows $\mathbf{a}_i$ of the matrix $\mathbf{A}$ corresponds to RSN and d is the number of RSNs. This decomposition can be performed by using the following objective function:

$$\text{argmin}_{\mathbf{D},\mathbf{A}} \| \mathbf{a}_i \|_1 \text{ s.t. } \|\mathbf{S} - \mathbf{DA}\|_F^2 < \epsilon. \tag{5}$$

Here l_1 norm ($\| \ \|_1$) induces the sparsity constraint on $\mathbf{a}_i$ for effective convergence of the rows onto distinct RSNs. $\| \ \|_F$ represents the Frobenius norm. ($\mathbf{S} - \mathbf{DA}$)

gives the error resulted due to decomposition of matrix **S**. Equation 5 is jointly non-convex in (**D, A**) and hence becomes an NP-hard problem which can be optimized using alternative iterations of Dictionary Update (DU) and Sparse Coding (SC) steps. The initialization of dictionary atom (temporal) is done by computing time series associated with an initial guess on activation maps obtained from known networks [14].

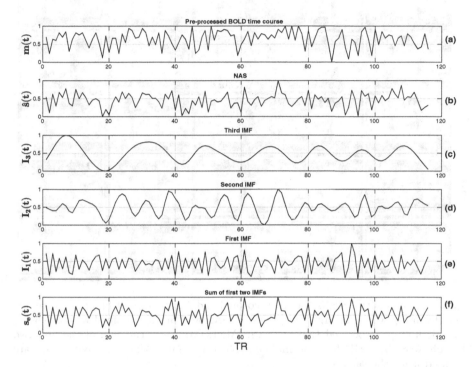

Fig. 2. Representative BOLD time course (voxel is taken from left lateral parietal cortex, Buckner dataset, sub00294) and it's EMD: (a) preprocessed BOLD time course, (b) neuronal activity signal, (c) third intrinsic mode function ($I_3(t)$), (d) second intrinsic mode function ($I_2(t)$), (e) first intrinsic mode function ($I_1(t)$) and (f) sum of $I_1(t)$ and $I_2(t)$

3   Experimental Results

To carry out the experiments, the datasets used are: 1. Cambridge_Buckner Dataset[1](Part 1): contains resting-state scans from 48 healthy subjects (21M/27F), age: 18–30 years. T1 - weighted images were collected using mprage with # slices = 192, max size = $256 \times 1.2 \times 1.0 \times 3.0$ mm^3. T2*-weighted

---

[1] http://fcon_1000.projects.nitrc.orgfcpClassicFcpTable.html.

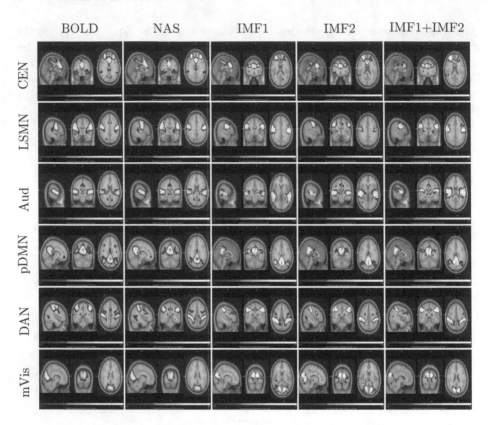

Fig. 3. Normal control RSNs: sagittal, coronal and axial views of functional connectivity (from top: CEN, LSMN, Aud, pDMN, DAN and mVis) obtained with DL using conventionally preprocessed BOLD, NAS, IMF1, IMF2 and the sum of the first two IMFs obtained by EMD from normal controlled rest data. All connectivity maps are presented using the same scale

images acquired using EPI with the TR (repetition time) = 3 s, # slices = 47, #scans =119, voxel resolution = $3 \times 3 \times 3$ mm^3. 2. ADHD Dataset[2]: Resting state scans from 40 subjects with ADHD (35M/5F) are considered, age: 7–21 years. T2*-weighted images acquired using EPI with the TR = 2 s, # slices = 47, #$scans$ = 77–261, voxel resolution = $\sim3 \times 3 \times 3$ mm^3 The datasets were preprocessed using SPM12[3] software with MATLAB R2019a. The initial 3 scans of all the subjects were discarded. Reorientation with respect to MNI space, realignment, slice time correction, co-registration (with the corresponding anatomical space), segmentation, normalization and smoothing (with Gaussian kernel, FWHM-6mm $\times$ 6mm $\times$ 6mm) of the data were done prior to analysis. Equation 5 was used to obtain the different RSNs using five different representa-

---

[2] http://fcon_1000.projects.nitrc.org/indi/adhd200/.

[3] http://www.fil.ion.ucl.ac.uk/spm/.

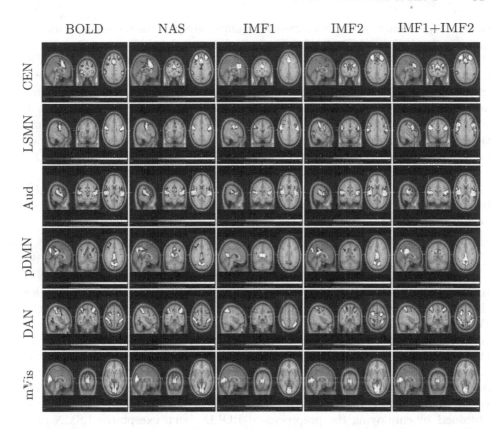

Fig. 4. ADHD RSNs: sagittal, coronal and axial views of functional connectivity (from top: CEN, LSMN, Aud, pDMN, DAN and mVis) obtained with DL using conventionally preprocessed BOLD, NAS, IMF1, IMF2 and the sum of the first two IMFs obtained by EMD from ADHD rest data. All connectivity maps are presented using the same scale

tions of BOLD signals, namely: $m(t)$, $\hat{s}(t)$, $I_1(t)$, $I_2(t)$ and $s_e(t)$. A model order (d) of 30 was chosen empirically in our experiments to estimate the spatial activation maps. Here, FSLeyes[4] was used to visualize the functional connectivity maps.

Six exemplary RSNs (central executive network - CEN, lateral sensorimotor network - LSMN, auditory network - Aud, posterior default mode network - pDMN, dorsal attention network - DAN and medial visual network - mVis) of healthy control data has been illustrated in Fig. 3. Again, out of the six presented RSNs, LSMN, DMN, DAN and mVis network appear well in the connectivity map for $s_e(t)$. Other two networks are also showing their symmetrical localization. The RSNs are shown for ADHD data where refined activity signal finds CEN, pDMN, DAN, mVis well and others also get appeared (Fig. 4). In every

---

[4] https://fsl.fmrib.ox.ac.uk/fsl/fslwiki/FSLeyes.

case, in the estimation of RSNs, results demonstrate that the refined activity signal, obtained after EMD of NAS from blind deconvolution method [18], where the neuronal information is not completely deconvolved as the assumption of HRF (in terms of three basis) to be uniform across time course do not hold true in practice, also capable of extracting FC well and hence underlying neuronal activities show a similar pattern for a particular RSN. We can also notice that in some cases, networks partially appear for individual IMF, but in the combination $(I_1(t) + I_2(t))$ it appears fully (e.g. ADHD, CEN). So, individual IMF may fails to produce a network entirely, but the proposed combination $(I_1(t) + I_2(t))$ can preserve all nodes of a RSN.

For quantitative comparison, we have measured the Jaccard distance [12] between the activation maps obtained using preprocessed BOLD and refined activity signal. Jaccard distance between two maps, is computed as

$$J(map_1, map_2) = \frac{Number\ of\ common\ active\ voxels\ in\ both\ map}{Total\ number\ of\ unique\ active\ voxels\ in\ both\ map} \quad (6)$$

In case of healthy control, the distances are 0.70, 0.43, 0.47, 0.68, 0.70, 0.56 for the given six networks (CEN, LSMN, Aud, pDMN, DAN, mVis) respectively. While measuring the Jaccard distances, we have noticed that active voxels in connectivity maps obtained using refined NAS are a subset of active voxels in the connectivity map obtained by using preprocessed BOLD. Similarly, In the case of ADHD data, the corresponding Jaccard distances are 0.48, 0.80, 0.64, 0.40, 0.62, 0.45. In this case, we have also observed the same trend that active voxels obtained by employing the refined NAS is a subset of that of active voxels obtained by employing the preprocessed BOLD signal except the LSMN map where 3275 active voxels are common with the connectivity map (PreBOLD) out of 4072 active voxels (refined NAS).

4   Summary

In this work, a novel method based on EMD is studied to further refine the NAS, which is highly influenced by varying HRF (spatially and temporally), for estimation of RSNs. The proposed method exploits that the neuronal activity has high varying characteristic in comparison to HRF, and hence can be estimated from the high-frequency region of the spectrum of the BOLD signal. The first two IMFs after EMD of NAS, provides complimentary RSNs and hence are combined together to provide a good estimate of the FC in the framework of DL. Moreover, it has been observed that there are significant similarities and total 11 out of 12 connectivity maps (both healthy control and ADHD) produced by refined NAS, are a subset of those produced by BOLD signal. So, the refined NAS can avoid false acceptance of active voxels. In future, spatial (3D) IMFs of NAS, along with temporal one, can be explored in extracting the neuronal activity for the estimation of the RSNs with different pathological conditions.

References

1. Beckmann, C.F., DeLuca, M., Devlin, J.T., Smith, S.M.: Investigations into resting-state connectivity using independent component analysis. Philos. Trans. R. Soc. B Biol. Sci. **360**(1457), 1001–1013 (2005)
2. Bijsterbosch, J., Smith, S.M., Beckmann, C.F.: Introduction to Resting State fMRI Functional Connectivity. Oxford University Press, Oxford (2017)
3. Bush, K., Cisler, J.: Decoding neural events from fMRI BOLD signal: a comparison of existing approaches and development of a new algorithm. Magn. Reson. Imaging **31**(6), 976–989 (2013)
4. Cordes, D., et al.: Advances in functional magnetic resonance imaging data analysis methods using empirical mode decomposition to investigate temporal changes in early Parkinson's disease. Alzheimer's Dement. Transl. Res. Clin. Interv. **4**, 372–386 (2018)
5. Dash, D., Abrol, V., Sao, A.K., Biswal, B.: The model order limit: deep sparse factorization for resting brain. In: IEEE 15th International Symposium on Biomedical Imaging (ISBI), pp. 1244–1247. IEEE (2018)
6. Dash, D., Biswal, B., Sao, A.K., Wang, J.: Automatic recognition of resting state fMRI networks with dictionary learning. In: Wang, S., et al. (eds.) BI 2018. LNCS (LNAI), vol. 11309, pp. 249–259. Springer, Cham (2018). https://doi.org/10.1007/978-3-030-05587-5_24
7. Deshpande, G., Sathian, K., Hu, X.: Effect of hemodynamic variability on granger causality analysis of fMRI. Neuroimage **52**(3), 884–896 (2010)
8. Glover, G.H.: Deconvolution of impulse response in event-related bold fMRI. Neuroimage **9**(4), 416–429 (1999)
9. Handwerker, D.A., Ollinger, J.M., D'Esposito, M.: Variation of bold hemodynamic responses across subjects and brain regions and their effects on statistical analyses. Neuroimage **21**(4), 1639–1651 (2004)
10. Huang, N.E., et al.: The empirical mode decomposition and the Hilbert spectrum for nonlinear and non-stationary time series analysis. Proc. R. Soc. Lond. Ser. Math. Phys. Eng. Sci. **454**(1971), 903–995 (1998)
11. Iqbal, A., Seghouane, A.K.: Dictionary learning algorithm for multi-subject fMRI analysis via temporal and spatial concatenation. In: Proceedings of International Conference on Acoustics, Speech and Signal Processing (ICASSP), pp. 2751–2755. IEEE (2018)
12. Jaccard, P.: The distribution of the flora in the alpine zone. 1. New Phytol. **11**(2), 37–50 (1912)
13. Karahanoğlu, F.I., Caballero-Gaudes, C., Lazeyras, F., Van De Ville, D.: Total activation: fMRI deconvolution through spatio-temporal regularization. Neuroimage **73**, 121–134 (2013)
14. Mensch, A., Varoquaux, G., Thirion, B.: Compressed online dictionary learning for fast resting-state fMRI decomposition. In: Proceedings of 13th International Symposium on Biomedical Imaging (ISBI), pp. 1282–1285. IEEE (2016)
15. Moradi, N., Dousty, M., Sotero, R.C.: Spatiotemporal empirical mode decomposition of resting-state fMRI signals: application to global signal regression. Front. Neurosci. **13** (2019)
16. Seghouane, A.K., Johnston, L.A.: Consistent hemodynamic response estimation function in fMRI using sparse prior information. In: IEEE 11th International Symposium on Biomedical Imaging (ISBI), pp. 596–599. IEEE (2014)

17. Sreenivasan, K.R., Havlicek, M., Deshpande, G.: Nonparametric hemodynamic deconvolution of fMRI using homomorphic filtering. IEEE Trans. Med. Imaging **34**(5), 1155–1163 (2014)
18. Wu, G.R., Liao, W., Stramaglia, S., Ding, J.R., Chen, H., Marinazzo, D.: A blind deconvolution approach to recover effective connectivity brain networks from resting state fmri data. Med. Image Anal. **17**(3), 365–374 (2013)

3D DenseNet Ensemble in 4-Way Classification of Alzheimer's Disease

Juan Ruiz[1], Mufti Mahmud[1]([⊠]), Md Modasshir[2], M. Shamim Kaiser[3],
and for the Alzheimer's Disease Neuroimaging Initiative

[1] Department of Computing and Technology, Nottingham Trent University, Clifton,
Nottingham NG11 8NS, UK
mufti.mahmud@ntu.ac.uk, muftimahmud@gmail.com
[2] Department of Computer Science, University of South Carolina,
Columbia, SC, USA
[3] IIT, Jahangirnagar University, Savar, 1342 Dhaka, Bangladesh

Abstract. One of the major causes of death in developing nations is
the Alzheimer's Disease (AD). For the treatment of this illness, is crucial
to early diagnose mild cognitive impairment (MCI) and AD, with the
help of feature extraction from magnetic resonance images (MRI). This
paper proposes a 4-way classification of 3D MRI images using an ensemble implementation of 3D Densely Connected Convolutional Networks
(3D DenseNets) models. The research makes use of dense connections
that improve the movement of data within the model, due to having
each layer linked with all the subsequent layers in a block. Afterwards, a
probability-based fusion method is employed to merge the probabilistic
output of each unique individual classifier model. Available through the
ADNI dataset, preprocessed 3D MR images from four subject groups
(i.e., AD, healthy control, early MCI, and late MCI) were acquired to
perform experiments. In the tests, the proposed approach yields better
results than other state-of-the-art methods dealing with 3D MR images.

Keywords: Convolutional neural network · Deep learning · Magnetic
resonance imaging · Machine learning · Neuroimaging

1 Introduction

Alzheimer's Disease (AD) is a neurodegenerative disease and the usual cause
of dementia in adult life. It is characterized by the deterioration of neurons,
affecting most of its functions, and producing the loss of immediate memory
[17]. One study has shown that the approximate number of individuals affected
by AD will duplicate in the next two decades, and by 2050, a diagnose of AD is
anticipated to approximately be produced every half minute, forecasting almost
one million new cases every year in the United States [3]. As a result of this, the
cost of treating and taking care of AD patients will be increasing, so it becomes
crucial to build computerized systems that can detect early AD accurately and
slow down its progress.

© Springer Nature Switzerland AG 2020
M. Mahmud et al. (Eds.): BI 2020, LNAI 12241, pp. 85–96, 2020.
https://doi.org/10.1007/978-3-030-59277-6_8

Artificial intelligence, in particular, machine learning (ML) has gained unprecedented attention during the last decade with applications such as anomaly detection [7,27,28], assay detection [23], biological data mining [14,16], disease diagnosis [2,18,19,29], education [25], financial prediction [20], natural language processing [21], trust management [15] and urban services [9]. Several of these ML methods (e.g., random forest [6], and auto-encoders [11]) have been employed for this type of research recently. This difficult research can be solved with Deep learning (DL) models that can be fed with 3D images and learn features to perform better with enhance detection. Studies done recently have shown that convolutional neural networks (CNNs) yield better results than the traditional approaches in computerized prediction of AD from MR images [8].

This paper proposes a novel approach of probability-based fusion of several CNN models to diagnose AD stages using brain 3D MRI scans. This model is able to perform a 4-way classification between the healthy brains (CN), brains with early MCI (EMCI), late MCI (LMCI) and diseased brains with AD (AD), (CN vs. EMCI vs. LMCI vs. AD) on the ADNI dataset.

In the rest of this paper, Sect. 2 reviews the literature, Sect. 3 describes the proposed method, Sect. 4 reports and discusses the results, and Sect. 5 concludes the paper along with some possible future research directions.

2   Related Works

The automatic classification of AD is an issue that has been under research for more than a decade. In recent years, there has been considerable progress in the field with DL models achieving near-perfect accuracy scores [4], thanks to the progress in the robust DL models, more specifically CNN-based models have been widely used for medical diagnosis research.

When DL was started to be employed in medical imaging classification, Liu et al. [12] used a stacked auto-encoder, to classify the early stage of AD. Applying 10-fold cross-validation to measure the model and achieved 47.42% accuracy in classifying 4 classes. Their dataset was unbalanced which was a limitation for the approach; thus classifying some groups was more complex than others for the auto-encoder. Moreover, with the popularity of predesigned CNN architectures that performed well on the ImageNet Large-Scale Visual Recognition Challenge, researchers started to focus in the potential that transfer learning has for computational biology applications. Farooq et al. [8] proposed an approach using predesigned CNNs and 2D segments of MRIs. The approach implemented complex CNN architectures from the ImageNet challenge, in this instance, two residual networks (Resnet-18 and ResNet-152) and Google's LeNet achieved astonishing accuracy, 98.01%, 98.14% and 98.88% respectively in a 3-way classification. Many of the reported AD classification methods were applied on 2D segments of MRIs, which in nature are 3D, and these approaches usually need multiple processes for feature extraction that help in future phases of training the model. Korolev et al. [10] developed powerful and altered adaptations of the VGG and Residual network architecture to work with 3D images. Additional research using

3D CNNs was conducted by Tang et al. [22] consisting of 1 ternary and 3 binary classification problems achieving 91.32% accuracy for the ternary classification, 88.43% for AD/MCI, 92.62% for MCI/NC and 96.81% for AD/NC. A different method researched by Wang et al. [24] achieved extraordinary performance in ternary classification with the application of an 3D ensemble approach. The approach consisted of merging the more efficient DenseNet classifiers that were trained individually and produced the probabilistic output through a softmax layer; lastly, the final classification was obtained by feeding the previous probability scores to the probability-based fusion approach.

3 Proposed Method

The proposed approach employs distinct 3D DenseNets that vary in their hyper-parameters and are fed with MR images that pass through the network and the networks classification probability goes to a probability-based fusion approach to make the last classification. Traditional network models comprises l layers, taking z_l as the output of the lth layer, and every layer implements a non-linear transformation $H_l(.)$, where l indexes the layer. To impede vanishing gradient and improve the information flow during the network training, the DenseNet employs the connections from a layer to all the following layers. In the approach

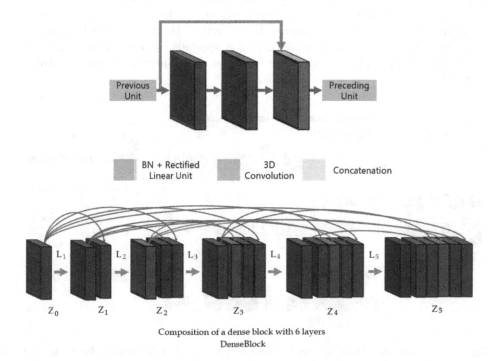

Fig. 1. Top: Architecture of a dense unit. Bottom: Composition of dense connectivity in a 6-layer dense block.

implemented for this study, the idea of dense connectivity is expanded to the 3D volumetric image classification task. Specifically, l is defined as:

$$z_l = H_l([z_0, z_1, z_2, ..., z_{l-1}])$$

where $z_0, z_1, ..., z_{l-1}$ are 3D feature volumes produced in previous layers, [...] refers to the concatenation function. The structure of a dense unit is shown in Fig. 1 (top). The function $H_l(.)$ has three main actions: a batch normalisation (BN) layer to decrease internal covariate transform, spatial convolution with k $3 \times 3 \times 3$ convolution kernels to produce 3D feature volumes, and to accelerate the training phase a rectified linear unit (ReLU). Figure 1 (bottom) shows a dense unit, that comprises one layer in a dense block, and each layer in the block connected with all the following layers. With dense connections between layers, feature utilisation is more efficient, and feature growth for each layer is lower than that of traditional CNNs. Thus, the models are compact and have less parameters than other networks.

In previous research it was shown that the hyper-parameters of the 3D DenseNet affects the performance [24]. Multiple tests were conducted with diverse hyper-parameter sets to produce individual networks with unique compositions, and that were able to extract different features. One sensible hyper-parameter demonstrated to enhance the outputs of the network was the growth rate. If each function H_l generates g volume-features, it means that the lth layer has $g_0 + g \times (l-1)$ input volume-features, where g_0 is the number of channels in the input layer. The 3D DenseNet can have compact layers, e.g., $g = 12$, where g is the growth rate of the network. Every layer appends g feature-maps of its own to the state given that every layer has access to all the previous volume-features in its block.

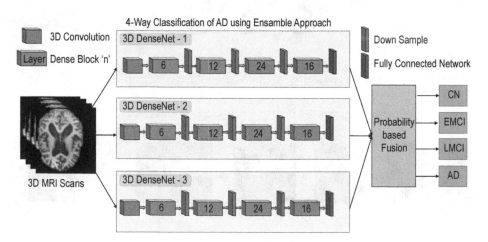

Fig. 2. Architecture of the proposed ensemble 3D DenseNet framework for 4-way AD classification.

The proposed method consists in the implementation of a probability-based fusion ensemble approach [26], having the probabilistic outcome of the last classification layer from the varying individual networks are combined (see Fig. 2). Compared to the usual majority voting method that uses as labels, the outcome that appeared the most in the models, in this ensemble method, every model is individually trained, thus the error margin among the different classifiers are insignificant, making the results of the approach superior compared to one single classifier. The error margin could rise for simple classifiers if the subject classification is complicated and there's incertitude among the distinct classes. As an example, take three classifiers, the output probabilities of the classifier layer for CN, EMCI, LMCI, and AD are: (1)0.8, 0.1, 0.1, 0.0 (2)0.4, 0.5, 0.0, 0.1 (3)0.3, 0.5, 0.1, 0.1, respectively. Making use of a majority voting approach, the classification result is Early MCI. On the other hand, this is not the most accurate answer, considering that the classification of the prediction model 1 is more certain in the prediction, while 2 and 3 had incertitude in theirs. The probability-based fusion approach will take the sum of the probabilistic output for each class of all the classifiers and then make a more certain prediction. For this research, u individual models were picked, and the probabilities of 3D DenseNet$_u$ assigned to classes on testing set were:

$$\Omega^u = (\beta_1^u, \beta_2^u, \beta_3^u, \beta_4^u)$$

where β_n^u indicates the probabilities of the class n. Then Ω^u is normalized by:

$$\Omega^k = \frac{Y^u}{\max[\beta_1^u, \beta_2^u, \beta_3^u, \beta_4^u]}$$

when outputs of the c-based 3D DenseNets have been calculated, the final prediction label is determined by the probability-based fusion method as:

$$a = \arg\ \max(\prod_{u=1}^{c} \beta_1^u, \prod_{u=1}^{c} \beta_2^u, \prod_{u=1}^{c} \beta_4^u, \prod_{u=1}^{c} \beta_4^u)$$

3.1 Experimentation

MRI Data. Structural brain MRI scans from the ADNI dataset (http://adni. loni.usc.edu/) were used (n=600 images) in this study. Preprocessed MRI scans (e.g., mask, intensity normalisation, reorientation, and spatial normalisation) were downloaded in NIfTI file format from ADNI2 and ADNIGO. For all the experiments the dataset was divided into 80% training and 20% validation, hence the training set consisted of 480 brain scans. With the goal of having an optimal dataset for the network, both the training and validation sets were balanced.

Parameter Selection. Multiple tests on the 3D DenseNet were carried out and the network hyper-parameters were optimised to obtain best results on the 4-way classification task. The following hyper-parameter settings were used during the training:

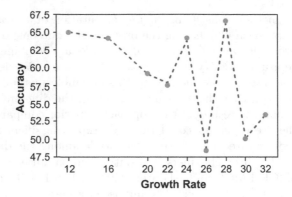

Fig. 3. Comparison of different growth rates.

- Adam stochastic optimisation algorithm;
- Pytorch's Cross-Entropy loss function;
- *Learning rate* = 0.0001;
- *Batch size* = 4;
- *Dropout* = 0.5;
- *Epochs* = 100.

Growth Rate Analysis. The number of new features incremented at each layer is determined by the hyper-parameter g known as the growth rate of the model. Figure 3 shows the considerable change in accuracy of the models depending of the number assigned to g. When $g = 28$, the model achieved the best performance; nonetheless, it can also be observed that with $g = 12$, the accuracy is near the result best performance. Previous research [24] shown that 3D DenseNet with low growth rate was incapable of learning crucial features for prediction and consequently, did not achieve good performance.

DenseNet Network Depth Selection. Different network depth configurations of DenseNet, specifically, the 121, 169 and 201 were compared for time and accuracy while making the executing the 4-way classification task. As shown in Fig. 4, DenseNet-121 was the most efficient network depth in both parameters, and hence was chosen to be the base classifier for this task.

3.2 Selecting Optimal Number of Models

The combination of different individual classifiers can reduce the error margin. Principally due to the probability-based fusion approach being able to combine the probabilistic output of different classifier models and produce a more certain decision based on more robust and reliable data, instead of producing predictions based on only one classifier or having a majority voting method (see Sect. 3).

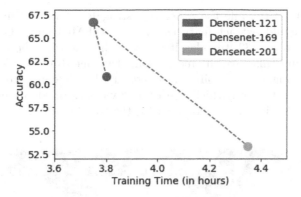

Fig. 4. Comparison of different network depths of the DenseNet model.

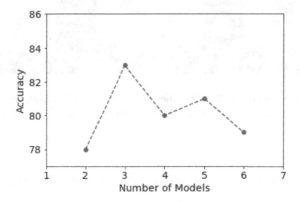

Fig. 5. Comparison of different number of models in the ensemble.

Various tests were carried out to probe the optimal number of models in creating the ensemble. As shown in Fig. 5, the ensemble with three models achieved the best accuracy. These experiments suggest that the quality of the models, i.e., how good is an individual model in predicting a specific class, is what actually is going to determine the number of models that produce the optimal performance.

4   Results and Discussion

4.1   Individual Classifier Performance

The test findings for the independent classifier models and their parameters are shown in Table 1. The best results out of the three was produced when $g = 28$, insinuating that 28 is the optimal growth rate to achieve higher results in 4-way classification with the DenseNet implementation of this study. Figure 6 shows that although classifier 1 was only 53.33% accurate in this task, it performed fine predicting EMCI, while the other two struggled. One justification to why the classifier 1 could extract features to predict EMCI subjects could be its growth rate. With $g = 32$, the classifier 1 was the one with the bigger number of parameters, and this gave the model some leverage to extract more complex features. This being said, classifier 1 struggled when it comes to predict more simple groups like CN, on which the other two performed better; this might occur when the classifier is too complex for the training data.

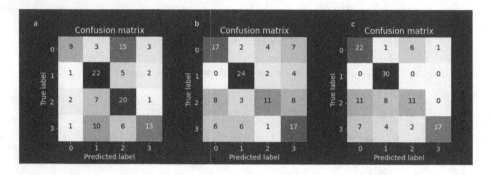

Fig. 6. Confusion matrices (a) for classifier-1 (accuracy = 53.33%), (b) for classifier-2 (accuracy = 57.50%), and (c) for classifier-3 (accuracy = 66.67%). Labels: 0 = CN, 1 = AD, 2 = EMCI, 3 = LMCI.

Table 1. Parameter comparison of different network structures.

Model	Growth rate	Convolutional kernel size	Parameters(n)	Layers	Training duration	Accuracy(%)
Classifier 1	32	$3 \times 3 \times 3$	11,226,500	121	3 h:35 min	53.33
Classifier 2	22	$7 \times 7 \times 7$	5,392,134	121	3 h:03 min	57.50
Classifier 3	28	$7 \times 7 \times 7$	8,649,224	121	3 h:45 min	66.67

4.2   Comparison with Residual Network

The results of the comparison between the DenseNet-121 and the ResNet-18 are presented in Fig. 7. The experiment demonstrated that DenseNet-18 has the quality to be trained faster and achieve more accuracy compared to the ResNet-18. The longer training time is probably due to the ResNet-18 network having around 108 million parameters to train compared to the 8.6 million of the DenseNet-121.

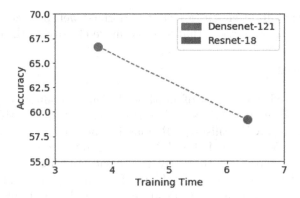

Fig. 7. Comparison of ResNet-18 and DenseNet-121.

Table 2. Test outcome of our approach compared with different methods in 4-way classification of AD.

Ref.	Architecture	Dataset (n)				Accuracy(%)
		CN	[s/E]MCI	[p/c/L]MCI	AD	
[12]	3D SAE	52	56	43	51	47.42
[5]	RF	60	60	60	60	61.9
[13]	MSDNN	360	409	217	238	75.44
[1]	3D ResNet	237	245	189	157	83.01
This work	3D DenseNet En	120	120	120	120	83.33

Legend: s = stable, p = progressive, c = converting, E = early, L = late, RF = Random Forest, MSDNN = Multi-scale Deep Neural Network, En. = Ensemble

4.3 Comparison with the State-of-the-Art

Test outcomes for this research approach compared to other similar research are shown in Table 2. While comparing with other models which use 3D MRI as input, our proposed model achieved the best performance (83.33%) which is 0.32% more than the test outcomes shown in [1]. However it becomes crucial to note here that this is not comparable in a straightforward fashion given that the other studies made use of stable MCI and converting or progressive MCI as two distinct phases of MCI, while in this research early MCI and late MCI were used, which seems to be different in literature.

Test results in the study show that the ensemble approach can lead to higher classification performance. Primarily because this approach can accumulate the probabilistic output of different classifier models and produce better predictions employing more robust and reliable data, instead of classifying based on only one classifier model.

Matched against the independent classifiers, a substantial increment in the accuracy is shown on the classification on both phases of MCI; as a result of merging the output from classifier 1 that performed well predicting EMCI and the other classifier's predictions that were accurate classifying the other groups.

5   Conclusion

This study presented an ensemble of multiple 3D densely connected convolutional neural networks to predict AD as well as two critical stages of MCI (known as early MCI and late MCI) utilising MR images. The prediction and discrimination between early MCI, late MCI and AD can aid in the recognition of different dementia's phases and allow the early treatment inn those early life phases. With the goal of figuring out the problem of having a limited number of MR images for the training phase, the proposed approach was implemented. The 3D DenseNet is more simple to train with its lower number of parameters due to having the type of connections that enhance the flow of gradients and data throughout the network. Various test were conducted to study the performance of the model with different parameters. Furthermore, these tests produced individual classifier models with diverse parameters and structures that could be used for the ensemble. A probability-based fusion approach was used to merge the probabilistic outputs from these models. The model's accuracy was enhanced while using the probability-based fusion approach, obtaining a final accuracy of 83.33%, in comparison to the individual member classifiers. This proofs that the approach of this study is a robust and reliable method in 4-way prediction tasks, while also outperforming some previous studies. In further research of this work, we would like to implement an increment in the training dataset, to test the classifier 1 of this research, and the ensemble approach to enhance the results. Otherwise further study could include implement less training data and finding an approach that yields the same or higher accuracy with the goal in mind of having a real-world environment where the data could be scarce.

Acknowledgment. *Data used in the preparation of this article were obtained from the Alzheimer's Disease Neuroimaging Initiative (ADNI) database (http://adni.loni.usc.edu/). For up-to-date information, see http://adni-info.org/.

References

1. Abrol, A., Bhattarai, M., Fedorov, A., Du, Y., Plis, S., Calhoun, V.: Deep residual learning for neuroimaging: an application to predict progression to Alzheimer's disease. J. Neurosci. Methods **339**, 108701 (2020)
2. Ali, H.M., Kaiser, M.S., Mahmud, M.: Application of convolutional neural network in segmenting brain regions from MRI data. In: Liang, P., Goel, V., Shan, C. (eds.) BI 2019. LNCS, vol. 11976, pp. 136–146. Springer, Cham (2019). https://doi.org/10.1007/978-3-030-37078-7_14
3. Association, A.: 2014 Alzheimer's disease facts and figures. Alzheimer's Dement. **10**(2), e47–e92 (2014)
4. Basaia, S., et al.: Automated classification of Alzheimer's disease and mild cognitive impairment using a single MRI and deep neural networks. NeuroImage Clin. **21**, 101645 (2019)

5. Dimitriadis, S.I., Liparas, D., Tsolaki, M.N., Initiative, A.D.N., et al.: Random forest feature selection, fusion and ensemble strategy: combining multiple morphological MRI measures to discriminate among healhy elderly, MCI, cMCI and Alzheimer's disease patients: from the Alzheimer's disease neuroimaging initiative (ADNI) database. J. Neurosci. Methods **302**, 14–23 (2018)

6. Dongren, Y., Calhoun, V., Fu, Z., Du, Y., Sui, J.: An ensemble learning system for a 4-way classification of Alzheimer's disease and mild cognitive impairment. J. Neurosci. Methods **302**, 75–81 (2018)

7. Fabietti, M., et al.: Neural network-based artifact detection in local field potentials recorded from chronically implanted neural probes. In: Proceedings of the IJCNN, pp. 1–8 (2020)

8. Farooq, A., Anwar, S., Awais, M., Rehman, S.: A deep CNN based multi-class classification of Alzheimer's disease using MRI. In: 2017 IEEE International Conference on Imaging Systems and Techniques (IST), pp. 1–6 (2017)

9. Kaiser, M.S., et al.: Advances in crowd analysis for urban applications through urban event detection. IEEE Trans. Intell. Transp. Syst. **19**(10), 3092–3112 (2018)

10. Korolev, S., Safiullin, A., Belyaev, M., Dodonova, Y.: Residual and plain convolutional neural networks for 3D brain MRI classification. In: 2017 IEEE 14th International Symposium on Biomedical Imaging (ISBI 2017), pp. 835–838 (2017)

11. Liu, S., et al.: ADNI: multimodal neuroimaging feature learning for multiclass diagnosis of Alzheimer's disease. IEEE Trans. Biomed. Eng. **62**(4), 1132–1140 (2015)

12. Liu, S., Liu, S., Cai, W., Pujol, S., Kikinis, R., Feng, D.: Early diagnosis of Alzheimer's disease with deep learning. In: 2014 IEEE 11th International Symposium on Biomedical Imaging, ISBI 2014, pp. 1015–1018, January 2014

13. Lu, D., Popuri, K., Ding, G.W., Balachandar, R., Beg, M.F.: Multimodal and multiscale deep neural networks for the early diagnosis of Alzheimer's disease using structural mr and FDG-PET images. Sci. Rep. **8**(1), 1–13 (2018)

14. Mahmud, M., Kaiser, M.S., Hussain, A.: Deep learning in mining biological data, pp. 1–36. arXiv:2003.00108 [cs, q-bio, stat], February 2020

15. Mahmud, M., Kaiser, M.S., Rahman, M.M., Rahman, M.A., Shabut, A., Al-Mamun, S., Hussain, A.: A brain-inspired trust management model to assure security in a cloud based IoT framework for neuroscience applications. Cogn. Comput. **10**(5), 864–873 (2018)

16. Mahmud, M., Kaiser, M.S., Hussain, A., Vassanelli, S.: Applications of deep learning and reinforcement learning to biological data. IEEE Trans. Neural Netw. Learn. Syst. **29**(6), 2063–2079 (2018)

17. McKhann, G., Drachman, D., Folstein, M., Katzman, R., Price, D., Stadlan, E.: Clinical diagnosis of Alzheimer's disease: report of the NINCDS-ADRDA work group under the auspices of department of health and human services task force on Alzheimer's disease. Neurology **34**(7), 939–944 (1984)

18. Miah, Y., Prima, C.N.E., Seema, S.J., Mahmud, M., Kaiser, M.S.: Performance comparison of machine learning techniques in identifying dementia from open access clinical datasets. In: Proceedings of the ICACIn, pp. 69–78. Springer, Singapore (2020)

19. Noor, M.B.T., Zenia, N.Z., Kaiser, M.S., Mahmud, M., Al Mamun, S.: Detecting neurodegenerative disease from MRI: a brief review on a deep learning perspective. In: Liang, P., Goel, V., Shan, C. (eds.) BI 2019. LNCS, vol. 11976, pp. 115–125. Springer, Cham (2019). https://doi.org/10.1007/978-3-030-37078-7_12

20. Orojo, O., Tepper, J., McGinnity, T., Mahmud, M.: A multi-recurrent network for crude oil price prediction. In: Proceedings of the SSCI, pp. 2940–2945, December 2019

21. Rabby, G., Azad, S., Mahmud, M., Zamli, K.Z., Rahman, M.M.: TeKET: a tree-based unsupervised keyphrase extraction technique. Cogn. Comput. (2020). https://doi.org/10.1007/s12559-019-09706-3

22. Tang, H., Yao, E., Tan, G., Guo, X.: A fast and accurate 3D fine-tuning convolutional neural network for Alzheimer's disease diagnosis. In: Zhou, Z.-H., Yang, Q., Gao, Y., Zheng, Yu. (eds.) ICAI 2018. CCIS, vol. 888, pp. 115–126. Springer, Singapore (2018). https://doi.org/10.1007/978-981-13-2122-1_9

23. Tania, M.H., et al.: Assay type detection using advanced machine learning algorithms. In: Proceedings of the SKIMA, pp. 1–8 (2019)

24. Wang, H., et al.: Ensemble of 3D densely connected convolutional network for diagnosis of mild cognitive impairment and Alzheimer's disease. Neurocomputing **333**, 145–156 (2019)

25. Watkins, J., Fabietti, M., Mahmud, M.: SENSE: a student performance quantifier using sentiment analysis. In: Proceedings of the IJCNN, pp. 1–6 (2020)

26. Wen, G., Hou, Z., Li, H., Li, D., Jiang, L., Xun, E.: Ensemble of deep neural networks with probability-based fusion for facial expression recognition. Cogn. Comput. **9**, 597–610 (2017). https://doi.org/10.1007/s12559-017-9472-6

27. Yahaya, S.W., Lotfi, A., Mahmud, M.: A consensus novelty detection ensemble approach for anomaly detection in activities of daily living. Appl. Soft Comput. **83**, 105613 (2019)

28. Yahaya, S.W., Lotfi, A., Mahmud, M., Machado, P., Kubota, N.: Gesture recognition intermediary robot for abnormality detection in human activities. In: Proceedings of the SSCI, pp. 1415–1421, December 2019

29. Zohora, M.F., et al.: Forecasting the risk of type II diabetes using reinforcement learning. In: Proceedings of the ICIEV, pp. 1–6 (2020)

Dynamic Functional Connectivity Captures Individuals' Unique Brain Signatures

Rohan Gandhi[1]([⊠]) [iD], Arun Garimella[1] [iD], Petri Toiviainen[2] [iD],
and Vinoo Alluri[1] [iD]

[1] International Institute of Information Technology, Hyderabad, Hyderabad, India
`rohan.gandhi@research.iiit.ac.in`
[2] Finnish Centre for Interdisciplinary Music Research, Department of Music, Art,
and Culture Studies, University of Jyvaskyla, Jyväskylä, Finland

Abstract. Recent neuroimaging evidence suggest that there exists a unique individual-specific functional connectivity (FC) pattern consistent across tasks. The objective of our study is to utilize FC patterns to identify an individual using a supervised machine learning approach. To this end, we use two previously published data sets that comprises resting-state and task-based fMRI responses. We use static FC measures as input to a linear classifier to evaluate its performance. We additionally extend this analysis to capture dynamic FC using two approaches: the common sliding window approach and the more recent phase synchrony-based measure. We found that the classification models using dynamic FC patterns as input outperform their static analysis counterpart by a significant margin for both data sets. Furthermore, sliding window-based analysis proved to capture more individual-specific brain connectivity patterns than phase synchrony measures for resting-state data while the reverse pattern was observed for the task-based data set. Upon investigating the effects of feature reduction, we found that feature elimination significantly improved results upto a point with near-perfect classification accuracy for the task-based data set while a gradual decrease in the accuracy was observed for resting-state data set. The implications of these findings are discussed. The results we have are promising and present a novel direction to investigate further.

Keywords: fMRI · Functional connectivity · Classification · Variance inflation factor · Individual differences

1 Introduction

Neuroscience has progressed by leaps and bounds in the past two decades. A growing interest to understand the structure and function of the brain has resulted in significant advancements in both data acquisition and analyses techniques. Central to one of the most common efforts to decipher brain function is

© Springer Nature Switzerland AG 2020
M. Mahmud et al. (Eds.): BI 2020, LNAI 12241, pp. 97–106, 2020.
https://doi.org/10.1007/978-3-030-59277-6_9

functional magnetic resonance imaging (fMRI), an indirect measurement of the neuronal activity.

Recent studies, however, have questioned the effectiveness of fMRI in understanding brain function and predicting future brain activity (although these studies primarily dealt with task based fMRI) [1,2] . Other studies have also shown that functional networks are dominated by stable individual features independent of task [3]. Gratton et al. [3] reported that an individual's brain network is dominated by stable group and individual factors while using a static functional connectivity approach(sFC). This would then imply that sFC patterns would represent an individual's functional connectivity signature thereby allowing us to identify an individual across tasks. However, it remains to be seen if this applies in a naturalistic paradigm wherein the participant performs a contiguous task like movie viewing [7] or music listening [8] thereby emulating real-life experiences. Moreover, Gratton et al. did not investigate individual-specific dynamic functional connectivity(dFC) patterns. Some of the most common approaches used are sFC analyses [4], and dFC analyses like Correlation-based Sliding Window (CSW) analysis [5] and the more recent Instantaneous Phase Synchrony (IPS) analysis [6].

The sFC analysis approach involves taking an average of the time series for region of interest (a voxel or parcel) and using this for further analysis with the primary assumption that networks are temporally stationary. While this leads to an ease in result interpretability, the primary problem encountered is the loss of the temporal dimension shifting the focus entirely to the spatial dimension.

Dynamic functional connectivity, on the other hand, incorporates temporal fluctuations, a clear improvement over it's static counterpart. In its most basic version, the CSW dynamic approach uses a sliding window of a fixed length in order to capture temporally varying functional networks. IPS is a novel approach introduced quite recently into fMRI based studies [10]. This method compares the phase angles for each brain voxel or region (depending on the area of interest) at every single time point thus providing the same temporal resolution as the original fMRI data. Another study has found CSW and IPS to convey comparable information [11], where IPS is preferred as it foregoes the need to select appropriate window length and overlap required for CSW. It remains to be seen as to which of these techniques captures individual-specific information better.

The main objective of our study is to identify individuals based on their functional connectivity patterns. To this end, we try to glean a functional signature from their sFC and the two dFC approaches. Subsequently, we compare the classification accuracy so as to determine the stronger approach. In order to assess the external validity of the proposed classification approach, we use two different datasets. Building on that, we have performed experiments to identify individuals based on their fMRI scans using 2 different data sets. One, a passive task based music listening data set (part of "Tunteet" data set), and the other a resting state data set (part of HCP data set). The passive music listening task is part of the naturalistic paradigm, so as to emulate real-life listening situations in addition to being comparable to resting-state while performing the task (music listening). This would help us in understanding whether a unique FC signature exists for a participant and whether it can be replicated over time. As far as we know, this is the first study to attempt identifying participants based on their intrinsic static and dynamic functional connectivity signatures.

2   Methods

The study was performed on two different data sets which were previously used in already published research papers. The first one, part of the data sets uploaded in the "Human Connectome Project", is a resting state data set [14] (henceforth referred to as the "HCP data set"). The second one, part of "Tunteet" data set, is a passive task based music listening data set [12,13] (henceforth referred to as the "musical data set"). Both the data sets were chosen for their difference between each other and their history of being used previously in published studies.

2.1   Data Set Specification

HCP Data Set: This data set consists of resting state fMRIs of 40 random participants from the much larger HCP1200 Young Adult data set [14] so as to keep it comparable to the musical data set. Each scan was 15 min long, done twice for every participant with a gap of 3 weeks. The subjects were asked to be at rest and think about nothing while undergoing the fMRI scan. The subjects were processed with the HCP minimal preprocessing pipeline [15]). More details can be found in the HCP documentation page [20].

Musical Data Set: The first set consisted of 36 participants, that included 18 musicians (9 females, age 28.2 ± 7.8 years) and 18 non-musicians (10 females, age 29.2 ± 10.7 years). All the participants were asked to listen to three instrumental pieces - Stream of Consciousness by Dream Theater (progressive rock), Adios Nonino by Astor Piazzolla (tango nuevo), and the first three dances of the Rite of Spring by Igor Stravinsky (modern classical). Each piece was roughly around 8 min long and belonged to a different genre.

The brain responses of participants were acquired while they listened to the musical stimuli presented in randomized order. Their only task was to attentively listen to the music delivered via MR-compatible insert earphones while keeping their eyes open. The data was preprocessed using well-established preprocessing methods [7].

2.2   Feature Extraction

The fMRI data from both the data sets were first parcellated using the AAL atlas which resulted in time-series of 116 regions to ease the computations required in the tasks ahead.

Static Functional Connectivity: For correlation-based static Functional Connectivity matrices (sFC), pair-wise Pearson correlation coefficients were calculated between the brain regions for the time series from each scanning session. This resulted in a symmetrical correlation matrix of size $116 \times 116 \times 2$ for every participant in the HCP data set, and $116 \times 116 \times 3$ for every participant in the musical data set. These matrices were converted to vectors by linearizing the lower-triangular matrix without the diagonal, resulting in $\frac{116 \times 115}{2} = 6670$ feature vector for every scanning session. This resulted in a feature set of size 6670×80 for the HCP data set, and 6670×108 for the musical data set.

Dynamic Functional Connectivity:

Correlation-Based Sliding Window. For this analysis, a rectangular window of size 10 time points with 50% overlap was employed as shown in Fig. 1. Pair-wise Pearson correlation was performed between the brain regions with all the time-points in a single window for every scanning session. The resultant 116×116 matrices were then linearized using the same method as used in sFC analysis. This was done for all the participants in both the data sets, which resulted in $6670 \times \omega 1 \times 40$ feature set for every scanning session for the HCP data set, and $6670 \times \omega 2 \times 36$ feature set for every stimulus in the musical data set, where $\omega 1$ *and* $\omega 2$ are the total number of windows for every participant in the HCP and musical data set respectively.

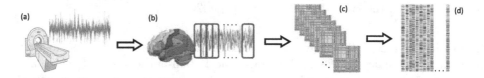

Fig. 1. For CSW analysis, every participant's data goes through the following steps: (a) Voxel based time series. (b) Parcellation into 116 regions and 50% overlapping window of 10 time points. (c) Region-wise correlation and generation of CSW matrices for every time window. (d) Linearization of lower triangular matrix for every time point to get a 2D matrix per participant per scanning session.

Instantaneous Phase Synchrony. As shown in Fig. 2, Hilbert transform was applied on the parcelled fMRI time series of every region for every participant to get the analytical signal, upon which phase angle was calculated. Then cosine of instantaneous phase angle difference was calculated between every pair of regions for all the time points which resulted in a 116×116 symmetrical distance matrix for every time-point. These IPS matrices were linearized using the same method as used for sFCs for every participant generating a dynamic IPS, resulting in $6670 \times \tau 1 \times 40$ feature set for every scanning session for the HCP data set, and $6670 \times \tau 2 \times 36$ feature set for every stimulus in the musical data set, where $\tau 1$ *and* $\tau 2$ are the total number of time points for every participant in the HCP and musical data set respectively.

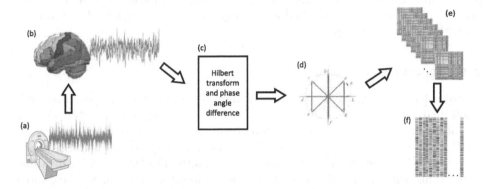

Fig. 2. For IPS analysis, every participant's data goes through the following steps: (a) Voxel based time series. (b) Parcellation into 116 regions. (c) Hilbert transform, phase angle calculation and region-wise angular difference. (d) cosine function on outcome of c. (e) IPS matrices for every time point. (f) Linearization of lower triangular matrix for every time point to get a 2D matrix per participant.

2.3   Classification

We used Linear Discriminant Analysis (LDA) from python's scikit-learn toolbox [16] for classification as it is a parameter-free method and is a simple model that is easy to interpret. The classification tasks were performed separately on both sets of data and both sets of static and dynamic matrices generated from the data sets. For the HCP data set, the classification accuracy was calculated using the feature set from the first scanning session for training the model and from the second scanning session done 3 weeks later for testing. The classification accuracy in musical data set was tested using leave-one-stimulus-out cross validation method for each stimulus, and a 50% cross validation method. For the first cross validation method, time points from two stimuli were used for training the classification models and the time points from the remaining stimulus were used for validation, where the cross validation methods would be denoted henceforth as S1, S2, and S3 for using Dreamtheater, Piazzolla, and Stravinsky scans for validation respectively. For 50% cross validation method, half of the time points from each stimulus were used for training and the other half were used for testing.

The classification accuracy for dynamic analyses were evaluated using two different techniques. For the first method, classification accuracy for classification of every time window was calculated for CSW (CSW-TW), and accuracy for classification of every time point in IPS (IPS-TP). For the second method, a majority voting method was applied to measure the overall classification accuracy of participants. In this technique, we take a majority vote of all the classes the time windows or time points for each participants are classified in, and the participants are classified in the class in which maximum number of their time points are classified. This method will be denoted by CSW-MV and IPS-MV for both the dynamic analyses.

2.4   Feature Elimination

In order to reduce the dimensionality of the feature set owing to potential multicollinearity, the Variance Inflation Factor (VIF) technique was used to identify a unique set of features from the original feature set. Variance Inflation Factor (VIF) is a technique used to evaluate multicollinearity in a set of regression variables [17], using which we repetitively eliminated the features with maximal multicollinearity among all the features at every iteration until we get the desired size of the feature set. The features identified using VIF feature elimination do not necessarily guarantee greater classification accuracy since it is purely a data-driven approach; however, it allows us to identify the contribution of subsets of the input feature set that provided us with the best classification accuracy for each data set.

For HCP data set, VIF elimination was performed on the training set of CSW as it had provided us with the best results. The feature set was reduced to 50%, 30%, 15%, 10%, 5%, and 1% of the original feature set and the remaining features were used to train and test the LDA classifier and classification accuracy was calculated. For the musical data set, VIF elimination was performed on the training set of IPS as it provided the best results. The feature set upon which VIF was to be performed was the one used for 50% cross validation method as it included time points from all three stimuli. The feature set was reduced to the same number of features as for the HCP data set and the resultant features were used to train and test the LDA classifier for all three of the S1, S2, and S3 cross validation methods.

3   Results

3.1   Classification

Overall, dynamic analyses approaches provided far better accuracy in classifying individuals than the static ones, as it can be observed in Table 1, which contains the classification results on the complete feature set. The classification accuracy on classification using CSW-MV was found to be most significant for the HCP data set with an accuracy score of 0.775. Whereas for the musical data set, classification accuracy for IPS-TP provided far better classification accuracy at an average of 0.8148 across all cross validation methods. This was also the highest classification accuracy found in classification among all the data sets and types of analyses.

Table 1. Overall classification accuracy for both data sets with different feature extraction techniques using complete feature set.

Data set	sFC	CSW-TW	CSW-MV	IPS-TP	IPS-MV
HCP 40	0.1625	0.386	0.775	0.2730	0.45
Musical	0.4814	0.2541	0.7129	0.3437	0.8148

For classification using IPS for the musical data set, the classification model performs varyingly for different cross-validation methods. Table 2 gives a summary of classification results on the musical data set for all cross validation methods using the LDA classifier on the IPS data.

Table 2. Cross-validation results using LDA classifier on IPS data of musical data set.

Cross validation method	IPS-TP	IPS-MV
50% Cross validation	0.335	0.9444
Leave Dreamtheater out	0.344	0.7778
Leave Piazzolla out	0.3508	0.8611
Leave Stravinsky out	0.3365	0.8056

3.2 VIF Feature Elimination

As seen in Fig. 3a, upon implementing VIF elimination for the HCP data set, the participant classification accuracy reduced as the number of features were reduced, while the sharpest drop in accuracy was seen on using the feature set with 2.5% of the original features. The accuracy trend for classification of IPS data in musical data set with different number of features and using different cross-validation methods can be seen in Fig. 3b for participant classification accuracy. Here, the overall participant classification accuracy increased as the number of features were reduced until it reached a peak on using 10% of the feature set (667 features from the original 6670 feature set), and the classification accuracy started decreasing again on using 2.5% features from the original feature set.

4 Discussion and Scope

Across both data sets, it was observed that dFC feature-based classification models outperformed their sFC counterpart. This supports the notion that the temporal dimension indeed captures nuanced individual-specific signatured brain organization patterns. The CSW approach exhibited comparable classification

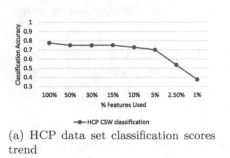

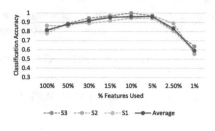

(a) HCP data set classification scores trend

(b) Musical data set classification scores trend

Fig. 3. VIF feature elimination based classification score trend

accuracies of around 70% accuracy in both datasets which is significantly higher than chance level, that is, 2.5% (1/40) for HCP and 2.8% (1/36) for Music datasets respectively. This is a notable result in particular for the HCP dataset since there exists a time lapse of three weeks between the acquisition of both rsfMRI sessions. This in fact indicates that short time periods, at least limited to weeks do not engender stark differences in brain functioning which manifest in fMRI data. CSW-based classification approach outperformed IPS-based classification for the HCP dataset while the opposite trend was observed for the musical dataset. Specifically, a 10% increase in accuracy was observed in the Music dataset as a result of the IPS-based classification. This can be attributed to the fact a rich stimulus like music requires an individual to process several elements in parallel such as melody, rhythm, timbre, and tonality in parallel, which are known to recruit large-scale networks with overlapping regions and hence would be captured better with a measure such as IPS. Additionally one could postulate that an external stimulus such as music evokes rapid temporal changes in brain states that cannot be so accurately captured with a sliding window approach.

Furthermore, music processing and experienced emotional states have been found to be modulated by several individual factors such as musical expertise, personality, empathy [18,19], which further potentially manifests as distinct synchronization between specific brain regions at an individual level. This would then allow us to postulate that IPS is more representative of dynamic brain functioning than the CSW approach as it captures minuscule changes owing to its ability to integrate data from a smaller timescale than CSW. The majority vote approach turned to be a more accurate approach for classification than the individual time-point classification approach. This implies that there indeed exist common dynamic FC patterns/states across individuals and hence a minimum number of observations per participant is required for successful classification. This calls for further investigation.

The feature elimination process resulted in differing trends in both datasets. While reduced number of features resulted in a decrease in classification accuracy in the HCP dataset, an increase in the classification accuracy approaching near-perfect classification (with top 5% = 333 features) was observed for the music dataset before evidencing a declining trend. A similar steep decrease was observed post 5% of the feature set related to the HCP dataset. The decrease in accuracy for the HCP dataset might imply that all pair-wise connection patterns are essential when using the CSW-approach. On the other hand, the increasing classification accuracy of the classification model for the musical data as a result of VIF feature elimination can be attributed to the removal of noise from the feature set thereby improving the overall quality of data. In fact, certain regions in the brain have been found to consistently process certain musical features across individuals [18], which, when removed, allows to better find intrinsic functional networks. However, it remains to be seen which regions con-tribute the most in correctly classifying the participants with a higher accuracy. This calls for a focused study in feature importance for classification, which is beyond the scope of the current study. In fact, identifying specific regions, the phase synchronization of which would be important in classifying individuals, would be valuable in contexts wherein severity of neurological conditions such as autism or mental health conditions such as depression, post-traumatic stress disorder, need to be predicted.

This work can be naturally extended to investigate other tasks such as naturalistic viewing, reading and language processing to check whether IPS does outperform CSW consistently across multiple tasks, especially in the same set of individuals. Furthermore, dFC-based features may be subjected to other classification models to compare performance while keeping in mind complexity and interpretability of the model. A concern with CSW is the lack of consensus on window length. Shorter windows are likelier to capture noise in the data while longer windows would generate more accurate results at the cost of temporal resolution. The effect of band-pass filtering (also based on the frequency range) of data before IPS also has to be investigated, but our ongoing pilot study using these steps in the feature extraction part has provided notably similar results. The AAL atlas used in the current study sacrifices a lot of spatial resolution for ease of computation, so a higher resolution atlas should also be looked into to investigate the spatial scales at which the individual brain networks differ. Other classification models can also be checked for improved classification accuracy.

References

1. Botvinik-Nezer, R., Holzmeister, F., Camerer, C.F., et al.: Variability in the analysis of a single neuroimaging dataset by many teams. Nature **582**, 84–88 (2020). https://doi.org/10.1038/s41586-020-2314-9
2. Elliott, M.L., et al.: What is the test-retest reliability of common task-functional MRI measures? New empirical evidence and a meta-analysis. Psychol. Sci. (2020). https://doi.org/10.1177/0956797620916786
3. Gratton, C., Laumann, T.O., Nielsen, A.N., et al.: Functional brain networks are dominated by stable group and individual factors, not cognitive or daily variation. Neuron **98**(2), 439–452.e5 (2018). https://doi.org/10.1016/j.neuron.2018.03.035

4. Biswal, B., Zerrin Yetkin, F.Z., Haughton, V.M., Hyde, J.S.: Functional connectivity in the motor cortex of resting human brain using echo-planar MRI. Magn. Resona. Med. **34**(4), 537–541 (1995). https://doi.org/10.1002/mrm.1910340409
5. Hutchison, R.M., et al.: Dynamic functional connectivity: promise, issues, and interpretations. NeuroImage **80**, 360–378 (2013). https://doi.org/10.1016/j.neuroimage.2013.05.079
6. Glerean, E., Salmi, J., Lahnakoski, J.M., Jääskeläinen, I.P., Sams, M.: Functional magnetic resonance imaging phase synchronization as a measure of dynamic functional connectivity. Brain Connect. 91–101 (2012). https://doi.org/10.1089/brain.2011.0068
7. Hasson, U., Nir, Y., Levy, I., Fuhrmann, G., Malach, R.: Intersubject synchronization of cortical activity during natural vision. Science **303**(5664), 1634–1640 (2004). https://doi.org/10.1126/science.1089506
8. Alluri, V., Toiviainen, P., Jääskeläinen, I.P., Glerean, E., Sams, M., Brattico, E.: Large-scale brain networks emerge from dynamic processing of musical timbre, key and rhythm. Neuroimage **59**(4), 3677–3689 (2012). https://doi.org/10.1016/j.neuroimage.2011.11.019
9. Yeo, B.T., et al.: The organization of the human cerebral cortex estimated by intrinsic functional connectivity. J. Neurophysiol. **106**(3), 1125–1165 (2011)
10. Omidvarnia, A., Pedersen, M., Walz, J.M., Vaughan, D.N., Abbott, D.F., Jackson, G.D.: Dynamic regional phase synchrony (DRePS). Hum. Brain Mapp. **37**, 1970–1985 (2016). https://doi.org/10.1002/hbm.23151
11. Pedersen, M., Omidvarnia, A., Zalesky, A., Jackson, G.D.: On the relationship between instantaneous phase synchrony and correlation-based sliding windows for time-resolved fMRI connectivity analysis. Neuroimage **181**, 85–94 (2018). https://doi.org/10.1016/j.neuroimage.2018.06.020
12. Burunat, I., Brattico, E., Puoliväli, T., Ristaniemi, T., Sams, M., Toiviainen, P.: Action in perception: prominent visuo-motor functional symmetry in musicians during music listening. PLoS ONE **10**(9), e0138238 (2015). https://doi.org/10.1371/journal.pone.0138238
13. Alluri, V., Toiviainen, P., Burunat, I., Kliuchko, M., Vuust, P., Brattico, E.: Connectivity patterns during music listening: evidence for action-based processing in musicians. Hum Brain Mapp. **38**(6), 2955–2970 (2017). https://doi.org/10.1002/hbm.23565
14. Van Essen, D.C., et al.: The WU-Minn Human Connectome Project: an overview. NeuroImage **80**(2013), 62–79 (2013)
15. GlasserGlasser, M.F., et al.: The minimal preprocessing pipelines for the Human Connectome Project. Neuroimage **80**, 105–124 (2013)
16. Pedregosa, F., et al.: Scikit-learn: machine learning in Python. J. Mach. Learn. Res. **12**, 2825–2830 (2011)
17. Snee, R.: Who Invented the Variance Inflation Factor? (1981). https://doi.org/10.13140/RG.2.1.3274.8562
18. Alluri, V., et al.: From Vivaldi to Beatles and back: predicting brain responses to music. Neuroimage **83**, 627–636 (2013). https://doi.org/10.1016/j.neuroimage.2013.06.064
19. Niranjan, D., Burunat, I., Toiviainen, P., Brattico, E., Alluri, V.: Influence of musical expertise on the processing of musical features in a naturalistic setting. In: 2019 Conference on Cognitive Computational Neuroscience. https://doi.org/10.32470/CCN.2019.1314-0
20. Human Connectome Project Homepage. http://www.humanconnectomeproject.org. Accessed 15 Jun 2020

Differential Effects of Trait Empathy on Functional Network Centrality

Vishnu Moorthigari[1]([ID]), Emily Carlson[2]([ID]), Petri Toiviainen[2]([ID]),
Elvira Brattico[3]([ID]), and Vinoo Alluri[1]([ID])

[1] International Institute of Information Technology, Hyderabad, Hyderabad, India
vishnu.moorthigari@research.iiit.ac.in, vinoo.alluri@iiit.ac.in
[2] Center for Interdisciplinary Music Research, Department of Music,
University of Jyväskylä, Jyväskylä, Finland
{emily.j.carlson,petri.toiviainen}@jyu.fi
[3] Center for Music In the Brain, Aarhus University, Aarhus, Denmark
elvira.brattico@clin.au.dk

Abstract. Previous research has shown that empathy, a fundamental component of human social functioning, is engaged when listening to music. Neuroimaging studies of empathy processing in music have, however, been limited. fMRI analysis methods based on graph theory have recently gained popularity as they are capable of illustrating global patterns of functional connectivity, which could be very useful in studying complex traits such as empathy. The current study examines the role of trait empathy, including cognitive and affective facets, on whole-brain functional network centrality in 36 participants listening to music in a naturalistic setting. Voxel-wise eigenvector centrality mapping was calculated as it provides us with an understanding of globally distributed centres of coordination associated with the processing of empathy. Partial correlation between Eigenvector centrality and measures of empathy showed that cognitive empathy is associated with higher centrality in the sensorimotor regions responsible for motor mimicry while affective empathy showed higher centrality in regions related to auditory affect processing. Results are discussed in relation to various theoretical models of empathy and music cognition.

Keywords: Eigenvector centrality · Cognitive empathy · Affective empathy · Naturalistic paradigm · Music listening

1 Introduction

It is clearly established that the human brain is organised into functional networks, acting as independent units [4]. Recent work has shown that these networks exhibit stable features and are dominated by individual-specific factors [13]. That is functional networks of an individual exhibit stable characteristics across tasks. Personality traits, defined as stable behavioural tendencies in individuals, have been found to correlate with these individual functional networks

© Springer Nature Switzerland AG 2020
M. Mahmud et al. (Eds.): BI 2020, LNAI 12241, pp. 107–117, 2020.
https://doi.org/10.1007/978-3-030-59277-6_10

[1]. Individual differences in the tendency to empathise has particularly interested social neuroscience over the last few decades [9]. Empathy refers to the ability to understand and share in the mental experiences of others. One mechanism for this is internal mimicry; a person perceives another's bodily movements or facial expressions and grasps their mental state by mentally simulating the same movements [36]. Empathy is generally agreed to be underpinned by two distinct subsystems: an affective, involuntary system and a cognitive, voluntary system [12], which are related but dissociable [26]. Tomasello [32] has suggested that the ability to understand the mental reality of others by imagining being "in their shoes," and subsequent ability to see others as "like me," represents the crucial step in human evolution that allowed for the development of species-specific cultural transmission systems. Empathy is vital to social functioning, and its dysfunction has been implicated in serious disorders such as autism, schizophrenia, and Borderline Personality Disorder [8], making the neural underpinnings of empathy an important area of research from many perspectives.

Multiple tests measuring trait empathy have been developed; the Interpersonal Reactivity Index (IRI) [6], is particularly useful as it includes subscales which distinguish between several aspects of empathy and has previously been used in neuroscientific studies of empathy [20]. The IRI's four subscales–Perspective-taking (PT), Fantasy-Seeking (FS), Empathic Concern (EC), and Personal Distress (PD)–have been used as a two-dimensional model comprising Emotional (EC, PD) and Cognitive (FS, PT) empathy [34]. However, in light of studies [17] showing PD to be inversely related to the concept of affective empathy, we limit ourselves to understanding affective empathy through EC.

Music represents a useful stimulus for studying empathy, due to its ability to evoke a variety of emotional responses in listeners [16]. Empathy is thought to play a role in these responses; music may express others' emotions or act as a virtual agent which can evoke empathy [16]. Music's close association with bodily movement makes it especially relevant to understanding internal mimicry [21]. Cross [5] has posited music as a mode of communication that privileges interaction and emotion, which places empathy as a fundamental aspect of musical experiences.

Studies have revealed a subnetwork of brain regions involved in processing empathy, referred to by Fan et al. [10] as the Core Empathy Network (CEmN). It includes the Medial cingulate cortex (MCC), Anterior cingulate cortex (ACC), Insula and Inferior frontal gyrus (IFG), and the Supplementary motor area (SMA). To date, only two studies have investigated the neurophysiological relationship between empathy and music processing. Wallmark et al. [34] found significant activation in both the cognitive and affective parts of the CEmN, related to trait empathy, albeit using very short (<3 s) music segments as stimuli. Sachs et al.'s [25] found greater synchronisation in individuals scoring high on FS in auditory, visual and prefrontal regions during listening to a full piece of sad music. Their study is an example of a recent shift in fMRI research towards naturalistic paradigms; that is, making use of real-world stimuli such as films or music, and not asking participants to perform any other tasks during recording [23]. However, their study was specific to sad music and focused on the FS subscale. Moreover, their measures comprised inter-subject correlation and phase synchronisation in addition to intra-subject pairwise (voxel/seed-based) synchronisation, which do not provide information about the global organisation of functional networks and their individual-specific properties [13].

The current study addresses this by examining global functional connectivity in order to clarify how individual differences in empathy modulate whole brain functional connectivity during music listening. Recent advances in graph theory provide a strong foundation for modelling whole-brain functional connectivity [2]. Centrality, a widely used graph metric, is a way of quantifying the relative importance of the role played by some nodes in a network [18] and have successfully been used in the analysis of social networks [14] and the spread of epidemics [27] in identifying crucial nodes. Specifically, eigenvector centrality helps in identifying crucial nodes that are responsible in the organisation of brain states and reflects global properties within the network [37]. To this end, we use an eigenvector centrality based approach to examine global functional connectivity and how individual differences in empathy modulate it thereof.

2   Methods

2.1   Data Acquisition and Pre-processing

The current study utilises a subset of the data used by Toiviainen et al. [31], with the fMRI scanning and pre-processing pipeline remaining the same. Thirty-six healthy participants (20 females, mean age = 28.6 yrs, std = 8.9) with no history of neurological or psychological disorders participated in the fMRI experiment. Participants' IRI scores, in addition to Familiarity and Liking, were collected along with other tests as a part of a larger project ("TUNTEET"). Participants' brain responses were acquired with fMRI while they listened to an 8-min long piece of Argentine tango, Adiós Nonino by Astor Piazzolla. This stimulus was chosen because of its long duration and its acoustic variations. The study protocol proceeded on acceptance by the ethics committee of the Coordinating Board of the Helsinki and Uusimaa Hospital District.

fMRI scanning was performed using a 3T MAGNETOM Skyra wholebody scanner at the Advanced Magnetic Imaging (AMI) Centre (Aalto University, Finland). Using a single-shot gradient echo-planar imaging (EPI) (33 slices; thickness: 4 mm, interslice skip: 0 mm; voxel size: $2 \times 2 \times 2$ mm^3, TR: 2 s). T1-weighted structural images (176 slices; slice thickness: 1 mm; interslice skip: 0 mm; pulse sequence: MPRAGE) were also collected for individual co-registration. The scans were then pre-processed on a Matlab platform using SPM8, VBM5 for SPM, and customised scripts developed by the present authors. Each participant's scans were realigned, segmented and normalised to the MNI template. Signal-to-noise ratio was enhanced by Gaussian spatial smoothing, and movement-related variance components were regressed out. Following this, spline interpolation and Gaussian temporal filtering were carried out.

2.2 Eigenvector Centrality Mapping

Eigenvector centrality of a node is indicative of its central role in coordinating whole-brain network functioning, which in addition to its parameter-free nature makes it the appropriate choice for the current study. Voxel-wise eigenvector centrality was computed for each participant, essentially modelling each voxel as a separate graph node. This was done by generating each participant's functional connectivity (FC) matrix by computing the Pearson correlation of the fMRI time series between every pair of voxels. This matrix was then made non-negative by incrementing each entry by 1. A power-iteration method (von Mises, 1929) was used to compute the first eigenvector for each participant's FC matrix. The result was a voxel-wise eigenvector centrality brain map for each participant (Refer to Eq. 1)(Fig. 1).

$$x_i = \frac{1}{\lambda} \sum_k FC_{k,i}\, x_k \tag{1}$$

Where, x_i is centrality of ith node and k denotes all voxels, $FC_{k,i}$ denotes the FC matrix value between nodes k and i.

The resultant eigenvector centrality maps were then correlated on a voxel-wise basis with the participants' IRI scores, using Spearman's partial correlation. We chose partial correlation due to the inherent correlation among the IRI sub-scales typically reported in studies. To correct for multiple comparisons, we used cluster size thresholding wherein the respective thresholds were obtained from a null distribution obtained via a permutation test. Specifically, we performed 1000 iterations, in which the IRI scores were randomised (with replacement) followed by correlation with EC values and recording the observed cluster sizes of significant correlations. Cluster sizes were calculated based on the resulting null distribution.

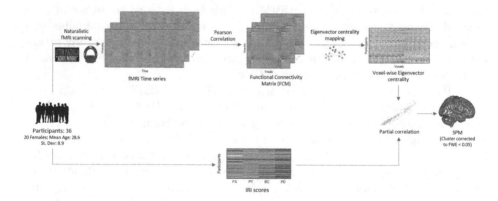

Fig. 1. Overview of the study

3 Results

Lilliefors test (as well as Jarque-Bera goodness-of-fit test) for normality showed that IRI scores were normally distributed across all four subscales (FS, PT, EC, PD) at a 5% significance level. Pearson's correlation revealed statistically significant correlations between the subscales, supporting our choice to use partial correlation. Mann-Whitney U test performed between the Liking and Familiarity scores between low and high empathy participants grouped by means of median-split of IRI scores revealed no statistically significant differences. The results for the partial correlation can be seen in Table 1.

Table 1. Summary of partial spearman correlation between eigenvector centrality and IRI. * denotes negative correlation. p < .01, Cluster size corrected at FWE < 0.05

Left hemisphere					Right hemisphere				
Region	n	MNI (mm)	z-val	BA	Region	n	MNI (mm)	z-val	BA
FS					*FS*				
MTG, ITG*	193	−60, −28, −16	−4.73	20	Precentral gyrus, SFG	100	20, −26, 62	4.07	6
MTG*	158	−62, −46, 8	−4.16	22	ACC extending to MFG	68	24, 34, 22	4.13	46
					Crus I, Crus II of Cerebellum*	290	16, −84, −28	−4.33	
PT					*PT*				
Pre/Postcentral gyrus	103	−32, −30, 72	4.28	4, 6	SMA, SFG, Pre/Postcentral gyrus	237	12, −14, 72	4.22	6
Putamen, Thalamus*	45	−16, −6, 10	−3.88		ACC, MCC (R/L), SFG (R/L)*	381	6, 10, 28	−3.83	24, 32
					Basal ganglia around Caudate nucleus, Globus pallidus, Thalamus*	122	10, 2, 0	−4.18	
					Insula, IFG*	112	44, 18, −10	−3.87	38
					Thalamus*	68	8, −22, −2	−4.30	
EC					*EC*				
ITG, MTG	86	−60, −28, −18	3.68	20	Inferior occipital gyrus, Fusiform gyrus, Crus I of Cerebellum	181	48, −70, −16	4.44	19, 37
Temporal pole, IFG	72	−42, 18, −16	3.57	38	WM around Precuneus*	315	18, −40, 44	−4.04	
Gyrus rectus, Orbitofrontal gyrus	61	−8, 58, −8	3.52	11	Superior occipital gyrus, Precuneus*	200	26, −66, 38	−4.54	7, 40
Precentral gyrus, Paracentral lobule*	164	−34, −22, 58	−4.74	4	MFG, IFG, Insula*	119	38, 40, 2	−3.51	47
Precuneus extending to occipital lobe*	141	−14, −58, 32	−4.49	7	Insula, Hippocampus, Basal ganglia*	62	38, −12, −10	−3.55	48, 20
Fusiform gyrus and WM extending to lingual gyrus*	99	−40, −44, −4	−4.18	37	Insula, IFG*	59	40, 10, 6	−3.49	48
Postcentral gyrus, Superior parietal gyrus, Precuneus*	90	−18, −34, 68	−3.70	2, 4	Thalamus*	58	24, −24, 6	−3.26	
IFG*	52	−34, 24, 14	−3.47	48	Postcentral gyrus*	51	18, −40, 72	−4.53	
ACC*	50	−16, 38, 6	−3.24	32					
PD					*PD*				
IFG, Insula	63	−34, 24, 14	3.37	48	MFG, IFG	65	38, 42, 2	3.24	47

High centrality in bilateral sensorimotor regions consisting of the Supplementary motor area (SMA), Precentral gyrus (BA 6) and the Postcentral gyrus (BA 4) was associated with higher scores on the PT subscale while low centrality was observed in bilateral clusters around the Basal ganglia and Thalamus, right Insula and Inferior frontal gyrus (IFG). Another cluster belonging to the bilateral CEmN, including the Anterior and Medial cingulate and paracingulate gyri extending to the Superior frontal gyrus also demonstrated low centrality in high scoring participants (Fig. 2).

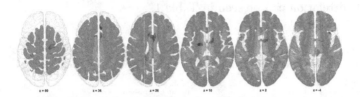

Fig. 2. Correlation results for PT. Red - Positive, Blue - Negative correlation. (Color figure online)

For the FS subscale (Fig. 3), higher centrality was associated with high scores in the right Premotor cortex (BA 6) as well as the white matter tract between the ACC and Middle frontal gyrus while low centrality was observed in left Middle/Inferior temporal gyrus (BA 20, 22) as well as the right cerebellum (Crus I, II).

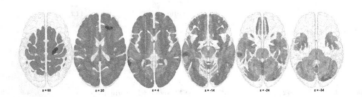

Fig. 3. Correlation results for FS. Red - Positive, Blue - Negative correlation (Color figure online)

For the EC subscale, high scoring participants showed increased centrality in the left Temporal pole (BA 38) and Orbitofrontal cortex (BA 11) as well as the right Occipital lobe extending along the Fusiform gyrus to the cerebellum (BA 19, 37). On the other hand, lower EC scores were associated with increased centrality in clusters centered bilaterally around the Precuneus, Primary motor cortex (BA 4) and IFG (BA 48); in the right hemisphere centered around the Precentral gyrus (BA 6) extending to the paracentral lobule, the left Insula and parts of the Occipital lobe. Some clusters were also found to extend into subcortical regions such as the Hippocampus, Thalamus and the Basal ganglia (Fig. 4).

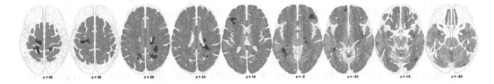

Fig. 4. Correlation results for EC. Red - Positive, Blue - Negative correlation (Color figure online)

Participants' PD scores were observed to be positively correlated with centrality in clusters around the left IFG extending to the Insula as well as the right MFG/IFG (BA 47, 48) (Fig. 5).

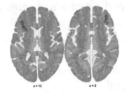

Fig. 5. Correlation results for PD. Red - Positive, Blue - Negative correlation (Color figure online)

4   Discussion

Using eigenvector centrality analysis, we unearthed brain nodes modulated by participants' IRI scores that are key in the coordination of global functional networks. Overall, we found differential trends in centrality between cognitive and affective IRI sub-scales. The key regions coordinating global brain functioning in participants with high cognitive empathy included cortical sensorimotor regions, which are involved in motor mimicry. By contrast, the decrease in centrality of these regions and the core DMN hub (Precuneus) in those with high affective empathy, in addition to the concurrent increase in centrality in the auditory and Orbitofrontal regions is reflective of its central role in higher engagement and affective coding of the stimulus.

These results seem to support the layered 'Russian-doll' model of evolution [7] in mammalian empathy processing. In this model, different components of empathy are processed by increasingly advanced layers built atop one another, with motor mimicry at its core observed in most mammals, surrounded by affective empathy and then by cognitive empathy, which is highly advanced in humans. Similarly, Panksepp [24] proposed that the human brain is organised into two systems; an affective, primitive subcortical/limbic system, which processes raw emotions and feelings across mammals and a more cognitive, neocortical system that deals with higher-order processes. Our results corroborate this model, as evidenced by the increased centrality in the sensorimotor regions of the neocortex in participants scoring high in cognitive empathy (FS, PT). Wallmark et al. [34] also found selective activations in the sensorimotor regions in high FS/PT participants, albeit using very short stimuli. The low centrality in the affective parts of the cerebellum [30] further supports the notion that such affective regions do not play a significant role in how high cognitive empathetic individuals process a stimulus.

Centrality in the subcortical regions, including the Thalamus, Basal ganglia, ACC-MCC and the Insula showed a characteristic negative correlation with both the affective and cognitive empathy. These regions are a part of the CEmN, integral to the processing of empathy. The decrease in centrality associated with empathy in these regions, therefore, suggests that they might act as intermediaries in the processing of empathy rather than as central coordination hubs. The Insula has also been shown to work in tandem with the Basal ganglia and Thalamus in the bottom-up encoding of affect, and to moderate communication with higher-level processing centres such as sensorimotor and the frontal regions [28]. Additionally, studies have shown that participants with lesions in the Basal ganglia scored significantly lower on the PT scale than the control group [35]; Basal ganglia abnormalities are also linked to autism, in which cognitive but not emotional empathy is deficient [3].

On the other hand, affective empathy was associated with a decrease in centrality in the sensorimotor regions and a concurrent increase in centrality in the auditory cortex and medial OFC, a critical region involved in appraising the hedonic value of a stimulus [22]. This suggests that participants scoring higher on affective empathy may automatically be coordinated by regions associated with the processing of affect. Moreover, the high centrality found in the Temporal pole, which has been termed an association cortex due to its connectivity with the limbic regions [19] further supports this notion that high EC is indeed associated with the automatic affective evaluation of any stimulus. Additionally, increased centrality in visual regions suggests that high EC participants are more prone to visual imagery, which in turn reflects higher susceptibility to musical affect [34]. To add to this, decreased centrality in the precuneus, the functional core of the Default mode network, indicates less mind-wandering and increased affective engagement in the stimulus [11].

The PD subscale showed positive correlations bilaterally in parts of the IFG (BA 47, 48) associated with the recognition of negative valence emotions such as fear, anger or disgust [29,33]. This finding is in line with several studies that report a negative affect bias in such individuals while processing any stimulus [15].

The graph-theory based approach employed in the present study offers insights about global network organisation in the human brain while allowing for greater interpretability of the results than more complex deep-learning-based models. The present study could be extended by looking at localised measures of connectivity, such as modularity, to better understand how empathy is locally processed. Moreover, a multi-modal approach looking into both structural (using voxel-wise gray matter densities) and functional measures of centrality would provide us with a better understanding. However, our results provide support for several key models of empathy and music processing, and merit further investigation into the topic.

References

1. Adelstein, J., et al.: Personality is reflected in the brain's intrinsic functional architecture. PLoS ONE (11), 6 (2011). https://doi.org/10.1371/journal.pone.0027633
2. Bullmore, E., Sporns, O.: Complex brain networks: graph theoretical analysis of structural and functional systems. Nat. Rev. Neurosci. **10**(3), 186–198 (2009). https://doi.org/10.1038/nrn2575
3. Calderoni, S., Bellani, M., Hardan, A., Muratori, F., Brambilla, P.: Basal ganglia and restricted and repetitive behaviours in autism spectrum disorders: current status and future perspectives. Epidemiol. Psychiatr. Sci. **23**(3), 235–238 (2014). https://doi.org/10.1017/S2045796014000171
4. Cox, C., Uddin, L., Martino, A., Castellanos, F., Milham, M., Kelly, C.: The balance between feeling and knowing: affective and cognitive empathy are reflected in the brain's intrinsic functional dynamics. Soc. Cogn. Affect. Neurosci. **7**(6), 727–737 (2012). https://doi.org/10.1093/scan/nsr051
5. Cross, I.: Music and communication in music psychology. Psychol. Music **42**(6), 809–819 (2014). https://doi.org/10.1177/0305735614543968
6. Davis, M.: A multidimensional approach to individual differences in empathy. JSAS Catalog Sel. Doc. Psychol. **10**, 85 (1980)
7. De Waal, F., Preston, S.: Mammalian empathy: behavioural manifestations and neural basis. Nat. Rev. Neurosci. **18**(8), 498–509 (2017). https://doi.org/10.1038/nrn.2017.72
8. Decety, J., Moriguchi, Y.: The empathic brain and its dysfunction in psychiatric populations: implications for intervention across different clinical conditions. BioPsychoSocial Med. **1**(1) (2007). https://doi.org/10.1186/1751-0759-1-22
9. Decety, J., Ickes, W. (eds.): The Social Neuroscience of Empathy. MIT Press, Cambridge (2009)
10. Fan, Y., Duncan, N., De Greck, M., Northoff, G.: Is there a core neural network in empathy? An fMRI based quantitative meta-analysis. Neurosci. Biobehav. Rev. **35**(3), 903–911 (2011). https://doi.org/10.1016/j.neubiorev.2010.10.00910.1016/j.neubiorev.2010.10.009
11. García-García, I., Jurado, M., Garolera, M.: Functional network centrality in obesity: a resting-state and task fMRI study. Psychiatr. Res. **233**(3), 331–338 (2015). https://doi.org/10.1016/j.pscychresns.2015.05.017
12. Goldman, A.I.: Understanding empathy: its features and effects. In: Two Routes to Empathy: Insights from Cognitive Neuroscience, chap., pp. 31–44. Oxford University Press (2011)
13. Gratton, C., Laumann, T., Nielsen, A.: Functional brain networks are dominated by stable group and individual factors, not cognitive or daily variation. Neuron **98**(2), 439–452 (2018). https://doi.org/10.1016/j.neuron.2018.03.035
14. Hage, P., Harary, F.: Eccentricity and centrality in networks. Soc. Netw. **17**(1), 248–257 (1995). https://doi.org/10.1016/0378-8733(94)10.1016/0378-8733(94)
15. John, O., Naumann, L., Soto, C.: Paradigm shift to the integrative Big Five trait taxonomy: history, measurement, and conceptual issues, pp. 114–158. Guilford, New York (2008)

16. Juslin, P., Västfjäll, D.: Emotional responses to music: the need to consider under-lying mechanisms. Behav. Brain Sci. **31**(5), 559–575 (2008). https://doi.org/10.1017/S0140525X08005293

17. Kim, H., Han, S.: Does personal distress enhance empathic interaction or block it? Personality Individ. Differ. **124**, 77–83 (2018). https://doi.org/10.1016/j.paid.2017.12.005

18. Koschützki, D., Lehmann, K.A., Peeters, L., Richter, S., Tenfelde-Podehl, D., Zlo-towski, O.: Centrality indices. In: Brandes, U., Erlebach, T. (eds.) Network Anal-ysis. LNCS, vol. 3418, pp. 16–61. Springer, Heidelberg (2005). https://doi.org/10.1007/978-3-540-31955-9_3

19. Kringelbach, M.L., Rolls, E.T.: The functional neuroanatomy of the human orbitofrontal cortex: evidence from neuroimaging and neuropsychology. Prog. Neu-robiol. **72**(5), 341–372 (2004). https://doi.org/10.1016/j.pneurobio.2004.03.006

20. Krämer, U.M., Mohammadi, B., Doñamayor, N., Samii, A., Münte, T.F.: Emo-tional and cognitive aspects of empathy and their relation to social cognition-an fMRI-study. Brain Res. **1311**, 110–120 (2010). https://doi.org/10.1016/j.brainres.2009.11.043

21. Leman, M.: Embodied Music Cognition and Mediation Technology. MIT Press, Cambridge (2008)

22. Liu, X., Hairston, J., Schrier, M., Fan, J.: Common and distinct networks underly-ing reward valence and processing stages: a meta-analysis of functional neuroimag-ing studies. Neurosci. Biobehav. Rev. **35**(5), 1219–1236 (2011). https://doi.org/10.1016/j.neubiorev.2010.12.012

23. Neuhaus, C.: Methods in neuromusicology: principles, trends, examples and the pros and cons. In: Schneider, A. (ed.) Studies in Musical Acoustics and Psychoa-coustics. CRSM, vol. 4, pp. 341–374. Springer, Cham (2017). https://doi.org/10.1007/978-3-319-47292-8_11

24. Panksepp, J.: Cross-species affective neuroscience decoding of the primal affective experiences of humans and related animals. PLoS ONE **6**(9) (2011). https://doi.org/10.1371/journal.pone.0021236

25. Sachs, M., Habibi, A., Damasio, A., Kaplan, J.: Dynamic intersubject neural syn-chronization reflects affective responses to sad music. NeuroImage (2019). https://doi.org/10.1016/j.neuroimage.2019.116512

26. Shamay-Tsoory, S.G., Aharon-Peretz, J., Perry, D.: Two systems for empa-thy: a double dissociation between emotional and cognitive empathy in inferior frontal gyrus versus ventromedial prefrontal lesions. Brain **132**(3), 617–627 (2009). https://doi.org/10.1093/brain/awn279

27. da Silva, R.A.P., Viana, M.P., Costa, L.: Predicting epidemic outbreak from indi-vidual features of the spreaders. J. Stat. Mech. Theory Exp. **2012**(07), P07005 (2012). https://doi.org/10.1088/1742-5468/2012/07/p07005

28. Singer, T., Lamm, C.: The social neuroscience of empathy. Ann. N. Y. Acad. Sci. **1156** (2009). https://doi.org/10.5167/uzh-25655

29. Sprengelmeyer, R., Rausch, M., Eysel, U.T., Przuntek, H.: Neural structures asso-ciated with recognition of facial expressions of basic emotions. Proc. R. Soc. Lond. B Biol. Sci. **265**(1409), 1927–1931 (1998). https://doi.org/10.1098/rspb.1998.0522

30. Stoodley, C., Schmahmann, J.: Evidence for topographic organization in the cere-bellum of motor control versus cognitive and affective processing. Cortex **46**(7), 831–844 (2010). https://doi.org/10.1016/j.cortex.2009.11.008

31. Toiviainen, P., Burunat, I., Brattico, E., Vuust, P., Alluri, V.: The chronnectome of musical beat. NeuroImage (2019). https://doi.org/10.1016/j.neuroimage.2019.116191

32. Tomasello, M.: The Cultural Origins of Human Cognition (2019). https://doi.org/10.2307/j.ctvjsf4jc.3
33. Vytal, K., Hamann, S.: Neuroimaging support for discrete neural correlates of basic emotions: a voxel-based meta-analysis. J. Cogn. Neurosci. **22**(12), 2864–2885 (2010). https://doi.org/10.1162/jocn.2009.21366. pMID: 19929758
34. Wallmark, Z., Deblieck, C., Iacoboni, M.: Neurophysiological effects of trait empathy in music listening. Front. Behav. Neurosci. **12**, 66 (2018). https://doi.org/10.3389/fnbeh.2018.00066
35. Yeh, Z.T., Tsai, C.F.: Impairment on theory of mind and empathy in patients with stroke. J. Neuropsychiatry Clin. Neurosci. **68**(8), 612–620 (2014). https://doi.org/10.1111/pcn.12173
36. Zahavi, D.: Beyond empathy: phenomenological approaches to intersubjectivity. J. Conscious. Stud. **8**(5–7), 151–167 (2001)
37. Zuo, X.N., et al.: Network centrality in the human functional connectome. Cereb. Cortex **22**(8), 1862–1875 (2011). https://doi.org/10.1093/cercor/bhr269

Classification of PTSD and Non-PTSD Using Cortical Structural Measures in Machine Learning Analyses—Preliminary Study of ENIGMA-Psychiatric Genomics Consortium PTSD Workgroup

Brian O'Leary[1]([✉]) [iD], Chia-Hao Shih[1] [iD], Tian Chen[1] [iD],
Hong Xie[1] [iD], Andrew S. Cotton[1] [iD], Kevin S. Xu[1] [iD],
Rajendra Morey[2] [iD], and Xin Wang[1] [iD] and ENIGMA-Psychiatric
Genomics Consortium PTSD Workgroup

[1] University of Toledo, Toledo, OH 43606, USA
brian.o'leary@rockets.utoledo.edu
[2] Duke University, Durham, NC 27710, USA

Abstract. Classification and prediction of posttraumatic stress disorder (PTSD) based on brain imaging measures is important because it could aid in PTSD diagnosis and clinical management of PTSD. The goal of the present study was to test the effectiveness of using cortical morphological measures (i.e. volume, thickness, and surface area) to classify PTSD cases and controls on 3571 individuals from the ENIGMA-Psychiatric Genomics Consortium PTSD Workgroup, the largest PTSD neuroimaging dataset to date. We constructed 6 feature sets from different demographic variables (age and sex) and cortical morphological measures and used four machine learning algorithms for classification: logistic regression, random forest, support vector machine, and multi-layer perceptron. We found that classifiers trained using only cortical morphological measures (any one of volume, thickness, or surface area) performed better than classifiers trained using only demographic variables. Among all 6 feature sets, combining demographic variables and all three cortical morphological measures yielded the best prediction accuracy, with area under the receiver operating characteristic curve (ROC AUC) scores ranging from 0.615 for logistic regression to 0.648 for random forest. These findings suggest that using cortical morphological measures only has modest prediction power for PTSD classification. Future studies that wish to produce clinically and practically significant findings should consider using whole brain morphological measures, as well as incorporating other neuroimaging modalities and relevant clinical and behavioral symptoms.

Keywords: Structural magnetic resonance imaging · Posttraumatic stress disorder · Cortical morphological measures · Logistic regression · Random forest · Support vector machine · Multi-layer perceptron

B. O'Leary and C.-H. Shih—Contributed equally.Contributing authors are listed in https://drive.google.com/file/d/1wO-WeUYGB_gWbFh5LIQsUP7H7ckEjeo1/view.

© Springer Nature Switzerland AG 2020
M. Mahmud et al. (Eds.): BI 2020, LNAI 12241, pp. 118–127, 2020.
https://doi.org/10.1007/978-3-030-59277-6_11

1 Introduction

Posttraumatic stress disorder (PTSD) is characterized by intrusive memories of a traumatic event, avoidance of trauma-related circumstances, hyperarousal, and negative alterations in mood and cognition. PTSD is a major health concern which produces negative impacts on both the individual and societal level [1]. Despite extensive neurobiological research efforts, diagnoses of PTSD still solely rely on behavioral assessments.

Magnetic resonance imaging (MRI) has been shown as a powerful tool for researchers to understand the pathophysiology of PTSD in the brain. Indeed, cortical morphological differences in patients with PTSD as compared to matched controls are well documented [2]. For example, structural MRI studies have revealed smaller volumes and thinner cortical thickness in cingulate, insula, and select parts of the prefrontal, parietal, temporal, and occipital cortices [3–6]. Functional neuroimaging studies have also reported alterations of brain activation associated with emotion responses in some of the above-mentioned regions [7–9]. Therefore, it has been speculated that alterations in cortical structures may associate with functional deficits in these cortical regions, which could underlie PTSD symptomatology. These findings suggest that cortical morphological measures may possess classification power to differentiate individuals with and without PTSD.

Recently, machine learning algorithms have been applied to classify PTSD cases and controls, which may help to improve the diagnosis of this psychiatric condition. However, the current PTSD diagnosis relays on the behavioral symptoms solely [10]. Adding other factors may greatly help PTSD classification. For example, demographic factors such as a combination of sex and age have been associated with the incidence of PTSD [11], and the inclusion of these demographic factors improve the classification accuracy of PTSD cases and controls [12, 13]. Studies using brain morphological measures including cortical volume, thickness, and surface area to classify neurological and psychiatric disorders such as Alzheimer's Disease and Bipolar Disorder have been accumulating rapidly [11–14]. However, to the best of our knowledge, these cortical morphological measures have not been tested for PTSD classification.

Therefore, the goal of the present study was to evaluate effectiveness of using cortical morphological measures in classification of PTSD cases and controls. Specifically, we compared model performance on the following 6 models, each corresponding to a different set of features for classification: 1) demographics (combining sex and age), 2) volume, 3) thickness, 4) surface area, 5) combining all three cortical morphological measures, and 6) combining demographics and cortical morphological measures together. Since there is currently no understanding on the relationship between cortical morphological measures and PTSD diagnosis, this exploratory study compares the classification accuracies of multiple machine learning algorithms to find the most effective algorithm for predicting the PTSD diagnosis. Previous studies tested a variety of classifiers including logistic regression, random forest, support vector machine (SVM), and multi-layer perceptron (MLP) to classify PTSD and other psychiatric disorders [15, 18–20]. We compare these 4 machine learning algorithms on each of the 6 feature sets in this study.

2   Methods

2.1   Samples

The ENIGMA-Psychiatric Genomics Consortium PTSD Workgroup collected data from 3571 individuals, including 1379 PTSD patients and 2192 controls without PTSD, from 43 cohorts assessed in 31 laboratories across 7 countries. Depending on the cohort, current PTSD was diagnosed according to the Diagnostic and Statistical Manual of Mental Disorders (DSM) IV criteria using the following standard instruments: Clinician-Administered PTSD Scale-IV (CAPS-4), Structured Clinical Interview, Mini International Neuropsychiatric Interview 6.0.0, PTSD Checklist (PCL)-4, Davidson Trauma Scale, PTSD Symptom Scale, and Anxiety Disorders Interview Schedule; or according to DSM-V criteria using CAPS-5 and PCL-5. The clinical, demographic, and brain imaging data were uploaded to the central site for analysis. Summary statistics from the data are shown in Table 1.

Table 1. Demographics and symptoms of PTSD and control groups.

	PTSD	Control	Difference
N (%)	1379 (39.5%)	2192 (60.5%)	
Female N (%)	554 (40.4%)	923 (42.2%)	$\chi^2 = 1.02$
Age (years)	36.0 ± 14.1	34.3 ± 15.5	$t = 3.35^*$
Age range (years)	6 – 82	6 – 85	
PTSD severity	49.8 ± 16.7	10.5 ± 12.8	$t = 64.91^*$
N of cohorts	43	42	

Note. Data are reported as mean $\pm$ standard deviation. *indicates statistical significance at $p < 0.05$ level.

2.2   Imaging Acquisition and Processing

At the participating laboratories, high resolution T1-weighted structural MRI scans were acquired and processed using a standard automated FreeSurfer (version 5.3 or 6.0) [21] processing stream to create individual vertex thickness maps. Each hemisphere is parcellated into 34 anatomical regions of interest (ROIs) using the Desikan–Killiany atlas [22]. The regional gray matter volume (i.e., product of cortical thickness and surface area), regional average cortical thickness, and other measures were calculated for each ROI. The data were visually inspected using ENIGMA imaging quality control protocols [23]. ROIs with segmentation or parcellation errors were excluded.

2.3   Analytical Approaches

In the present study, we studied four classifiers, logistic regression, random forest, support vector machine (SVM), and multi-layer perceptron (MLP), to classify PTSD versus non-PTSD cases. Logistic regression is perhaps the most commonly used linear classifier, while the other three allow for non-linear classification. We evaluated prediction performance using 6 different sets of features: demographic variables alone, three cortical morphological measures separately, a combination of all three, and a combination of demographic variables and all cortical morphological measures together. The feature sets contain different numbers of features, as shown in Table 2.

Table 2. The number of features used in each model (feature set).

Model	Feature count
Demographics (D)	2
Volume (V)	68
Thickness (T)	68
Surface Area (SA)	68
V + T + SA	204
V + T + SA + D	206

2.4 Machine Learning Algorithms

Logistic regression, random forest, SVM, and MLP classifiers were chosen to predict whether a patient belongs to the PTSD or non-PTSD group. We used the implementations in the scikit-learn Python package [24].

The initial dataset was split into a training and testing dataset. 75% of the data was allocated to training, and the remaining 25% of the data was allocated for testing. These splits were stratified by diagnosis to ensure that each set had roughly the same proportion of control to confirmed PTSD diagnosis.

Hyperparameter tuning for each model was performed by using 5-fold cross-validation (CV) on the training data to optimize the area under the receiver operating characteristic curve (ROC AUC) metric. To ensure consistency across models, the same cross-validation splits were used for each classifier and feature set, again stratified on the PTSD diagnosis. The hyperparameters that resulted in the highest 5-fold CV accuracy were then used to train a model on the entire training data set. The ROC AUC of predictions on the testing dataset was then used to evaluate each model.

Logistic Regression
Logistic regression is perhaps the most widely used linear classifier. We considered a logistic regression model with an elastic net (combined ℓ_1 and ℓ_2) regularization on the coefficients [25]. This regularization helps prevent overfitting and promotes sparsity in the coefficients. This formulation corresponds to:

$$\min_{\{w,c\}} \frac{1-\rho}{2} w^T w + \rho \|w\|_1 + C \sum_i^N \log\left(\exp\left(-y_i\left(X_i^T w + c\right)\right) + 1\right)$$

where X_i and y_i denote the features and the class (either $+1$ for PTSD or -1 for control), respectively, for the i th subject; w denotes the model coefficients; C controls the regularization strength; and ρ controls the tradeoff between the ℓ_1 and ℓ_2 penalties [24]. Hyperparameter tuning was performed using cross-validation by a 2-dimensional grid search on ρ and C.

Random Forest

A random forest is an ensemble supervised learning method that fits a number of decision tree classifiers that have been trained on different random subsets of the features [26]. Training on subsets of the features helps avoid overfitting, and as the number of trees increases, the overall variance of the model will decrease.

Random forests allow for learning non-linear decision boundaries. We used 1000 trees with the Gini impurity as the splitting criterion. The maximum number of features to consider on each split was optimized using cross-validation by a linear grid from 1 to the feature count (shown in Table 2).

Support Vector Machine

A support vector machine (SVM) is a supervised learning method that attempts to find an optimal linear decision boundary between the two classes. When used with a non-linear kernel, SVMs can find non-linear decision boundaries. Common non-linear kernels include polynomial, sigmoid, and radial basis functions. These kernels can be included in the search space when performing hyperparameter tuning.

The SVM formulation we consider has the form:

$$\min_{w,b,\zeta} \frac{1}{2} w^T w + C \sum_{i=1}^{n} \zeta_i$$

$$\text{Subject to} : y_i \left(w^T \phi(X_i) + b \right) \geq 1 - \zeta_i, \zeta_i \geq 0$$

where w are the coefficients corresponding to each feature in X_i, $\phi(\cdot)$ is the non-linear mapping corresponding to the selected kernel, C is the strength of regularization, and ζ_i denotes the slack variable for the i th subject, which is used to allow for some misclassification on the training data in the case where the two classes (PTSD and control) are not perfectly separable. In the case of polynormal, radial basis function, and sigmoid kernels, there is an additional hyperparameter γ. γ is the scale parameter of these kernels and interacts with the regularization strength of C.

The kernel, C, and γ are optimized using cross-validation by grid search. Additionally, the degree of the polynomial kernel is optimized in the same manner.

Multi-layer Perceptron

A multi-layer perceptron (MLP) is a type of feedforward neural network that is also commonly referred to as a fully connected or dense network. It consists of three main components: (1) an input layer, (2) one or more hidden layers, and (3) an output layer. By using non-linear activation functions in the hidden layers, MLPs are able to learn non-linear decision boundaries between classes.

The hyperparameters optimized for in the multi-layer perceptron were the batch size, the number of nodes in each hidden layer, the number of hidden layers, the validation fraction used for early stopping, the non-linear activation function, and the amount of ℓ_2 regularization. These were all optimized using cross-validation by grid search. The Adam optimizer [27] was used with initial learning rate of 0.001 and exponential decay rates of $\beta_1 = 0.9, \beta_2 = 0.999$.

3 Results

Model performance was evaluated using ROC AUC and is summarized in Table 3. For the 6 models (feature sets) compared in the present study, using demographics alone showed the worst model performance with ROC AUC scores in the range of 0.527 to 0.558 on the test set. Models using individual cortical morphological measures showed better performance than using demographics alone; training a classifier on any of volume, thickness, or surface area resulted in a higher ROC AUC score than training that same classifier on demographics. The highest ROC AUC score for any individual cortical morphological measure was 0.621 achieved by random forest on thickness.

Combining three cortical morphological measures did not improve model performance notably except for logistic regression, which is a linear classifier and benefits from the additional features. Finally, using both demographics and the three cortical morphological measures resulted in the best model performance for each classifier, although the classification accuracy was still not very strong. The highest ROC AUC score of 0.648 was achieved using random forest. The specificity and sensitivity of this model are 0.868 and 0.275, respectively, for a threshold at probability 0.5 for both classes. This random forest model was fit by considering a random subset of 69 features (out of 206 total) at each split.

The ROC curves for logistic regression (the least accurate classifier) and random forest (the most accurate classifier) when using both demographics and the three cortical morphological measures are shown in Fig. 1. Aside from a small interval between false positive rate = 0.2 to 0.3, the random forest classifier is superior overall.

Table 3. Classification ROC AUC for all 6 models (feature sets) and 4 classifiers compared in the present study. Both cross-validation (CV) and test set ROC AUC scores are shown. Most accurate classifier on the test set shown in bold.

	Logistic regression		Random forest		Support vector machine		Multi-layer perceptron	
Models	CV	Test	CV	Test	CV	Test	CV	Test
Demographics (D)	0.533	0.534	0.523	0.527	0.546	0.558	0.537	0.550
Volume (V)	0.592	0.573	0.576	0.576	0.569	0.582	0.578	0.514
Thickness (T)	0.609	0.576	0.572	0.621	0.587	0.610	0.585	0.606
Surface Area (SA)	0.619	0.566	0.568	0.592	0.571	0.576	0.569	0.572
V + T + SA	0.655	0.613	0.609	0.614	0.605	0.626	0.606	0.602
V + T + SA + D	0.656	0.615	0.609	**0.648**	0.609	0.633	0.605	0.626

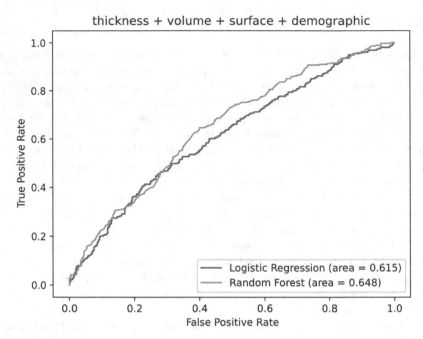

Fig. 1. ROC curves for logistic regression and random forest classifiers with cortical volume, thickness, surface area, and demographics as model features. The PTSD group is treated as the positive group.

4 Discussion

Cortical morphological differences have been reported in individuals with and without PTSD. The present study aimed to test whether cortical morphological measures are useful to classify PTSD using machine learning algorithms with more than 3000 PTSD cases and controls from the ENIGMA-Psychiatry Genomics Consortium PTSD Workgroup, the largest PTSD neuroimaging dataset to date. The results suggest that cortical volume, thickness, or surface area separately have modest prediction accuracies when used as features for logistic regression, random forest, SVM, and multi-layer perceptron classifiers. On the other hand, the classification using demographics alone is poor and only slightly better than a random guess. Combining all of the features does improve the prediction accuracy, but not by a significant amount.

For individual cortical morphological measures, we found that prediction accuracy on the test dataset is best using cortical thickness as compared to using cortical volume or surface area. Existing literature suggests that more PTSD-related cortical morphological differences were reported in cortical volume and in cortical thickness, and less in surface area [2]. Importantly, these different prediction accuracies may suggest that cortical thickness possesses more PTSD differences than cortical volume and surface area.

Despite combining all three cortical morphological measures with demographic factors yielding the best prediction accuracy, these findings are still lacking clinical and practical meaning. This low accuracy issue has also been reported by studies using machine learning analyses on brain morphological measures to classify PTSD and other disorders [15, 28–31]. We provide potential explanations and future suggestions here. First, PTSD brain morphological abnormalities have also been reported in subcortical regions, such as smaller hippocampus volume [32]. Therefore, we speculate that models using whole brain morphological measures would improve the prediction power. Second, previous research using machine learning analyses with behavioral symptoms obtained from self-reported questionnaires shows great predictive power for identifying those at risk for developing PTSD [33]. Third, advanced neuroimaging techniques, such as multimodal data fusion [34, 35], can combine non-redundant brain imaging data and possibly improve the accuracy of classification. Finally, this study pooled data from multiple cohorts that vary in inclusion/exclusion criteria, MRI scanners, and PTSD assessments. These factors may confound the classification. Future studies using machine learning algorithms to classify PTSD cases and controls should consider incorporating neuroimaging measures with behavioral symptoms and eliminate the confound factors to produce meaningful findings.

References

1. Sareen, J.: Posttraumatic stress disorder in adults: impact, comorbidity, risk factors, and treatment. Can. J. Psychiatry **59**, 460–467 (2014). https://doi.org/10.1177/070674371405 900902
2. Liberzon, I., Wang, X., Xie, H.: Brain structural abnormalities in posttraumatic stress disorder and relations with sleeping problems. In: Vermetten, E., Germain, A., Neylan, T.C. (eds.) Sleep and Combat-Related Post Traumatic Stress Disorder, pp. 145–167. Springer, New York (2018). https://doi.org/10.1007/978-1-4939-7148-0_12
3. Eckart, C., Stoppel, C., et al.: Structural alterations in lateral prefrontal, parietal and posterior midline regions of men with chronic posttraumatic stress disorder. J. Psychiatry Neurosci. **36**, 176 (2011)
4. Rauch, S.L., et al.: Selectively reduced regional cortical volumes in post-traumatic stress disorder. NeuroReport **14**, 913–916 (2003)
5. Kitayama, N., Quinn, S., Bremner, J.D.: Smaller volume of anterior cingulate cortex in abuse-related posttraumatic stress disorder. J. Affect. Disord. **90**, 171–174 (2006)
6. Chao, L., Weiner, M., Neylan, T.: Regional cerebral volumes in veterans with current versus remitted posttraumatic stress disorder. Psychiatry Res. Neuroimaging **213**, 193–201 (2013)
7. Liberzon, I., Abelson, J.L.: Context processing and the neurobiology of post-traumatic stress disorder. Neuron **92**, 14–30 (2016). https://doi.org/10.1016/j.neuron.2016.09.039
8. Garfinkel, S.N., et al.: Impaired contextual modulation of memories in PTSD: an fMRI and psychophysiological study of extinction retention and fear renewal. J. Neurosci. **34**, 13435–13443 (2014)
9. Greco, J.A., Liberzon, I.: Neuroimaging of fear-associated learning. Neuropsychopharmacol. **41**, 320–334 (2016)
10. Kessler, R.C., et al.: How well can post-traumatic stress disorder be predicted from pre-trauma risk factors? an exploratory study in the WHO World Mental Health Surveys. World Psychiatry **13**, 265–274 (2014)

11. Ditlevsen, D.N., Elklit, A.: The combined effect of gender and age on post traumatic stress disorder: do men and women show differences in the lifespan distribution of the disorder? Ann. Gen. Psychiatry **9**, 32 (2010). https://doi.org/10.1186/1744-859X-9-32

12. Galatzer-Levy, I.R., Karstoft, K.-I., Statnikov, A., Shalev, A.Y.: Quantitative forecasting of PTSD from early trauma responses: a machine learning application. J. Psychiatry Res. **59**, 68–76 (2014)

13. Mor, N.S., Dardeck, K.L.: Quantitative forecasting of risk for PTSD using ecological factors: a deep learning application. J. Soc. Behav. Health Sci. **12**, 4 (2018)

14. Choi, J.S., Lee, E., Suk, Hl: Regional abnormality representation learning in structural MRI for AD/MCI diagnosis. In: Shi, Y., Suk, Hl, Liu, M. (eds.) MLMI 2018. LNCS, vol. 11046, pp. 64–72. Springer, Cham (2018). https://doi.org/10.1007/978-3-030-00919-9_8

15. A. Nunes, et al: Using structural MRI to identify bipolar disorders – 13 site machine learning study in 3020 individuals from the ENIGMA bipolar disorders working group. Mol. Psychiatry, 1–14 (2018). https://doi.org/10.1038/s41380-018-0228-9

16. Lee, J.S., et al.: Machine learning-based individual assessment of cortical atrophy pattern in alzheimer's disease spectrum: development of the classifier and longitudinal evaluation. Sci. Rep. **8**, 4161 (2018)

17. Menikdiwela, M., Nguyen, C., Shaw, M.: Deep learning on brain cortical thickness data for disease classification. In: 2018 Digital Image Computing: Techniques and Applications (DICTA), pp. 1–5. IEEE (2018)

18. Ramos-Lima, L.F., Waikamp, V., Antonelli-Salgado, T., Passos, I.C., Freitas, L.H.M.: The use of machine learning techniques in trauma-related disorders: a systematic review. J. Psychiatr. Res. **121**, 159–172 (2020). https://doi.org/10.1016/j.jpsychires.2019.12.001

19. Gosnell, S.N., Fowler, J.C., Salas, R.: Classifying suicidal behavior with resting-state functional connectivity and structural neuroimaging. Acta Psychiatry, Scand (2019)

20. Kessler, R.C., et al.: Predicting suicides after outpatient mental health visits in the Army Study to Assess Risk and Resilience in Servicemembers (Army STARRS). Mol. Psychiatry. **22**, 544–551 (2017)

21. Fischl, B.: FreeSurfer. NeuroImage. **62**, 774–781 (2012). https://doi.org/10.1016/j.neuroimage.2012.01.021

22. Desikan, R.S., et al.: An automated labeling system for subdividing the human cerebral cortex on MRI scans into gyral based regions of interest. NeuroImage. **31**, 968–980 (2006). https://doi.org/10.1016/j.neuroimage.2006.01.021

23. Genetics Protocols « ENIGMA, (n.d.). http://enigma.ini.usc.edu/protocols/genetics-protocols/. Accessed 15 June 2020

24. Pedregosa, F., et al.: Scikit-learn: machine learning in Python. J. Mach. Learn. Res. **12**, 2825–2830 (2011)

25. Zou, H., Hastie, T.: Regularization and variable selection via the elastic net. J. R. Stat. Soc. Ser. B Stat. Methodol. **67**(2), 301–320 (2005)

26. Breiman, L.: Random forests. Mach. Learn. **45**, 5–32 (2001)

27. Kingma, D.P., Ba, J., Adam: A method for stochastic optimization. ArXiv14126980 Cs (2017). http://arxiv.org/abs/1412.6980

28. Hajek, T., Cooke, C., Kopecek, M., Novak, T., Hoschl, C., Alda, M.: Using structural MRI to identify individuals at genetic risk for bipolar disorders: a 2-cohort, machine learning study. J. Psychiatry Neurosci. JPN. **40**, 316–324 (2015). https://doi.org/10.1503/jpn.140142

29. Costafreda, S.G., Chu, C., Ashburner, J., Fu, C.H.: Prognostic and diagnostic potential of the structural neuroanatomy of depression. PLoS ONE 4, e6353 (2009)

30. Gong, Q., et al.: Prognostic prediction of therapeutic response in depression using high-field MR imaging. Neuroimage. **55**, 1497–1503 (2011)

31. Ecker, C., et al.: Investigating the predictive value of whole-brain structural MR scans in autism: a pattern classification approach. Neuroimage **49**, 44–56 (2010)
32. Logue, M.W., et al.: Smaller hippocampal volume in posttraumatic stress disorder: a multisite ENIGMA-PGC study: subcortical volumetry results from posttraumatic stress disorder consortia. Biol. Psychiatry **83**, 244–253 (2018). https://doi.org/10.1016/j.biopsych.2017.09.006
33. Wshah, S., Skalka, C., Price, M.: Predicting posttraumatic stress disorder risk: a machine learning approach. JMIR Ment. Health. **6**, e13946 (2019). https://doi.org/10.2196/13946
34. Calhoun, V.D., Sui, J.: Multimodal fusion of brain imaging data: a key to finding the missing link(s) in complex mental illness. Biol. Psychiatry Cogn. Neurosci. Neuroimaging. **1**, 230–244 (2016). https://doi.org/10.1016/j.bpsc.2015.12.005
35. Uludağ, K., Roebroeck, A.: General overview on the merits of multimodal neuroimaging data fusion. NeuroImage. **102**, 3–10 (2014). https://doi.org/10.1016/j.neuroimage.2014.05.018

Segmentation of Brain Tumor Tissues in Multi-channel MRI Using Convolutional Neural Networks

C. Naveena[1] , S. Poornachandra[2] , and V. N. Manjunath Aradhya[3]([✉])

[1] SJB Institute of Technology, Bengaluru, India
naveena.cse@gmail.com
[2] Srinivas University College of Engineering & Technology, Mangaluru, India
poorna.sandur18@gmail.com
[3] JSS Science and Technology University, Mysuru, India
aradhya.mysore@gmail.com

Abstract. Unmanned segmentation of brain tumors is one of the hardest tasks to be solved in Computer Vision. In this work, we focus on Convolutional Neural Network model to segment tumorous cells in MRI brain scans. The inputs to the network are multi-channel MR image intensity information extracted from patches around each point to be predicted. The pre-processing steps are employed to precise the magnetic field bias and then intensity values are normalized using Z-score technique. The training was done for both HGG and LGG and the network was optimized with SGD in which the gradients are calculated using Nesterov Accelerated Gradient. The obtained results are promising for the complete tumor, the core tumor and the enhancing tumor segmentation. The propounded model achieved a dice score of 0.86, 0.62 and 0.65 for complete, core and enhancing tumor.

Keywords: Gliomas · Convolutional Neural Network · Brain Tumor · MRI · SGD

1 Introduction

Malignant primary brain tumors gliomas are one of the most dreadful cancers on the humanity. Brain tumors not only lead to miserable prognosis but also decreases the cognitive activity of the patient, which directly influences the well being of the patient under consideration. The primary brain tumors are termed as low grade astrocytomas or oligoastrocytomas (Low Grade Gliomas, LGG) and high grade tumors are anaplastic astrocytomas and glioblastoma multiforme (High Grade Gliomas, HGG). Brain tumors are abnormality in healthy human brain. The healthy brain comprises of white matter, grey matter and cerbrospinal fluid if instead of these three components the other mass of tissues (tumor cells) occur in the brain, they can be termed as tumors. Brain tumor

© Springer Nature Switzerland AG 2020
M. Mahmud et al. (Eds.): BI 2020, LNAI 12241, pp. 128–137, 2020.
https://doi.org/10.1007/978-3-030-59277-6_12

tissues grow rapidly and get multiplied uncontrollably. The World Health Organization (WHO) classifies brain tumors into 4 grades. Grade I and Grade II (astrocytomas and oligoastrocytomas) are low-categorized tumors, and anaplastic astrocytomas and glioblastoma multiforme (GBM) are termed as Grade III and Grade IV tumors. Grade III and Grade IV tumor are termed as HGG which are dreadful with a highest mortality rate of 2 years.

The major challenge in the treatment planning and quantitative assessment of brain tumors is the determination of tumor extent and accurate delineation of brain tumors from MRI scans is necessary for treatment planning and to monitor the progression of the disease. Manual delineation of these brain tumors is time consuming and requires an human expert to segment them manually. Hence, an automated segmentation method is helpful in large clinical facilities. Gliomas which comprise of different tumor sub-regions with fuzzy and irregular shapes cannot be detected with a single MRI modality. Hence, four different MRI modalities are used namely, T1, T2, T1c and Fluid Attenuation Inversion Recovery (FLAIR). These multi-modal MRI images consists complementary information about different tumor tissues. Segmentation of brain tumors using automatic methods is of prime importance for assessing the tumor structures. They often pose a great challenge because of the variability of appearance and fuzzy structure of the intra-tumorous cells in the brain. Recently, Convolutional Neural Networks (CNNs) have proven remarkably good results for various image segmentation and classification problems in different domains. With this motivation, we propose a patch-based fully connected 2D CNN model to categorize pixels in an MR image by applying the advanced concepts in discipline of neural networks. The 2D patches are extracted from the tumoral sub-regions to avoid class imbalance. The remainder of this paper focusses on different researchers encompassing in the domain of brain tumor image analysis in Sect. 2. In Sect. 3 we discuss about the methodologies used in the proposed work. Section 4 emphasizes on the experimental organization for the proposed work. Section 5 we focus on the Results and Discussion for the proposed work. In Sect. 6 we conclude the paper discussing on the future enhancement.

2   Related Work

This section discusses about the distinct researchers encompassing in the domain of automatic brain tumor segmentation. Acclaimed by Menze et al. [1] the work in the domain of automatic brain tumor categorization has fattened widely in the recent years.

Ayush Karnawat et al. [3] proposed radiomics based CNN for brain tumor segmentation in which primarily the radiomic features were extracted and further was trained with the Adam optimizer. Yuexiang Li et al. [7] focussed on multiview Deep Learning framework for multi-modal brain tumor segmentation in which 3 sub-networks are used for processing multi-modal brain images in three different axis (x, y, z). Ashish Phoplaia et al. ashish proposed ensemble of forest method, in which numerous trained decision trees was used for segmenting brain tumors. Reza Pourreza et al. [9] investigated on deeply supervised neural networks for brain tumor categorization in which holistically-nested edge detection methods was used.

Mohammad Hamghalam et al. [27] proposed 2D Convolutional Neural Network for prediction of central pixel using 3D to 2D patch conversions. Xiaowei Xu et al. [28] focussed on attention based network to partition glioma sub-regions. Xiaochuan Li [29] proposed multistage segmentation for exact delineation of tumor sub-regions based on Cascaded modified U-net. Mingyuan Liu [31] focussed on two stage model to obtain the overall shape of region-of-interest and the second one to identify pixel level details. Michal Marcinkiewicz et al. [32] worked on two stage fully convolutional neural network in which the first stage detects target region and the second one performs multiclass classification.

The above discussed are some of the different researchers encompassing in the domain of automatic brain tumor categorization.

3   Methodology

The methodology proposed is based on convolutional neural networks for brain tumor categorization. The methodology is as follows:

3.1   Pre-processing

The intensity inhomogeneity generated owing to varying magnetic field strengths is corrected using the non-parametic, non-uniform intensity normalization technique (N4) [16]. Further, the intensities are normalized using Z-score technique to settle the data in proportion [30]. The normalization technique applied is shown in Eq. (1):

$$X_n = \frac{X - \mu}{\sigma} \tag{1}$$

Here, X is the loaded image, μ and σ constitute mean and the standard deviation of X respectively and X_n represent the normalized accomplished image.

3.2   Convolutional Neural Network

In this work, we investigate a 2D CNN model comprising of 5 layer architecture for the categorization of brain tumors. The proposed model takes 2D patches from 4 MRI modalities T1, T2, T1c and FLAIR for predicting the output for each pixel in the patch, thus accomplishing categorization of entire brain tumor region. The patches extracted from MRI modalities are inputs for the first layer and the successive layers employ feature maps spawned by the previous layer as input. The feature map O_p is obtained by the following relation,

$$O_p = b_p + \sum_n F_{pn} * I_n \tag{2}$$

Where I_n is the input plane, F_{pn} is the convolution kernel, b_p is the bias and $*$ is the convolution function. In this method, the input patches are feed-forwarded through the network and the output predictions are compared to the ground truth. The weight updates are backpropogated from the last layer and move towards the input. The max-pooling layer retains the maximum value in a specified window. Thus, the max-pooling layer calculates every point in the feature map I, by picking a max value in the window of length k.

$$O_{a,b} = max(I_{i+k,j+k}) \tag{3}$$

At the end of the network a softmax function is applied to obtain a distribution over segmented labels. The probability P of each class c, for n classes is given by,

$$P(y = c|x) = \frac{exp(xw_c)}{\sum_{n=1}^{N} exp(xw_n)} \tag{4}$$

where x and w are feature and weight vectors. The 2D spatial convolution is used in this convolutional neural network. The two spatial dimensions in the data are (x, y) and one dimension for each input sequence (T1, T2, T1c, FLAIR). Hence, 3D data (x, y, c) is analysed during the convolution operation.

Firstly, the patches are extracted from the tumoral sub-regions to avoid class imbalance. Then, the Convolutional Neural Network consists of stack of layers, in which the inputs are convolved with a set of filters. These filters are optimized on training data using Stochastic Gradient Descent (SGD). After, the convolution operation is applied, then ReLu activation is applied. The 3D blocks of the preceding layer is reduced to filtered 2D blocks. All the filtered 2D block are combined to serve as 3D input in the successive layer. Finally, the softmax function is applied, so that the values of the output sum to one, thus enabling the outputs to be interpreted as probablities.

The scheme of the proposed Convolutional Neural Network is described below.

- Layer 0: The input patches of size $19 \times 19 \times 4$ are fed into the input layer.
- Layer 1: In the convolutional layer 64 kernels of size $5 \times 5 \times 4$ are convolved with the inputs.
- Layer 2: The max pooling layer with kernel size 3 and stride of 3 is applied which results in $5 \times 5 \times 64$ nodes.
- Layer 3: The convolution operation is applied using 64 kernels of size $3 \times 3 \times 64$.
- Layer 4: In this layer the pixels from layer 3 are fully connected with 512 nodes and the weights are determined by Backpropogation.
- Layer 5: Fully connected Softmax layer is implemented with 5 output nodes (for the 5 intra-tumoral classes).

4   Experimental Setup

4.1   Dataset

The proposed work is accomplished on BRATS 2015 dataset, every subject in the BRATS dataset consists of 4 MRI modalities T1, T2, T1c and FLAIR.

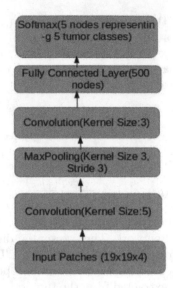

Fig. 1. The CNN architecture for the proposed model.

Images are skull stripped and aligned to T1 with 1mm isotropic resolution in each direction. The BRATS 2015 dataset consists of 220 high grade gliomas (HGG) and 54 are low grade gliomas (LGG) subjects. The segmentation is performed on the complete tumor (all tumor classes), enhancing and the core (non-enhancing + enhancing + necrosis). The ground truth has a label value 0-healthy tissue, 1-necrotic, 2-edema, 3- non-enhancing and 4-enhancing (Fig. 1).

4.2 Performance Metrics

The dice score, sensitivity and specificity metrics are employed to compute the performance of the proposed model.

$$D(P,T) = 2 \times \frac{(|P_1 \wedge T_1|)}{(|P_1| + |T_1|)} \tag{5}$$

Where P_1-predicted lesion area, T_1-true lesion area. The sensitivity is calculated enrolling the ensuing equation.

$$Sensitivity(P,T) = \frac{|P_1 \wedge T_1|}{T_1} \tag{6}$$

The true negative rate or specificity is computed enrolling the ensuing relation.

$$Specificity(P,T) = \frac{|P_0 \wedge T_0|}{|T_0|} \tag{7}$$

Where P_0 is the predicted healthy area and T_0 is the true healthy area.

5   Implementation Details

In this work, the implementation is done using the Keras Python library [18], which has enormous methods and pre-trained models to implement the CNNs. Theano [12] is enrolled as backend for Keras library. The Theano library uses the underlying cuDNN [2] library for the computation of mathematical expressions in n-Dimensional tensors. The model is trained on CUDA [22] enabled GPU device and Intel Core-i5 machine with 16 GB of RAM.

The ReLu activation function [11] is employed for neuronal activation. The Batch Normalization [13] technique is used to normalize the input data. The dropout layer [15] is introduced on feature maps. And, Backpropogation along with Stochastic Gradient Descent is used as an optimization technique.

The focus of the network training is to minimize the incorrect classification while training and increase the chance of accurate classification. The CNN depicts the probability allotment of all labels with an intent to increase the probability of forecasting actual label. The Stochastic Gradient Descent (SGD) [21] is enrolled for training the network. Further, Mini-batch approach is enrolled during training wherein it decimates the computation and memory requirements. The SGD was additionally modified enrolling the Nesterov accelerated gradient algorithm [17], which computes the variation in the gradient and then forwards in the control of the gradient. This allows the Nesterov Accelerated Gradient to calculate the gradient in prior to updating it, making it more active. The gradient and velocity are calculated using following two equations:

$$v_{t+1} = \mu v_t - lr \, \triangledown f(\theta_t + \mu v_t) \tag{8}$$

$$\theta_{t+1} = \theta_t + v_{t+1} \tag{9}$$

6   Results and Discussion

This section focusses on the results acquired for the BRATS 2015 dataset by using the proposed architecture. The 2D patches extracted from the four MRI sequences T1, T2, T1c and FLAIR are employed for training and testing. The dataset is divided randomly into training, validation and testing sets. The train dataset consists of 70% of the data, the validation dataset consists of 15% of the data and the testing dataset consists of 15% of the data. The training is done using 5 fold cross validation repeated 10 times, so that bias can be prevented. The network is assessed for 3 tumoral sub-regions complete tumor, core tumor and enhancing. The proposed method has yielded promising results for segmenting intra-tumoral cells in brain MR images, specifically in complete tumor segmentation the Dice score, specificity and sensitivity results are promising. I The dice score for complete, core and enhancing tumor is 0.86,0.62 and 0.65 accordingly. The sensitivity for complete, core and enhancing tumor is 0.73, 0.67 and 0.63 accordingly. The specificity for complete, core and enhancing tumor is 0.74, 0.72 and 0.75 accordingly. The evaluated results are compared with the models of other researchers and tabulated in Table 1, Table 2 and Table 3 (Fig. 2).

Table 1. Comparison of dice scores for complete, core & enhancing tumor

Dice score			
Method	Complete	Core	Enhancing
Proposed	0.86	0.62	0.65
Pereira [6]	0.87	0.73	0.68
Davy [23]	0.0.72	0.63	0.56
Isensee [24]	0.85	0.74	0.64
Jesson [25]	0.88	0.78	0.68
Li [26]	0.86	0.86	0.77

Table 2. Comparison of sensitivity for complete, core & enhancing tumor

Sensitivity			
Method	Complete	Core	Enhancing
Proposed	0.73	0.67	0.63
Pereira [6]	0.86	0.77	0.70
Davy [23]	0.72	0.63	0.56
Isensee [24]	0.91	0.73	0.72
Jesson [25]	0.87	0.78	0.75
Li [26]	0.90	0.80	0.80

Table 3. Comparison of specificity for complete, core & enhancing tumor

Specificity			
Method	Complete	Core	Enhancing
Proposed	0.74	0.72	0.75
Pereira	0.89	0.74	0.72
Davy [23]	0.69	0.64	0.50
Isensee [24]	0.83	0.80	0.63
Jesson [25]	0.99	0.99	0.99
Li [26]	0.82	0.85	0.74

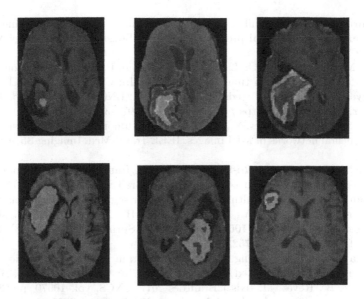

Fig. 2. Segmentation results obtained for HGG & LGG data

7   Conclusion

In this work, we proposed the successful application of Convolutional Neural Networks for segmenting intra-tumoral regions in brain MR scans yielding better results for complete tumor, tumor core and enhancing tumor regions. The clear benefit of this approach is that it does not depend on the manual feature extrication. As the convolution kernels learns the features automatically. The MR scans were pre-processed to remove magnetic field bias and intensity values are standardized using Z-score normalization. To prevent overfitting Dropout technique is used. The network is accelerated by enrolling SGD with Nesterov Accelerated Gradient calculation which helped the network to converge faster. As a future work, we plan to institute 2 nodes in the output for low and high grade tumors which help in delineating tumor sub regions accurately.

References

1. Menze, B.H., Jakab, A., Bauer, S., Kalpathy-Cramer, J., Farahani, K., et al.: The multimodal brain tumor image segmentation benchmark (BRATS). IEEE Trans. Med. Imaging **34**, 1993–2024 (2015)
2. Chetlur, S., et al.: cuDNN: efficient primitives for deep learning. arXiv:1410.0759 (2014)
3. Karnawat, A., Prasanna, P., Madabushi, A., Tiwari, P.: Radiomics-based convolutional neural network (RadCNN) for brain tumor segmentation on multiparametric MRI. In: Proceedings MICCAI BraTS Conference (2017)

4. Revanuru, K., Shah, N..: Fully automatic brain tumour segmentation using random forests and patient survival prediction using XGBoost. In: Proceedings MICCAI BraTS Conference (2017)

5. Havaei, M., Dutil, F., Pal, C., Larochelle, H., Jodoin, P.-M.: A convolutional neural network approach to brain tumor segmentation. In: Crimi, A., Menze, B., Maier, O., Reyes, M., Handels, H. (eds.) BrainLes 2015. LNCS, vol. 9556, pp. 195–208. Springer, Cham (2016). https://doi.org/10.1007/978-3-319-30858-6_17

6. Pereira, S., Pinto, A., Alves, V., Silva, C.: Brain tumor segmentation using convolutional neural networks in MRI images. IEEE Trans. Med. Imaging 35, 1240–1251 (2016)

7. Li, Y., Shen, L.: MvNet: multi-view deep learning framework for multimodal brain tumor segmentation. In: Proceedings MICCAI BraTS Conference (2017)

8. Phophalia, A., Maji, P.: Multimodal brain tumor segmentation using ensemble of forest method. In: Crimi, A., Bakas, S., Kuijf, H., Menze, B., Reyes, M. (eds.) BrainLes 2017. LNCS, vol. 10670, pp. 159–168. Springer, Cham (2018). https://doi.org/10.1007/978-3-319-75238-9_14

9. Pourreza, R., Zhuge, Y., Ning, H., Miller, R.: Brain tumor segmentation in MRI scans using deeply-supervised neural networks. In: Crimi, A., Bakas, S., Kuijf, H., Menze, B., Reyes, M. (eds.) BrainLes 2017. LNCS, vol. 10670, pp. 320–331. Springer, Cham (2018). https://doi.org/10.1007/978-3-319-75238-9_28

10. Krizhevsky, A., Sutskever, I., Hinton, G.E.: ImageNet classification with deep convolutional neural networks. In: Advances in Neural Information Processing Systems, pp. 1097–1105 (2012)

11. Ramachandran, P., Zoph, B., Le, Q.V.: Searching for Activation Functions. arXiv:1710.05941 (2017)

12. Theano Development Team.: Theano: a Python framework for fast computation of mathematical expressions. arXiv:1605.02688 (2016)

13. Ioffe, S., Szegedy, C.: Batch normalization: accelerating deep network training by reducing internal covariate shift. arXiv:1502.03167 (2015)

14. Prastawa, M., Bullitt, E., Ho, S., Gerig, G.: A brain tumor segmentation framework based on outlier detection. Med. Image Anal. 8(3), 275–283 (2004)

15. Srivastava, N., Hinton, G., Krizhevsky, A., Sutskever, I., Salakhutdinov, R.: Dropout: a simple way to prevent neural networks from overfitting. J. Mach. Learn. Res. 15(56), 1929–1958 (2014)

16. Tustison, N.J., et al.: N4ITK: improved N3 bias correction. IEEE Trans. Med. Imaging 29(6), 1310–1320 (2010)

17. Botev, A., Lever, G., Barber, D.: Nesterov's accelerated gradient and momentum as approximations to regularised update descent. arXiv:1607.01981 (2017)

18. Chollet, F. (2015). https://github.com/keras-team/keras

19. Havaei, M., Larochelle, H.: Brain tumor segmentation with deep neural networks. Med. Image Anal. 35, 18–31 (2017)

20. Riedmiller, M.: 10 steps and some tricks to set up neural reinforcement controllers. In: Montavon, G., Orr, G.B., Müller, K.-R. (eds.) Neural Networks: Tricks of the Trade. LNCS, vol. 7700, pp. 735–757. Springer, Heidelberg (2012). https://doi.org/10.1007/978-3-642-35289-8_39

21. Bottou, L.: Large-scale machine learning with stochastic gradient descent. In: Proceedings of COMPSTAT 2010. Physica-Verlag HD, Heidelberg (2010). https://doi.org/10.1007/978-3-7908-2604-3_16

22. Nickolls, J.: Scalable parallel programming with CUDA introduction. In: 2008 IEEE Hot Chips 20 Symposium (HCS), Stanford, CA, pp. 1–9 (2008)

23. Davy, A., Bengio, Y.: Brain tumor segmentation with deep neural networks. In: Proceedings MICCAI BraTS Conference, pp. 01–05 (2014)
24. Isensee, F., et al.: Brain tumor segmentation and radiomics survival prediction: contribution to the BRATS 2017 challenge. arXiv:1802.10508 (2018)
25. Jesson, A., Arbel, T.: Brain tumor segmentation using a 3D FCN with multi-scale loss. In: Crimi, A., Bakas, S., Kuijf, H., Menze, B., Reyes, M. (eds.) BrainLes 2017. LNCS, vol. 10670, pp. 392–402. Springer, Cham (2018). https://doi.org/10.1007/978-3-319-75238-9_34
26. Li, X., Zhang, X., Luo, Z.: Brain tumor segmentation via 3D fully dilated convolutional networks. In: MICCAI BraTs conference (2017)
27. Hamghalam, M., Lei, B., Wang, T.: Convolutional 3D to 2D patch conversion for pixel-wise glioma segmentation in MRI scans. In: Crimi, A., Bakas, S. (eds.) BrainLes 2019. LNCS, vol. 11992, pp. 3–12. Springer, Cham (2020). https://doi.org/10.1007/978-3-030-46640-4_1
28. Xu, X., Zhao, W., Zhao, J.: Brain tumor segmentation using attention-based network in 3D MRI images. In: Crimi, A., Bakas, S. (eds.) BrainLes 2019. LNCS, vol. 11993, pp. 3–13. Springer, Cham (2020). https://doi.org/10.1007/978-3-030-46643-5_1
29. Li., X.: Fused U-Net for brain tumor segmentation based on multimodal MR images. In: MICCAI BraTs Conference (2018)
30. Poornachandra, S., Naveena, C., Aradhya, M.: Intensity normalization—a critical pre-processing step for efficient brain tumor segmentation in MR images. In: Bhateja, V., Nguyen, B.L., Nguyen, N.G., Satapathy, S.C., Le, D.-N. (eds.) Information Systems Design and Intelligent Applications. AISC, vol. 672, pp. 885–893. Springer, Singapore (2018). https://doi.org/10.1007/978-981-10-7512-4_87
31. Liu, M.: Coarse-to-fine deep convolutional neural networks for multi-modality brain tumor semantic segmentation. In: MICCAI BraTs Conference (2018)
32. Marcinkiewicz, M., Mrukwa, G.: Automatic brain tumor segmentation using a two-stage multi-modal FCNN. In: MICCAI BraTs Conference (2018)

Brain Big Data Analytics, Curation and Management

Resolving Neuroscience Questions Using Ontologies and Templates

Aref Eshghishargh$^{(\boxtimes)}$ (iD), Kathleen Gray (iD), and Scott C. Kolbe (iD)

University of Melbourne, Melbourne, Australia
aref.cs@gmail.com,
{kgray,kolbes}@unimelb.edu.au

Abstract. Neuroscience is a vast field of study, important for its role in human body and brain disorders. Neuroscientists tend to ask complicated questions that need a complex set of actions and multiple resources. A question resolution approach in this field should be able to address these issues.

This study uses an ontology-based approach and creates codes that mirror the internal structure of questions, called templates, to translate questions to machine-understandable language. This research uses ontologies to expand queries, disambiguate terms, integrate resources, explore brain structures and create templates.

Keywords: Ontologies · Templates · Neuroscience · Question resolution · Question answering

1 Background

Scientists in neuroscience ask sophisticated questions that need multiple resources and are time-consuming to answer. Ontologies are one of the tools that can assist scientists in answering those questions. Template-based question resolution is also a method for translating questions to machine language.

This chapter reports an approach for resolving neuroscience questions. Ontologies can be used to characterize and classify neuroscience questions. They can also be used in disambiguation, query translation and resolving questions.

Ontologies can help resolve neuroscience questions by assisting resources integration and question-oriented tasks. As [4] states, a problem with answering neuroscience questions is that simple questions might need several time consuming searches on different resources. Resource integration addresses this problem.

In question-oriented tasks, query disambiguation, expansion and translation capabilities of ontologies are used to disambiguate neuroscience terms and resolve questions, such as the approach used by [5]. Question resolution systems can benefit from both resource integration and question-oriented tasks at the same time, like the system described in [12,13].

Questions should be translated to machine language. A template-based approach [10], is one that reduces and represents a question as a template, mirroring

© Springer Nature Switzerland AG 2020
M. Mahmud et al. (Eds.): BI 2020, LNAI 12241, pp. 141–150, 2020.
https://doi.org/10.1007/978-3-030-59277-6_13

the internal structure of questions [32]. Templates include some missing elements called slots, which are filled according to the question. After filling the slots, the template is queried against the data. AskHermes [7], papers such as [1] and some systems trying to reduce questions to templates in a textual entailment process [18], such as work performed in [25], are examples of such systems.

In the remainder of this paper, Sect. 2 describes how this study was performed, and Sect. 3 shows the outputs. In Sect. 4, results will be further analysed; also, achievements and future goals will be discussed.

2   Methods

Neuroscience questions can be represented by their features (dimensions) [12,13]. Dimensions, which are selected through a careful question analysis process, include entities, domain-specific phrases, data references, aggregation and statistical phrases and conditional phrases. For example, the token 'hippocampus' is tagged as an entity. Using dimensions, questions were classified into a hierarchy. The question hierarchy is created based on the number, formation and plausibility of different dimensions in a question. Each dimension is represented by a Resource Description Framework (RDF) triple, which adds to the complexity of the data. With regard to the formation and plausibility, the hierarchy was informed by definition of a valid question [11], Bloom's Taxonomy [3], Web Ontology Language (OWL) definition and classes, and to some extent, Aristotelian categories and relationships explained in [28,30]. The hierarchy is as follows:

- Level 0: Questions with only entities in them.
- Level 1: Level 0 plus domain-specific phrases.
- Level 2: Level 1 plus references to data.
- Level 3: Level 2 plus aggregation/ statistical phrases.
- Level 4: Level 3 plus conditions, changes or comparison.

Once a question was received, it was processed by processes depicted in the left circle of Fig. 1. There, it was parsed and tokenized, stop-words were removed and tokens were tagged by dimensions. Then, the question was classified according to the question hierarchy. For more details on processes involved in this part, please refer to [12].

In a question resolution system, following the initial pre-processing and classification, questions are passed to the processes located inside the right circle of Fig. 1 to be translated by templates and eventually get resolved.

Templates were made based on the question hierarchy. A general high-level template was created per each level, accompanied by several specific ones, except level 4 that included changes, comparisons and conditional questions and needed three. SPARQL was used for querying ontologies and Python was used for creating the overall templates and communicating with other applications such as Freesurfer [14]. The right circle processes were responsible for question-oriented tasks, such as query expansion and resource integration too.

Query expansion seeks to remove ambiguities. Moreover, if the user wants to receive more information, query expansion can help in increasing the recall. Upon detecting terms such as 'subparts' in the questions or having the query expansion selected by the user, queries were expanded in several aspects such as synonyms, parent and child nodes of the dimension. Query expansion and string matching can be performed using various methods and tools such as programming languages, libraries, APIs and even standalone applications. Here, SPARQL functions and filters were used, and then, the information was passed to templates. Codes are available from https://github.com/Aref-cs/Templates.

To better resolve the questions, different resources, including the NIFSTD [17] ontology and the Freesurfer application were integrated, using a subsection of the Foundational Model of Anatomy (FMA) ontology [27], called NeuroFMA, and according to the directions described in [23,24].

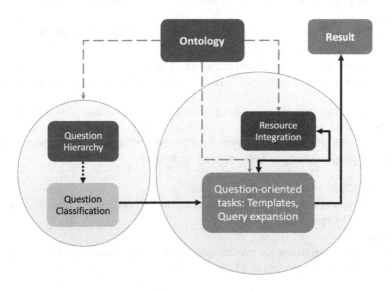

Fig. 1. The process of resolving a question

3   Results

First, a data-set, created from literature and questions posed by expert was gathered and examined by an expert. This data-set, and methods used in gathering it can be accessed via ~/Dataset-ch4-p3.

Then, templates were created to cover and translate as many questions as possible. As described in Sect. 2, each template was created based on a level from the question hierarchy. Table 1 matches questions to hierarchy levels.

For example, a level 0 question had one template, since based on definitions in question hierarchy levels, a question was located under this group if it included

Table 1. Questions, their dimensions and level

Question number	Question contains	Level
7	Only 1 dimension	0
1, 6, 8, 9, 10, 13, 14, 22, 28,30	Entity + Domain-specific (attribute) phrase	1
2, 3, 5, 15, 16, 21	Entity + Domain-specific phrase + Data-reference	2
17, 18, 19, 20, 26, 29	Previous formations + Aggregation phrases	3
4, 11, 12, 23, 24, 25, 27, 31, 32	Previous formations + Conditions/Changes/Comparisons	4

only one dimension. "What is the amygdala?" is an example for this level. The general pseudocode for this template is as follows:

```
SELECT distinct (?dim as ?Part) (Str(?label) as
?Name) (?def as ?Definition) (?com as ?Additional_Info)
  WHERE {
    GRAPH <http://localhost:3030/myDataset/data/NeuroFMA> {
        dim rdfs:label ?label .
        optional {?dim rdfs:comment ?com}
        ?dim fma:definition (or skos:definition for nif) ?def}
```

"What are the synonyms of hippocampus?" was a sample of level 1 questions. This question contained an entity and a domain-specific phrase, with the dimension searching for, being 'synonym', which was a domain-specific phrase. The general pseudocode for level 1, was as follows:

```
SELECT DISTINCT (?dim as ?Result) {
  {VALUES ?type {ontology1 namespace (nif) :related predicates}.
    ?subject ?type ?dim.
  } UNION {
  VALUES ?type {ontology2 namespace (fma):related predicates}.
      ?subject ?type ?dim. } }
```

Level 2 was a little bit different from previous levels, since it worked with data outputs of neuroimaging applications such as the Freesurfer. A sample of such a file is available via `~/FreesurferDataFile.jpg`.

"What is the volume of the insula in the data?" is a sample question for level 2. This question contains entity, domain-specific phrase and data reference. Here, 'insula' was found in Fressurfer data, using the mapping provided by the NeuroFMA ontology, with Code 1.1.

Then, the information regarding the Freesurfer IDs was passed to Python and using the Pandas library, the final result of this question was calculated and returned to the user. Instructions on pandas library is available via `~/general-panadas.py`.

Level 3 codes were based on, and similar to level 2, since it was related to aggregation and statistical phrases and only needed some extra calculations.

SPARQL could implement those phrases conventionally with its statistical functions such as Count, Min, Max, Avg and other related functions. Codes related to this level can be accessed from the Github link, provided above.

Level 4 contained different subgroups including changes, comparisons and conditions. Since changes in the data usually happen across different experiments or readings, more than one data-set was needed while resolving such questions. However, codes shared foundations with previous ones. A sample questions associated with level 4 was "What region of the premotor cortex shows atrophy?". Atrophy can be measured only by looking at different data-sets from different times or groups of patients. The same goes with groups of patients.

According to each of these, after the query expansion, the Python code with the Pandas library will get the information regarding the sizes of the parts in a loop using the pseudocode below:

```
# Load Pandas as shown in Github link
# Read data from related files 'file1.csv', 'file2.csv'
data1 = pd.read_csv("filename.csv")
#one file per subject data (data2 for the second one)
count = 0
while (count < 'number of loops needed
  for reading the data'): count += 1
    Read the data from the file as shown in
https://~/general_panadas.py
# Compare and calculate the result
# print out the result
```

Then the results of the loops were compared together. Please note that each loop could consist of a number of available data-sets. Also, it is obvious that all these loading and calculations add to the cost of calculations. Another type of level 4 questions are the comparison questions, which were very similar to the one above.

The last template for questions containing conditions was a little bit different, because in questions containing conditions, the condition had to be resolved first, since the rest of the question was basically a question from other levels, queried on the result of the condition.

An example for a conditional question is "Which subjects show more atrophy in cortical regions that are connected by the superior longitudinal fasciculus?" In these types of questions, first the condition should be satisfied. Therefore, regions that are connected by superior longitudinal fasciculus had to be found as a separate query and stored as a graph first, and then the rest was queried against it.

Altogether, around 10 main templates and several extra templates were made in order to cover and resolve different types of questions. Main templates included four templates for levels 0 to 3, and six different templates for level 4 questions containing comparison, change and conditions.

As discussed, resource integration enables users to ask more complex questions with a wider scope and contributes to richer results. Here, NIFSTD ontology and Freesurfer were connected using NeuroFMA ontology, using directions provided by [24]. The general form for mapping resources was as follows:

Code 1.1. Code for mapping between resources

```
SELECT DISTINCT ?fmaS   ?fmaName ?neurolexId ?nlxName
     WHERE {? fmaS    fma:preferred_name ?fmaName;
                      fma:Neurolex ?neurolexId .
     OPTIONAL {?nlxAnt owl:annotatedTarget ?neurolexId;
                      fma:name ?nlxName .} }
```

The approach presented in this study could resolve 78% of questions in the data-set. One important outcome of this study, was its success in resolving different types of questions via templates.

4 Discussion

Here are several issues, including related works and a critical reflection on results, which explores role and effects of different elements in this study such as templates and ontologies; moreover, limitations and future work is discussed.

Related works to this study included AquaLog [21, 22] and later, PowerAqua [20] and Freebase [9, 33], which were systems designed for tackling queries on the semantic web. They were among the first systems using ontologies. One other system that was related to this study, was NIF search [2, 16, 17]. NIF queries included searching for synonyms; some conjunctive queries; searching hierarchies and seeking for collection of terms. BioDB [15] is another ontology-based system in the biological domain.

There are other related studies outside neuroscience field, such as the KA-SB [26] that integrates resources and performs reasoning in biology, or works presented in [6, 31] towards general question answering.

Critical reflection on results show that a noticeable feature of the approach discussed here, is its flexibility and ability to be extended as a result of using a modular design and usage of ontologies. Furthermore, its comprehensiveness is a result of bringing different resources together.

The approach discussed in this study has the ability to resolve complex free-text questions containing synonyms, descriptions, hierarchical terms such as parents and children of a term, comparisons, patient related data, changes in the data, condition and aggregation phrases. Therefore, this study covers a wide range of questions. It can potentially answer more questions.

Answering more questions needs creating separate templates for unique questions or using user-interaction. For example, "What are the positive effects of aspirin on elderly people?" was not resolvable because of abstract terms such as 'positive' and 'elderly'. However, this question might be potentially resolvable through simple methods like user-interaction, or more sophisticated methods such as using knowledge graphs according to methods investigated by [8].

Something that is worth discussing is the resolution of questions containing temporal phrases. In this study, they were resolved using a mixture of Python and SPARQL. There are ontologies that contain information on temporal and other aspects of the neurosience, and can assist in resolving questions, including the DICOM ontology, which contains information regarding the patient and imaging procedures; OBO-RO, which contains information regarding relations in biomedical ontologies and RadLex ontology [19], that includes information regarding neuroimages. Fortunately, the approach of this study allows adding other ontologies.

Templates being based on the question hierarchy, inherited its hierarchical form, which allowed templates on higher levels to be built based on lower-level templates. This, simplified the implementation by making it a modular one and decreased coding and debugging. Templates played a significant role in automating the process of resolving questions. However, correct classification of questions is also important in its success.

Ontologies worked as sources of data, complementary data and means of disambiguation and a bridge to other sources. Figure 2 demonstrates a high-level view on how the model and ontologies assisted in finding answers for questions. It shows how processes such as query expansion and disambiguation benefited from ontolgies, apart from the benefit of synonyms and string matching. It shows what sorts of problems would have been faced if ontologies were not present. Furthermore, it depicts why answering certain questions was not possible without ontologies due to the level of MRI image resolution; for example, in "What is the white matter volume of subparts of the fusiform gyrus in the patient?", 'subparts', which are visible in MRI images can be found using ontologies. The role of ontology in resource integration was discussed previously. Please note that, these uses rely on the expressive power, comprehensiveness and quality of the ontology.

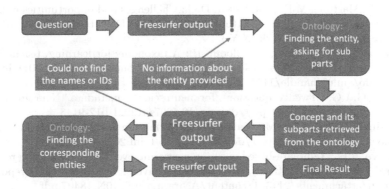

Fig. 2. How ontologies assisted query expansion, disambiguation, and finding new information

Ontologies are getting more popular and are showing prominent benefits. However, a standard method of accessing and handling ontologies, also removing redundancies, would make ontology-based applications flourish. Innovation such as the OBO foundry [29] has helped this, but the process is still slow.

Introducing other image modalities such as fMRI, and moving towards a multi-modal approach can be a future direction for this research. Another future direction can be to factor issues that arose during implementation of templates and updating the question hierarchy.

5 Conclusion

A background for answering questions in neuroscience in an automated way, using ontologies and templates was given. Methods were described, and as a result, a set of multi-level templates were created according to a question hierarchy, which was based on ontologies.

The outcome was an approach that could answer 78% of questions in the data-set successfully. Results were further discussed and related works were pointed out. Roles of each element and its advantages and disadvantages were explained. Future directions and ways of continuing the research were mentioned.

Acknowledgements. We would like to thank Dr. Nolan Nichols (Genentech, Inc.), for providing us with technical information. Support for this work was provided by The University of Melbourne School of Computing and Information Systems.

References

1. Abacha, A.B., Zweigenbaum, P.: Medical question answering: translating medical questions into SPARQL queries. In: IHI 2012 - Proceedings of the 2nd ACM SIGHIT International Health Informatics Symposium, pp. 41–49 (2012). https://doi.org/10.1145/2110363.2110372
2. Akil, H., Martone, M.E., Van Essen, D.C.: Challenges and opportunities in mining neuroscience data. Science **331**(6018), 708–712 (2011). https://doi.org/10.1126/science.1199305. (New York, N.Y.)
3. Anderson, L., Krathwohl, D., Bloom, B.: A taxonomy for learning, teaching, and assessing: a revision of Bloom's taxonomy of educational objectives (2001). https://eduq.info/xmlui/handle/11515/18345
4. Ascoli, G.A.G.: Twenty questions for neuroscience metadata. Neuroinformatics **10**(2), 115–117 (2012). https://doi.org/10.1007/s12021-012-9143-4
5. Ashish, N., Toga, A.W.: Medical data transformation using rewriting. Front. Neuroinform. **9**, 1 (2015). https://doi.org/10.3389/fninf.2015.00001
6. Athreya, R.G.: Template-based question answering over linked data using recursive neural networks. Ph.D. thesis, Arizona State University (2018). https://repository.asu.edu/attachments/211341/content/Athreya_asu_0010N_18407.pdf
7. Cao, Y.G., et al.: AskHERMES: an online question answering system for complex clinical questions. J. Biomed. Inform. **44**(2), 277–288 (2011). https://doi.org/10.1016/j.jbi.2011.01.004
8. Cimiano, P.: Knowledge graph refinement: a survey of approaches and evaluation methods. Semantic Web **8**(3), 489–508 (2017). https://doi.org/10.3233/sw-160218

9. Cui, W., Xiao, Y., Wang, W.: KBQA: an online template based question answering system over freebase. In: IJCAI International Joint Conference on Artificial Intelligence, January 2016, pp. 4240–4241 (2016). https://www.ijcai.org/Proceedings/16/Papers/640.pdf

10. Dwivedi, S.K., Singh, V.: Research and reviews in question answering system. Procedia Technol. **10**, 417–424 (2013). https://doi.org/10.1016/j.protcy.2013.12.378

11. Ely, J.W., et al.: Obstacles to answering doctors' questions about patient care with evidence: qualitative study. BMJ **324**(7339), 710–710 (2002). https://doi.org/10.1136/bmj.324.7339.710

12. Eshghishargh, A., Gray, K., Milton, S.K., Kolbe, S.C.: A semantic system for answering questions in neuroinformatics. In: ACM International Conference Proceeding Series, pp. 1–5. ACM Press, New York (2018). https://doi.org/10.1145/3167918.3167960

13. Eshghishargh, A., et al.: An ontology-based semantic question complexity model and its applications in neuroinformatics. Front. Neurosci. **9**, (2015). https://doi.org/10.3389/conf.fnins.2015.91.00015

14. Fischl, B.: FreeSurfer. Neuroimage (2012). http://www.sciencedirect.com/science/article/pii/S1053811912000389

15. Gupta, A., Condit, C., Qian, X.: BioDB: an ontology-enhanced information system for heterogeneous biological information. Data Knowl. Eng. **69**(11), 1084–1102 (2010). https://doi.org/10.1016/j.datak.2010.07.003

16. Imam, F.T., Larson, S.D., Bandrowski, A., Grethe, J.S., Gupta, A., Martone, M.E.: Development and use of ontologies inside the neuroscience information framework: a practical approach. Frontiers Genet. **3**(JUN), 111 (2012). https://doi.org/10.3389/fgene.2012.00111

17. Imam, F.T., Larson, S.D., Grethe, J.S., Gupta, A., Bandrowski, A., Martone, M.E.: NIFSTD and NeuroLex: a comprehensive neuroscience ontology development based on multiple biomedical ontologies and community involvement. In: CEUR Workshop Proceedings of the Neuroscience Information Framework, Center for Research in Biological Systems, ICBO, vol. 833, pp. 349–356, University of California, San Diego (2011)

18. Kouylekov, M., Negri, M., Magnini, B., Coppola, B.: Towards entailment-based question answering: ITC-irst at CLEF 2006. In: Peters, C., et al. (eds.) CLEF 2006. LNCS, vol. 4730, pp. 526–536. Springer, Heidelberg (2007). https://doi.org/10.1007/978-3-540-74999-8_64

19. Langlotz, C.P.: RadLex: a new method for indexing online educational materials. Radiographics **26**(6), 1595–1597 (2006). https://doi.org/10.1148/rg.266065168

20. Lopez, V., Fernandez, M., Stieler, N., Motta, E.: PowerAqua : supporting users in querying and exploring the semantic web content. Semant. Web J. (2011). https://doi.org/10.3233/sw-2011-0030

21. Lopez, V., Pasin, M., Motta, E.: AquaLog: an ontology-portable question answering system for the semantic web. In: Gómez-Pérez, A., Euzenat, J. (eds.) ESWC 2005. LNCS, vol. 3532, pp. 546–562. Springer, Heidelberg (2005). https://doi.org/10.1007/11431053_37

22. Lopez, V., Uren, V., Motta, E., Pasin, M.: AquaLog: an ontology-driven question answering system for organizational semantic intranets. Web Semant. 5(2), 72–105 (2007). https://doi.org/10.1016/j.websem.2007.03.003

23. Nichols, B.N., et al.: Neuroanatomical domain of the foundational model of anatomy ontology. J. Biomed. Semant. 5(1), 1 (2014). https://doi.org/10.1186/2041-1480-5-1

24. Nichols, B.N., Mejino Jr, J.L.V., Brinkley, J.F.: The foundational model of neuroanatomy ontology: an ontology framework to support neuroanatomical data integration. In: ICBO (2011). http://ceur-ws.org/Vol-833/paper92.pdf
25. Ou, S., Orasan, C., Mekhaldi, D., Hasler, L.: Automatic question pattern generation for ontology-based question answering. In: Proceedings of the 21st International Florida Artificial Intelligence Research Society Conference, pp. 183–188 (2008)
26. Roldán-García, M.D.M., Navas-Delgado, I., Kerzazi, A., Chniber, O., Molina-Castro, J., Aldana-Montes, J.F.: KA-SB: from data integration to large scale reasoning. BMC Bioinform. **10**(SUPPL. 10), S5 (2009). https://doi.org/10.1186/1471-2105-10-S10-S5
27. Rosse, C., Mejino, J.L.: The foundational model of anatomy ontology. In: Burger, A., Davidson, D., Baldock, R. (eds.) Anatomy Ontologies for Bioinformatics, vol. 6, pp. 59–117. Springer, London (2008). https://doi.org/10.1007/978-1-84628-885-2_4
28. Ryle, G.: Categories. JSTOR **38**, 189–206 (1937). https://doi.org/10.1093/oseo/instance.00258580
29. Smith, B., et al.: The OBO foundry: coordinated evolution of ontologies to support biomedical data integration. Nat. Biotechnol. **25**(11), 1251–1255 (2007). https://doi.org/10.1038/nbt1346
30. Studtmann, P.: Aristotle's Categories (2018). https://plato.stanford.edu/archives/fall2018/entries/aristotle-categories/
31. Pellissier Tanon, T., de Assunção, M.D., Caron, E., Suchanek, F.M.: Demoing platypus – a multilingual question answering platform for wikidata. In: Gangemi, A., et al. (eds.) ESWC 2018. LNCS, vol. 11155, pp. 111–116. Springer, Cham (2018). https://doi.org/10.1007/978-3-319-98192-5_21
32. Unger, C., Bühmann, L.: Template-based question answering over RDF data. In: Proceedings of the 21st International Conference on World Wide Web, pp. 639–648 (2012). https://doi.org/10.1145/2187836.2187923
33. Yao, X., Van Durme, B.: Information extraction over structured data: question answering with freebase. In: Proceedings of the Conference on 52nd Annual Meeting of the Association for Computational Linguistics, ACL 2014, vol. 1, pp. 956–966 (2014). https://doi.org/10.3115/v1/p14-1090

Machine Learning in Analysing Invasively Recorded Neuronal Signals: Available Open Access Data Sources

Marcos Fabietti⬤, Mufti Mahmud(✉)⬤, and Ahmad Lotfi⬤

Department of Computing and Technology, Nottingham Trent University,
Clifton Lane, Clifton, Nottingham NG11 8NS, UK
mufti.mahmud@ntu.ac.uk,muftimahmud@gmail.com

Abstract. Neuronal signals allow us to understand how the brain operates and this process requires sophisticated processing of the acquired
signals, which is facilitated by machine learning-based methods. However, these methods require large amount of data to first train them on
the patterns present in the signals and then employ them to identify
patterns from unknown signals. This data acquisition process involves
expensive and complex experimental setups which are often not available to all – especially to the computational researchers who mainly deal
with the development of the methods. Therefore, there is a basic need for
the availability of open access datasets which can be used as benchmark
towards novel methodological development and performance comparison
across different methods. This would facilitate newcomers in the field to
experiment and develop novel methods and achieve more robust results
through data aggregation. In this scenario, this paper presents a curated
list of available open access datasets of invasive neuronal signals containing a total of more than 25 datasets.

Keywords: Computational neuroscience · Neuroinformatics ·
Neuronal spikes · Neurophysiological signals

1 Introduction

Neuronal signals are the electrical activity of neurons, which can be recorded
at different depths of the brain. They are key to understand its functioning,
and are used for diagnosis, brain-computer interface (BCI), biofeedback therapy,
rehabilitation and other applications [51].

The non-invasive signals, namely electroencephalography (EEG) and magne-
toencephalography (MEG), are more susceptible to noise but have the advantage
that are easier to acquire than their invasive counterparts [18,19,22]. Because of
it, there is a bigger amount of open datasets of them available for researchers. On
the other hand, the invasively recorded signals, i.e. electrocorticogram (ECoG),
local field potentials (LFP) and neuronal spikes, give us insight into specific
structures of the brain but are less represented [17].

© Springer Nature Switzerland AG 2020
M. Mahmud et al. (Eds.): BI 2020, LNAI 12241, pp. 151–162, 2020.
https://doi.org/10.1007/978-3-030-59277-6_14

In the case of BCI applications, the use of invasive signals offers accurate control, which is a prerequisite for user acceptance, combined with restoration of somatosensation [53]. In contrast, EEG signals suffer from limited spatial resolution, susceptibility to artifacts, and low information transfer rate which makes them too slow for controlling complex devices [26].

The complexity of the spatio-temporal patterns of these signals calls for the need of computational models to predict, classify and analyze these signals in order to aid patients and researchers alike. In recent years machine learning has contributed in many different disciplines including anomaly detection [10,58], biological data mining [20], medical image analysis [2], natural language processing [40,54], and disease detection [25,31]. These techniques have also helped to develop powerful tools for neuroscience, but these methods rely on big amounts of information [21]. A robust model requires ample data from different subjects, of sufficient length to remove possible artifacts and with enough samples per categories the study is looking to identify [23].

In the computational field, the use of public datasets to train, improve or validate a model is a common procedure. However, the acquisition process of invasive neuronal signal requires costly and complicated experimental setups that are often not accessible to everyone, especially computational researchers who are primarily interested in the creation of methods. This raises the need for open data sources of invasively recorded neuronal signal in order to widen the possibilities of research and to incorporate newcomers in the field.

On a wider scope, the importance of data availability lies in enhancing scientific progress via reproducibility and self-correction, leading to credible findings [13]. Other benefits are that the aggregation of data from different sources may lead to new findings, being able to draw out more robust conclusions and not having to employ resources on collecting similar data. Therefore, scientific communities should strive to make data available for everyone.

The goal of this paper is to analyze the current state of publicly available data of invasive neuronal signals, and provide an up to reference for future researches. In the following sections we will describe the invasive neuronal signals, give an overview of machine learning methods, detail and compare the data sets, discuss current challenges of open data sharing and selection of datasets, and finally draw out conclusive remarks.

2   Neuronal Signals and Analysis

There are several methods for recording invasive neuronal signals, and depending on which one is used, the signals have different properties, such as frequency and amplitudes. Their characteristics are described following paragraphs.

The acquisition of electrical activity by the placement of electrodes at the epidural or subdural level of the brain is denominated ECoG. It has the benefit of not suffering the distortions generated by the skull and intermediate issue and possessing more amplitude than EEG. At the epidural level it has a spatial resolution of 1.4 mm, while at the subdural level of 1.25 mm. It allows for the acquisition of a wide range of frequencies, between 0 to 500 Hz [42].

Through the low pass filtering of the extracellular electrical potential to under 100–300 Hz, in deep layers of the brain, LFP are obtained. The recording contains a mixture of neuronal processes, for instance synchronized synaptic potentials, after-potentials of somato-dendritic spikes and voltage-gated membrane oscillations. Thus, it is composed of the contribution of several different neuronal processing pathways and they posses the advantage of providing stable signal for longer period of time than multi-unit spiking activity [24].

The acquisition of neuronal spikes can be done through different techniques. The patch clamp technique is used to measure ionic currents with a micropipette in patches of cell membrane, tissue sections or individual isolated living cells. When the detection of neuronal activity is performed with a microelectrode it is referred to as single-unit recording, but if the electrode is of a bigger size than micrometers then the activity of a group of neurons can be detected, and this is named multi-unit recording [16].

The interpretation of these signals requires an experienced neurophysiologist to visually examine them, which is a time consuming and monotonous task, as well as prone to inter-observer variations. In order to aid the analysis, several signal analysis techniques such as linear, non-linear, time domain and frequency domain methods have been developed [1] to extract useful information from the recorded neural activity. As machine learning techniques can make use of this information to analyze large volumes of data, and automate the process, they are increasingly used in many applications, e.g. the detection of noisy segments [10]. Figure 1 illustrates the different steps of manual and automated diagnosis as an example. In the subsequent section, we will describe these techniques and their properties.

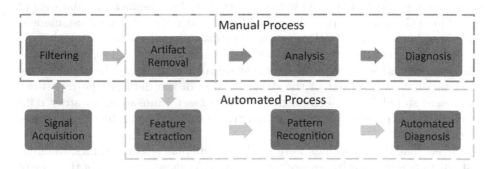

Fig. 1. Steps from signal acquisition to diagnosis via manual and automated processes.

3   Machine Learning Techniques

Machine learning techniques are algorithms that learn from patterns in data and are able to make predictions based on it. There are three main types of learning problems. First, supervised, is task driven such as a classification or regression problem where the data has previously been annotated. Examples of these algorithms are: linear discriminant analysis, support vector machines, k-nearest neighbours and random forest.

Second, unsupervised, the algorithm groups unlabeled data so that the properties of objects within a group are resembling and properties in other groups are different. This includes partitioning methods (k-means), hierarchical methods, density based methods, fuzzy clustering and others.

Lastly, reinforcement, an agent learns to interact with an environment. It is important to point out neural networks, due to their massive success and popularity, and that they are used across all three learning problems. Neural networks are composed of multiple layers of neurons for processing of non-linear information and were inspired by how the human brain works.

In spite of the success of machine learning, the complexity of the problem increases the amount of information these techniques require. Therefore, in the following section we present accessible sources of data that can be used to address this, via their direct use or their incorporation to private datasets.

4   Open-Access Datasets

While datasets found online range from a few kilobytes to several terabytes, we have included those of intermediate size of 1 to 10 GB. This inclusion criteria was selected based on the 2018 online poll "Largest Dataset Analyzed/Data Mined" [15], conducted by a popular site on AI, Analytics, Big Data, Data Science and Machine Learning. The survey received a total of 1108 votes from students, members of academia, researchers in the private sector, governmental or non-profit members, and others; where the majority voted the 1.1 to 10 GB range, as depicted in Fig. 2. This can be attributed to the fact that datasets of less than 1 GB may not provide enough information to extract robust models, and those bigger than 10 GB can prove difficult to handle, store and analyze.

Table 1 contain the selected list the LFP, neuronal spikes and ECoG datasets. The table includes the type of neuronal signal, the subjects the signals were acquired from, the format of the data, the size of the dataset, the repository they were stored in, the complexity of the dataset from an exploratory data analysis (EDA) perspective, the research area of the study and the corresponding reference.

Given that the recordings were made for different research topics, different test subjects were used by researchers. Figure 3(A) shows the ratio of the type of subjects signals were acquisition from, sorted by each type of signal. The three most used subjects are rodents in 12 datasets, followed by humans and monkeys in 7 datasets each. Because of the availability of subjects, ethical approvals, and the risks damage to the neuronal tissue, the most human datasets are in ECoG, as they are the least invasive.

The Fig. 3(B), on the other hand, indicates the proportion of the different data formats used to store neuronal recordings in the surveyed datasets. The format .mat is an overwhelming majority, suggesting that Matlab software is the preferred programming language used in the neuroscience field.

Table 1. Open-Access Invasive Neuronal Datasets

Signal	Subjects	Type	Size (GB)	Host	EDA	Research area	Ref.
LFP	Rodent	.mat	3	Dryad	Medium	Cortical responses to sensory inputs	[43]
	Rodent	.mat	10	Dryad	Complex	Intracellular dynamics of interneurons and pyramidal cells during spontaneous and visually evoked gamma activity	[36]
	Rodent	.mat	2	Dryad	Complex	Connectivity patterns underlying replay in a network model of place cells	[49]
	Rodent	.mat	3	Dryad	Simple	Predicting behavior across tasks and species	[45]
	Rodent	.mat	1.3	Zenodo	Medium	Neocortical inhibitory neuron function in awake mice	[34]
	Rodent	.mat	3.6	Figshare	Medium	Not specified	[56]
	Rodent	.mat	1.4	Harvard Dataverse	Complex	Ketamine and walking induced gamma oscillations	[12]
	Rodent	.mat	1.5	CRCNS	Complex	Auditory cortex response	[8]
	Rodent	.mat/.csv	8.3	CRCNS	Complex	Network Homeostasis and State Dynamics of Neocortical Sleep	[55]
	Human	.h5	3	Dryad	Complex	Tracking the lead-up to impulsive choices	[35]
	Ferret	.csv	2	Dryad	Simple	Anesthesia effects	[57]
Spikes	Rodent	.mat	2.4	DIR	Medium	Spike and burst coding in thalamocortical relay cells	[59]
	Human	.mat	6	OSF	Complex	Memory Task	[5]
	Simulated	.mat	2.2	Zenodo	Simple	Spike sorting	[4]
	Monkey	.mat	9	Dryad	Complex	Effects of transcranial magnetic stimulation	[41]
ECoG	Rodent	.h5	3.94	Brainliner	Simple	Visual cortex stimulation	[50]
	Human	.mat	6	Kaggle	Simple	Classification of graphoelements and artifactual signals	[27]
	Human	.mat	3.5	Zenodo	Complex	Visual episodic recollection	[32]
	Human	.mat	1.12	MNI Open iEEG Atlas	Simple	Sleep study	[9]
	Human	.mat	2.15	MNI Open iEEG Atlas	Simple	Are high frequency oscillations biomarkers for seizure	[7]
	Human and Dog	.mat	10	Kaggle	Simple	Seizure detection	[48]
	Monkey	.mat	3.3	Neurotycho	Simple	Artifact removal	[33]
	Monkey	.mat	5.96	Neurotycho	Simple	BMI decoding	[44]
	Monkey	.mat	1.1	Neurotycho	Medium	BMI decoding	[6]
	Monkey	.mat	1.76	Neurotycho	Medium	Visual grating task	[30]
	Monkey	.mat	3.98	Neurotycho	Simple	Emotional movie task	[28]
	Monkey	.mat	1.9	Neurotycho	Simple	Fixiation task	[29]

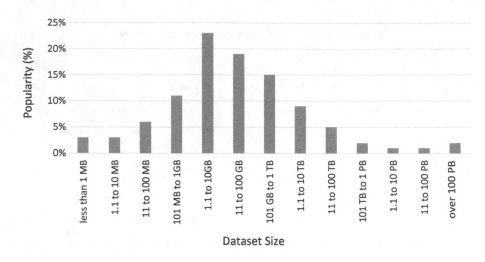

Fig. 2. Popularity of dataset size while using them for machine learning based methods. Modified from [15] .

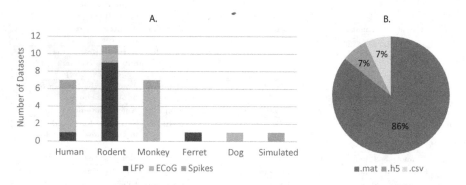

Fig. 3. Number of datasets per subject type, sorted by signal (A) and the distribution of format types (B).

When it comes to ECoG records, it is worth mentioning IEEG.ORG, a collaborative initiative funded by the National Institutes of Neurological Disorders and Stroke. It includes 819 public ECoG datasets, however it is currently not possible to download entire datasets directly. Outside these open access datasets, there are others which can be accessed upon request to their owners: Henin et al. [14] and the RAM initiative by the University of Pennsylvania [39]. Lastly, the European Epilepsy Database [38], consisting of more than 250 patient datasets, is also available for purchase.

On regards to spikes and LFP data, Buzsáki Labs [37] have shared on their platform approximately 40 Tb of data of from freely moving rodents recorded over the course of several years. It was acquired across different brain structures such as the hippocampus, thalamus, amygdala, post-subiculum, septal region and the entorhinal cortex and various neocortical regions. Lastly, other repositories that host invasive neuronal recordings but were not included in the table are GigaDB, IEEE DataPort, Standford Digital Repository and SWEC-ETHZ.

5 Discussion

Currently, there are many challenges in both data sharing and in the selection of open access data sources. In this section we will be discussing them, with inputs of what has been mentioned in the literature and our findings.

5.1 Data Sharing

The sharing of experimental data has been a topic of discussion in neuroscience. Wagenaar et al. [52] identified integrating different file formats, de-identifying protected health information, and adhering to government regulations as obstacles. They argued that the lack of a platform to share data and the enforcement of sharing data after publishing causes a slower scientific progress.

Ferguson et al. [11] encouraged the sharing of small data sets produced by individual neuroscientists, so-called long-tail data, for different approaches or to aggregate them and learn new insights. Furthermore, they raise the need for a scholarly system for credit attribution for data, equivalent to the system for literature citations. They discussed as well negative aspects of data sharing, such as: researchers fearing sharing data may lead to question the validity of the analysis, the costs associated with managing, hosting and curating data and the concern that re-analysis of data sets by non-experts will lead to a big amount of poor contributions in the literature.

Amari et al. [3] have pointed out that the main challenges of shared databases are publication methods, quality assurance, metadata, tools and ethical and legal aspects. On the first subject, current publications contain selected parts of the original data, and limited descriptions of the processes used. Second, quality control is difficult when there is a lack of heterogeneity of data formats, large variability of data and differences among data providers. Third, there is a need for complete and standardized metadata in contrast of the free text format used in journals. Fourth, it is not common for non-commercial coding to achieve being generally recognised and used. Lastly, human subject anonymity must be protected to avoid misuse of sensible information.

Teeter et al. [47] establishes key points of a discussion held on a workshop of ways to advance public data sharing for computational neuroscience. While similar aforementioned challenges and benefits are addressed, they also voiced that new data sharing initiatives should aim for less represented data types, which correlates with the aim of this paper. Additionally, they stated that progress in the field could accelerate through the creation of test beds for improving and benchmarking methods for analyzing and modeling neuroscience data.

On the topic of data format, the Berkeley Institute for Data Science conducted a survey[1] of 440 responses from nearly 90 unique universities and institutions of the EEG, MEG, and ECoG communities. The poll show that the top 80% of responses for which format they used for ECoG signals are: eeglab (.set), elekta (.fif), european data format (.edf) and fieldtrip (.mat). Results indicate as well that .mat is the format most respondents would be willing to share files, followed by .set and .edf, as it is likely the format they're already utilizing. This coincides with our findings, as was previously shown in Fig. 3(B).

In the case of researchers aiming to create new public datasets, we encourage the use of the Neurodata Without Borders structure formulated by Teeter et al. [46], made specifically to address the problem of heterogeneous metadata and format.

5.2   Selecting Neuronal Open Access Data Sources

While a search engine for datasets[2] has been recently developed, we identified the challenge that datasets may be difficult to locate without the correct keywords or prior knowledge of the available repositories. As there can be many possible search results regardless of the input, the search through large quantities of datasets and repositories in hopes to find a useful one can result in newcomers being put off.

Even after locating datasets that include the information of interest, difficulties arise. Through our research for this article, we found that common quality problems of open datasets are not having sufficient data, possessing missing or duplicate values, that the format of the data is not easy to manipulate, having to match and standardize data when using multiple sources, that the database is poorly structured and the lack of metadata, which narrows down the list of possible options substantially.

Regarding metadata, in a few of the datasets we inspected it was only found within published papers which laid behind paywalls. So while the data is accessible, the process of acquisition and its explanation are not. This restricts the use of the data by limiting its comprehension, which may lead to data being used for something that it is not intended for.

6   Conclusion

Invasive neuronal recording show promise for understanding the underlying circuits of brain disorders and the development of a broad number of neural interface technologies. This being said, research employing invasive recordings are often limited by the number of subjects and resources available to implement complex experimental protocols. Because of this, open datasets are necessary to advance neuroscience.

---

[1] https://bids.berkeley.edu/news/bids-megeegieeg-data-format-survey.
[2] https://datasetsearch.research.google.com/.

Given the success of machine learning tools in the analysis of neuronal signals, shared data can be used for the validation of published methodologies, creating a testbed to find a new state-of-the-art, or by means of breakthrough findings rendered possible by combined resources that outweigh the capacities of independent labs or even institutional projects. However, the datasets may suffer from poor quality, lack standardized structure and contents, provide no direct benefit to the proprietary researchers, and other difficulties that may hinder their use.

In this paper we have presented a curated list of open invasive neuronal signals datasets, given their under-representation. We have outlined the many challenges that have risen with this modality, which have also been pointed out by other authors in the field. We expect this work to function as a practical reference for those interested to access this type of data to develop an approach via machine learning.

References

1. Acharya, U.R., et al.: Automated EEG analysis of epilepsy: a review. Knowl. Based Syst. **45**, 147–165 (2013)
2. Ali, H.M., Kaiser, M.S., Mahmud, M.: Application of convolutional neural network in segmenting brain regions from MRI data. In: Liang, P., Goel, V., Shan, C. (eds.) BI 2019. LNCS, vol. 11976, pp. 136–146. Springer, Cham (2019). https://doi.org/10.1007/978-3-030-37078-7_14
3. Amari, S.I., et al.: Neuroinformatics: the integration of shared databases and tools towards integrative neuroscience. J. Integr. Neurosci. **1**(02), 117–128 (2002)
4. Bernert, M., Yvert, B.: An attention-based spiking neural network for unsupervised spike-sorting. Int. J. Neural Syst. **29**(08), 1850059 (2019). https://doi.org/10.5281/zenodo.888977
5. Chandravadia, N., et al.: A NWB-based dataset and processing pipeline of human single-neuron activity during a declarative memory task. Sci. Data **7**(1), 1–12 (2020). https://doi.org/10.17605/OSF.IO/HV7JA
6. Chao, Z.C., Nagasaka, Y., Fujii, N.: Long-term asynchronous decoding of arm motion using electrocorticographic signals in monkey. Front. Neuroeng. (2010). http://neurotycho.org/food-tracking-task. Accessed 14 June 2020
7. Cimbalnik, J., et al.: Physiological and pathological high frequency oscillations in focal epilepsy. Ann. Clin. Transl. Neurol. **5**(9), 1062–1076 (2018). https://doi.org/10.1002/acn3.618
8. Deweese, M.R., Zador, A.M.: Whole cell recordings from neurons in the primary auditory cortex of rat in response to pure tones of different frequency and amplitude, along with recordings of nearby local field potential (LFP) (2011). https://doi.org/10.6080/K0G44N6R
9. Ellenrieder, N., et al.: How the human brain sleeps: direct cortical recordings of normal brain activity. Ann. Neurol. **87**(2), 289–301 (2019). https://doi.org/10.1002/ana.25651
10. Fabietti, M., et al.: Neural network-based artifact detection in local field potentials recorded from chronically implanted neural probes. In: Proceedings of IJCNN, pp. 1–8 (2020)

11. Ferguson, A.R., et al.: Big data from small data: data-sharing in the 'long tail' of neuroscience. Nat. Neurosci. **17**(11), 1442–1447 (2014)
12. Furth, K.: Replication data for: neuronal correlates of ketamine and walking induced gamma oscillations in the medial prefrontal cortex and mediodorsal thalamus (2017). https://doi.org/10.7910/DVN/MIBZLZ
13. Hardwicke, T.E., et al.: Data availability, reusability, and analytic reproducibility: evaluating the impact of a mandatory open data policy at the journal cognition. Roy. Soc. Open Sci. **5**(8), 180448 (2018)
14. Henin, S., et al.: Hippocampal gamma predicts associative memory performance as measured by acute and chronic intracranial EEG. Sci. Rep. **9**(1), 1–10 (2019)
15. KDnuggets: Amazing consistency: largest dataset analyzed/data mined - poll results and trends. https://www.kdnuggets.com/amazing-consistency-largest-dataset-analyzed-data-mined-poll-results-and-trends.html/. Accessed 14 June 2020
16. Maguire, Y.G., et al.: Physical principles for scalable neural recording. Front. Comput. Neurosci. **7**, 137 (2013)
17. Mahmud, M., Cecchetto, C., Vassanelli, S.: An automated method for characterization of evoked single-trial local field potentials recorded from rat barrel cortex under mechanical whisker stimulation. Cogn. Comput. **8**(5), 935–945 (2016). https://doi.org/10.1007/s12559-016-9399-3
18. Mahmud, M., Girardi, S., Maschietto, M., Vassanelli, S.: An automated method to remove artifacts induced by microstimulation in local field potentials recorded from rat somatosensory cortex. In: Proceedings of BRC, pp. 1–4 (2012). https://doi.org/10.1109/BRC.2012.6222169
19. Mahmud, M., Girardi, S., Maschietto, M., Rahman, M.M., Bertoldo, A., Vassanelli, S.: Slow stimulus artifact removal through peak-valley detection of neuronal signals recorded from somatosensory cortex by high resolution brain-chip interface. In: Dössel, O., Schlegel, W.C. (eds.) World Congress on Medical Physics and Biomedical Engineering. IFMBE, vol. 25/4, pp. 2062–2065. Springer, Heidelberg (2009). https://doi.org/10.1007/978-3-642-03882-2_547
20. Mahmud, M., Kaiser, M.S., McGinnity, T.M., Hussain, A.: Deep learning in mining biological data. arXiv:2003.00108, pp. 1–36, February 2020
21. Mahmud, M., Kaiser, M.S., Hussain, A., Vassanelli, S.: Applications of deep learning and reinforcement learning to biological data. IEEE Trans. Neural Netw. Learn. Syst. **29**(6), 2063–2079 (2018)
22. Mahmud, M., Vassanelli, S.: Processing and analysis of multichannel extracellular neuronal signals: state-of-the-art and challenges. Front. Neurosci. **10**, 248 (2016)
23. Mahmud, M., Vassanelli, S.: Open-source tools for processing and analysis of in vitro extracellular neuronal signals. In: Chiappalone, M., Pasquale, V., Frega, M. (eds.) In Vitro Neuronal Networks: From Culturing Methods to Neuro-Technological Applications. AN, vol. 22, pp. 233–250. Springer, Cham (2019). https://doi.org/10.1007/978-3-030-11135-9_10
24. Mazzoni, A., Logothetis, N.K., Panzeri, S.: The information content of local field potentials: experiments and models (2012)
25. Miah, Y., Prima, C.N.E., Seema, S.J., Mahmud, M., Kaiser, M.S.: Performance comparison of machine learning techniques in identifying dementia from open access clinical datasets. In: Proceedings of ICACIn, pp. 69–78. Springer, Singapore (2020)
26. Milan, J.D.R., Carmena, J.M.: Invasive or noninvasive: understanding brain-machine interface technology [conversations in BME]. IEEE Eng. Med. Biol. Mag. **29**(1), 16–22 (2010)

27. Nejedly, P.: Multicenter intracranial EEG dataset (2019). https://www.kaggle.com/nejedlypetr/multicenter-intracranial-eeg-dataset. Accessed 14 June 2020
28. Neurotycho: neurotycho - emotional movie task (2016). http://neurotycho.org/emotional-movie-task. Accessed 14 June 2020
29. Neurotycho: neurotycho - fixation task (2016). http://neurotycho.org/fixation-task. Accessed 14 June 2020
30. Neurotycho: neurotycho - visual grating task (2016). http://neurotycho.org/visual-grating-task. Accessed 14 June 2020
31. Noor, M.B.T., Zenia, N.Z., Kaiser, M.S., Mahmud, M., Al Mamun, S.: Detecting neurodegenerative disease from MRI a brief review on a deep learning perspective. In: Liang, P., Goel, V., Shan, C. (eds.) BI 2019. LNCS, pp. 115–125. Springer, Cham (2019). https://doi.org/10.1007/978-3-030-37078-7_12
32. Norman, Y., et al.: Data related to the article: "hippocampal sharp-wave ripples linked to visual episodic recollection in humans" (2019). https://doi.org/10.5281/ZENODO.3259369
33. Oosugi, N., et al.: A new method for quantifying the performance of EEG blind source separation algorithms by referencing a simultaneously recorded ECoG signal. Neural Netw. **93**, 1–6, September 2017. http://neurotycho.org/eeg-and-ecog-simultaneous-recording. Accessed 14 June 2020
34. Pala, A., Petersen, C.C.: Data set for "state-dependent cell-type-specific membrane potential dynamics and unitary synaptic inputs in awake mice" (2018). https://doi.org/10.5281/ZENODO.1304771
35. Pearson, J.M., et al.: Data from: local fields in human subthalamic nucleus track the lead-up to impulsive choices (2018). https://doi.org/10.5061/DRYAD.54TP8Q5
36. Perrenoud, Q., Pennartz, C.M.A., Gentet, L.J.: Data from: membrane potential dynamics of spontaneous and visually evoked gamma activity in v1 of awake mice (2016). https://doi.org/10.5061/DRYAD.4754J
37. Petersen, P.C., Hernandez, M., Buzsaki, G.: Public data repository with electrophysiological datasets collected in the Buzsaki lab (2018). https://doi.org/10.5281/ZENODO.3629881
38. Project, E.: European epilepsy database (2007). http://epilepsy-database.eu. Accessed 14 June 2020
39. Project, R.: Restoring Active Memory (RAM) (2018). http://memory.psych.upenn.edu/RAM. Accessed 14 June 2020
40. Rabby, G., Azad, S., Mahmud, M., Zamli, K.Z., Rahman, M.M.: Teket: a tree-based unsupervised keyphrase extraction technique. Cogn. Comput. **12**, 811–833 (2020). https://doi.org/10.1007/s12559-019-09706-3
41. Romero, M.C., Davare, M., Armendariz, M., Janssen, P.: Neural effects of transcranial magnetic stimulation at the single-cell level. Nat. Commun. **10**(1), 1–11 (2019). https://doi.org/10.5061/dryad.g54381n
42. Schalk, G., Leuthardt, E.C.: Brain-computer interfaces using electrocorticographic signals. IEEE Rev. Biomed. Eng. **4**, 140–154 (2011)
43. Sederberg, A.J., Pala, A., Zheng, H.J.V., He, B.J., Stanley, G.B.: Data from: state-aware detection of sensory stimuli in the cortex of the awake mouse (2019). https://doi.org/10.5061/DRYAD.46CG87C
44. Shimoda, K., Nagasaka, Y., Chao, Z.C., Fujii, N.: Decoding continuous three-dimensional hand trajectories from epidural electrocorticographic signals in Japanese macaques. J. Neural Eng. **9**(3), 036015, May 2012. http://neurotycho.org/epidural-ecog-food-tracking-task. Accessed 14 June 2020
45. Shin, H., et al.: Data from: the rate of transient beta frequency events predicts behavior across tasks and species (2017). https://doi.org/10.5061/DRYAD.PN931

46. Teeters, J.L., et al.: Neurodata without borders: creating a common data format for neurophysiology. Neuron **88**(4), 629–634 (2015)
47. Teeters, J.L., et al.: Data sharing for computational neuroscience. Neuroinformatics **6**(1), 47–55 (2008). https://doi.org/10.1007/s12021-008-9009-y
48. Temko, A., Sarkar, A., Lightbody, G.: Detection of seizures in intracranial EEG: UPenn and mayo clinic's seizure detection challenge. In: Proceedings of EMBC, pp. 6582–6585 (2015). https://www.kaggle.com/c/seizure-detection. Accessed 14 June 2020
49. Theodoni, P., Rovira, B., Wang, Y., Roxin, A.: Data from: theta-modulation drives the emergence of connectivity patterns underlying replay in a network model of place cells (2018). https://doi.org/10.5061/DRYAD.N9C1RB0
50. Toda, H., et al.: Simultaneous recording of ECoG and intracortical neuronal activity using a flexible multichannel electrode-mesh in visual cortex (2011). http://brainliner.jp/data/brainliner/Rat_Eye_Stimulation. Accessed 14 June 2020
51. Vassanelli, S., Mahmud, M.: Trends and challenges in neuroengineering: toward "intelligent" neuroprostheses through brain-"brain inspired systems" communication. Front. Neurosci. **10**, 438 (2016)
52. Wagenaar, J.B., et al.: Collaborating and sharing data in epilepsy research. J. Clin. Neurophysiol. **32**(3), 235 (2015)
53. Waldert, S.: Invasive vs. non-invasive neuronal signals for brain-machine interfaces: will one prevail? Front. Neurosci. **10**, 295 (2016)
54. Watkins, J., Fabietti, M., Mahmud, M.: Sense: a student performance quantifier using sentiment analysis. In: Proceedings of IJCNN, pp. 1–6 (2020)
55. Watson, B., Levenstein, D., Greene, J., Gelinas, J., Buzsáki, G.: Multi-unit spiking activity recorded from rat frontal cortex (brain regions mPFC, OFC, ACC, and M2) during wake-sleep episode wherein at least 7 minutes of wake are followed by 20 minutes of sleep. CRCNS.org (2016). https://doi.org/10.6080/K02N506Q
56. Whittington, M., Adams, N., Hawkins, K., Hall, S.: 32 channel field array recording of V1 alpha rhythm in vitro (2020). https://doi.org/10.6084/m9.figshare.11762508.v1
57. Wollstadt, P., et al.: Data from: breakdown of local information processing may underlie isoflurane anesthesia effects (2018). https://doi.org/10.5061/DRYAD.KK40S
58. Yahaya, S.W., Lotfi, A., Mahmud, M.: A consensus novelty detection ensemble approach for anomaly detection in activities of daily living. Appl. Soft Comput. **83**, 105613 (2019)
59. Zeldenrust, F., Chameau, P., Wadman, W.J.: Spike and burst coding in thalamocortical relay cells. PLoS Comput. Biol. **14**(2), e1005960 (2018). https://data.donders.ru.nl/collections/di/dcn/DSC_626840_0002_144?4. Accessed 14 June 2020

Automatic Detection of Epileptic Waves in Electroencephalograms Using Bag of Visual Words and Machine Learning

Marlen Sofía Muñoz[1] , Camilo Ernesto Sarmiento Torres[1] ,
Diego M. López[2(✉)] , Ricardo Salazar-Cabrera[2] ,
and Rubiel Vargas-Cañas[1]

[1] Physics Department, Universidad del Cauca, Calle 5 #4-70, 190003 Popayán,
Cauca, Colombia
{marlensm, csarmiento, rubiel}@unicauca.edu.co
[2] Telematics Department, Universidad del Cauca, Calle 5 #4-70,
190003 Popayán, Cauca, Colombia
{dmlopez, ricardosalazarc}@unicauca.edu.co

Abstract. Epilepsy is one of the most recurrent brain disorders worldwide and mainly affects children. As a diagnostic support, the electroencephalogram is used, which is relatively easy to apply but requires a long time to analyze. Automatic EEG analysis presents difficulties both in the construction of the database and in the extracted characteristics used to build models. This article a machine learning-based methodology that uses a visual word bag of raw EEG images as input to identify images with abnormal signals. The performance introduces of the algorithms was tested using a proprietary pediatric EEG database. Accuracy greater than 95% was achieved, with calculation times less than 0.01 s per image. Therefore, the paper demonstrates the feasibility of using machine learning algorithms to directly analyze EEG images.

Keywords: Childhood epilepsy · Feature extraction and selection · Supervised classification · Visual categorization · Semantic categorization

1 Introduction

Epilepsy is one of the most recurrent chronic brain diseases worldwide [1]. It has an idiopathic origin, although it is believed to be caused by one of many causes, such as genetic origins, perinatal or prenatal injuries, brain, and congenital malformations and/or brain infections [2]. Epilepsy is characterized by abnormalities in brain electrical activity, generating unexpected, irregular, or involuntary movements of the muscles or other manifestations such as increases in body temperature above 38 °C. In children, it generally manifests for a first time from one month to six years [3] and can lead to loss of consciousness. Depending on the period of each convolution, abnormalities can have serious consequences, such as brain injuries, alterations in the neural network or even deaths [3]. Epilepsy is a disease that mainly affects the child population: 10.5 million

© Springer Nature Switzerland AG 2020
M. Mahmud et al. (Eds.): BI 2020, LNAI 12241, pp. 163–172, 2020.
https://doi.org/10.1007/978-3-030-59277-6_15

children in the world suffer epilepsy [4] with negatively involvement in the emotional, behavioral, and social aspects of their lives [5].

Approximately 75% of the population suffering the disease live a healthy life, as it can be controlled with early administration of antiepileptic drugs [3], or through pediatric epilepsy surgery [5]. Therefore, early detection is critical in children to improve their quality of life. Diagnosis of the disease is mainly based on clinical records and, when more than two unprovoked seizures appear [1], the neurologist confirms the case with the help of the electroencephalogram (EEG). The EEG shows brain activity through electrodes placed in the scalp's area, using the protocol of the international system 10–20 [6]. However, neurologists or specialized healthcare professional require a great deal of time reading the EEG. This affects the early detection of the disease, mainly in developing countries, where there is a lack of trained healthcare specialist [2].

Although EEG is relatively easy to implement and at affordable cost solution, it has drawbacks when reading and analyzing it, because interpretation is performed by direct visual inspection, which is a slow and time-consuming task [7]. In this regard, there are proposals for EEG automatic analysis, most of which are adaptations of techniques used in cardiology [8]. However, EEG signals represent a challenge, due to the large number of channels that are used, the low amplitude per channel, and the non-stationarity of each channel in the signal [9]. Because of these problems, many of the analytical tools used in EEG studies have used machine learning to discover relevant information in neuronal analysis, classification, and neuroimaging. The studies carried out, according to the input data, can be classified into three types of categories: those that use the signal values for each channel (39%), those that use characteristics calculated from the channel to compute descriptors and properties for a specific event (41%) and those which use images, mathematical transformations are applied to the signal to convert it into an image (20%) [10].

A restriction on the use of machine learning methods, regardless of the type of data used for the analysis, is the limited availability of a large volume of EEG records. To solve this, many proposals have tried to apply these techniques with publicly available databases [9]. However, these databases mostly contain adult EEGs recorded in intensive care units [11]. Besides, their annotations correspond to the complete record, and do not include annotations of specific segments. Regarding the type of data, almost half of the proposals extract characteristics of each signal/channel such as spectral density or statistical measurements, often analyzed in the frequency domain [10]. Proposals that use images generally transform the signal, or one of its attributes, into an image such as a spectrogram that is then used in the analysis [12]. This paper reports a methodology based on machine learning that uses the image of an EEG page as input. A bag of visual words, extracted from this image, feeds a classification algorithm to identify images (pages) with abnormal signals. The methodology was tested using a pediatric EEG database collected and annotated in the development of the project "NeuroMoTIC: system for the diagnostic support of epilepsy" [13, 16].

The rest of this paper is divided into three more sections: section two shows the details of collecting EEGs, obtaining the visual word bag, and the algorithm performance evaluation protocol. Section three presents the results obtained in each stage of the methodology. Finally, section four discusses the results, concludes this article, and presents some guidelines for future work.

2   Materials and Methods

The implemented methodology consists of four stages (Fig. 1). In the first one, the data set was collected and annotated. Then, in a preprocessing stage, each EEG page (the images) was segmented, and the visual characteristics were extracted from them. Later, in the modeling stage, several classification models were trained, and the model with the best performance in the training stage was selected. Finally, in the evaluation stage, the performance of the model was estimated with images of new patients.

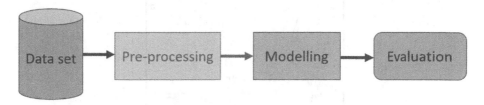

Fig. 1. Block diagram of the methodology used.

2.1   Acquisition of Encephalograms

The dataset was constructed from EEG tests performed on 100 children, aged between one month and 17 years old, with suspected epilepsy. This compilation was carried out as part of the NeuroMoTIC project. The project's objective was to propose and create a system that allows the collection, management, and classification of clinical information and EEG signals to support the diagnosis of epilepsy [13].

Data collection was carried out in compliance with the Declaration of Helsinki, with bioethical standards, obtaining informed consent for each EEG record, which were approved by the Ethics Committee of the University of Cauca, Colombia.

The device used in the acquisition was the BWII EEG with Neurovirtual BWII Analysis software (https://neurovirtual.com/). The EEG was recorded following the 10–20 standard and a sampling frequency of 200 Hz, with a 50/60 Hz filter and digital filter provided by the manufacturer's software. The exams were taken at the premises of the healthcare provider AXON PED S.A.S by a specialized technician. The duration of each exam was 30 min and was interpreted and annotated by a pediatric neurologist, who read it page by page and made different annotations that describe the observed events, i.e. the name of the event, the duration, and the channel where it was recorded (Table 1).

Table 1. Sample annotations for an electroencephalography exam.

Exam 1			
Event	Channel	Time	Observation
Poly-pikes	FP1-F7	3 s	Abnormality

The events were divided into normal and abnormal. The normal exams contained signs of patients without epilepsy, both in wakefulness and in sleep. The abnormal signals presented four different types of patterns (Fig. 2): sharp waves, spikes, poly-pikes, and spikes with slow-wave spikes.

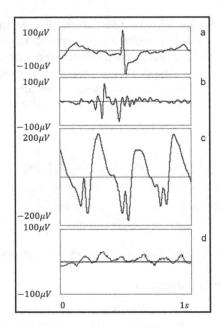

Fig. 2. Set of abnormalities considered in the study, a) spikes, b) poly-pikes, c) spikes with slow-waves, and d) normal.

2.2   Image Pre-processing

In this stage, we adapted and standardized the set of collected signals to implement it in the modeling stage. First, all EEGs were converted to the *edf* format (European Data Format) and stored using the device configuration of AXON PED S.A.S. according to the 10–20 standard. Subsequently, we selected the exam visualization tool, which was the software named EDFBrowser (https://www.teuniz.net/edfbrowser/). This tool is a free, open-source, multiplatform, universal viewer, capable of displaying time series such as EEG, EMG, ECG, among others. Besides, it has a set of different tools to interact and modify the display parameters in a user-friendly manner (Table 2).

Dataset Partition. The data set was divided into two parts. First, a training dataset with the EEG images of 70% of the patients. Second, a test dataset with the EEG images of the 30% of the remaining patients. Data partition was randomly performed.

Feature Extraction and Selection. To extract the visual vocabulary from each image package, we used the visual categorization technique of key points bag proposed in [14]. To do this, we create a visual vocabulary of 500 words. This method was based on the construction of a vector of semantic descriptors invariant to rotation and translation, taken from different parts of the images. We performed a semantic classification using two classifiers, Naïve Bayes and a Vector Support Machine (SVM), which, according to the authors, is robust for disorganized backgrounds without making use of geometric information.

Table 2. Display parameters for capturing each image.

Parameters	Description
Timeline	10 s/page
Amplitude	100 μV
Background	White
Axes	Hidden
Channels	19
Channel nomenclature	Visible
Electrooculogram	Visible
Electrocardiogram	Visible
Tonality	Blue
Edges and software interface	Hidden

2.3 Modeling

In the modeling stage, we tested 24 supervised classification algorithms for which we adjusted and varied their different parameters. We select the model with the best performance in the training stage, in terms of average accuracy. Some of the varied settings were:

- Cross-validation: the value of the folds varied between 5 and 15.
- K-nearest neighbor (KNN): the Euclidean distance was applied, and k varied from 3 to 10.
- Support Vector Machine: two types of kernel were applied, linear and polynomial with the degree of the polynomial varied from 2 to 5.
- Assembly of Classifiers: the size of the subspaces varied from 1 to 4.

2.4 Performance Evaluation

In this stage, we evaluated the best model from different performance indices, using the k-fold method with cross-validation, because this test guarantees that the results are independent of the partitions between training and testing datasets [15].

Using the test set, we calculated the confusion matrix, and later the following indices were derived: Accuracy, Sensitivity, Specificity, Precision, F1-Score and Matthews Correlation Coefficient (CCM).

3   Results and Discussion

This section presents the results obtained in each of the stages proposed in the methodology.

3.1   Dataset

A total of 100 EEG tests were collected with a duration of 30 min each. Besides, interpretation and annotations were performed with the follow-up of a pediatric neurologist, and the main characteristics of the patients contained in the dataset were identified. The data was divided into demographic data and the conclusion of the diagnostic test, i.e., abnormal, or normal (Table 3).

Table 3. Patient Demographics

Number of patients	Min. age	Max. age	Mean age	Gender		Conclusion
				M	F	
34	24 days	14 years	5, 86 years	21	13	Abnormal
66	22 days	17 years	6, 6 years	39	27	Normal

3.2   Pre-processing

In total, 401 images were obtained in jpg format with 1920 × 906 pixels, where the acquired signals were grouped into normal and abnormal (Fig. 3).

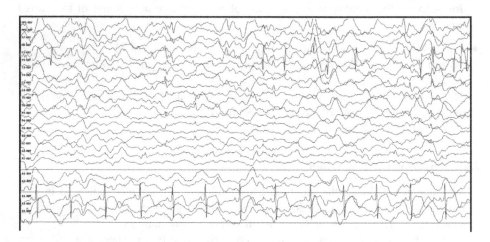

Fig. 3. Example of an EEG page annotated as abnormal.

Likewise, the abnormal category consisted of sharp waves, spikes, poly-pikes, and spikes with slow-waves, 166 images of abnormalities were collected in total (Table 4).

Table 4. Dataset composition according to diagnosis.

EEG	No. patients	EEG pages
Normal	66	235
Abnormal	34	166

Each EEG page was represented with a vector containing a bag of 500 visual words (Fig. 4). The visual word vector set was used as input for the classification stage.

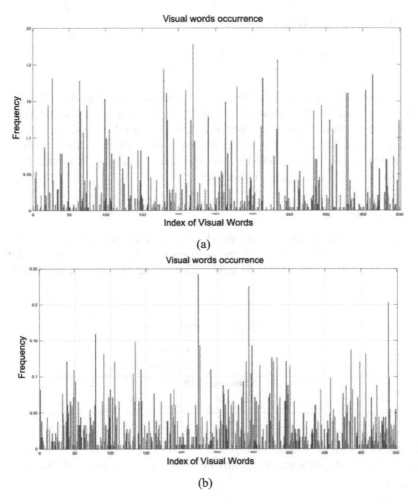

(a)

(b)

Fig. 4. Examples of the occurrence of visual words for an EEG page with abnormalities (a) and a normal one (b).

3.3   Modeling

At this stage, 24 classifiers were compared and to assure the best performance, their parameters were varied as stated in Sect. 2.3. Table 5 shows the results of the top five, according to their performance in the training stage.

Table 5. Training results of the five best classifiers.

Classifier	Configuration	Accuracy (%)	Precision (%)	Recall (%)
Assemble	Two KNN subspaces.	96.8	96.8	95.2
SVM	Quadratic Kernel	92.0	91.8	87.7
SVM	Cubic Kernel	91.2	91.2	87.0
KNN	k = 3	91.2	91.2	87.0
SVM	Linear Kernel	90.0	90.4	85.6

For the assembly of classifiers, the cross-validation method with $k = 10$ was used in their training, because this method guarantees that the results are independent of the partition of the data and got higher performance. On the other hand, the cubic kernel vector support machine (SVM) ranked third having the same classification performance as the KNN. However, the SVM's computational cost was less than the KNN, 0.0007 s/page vs. 0.0014 s/page, respectively.

3.4   Evaluation

According to the data in Table 5, the best classifier was the assembly of classifiers with the k-folds method. With this model, the performance was estimated thought test data set, the confusion matrix (Table 6) was obtained and the indices derived from it (Table 7).

Table 6. Confusion matrix for test data.

		Prediction	
		Abnormal	Normal
True class	**Abnormal**	40	1
	Normal	3	38

This data set allowed determining that the model is capable of generalizing and estimating its good performance against new data that was not implemented in the training stage.

Table 7. Performance indices obtained from the confusion matrix.

Index	Value (%)
Sensitivity/recall	93.0
Specificity	97.4
Precision	97.5
Accuracy	95.1
F1 score	95.2
MCC	90.3

4 Conclusions

This work's main contribution is a methodology capable of detecting and identifying EEG pages with different abnormalities that are useful for diagnosing epilepsy. These abnormalities include sharp waves, spikes, poly-pikes, and spikes with slow-waves. Also, a novel approach based on digital image processing and machine vision was introduced, which has a methodological advantage as it is an alternative to classic signal processing. It also saves the feature engineering process that was applied in other approaches to EEG signals. The methodology's performance reached an average accuracy of over 95%, demonstrating the feasibility of analyzing electroencephalograms using the images directly.

The direct use of EEG images with complex algorithms such as deep learning algorithms is proposed as future work. Moreover, this methodology needs to be tested in other databases with which comparisons can be made. Finally, after complying with the previous steps, this methodology can be adapted to be implemented in a clinical setting for the semi-automatic detection of epilepsy. Furthermore, the proposed method is expected to have a major impact on the diagnosis and treatment of epilepsy patients, for example, in low-income countries with high patient volumes and regions with limitations in the provision of neurology services.

Acknowledgment. This work was funded by the Colombian Agency for Science, Technology, and Innovation - COLCIENCIAS - in call 715-2015, "Call for Research and Development Projects in Engineering" Project "NeuroMoTIC: Mobile System for Diagnostic Support of Epilepsy," contract number FP44842-154-2016.

References

1. Perucca, P., Scheffer, I.E., Kiley, M.: The management of epilepsy in children and adults. Med. J. Aust. **208**(5), 226–233 (2018)
2. World Health Assembly, 68. Global burden of epilepsy and the need for coordinated action at the country level to address its health, social, and public knowledge implications: report by the Secretariat. World Health Organization, https://apps.who.int/iris/handle/10665/252840. Accessed 10 June 2020
3. Minardi, C., et al.: Epilepsy in children: from diagnosis to treatment with focus on emergency. J. Clin. Med. **8**(1), 39 (2019)

4. Guerrini, R.: Epilepsy in children. Lancet **367**(9509), 499–524 (2006)
5. Reilly, C., Hallböök, T., Viggedal, G., Rydenhag, B., Uvebrant, P., Olsson, I.: Parent reported health related quality of life (HRQoL) and behaviour in young people with epilepsy before and two years after epilepsy surgery. Seizure **74**, 1–7 (2020)
6. Alotaiby, T.N., Alshebeili, S.A., Alotaibi, F.M., Alrshoud, S.R.: Epileptic seizure prediction using CSP and LDA for scalp EEG signals. Comput. Intell. Neurosci. **2017**, 1–11 (2017)
7. Ullah, I., Hussain, M.Y., Aboalsamh, H.: An automated system for epilepsy detection using EEG brain signals based on deep learning approach. Expt. Sys. App. **107**, 61–71 (2018)
8. Uys, P.J.: Image classification from EEG brain signals using machine learning and deep learning techniques. MSc Thesis. Stellenbosch University, South Africa (2019)
9. Merlin Praveena, D., Angelin Sarah, D., Thomas George, S.: Deep learning techniques for EEG signal applications–a review. IETE J. Res. 1–8 (2020)
10. Craik, A., He, Y., Contreras-Vidal, J.L.: Deep learning for electroencephalogram (EEG) classification tasks: a review. J. Neural Eng. **16**(3), 031001 (2019)
11. Acharya, U.R., Oh, S.L., Hagiwara, Y., Tan, J.H., Adeli, H.: Deep convolutional neural network for the automated detection and diagnosis of seizure using EEG signals. Comput. Biol. Med. **100**, 270–278 (2018)
12. Jiao, Z., Gao, X., Wang, Y., Li, J., Xu, H.: Deep convolutional neural networks for mental load classification based on EEG data. Pattern Recognit. **76**, 582–595 (2018)
13. Molina, E., Sarmiento Torres, C.E., Salazar-Cabrera, R., López, D.M., Vargas-Cañas, R.: Intelligent telehealth system to support epilepsy diagnosis. J. Multi. Healthc. **13**, 433–445 (2020)
14. Fan, C.D., Bray, W.: Visual categorization with bags of keypoints. In: Workshop on statistical learning in computer vision, ECCV, vol. 1, pp. 1–2 (2004)
15. Refaeilzadeh, P., Tang, L., Liu, H.: Cross-Validation Encyclopedia of database systems. Arizona State University, Springer, USA (2009)
16. Mera, M., López, D.M., Vargas-Cañas, R., Mino, M.: Epileptic spikes detector in pediatric EEG based on matched filters and neural networks. Brain Inform. **7**, 1–10 (2020)

UPDRS Label Assignment by Analyzing Accelerometer Sensor Data Collected from Conventional Smartphones

Md. Sakibur Rahman Sajal[1,2]([✉]) [iD], Md. Tanvir Ehsan[1,2] [iD],
Ravi Vaidyanathan[3] [iD], Shouyan Wang[4] [iD], Tipu Aziz[5] [iD],
and Khondaker A. Mamun[1,2] [iD]

[1] United International University (UIU), Dhaka, Bangladesh
sakibur@cse.uiu.ac.bd
[2] Advanced Intelligent Multidisciplinary Systems Lab (AIMS Lab),
Institute of Advanced Research, United International University, Dhaka, Bangladesh
[3] Imperial College London, London, UK
[4] Fudan University, Shanghai, People's Republic of China
[5] University of Oxford, Oxford, UK

Abstract. The study of the characteristics of hand tremors of the patients suffering from Parkinson's disease (PD) offers an effective way to detect and assess the stage of the disease's progression. During the semi-quantitative evaluation, neurologists label the PD patients with any of the (0–4) Unified Parkinson's Diseases Rating Scale (UPDRS) score based on the intensity and prevalence of these tremors. This score can be bolstered by some other modes of assessment as like gait analysis to increase the reliability of PD detection. With the availability of conventional smartphones with a built-in accelerometer sensor, it is possible to acquire the 3-axes tremor and gait data very easily and analyze them by a trained algorithm. Thus we can remotely examine the PD patients from their homes and connect them to trained neurologists if required. The objective of this study was to investigate the usability of smartphones for assessing motor impairments (i.e. tremors and gait) that can be analyzed from accelerometer sensor data. We obtained 98.5% detection accuracy and 91% UPDRS labeling accuracy for 52 PD patients and 20 healthy subjects. The result of this study indicates a great promise for developing a remote system to detect, monitor, and prescribe PD patients over long distances. It will be a tremendous help for the older population in developing countries where access to a trained neurologist is very limited. Also, in a pandemic situation like COVID-19, patients from developed countries can be benefited from such a home-oriented PD detection and monitoring system.

Keywords: Parkinson's disease · Tremor and gait analysis · UPDRS label · Accelerometer sensor · Machine learning

This project was funded by the innovation fund of ICT division, Ministry of Posts, Telecommunications and Information Technology, People Republic of Bangladesh

© Springer Nature Switzerland AG 2020
M. Mahmud et al. (Eds.): BI 2020, LNAI 12241, pp. 173–182, 2020.
https://doi.org/10.1007/978-3-030-59277-6_16

1   Introduction

Parkinson's disease (PD) is one of the most concerning neurological disorders after Alzheimer's disease for the elderly population around the world [1]. People aging over 65 years are more likely to fall victim to PD that does not have any permanent remedy yet. While global statistics show that the number of PD patients is increasing rapidly every year, authentic data are not available for an underdeveloped country like Bangladesh [2]. However, it has been roughly estimated that around 1600 people in Bangladesh die while many more suffer from this illness every year [3]. Still, we do not have adequate resources to detect and support these patients with continuous monitoring.

The most obvious symptoms of PD are tremor, rigidity, slowness of movement, difficulty with walking, and gait impairments caused by the loss of nerve cells that produce a chemical call dopamine [4]. Among all of these symptoms, tremor significantly affects the activities of daily life and the mainstay of treatment for it is medication [5]. However, the dose of the medicine prescribed for the patients needs to be adjusted based on the disease's progression for which a patient might need to be routinely checked which might not be possible for the people of an underdeveloped country like Bangladesh.

Telemonitoring could be an effective alternative to remotely assess the symptoms of PD patients for detecting and monitoring the progression of this disease in underdeveloped countries. Especially in the time of pandemic situations like in COVID-19, in-person health checks might not be accessible even in the well-developed countries as well. To develop a home-oriented assessment system, many researchers have studied and proposed different frameworks in the past decade. Among these works, tremor and gait impairment analysis gained significant interest. However, some of the data collection devices or setups are not feasible to be accessed by the rural population both in the developed and underdeveloped countries.

Therefore, in this study, we have focused on tremor and gait data collection by the accelerometer sensor which is very common in today's conventional smartphones. We have developed a mobile application that records the data from a suspected PD patient and uploads it to the cloud where the feature extraction and analysis is performed. After the result generation, the patient is notified about his/her disease status according to the Unified Parkinson's Diseases Rating Scale (UPDRS) revised by Movement Disorder Society (MDS) [6]. Also, the patient is connected to a neurologist for a proper recommendation via the same smartphone.

2   Related Works

Almost 75% of PD patients exhibit tremors during rest or action [7]. Classically, PD tremor is reported as an asymmetric resting tremor (RT) within a frequency range of 4–7 Hz that ceases with volitional movement [8]. However, the author in [5] showed that the frequency of the tremors experienced in Parkinson's disease lies between a slightly broader range of 3–8 Hz. Therefore, most of the studies on tremor analysis focused on this range for feature extraction. Although resting tremor is a positive diagnostic criterion for PD, postural tremor (PT) is also found to be mixed with it in almost 90% cases [9]. Recent work by Bazgir [10] has considered both types of tremors in classifying PD patients with different UPDRS levels for developing a home-monitoring system. There have been other studies on hand tremor acquisition using accelerometer sensors and analysis with computers for remote detection of PD and development of suppressor devices [11–13], however, most of these works did not include any other assessment along with tremor.

Along with the tremor assessment, gait impairments are also evaluated in MDS-UPDRS sub-scales. However, in most cases, gait analysis is performed as a subjective measure. For quantitative measures, researchers looked into different gait impairments throughout the disease's progression such as the reduced amplitude of arm swing and smoothness of locomotion [14], the decrease in speed and step length, increased cadence [15], de-fragmentation of turn and problems with gait initiation [16], freezing of gait and reduced balance [15], etc. To assess these symptoms, non-wearable technologies have been used in many studies [17–19], however, those systems are not feasible to be implemented in the rural house-hold setup and can be costly for most of the people. Even some wearable technologies [20–22] could be expensive though they can generate reliable data for higher accuracy PD detection. Gait analysis from accelerometer sensor data was presented in [23,24] with extensive study. The accelerometer sensors used in these works were worn by the patients during data recording.

A combination of tremor and gait data for PD detection is found in several works as in [25,26]. However, they have used data from different sensors (accelerometer and pressure) for tremor and gait. Therefore, we were interested to use accelerometer sensor data for tremor and gait impairment analysis in a smartphone-based recording framework to make it a feasible and widely accessible system for telemonitoring PD patients.

3 Materials and Methods

We have been actively working for the last five years to develop a telemonitoring system for the people of Bangladesh [27]. As a part of our study, this paper presents a framework on the analysis of accelerometer sensor data collected by conventional smartphones to investigate different motor impairments such as rest tremor, postural tremor, and gait of the suspected PD patients. To collect the data, a smartphone is to be attached to the hand and the leg, respectively, using a moderately tight band for capturing the tremor and gait (see Fig. 1 for data collection procedure).

3.1 Data Collection, Storing and Transfer

During the rest tremor recording, the patient has to sit quietly in a chair and place the arms on a comfortable place (the arms of the chair or on their thighs)

Rest Tremor Capture
(a) Side view (b) Front view

Postural Tremor Capture
(c) Side view (d) Front view

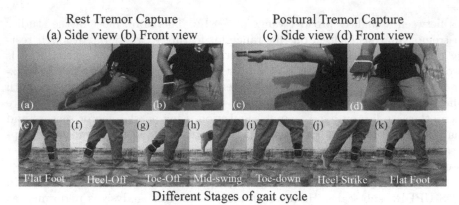

Different Stages of gait cycle

Fig. 1. Data collection procedure: (a–b) rest tremor, (c–d) postural tremor, and (e–k) gait data collection. Data collection protocol was adopted from the guidelines set by International Parkinson and Movement Disorder Society [6]

with a smartphone attached to the arm being examined. The feet should be comfortably supported on the floor for the whole 20 s of data collection (see Fig. 1 (a–b)). Rest tremor can be assessed separately for both hands and both legs, however, the name of the limb has to be mentioned in the data file.

For recording the postural tremor, the patients have to stretch both arms in front of them keeping the smartphone attached to one of the arms under examination (see Fig. 1 (c–d)) and hold this position for 20 s. In case of difficulty, data can be collected for at least 10 s as well.

The same smartphone can be strapped on the leg to collect the gait data of the patient. In this case, the patient is to walk for at least 30 m at a natural pace. For severe walking difficulty, this length can be reduced to 15 m as well. The sensor data will be used to get an insight of the gait characteristics. However, the data collector has to add notes on whether the patient needed any assistance (i.e. walking stick) during data recording. Figure 1 (e–k) shows different stages of the gait cycle which will be assessed from the accelerometer data to predict the presence of PD.

We used HUAWEI Y6 pro which is a very lightweight smartphone (150 g/5.29 oz) with a built-in 3-axes accelerometer sensor for data collection from 20 healthy subjects during development of the system. The sensor has a resolution of $0.0012 \, m/s^2$ with a recording range of $78.4532 \, m/s^2$. The sampling frequency of the mobile application used for data collection was 100 Hz. The acceleration data were recorded in absolute unit (m/s^2) and saved in a .txt files which were later transferred to a laptop for signal processing and analysis using MATLAB 2019b. However, for the purpose of comparison of the proposed system, we used tremor dataset of 52 PD patients collected by [10] using Sony Xperia SP Android smartphone 100 Hz sampling frequency and UPDRS label assigned by the expert neurologists of Hazrat Rasoul Akram Hospital of Tehran. The data collection protocol followed the instructions mentioned in the MDS-UPDRS guideline [6].

3.2   Signal Processing and Feature Extraction

Data Trimming, Detrending, and Filtering. As the beginning and the end of each recorded session might be contaminated by sudden limb movements from the patient (i.e. failing to maintain the posture) or intervention of the data collector (for turning on/off the data recording application), we truncated the first 2 s and the last 3 s from each sample files for increasing the data reliability.

These trimmed signals are usually biased by the orientation of the phone (i.e. acceleration due to gravity in z-axis data) unless data is collected using alternate coupling (AC) mode. Therefore, the raw data is passed through a detrend filter during pre-processing. The detrending is done by eliminating the DC component from the Fourier co-efficient by windowing the total duration of tremor in 200 samples per window without any overlap.

Finally, we used a wavelet filter bank to isolate the region-of-interest (ROIs) frequency bands (0–12.5 Hz for gait analysis, RT & PT) and discarded the noise (high-frequency bands). Debauchies mother wavelet of order 10 was used for a 3 level wavelet decomposition since the sampling frequency was 100 Hz. The approximation and the detailed signal at level 3 were used for feature extraction for gait impairment-rest tremor and postural tremor respectively.

Table 1. UPDRS label based on tremor characteristics and primary features

Label	Amplitude	Ampl. Features	Consistency (%time)	Freq. Features
0	Low (almost 0)	**Avg. Energy**	Inconsistent (almost none)	Rate change of F **Max. energy F**
1	Medium (<1 cm)	Avg. amplitude Variance of P*	Intermittent (<25%)	**Trigger percent***
2	Medium or High (>1 cm, <3 cm)	Mean of P **Rate change of P***	Intermittent (>25%, <50%)	
3	Medium or High (> 3 cm, <10 cm)	Max. amplitude	Continuous (>50%, <75%)	**Mode of F** **Skewness of F**
4	Very High (>10 cm)		Continuous (>75%)	Range of F Variance of F

Choice of Features and Feature Selection. As per the MDS-UPDRS labeling scheme, neurologists assess the quantitative measures of tremor mentioned in Table 1 for assigning scores. Therefore we have chosen the mentioned features primarily (some were used by other researchers while *marked features were introduced by us) for differentiating between different UPDRS levels. The amplitude features were chosen to separate 0, 1/2, and 3/4 as labels 1 and 2, and labels 3 and 4 can pose very subtle distinction during discrimination. Frequency features were chosen for discriminating between 1 and 2, and 3 and 4. Here, F = the dominating frequency in each data window, P = maximum peak value in each window. trigger percent = the rate of recurrence of tremors to detect the intermittent nature of it.

After extraction of these primary features, most informative ones were selected using Minimum Redundancy Maximum Relevance (MRMR) algorithms [28]. Table 1 shows the selected top 6 features (in bold) based on the ranks generated by the algorithm.

Since MDS-UPDRS has prescribed only subjective evaluation for gait and freezing of gait assessment, we adopted the conventional temporal gait features to keep the proposed system computationally simpler (and also because of the fact that we are using accelerometer sensor data only) and implementable using smartphone sensor data (Table 2).

Table 2. Temporal features for gait impairment analysis

Name of the feature	Short definition for the time duration
Gait cycle	Initial contact to initial contact on the same foot
Stance phase	The foot is in contact with the support surface
Swing phase	The foot is airborne
Step duration	2 successive events of the same type on opposite limbs

3.3   Models Training, Optimization and Extraction

Using different supervised machine learning algorithms we primarily selected top three best performing classifiers for PD vs Non-PD detection from the tremor data. Later, the PD positive patients were again classified using new models for 3 levels UPDRS label assignment where label 1 and 2 were merged together and label 3 and 4 were merged together as they had subtle distinction threshold. Finally, another training was performed on the PD positive patients for 5 levels classification for UPDRS labels 0 to 4. All these models were trained using 5-Fold classification and the model parameters were optimized by the machine learning toolbox of MATLAB.

As for the gait analysis, we extracted the feature values from the time domain analysis of the acceleration signal in each of the three axes. Gait cycle = the time difference from Heel Strike (HS) to Heal Strike, Stance Phase = the time difference from HS to Toe-off (TO). Swing phase = the time difference from TO to next HS. Step duration = time difference between HS and Heel off (HO). These are the typical temporal features for assessing different gait phases (see Fig. 1 and the nominal values can be compared with the feature values obtained from the suspected PD patient.

We could have used ML on the temporal feature values from gait analysis, however, we kept this assessment as an alternative to the subjective evaluation of gait according to the guidelines of MDS-UPDRS. Figure 2 shows the different phases of gait on the acceleration sensor data. These phases can be easily identified from the abrupt changes in the acceleration values in the 3-axes.

4   Results

Table 3. Classification accuracy, specificity and sensitivity from the tremor analysis

Used	PD vs Non-PD			3 levels			5 levels		
Classifier	Accu.	Spec.	Sens.	Acc.	Spec.	Sens.	Accu.	Spec	Sens.
kNN	98.5	100	94.0	96.7	99.5	92.5	90.5	96.0	87.5
SVM	96.8	98.0	92.0	94.3	96.5	90.0	87.0	91.0	86.5
Naive Bayes	91.6	95.5	89.5	88.4	92.0	85.5	77.0	72.0	81.5

From the tremor data analysis, we got a maximum of 98.5% accuracy in determining PD vs non-PD (or healthy) using kNN. For SVM and Naive Bayes, the accuracy was 96.8% and 91.6%, respectively as shown in Table 3. The highest specificity and sensitivity were found to be 100% and 94.0%, respectively for kNN. However, when we moved on to 3 levels classification by joining UPDRS levels 1 and 2 together and also joining UPDRS levels 3 and 4 together, the accuracy dropped a little for all the classifiers. The results are shown under the columns of '3 levels' in Table 3. Also, in this case, kNN performed better than SVM and NB with the highest accuracy, specificity, and sensitivity of 96.7%, 99.5%, and 92.5%, respectively.

Finally, for 5 level classifications (UPDRS labels 0 to 4), the accuracy was found to be 90% using kNN while others exhibit below 90% (see Table 3 for details). This time kNN provided the highest specificity and sensitivity of 96.0% and 87.5%, respectively. The subtle difference between UPDRS levels 1 and 2 can be misdiagnosed very easily as in differentiating between levels 3 and 4.

As for the gait analysis, we adopted a very simple approach of temporal features calculation from the gait events on the acceleration sensor data. The gait events are shown in Fig. 2 which can be easily detected from the remarkable changes in the value of acceleration in one or two axes. From the figure, we see that the acceleration in the z-axis was not very prominent since the position of the smartphone aligned the z-axis along the lateral direction (from side to side). During straight walking, this direction does not observe much of an acceleration. The calculated feature values can be compared with the pre-defined ranges for PD and Non-PD patients to support the result (PD positive/negative or severe stage of disease progression) obtained from the hand tremor analysis.

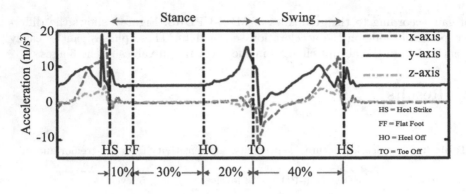

Fig. 2. Different phases and events of gait cycle: the toe-down and heel-down take place in between Toe-off and Heel Strike which is not shown in the figure

5   Discussion

Tremor data collected by smartphones might vary for different hand-sets that vary widely in weights. Also, the elastic band used to attach the phone to the hand might cause irritation or discomfort for some patients if fastened too tightly. This might also cause a variation in the tremor data for those patients. Therefore, an extensive study has to be performed on the same group of patients using mobile phones from various vendors so that detection accuracy variation due to phone/sensor model variation can be measured reliably. Besides, the accuracy might degrade in particular patients who might consciously or subconsciously try to suppress their tremor during data recording.

Although it is unlikely that the tremor data after ends-trimming will have unwanted fluctuations in it, the data collectors have to carefully monitor the patient's limbs to notice whether any disruption or sudden movement had taken place during the whole period of data recording. If necessary, new data has to be recorded after discarding the contaminated one for reliable detection and assessment of PD.

As for the gait data collection, the smartphone could be attached to the hands as well to collect the hand-swing patterns during walking. However, the patients have to be instructed to try and maintain the rhythm of hand-swing with maximum possible amplitude so that the impairment becomes well pronounced in the accelerometer sensor data. Although advanced gait analysis consists of complex signal processing on the simultaneously collected data from different body parts, the simplified approach of analyzing gait impairment from the lower leg can effectively corroborate the result generated from the tremor data analysis.

6   Conclusion

Hand tremors from 52 PD patients with 20 healthy persons have been studied in both time and frequency domains. Features were extracted and analyzed to distinguish among different UPDRS levels of PD. Based on the limitations observed, further analysis incorporating reliable features from amplitude information is believed to improve labeling accuracy. However, the obtained accuracy is high enough to launch a pilot application for further improvement of this project in the rural setup of a developing country like Bangladesh. The incorporation of gait analysis has increased the reliability of PD detection. As for future development, incorporation of finger-tapping and leg-kicking is now under investigation. The data could be collected using the same accelerometer sensor to provide more information about the condition of the suspected PD patient.

References

1. Elias, W.J., Shah, B.B.: Tremor. JAMA **311**, 948–954 (2014)
2. Parkinson's Disease Statistics, Parkinson's News Today. https://parkinsonsnewstoday.com/parkinsons-disease-statistics/. Accessed 20 Jan 2020
3. Deep brain stimulation: a chance to thrive, The Daily Star. https://www.thedailystar.net/health/disease/deep-brain-stimulation-chance-thrive-1466578. Accessed 2 Feb 2020
4. Rascol, O., et al.: A five-year study of the incidence of dyskinesia in patients with early Parkinson's disease who were treated with ropinirole or levodopa. New Engl. J. Med. **342**, 1484–1491 (2000)
5. Bhat, M., Inamdar, S., Kulkarni, D., Kulkarni, G., Shriram, R.: Parkinson's disease prediction based on hand tremor analysis. In: 2017 International Conference on Communication and Signal Processing, pp. 0625–0629. IEEE, India (2017)
6. MDS-Unified Parkinson's Disease Rating Scale, Movement Disorder Society. https://www.movementdisorders.org/. Accessed 25 Jan 2020
7. Politis, M., Wu, K., Molloy, S.P.G.B., Chaudhuri, K.E., Piccini, P.: Parkinson's disease symptoms: the patient's perspective. Mov. Disord. **25**(11), 1646–1651 (2010)
8. Teravainen, T., Calne, D.B.: Action tremor in Parkinson's disease. J. Neurol. Neurosurg. Psychiatry **43**(3), 257–263 (1980)
9. Koller, W.E., Veter-Overfield, B., Barter, R.: Tremors in early Parkinson's disease. Clin. Neuropharmacol. **12**(4), 293–297 (1989)
10. Bazgir, O., Habibi, S.A.H., Palma, L., Pierleoni, P., Nafees, S.: Classification system for assessment and home monitoring of tremor in patients with Parkinson's disease. J. Med. Signals Sens. **8**(2), 65–72 (2018)
11. Rocon, E., et al.: Rehabilitation robotics: a wearable exo-skeleton for tremor assessment and suppression. In: 2005 IEEE International Conference on Robotics and Automation, pp. 2271–2276. IEEE, Barcelona, Spain (2005)
12. Seki, M., et al.: Development of robotic upper limb orthosis with tremor suppressiblity and elbow joint movability. In: 2011 IEEE International Conference on Systems. Man, and Cybernetics, pp. 729–735. IEEE, Anchorage (2011)
13. Morrison, S., et al.: Bilateral tremor relations in Parkinson's disease: effects of mechanical coupling and medication. Parkins. Relat. Disord. **14**, 298–308 (2008)
14. Pistacchi, M., et al.: Gait analysis and clinical correlations in early Parkinson's disease. Funct. Neurol. **32**, 28–34 (2017)
15. Mirelman, A., et al.: Gait impairments in Parkinson's disease. Lancet Neurol. **18**, 697–708 (2019)
16. Son, M., et al.: Evaluation of the turning characteristics according to the severity of Parkinson disease during the timed up and go test. Aging Clin. Exp. Res. **29**, 1191–1199 (2017)

17. Leusmann, P., Mollering, C., Klack, L.,'Kasugai, K., Ziefle, M., Rumpe, B.: Your floor knows where you are: sensing and acquisition of movement data. In: 2011 IEEE 12th International Conference Mobile Data Management, vol. 2, pp. 61–66 (2011)

18. Vera-Rodriguez, R., Mason, J.S., Fierrez, J., Ortega-Garcia, J.: Comparative analysis and fusion of spatiotemporal information for footstep recognition. IEEE Trans. Pattern Anal. Mach. Intell. **35**, 823–834 (2013)

19. Colyer, S.L., Evans, M., Cosker, D.P., Salo, A.I.T.: A review of the evolution of vision-based motion analysis and the integration of advanced computer vision methods towards developing a markerless system. Sports Med. Open **4**, 24 (2018)

20. Tao, W., Liu, T., Zheng, R., Feng, H.: Gait analysis using wearable sensors. Sensors **12**, 2255–2283 (2012)

21. Dominguez, G., Cardiel, E., Arias, S., Rogeli, P.: A digital goniometer based on encoders for measuring knee-joint position in an orthosis. In: Proceedings of the: World Congress on Nature and Biologically Inspired Computing (NaBIC) 2013, Fargo (2013)

22. Bae, J., Tomizuka, M.: A tele-monitoring system for gait rehabilitation with an inertial measurement unit and a shoe-type ground reaction force sensor. Mechatronics **23**, 646–651 (2013)

23. Godfrey, A., Del Din, S., Barry, G., Mathers, J.C., Rochester, L.: Instrumenting gait with an accelerometer: a system and algorithm examination. Med. Eng. Phys. **37**(4), 400–407 (2015)

24. Xuan, Y., et al.: Gait cycle recognition based on wireless inertial sensor network. IERI Procedia **4**, 44–52 (2013)

25. Perumala, S.V., Sankarb, R.: Gait and tremor assessment for patients with Parkinson's disease using wearable sensors. ICT Express **2**(4), 168–174 (2016)

26. Abdulhay, E., Arunkumar, N., Narasimhan, K., Vellaiappan, E., Venkatraman, V.: Gait and tremor investigation using machine learning techniques for the diagnosis of Parkinson disease. Future Gener. Comput. Syst. **83**, 366–373 (2018)

27. Mamun, K.A., Alhussein, M., Sailunaz, K., Islam, M.S.: Cloud based framework for Parkinson's disease diagnosis and monitoring system for remote healthcare applications. Future Gener. Comput. Syst. **66**, 36–47 (2017)

28. Radovic, M., et al.: Minimum redundancy maximum relevance feature selection approach for temporal gene expression data. BMC Bioinform. **18**, 1–4 (2017)

Effectiveness of Employing Multimodal Signals in Removing Artifacts from Neuronal Signals: An Empirical Analysis

Marcos Fabietti⑩, Mufti Mahmud$^{(\boxtimes)}$⑩, and Ahmad Lotfi⑩

Department of Computing and Technology, Nottingham Trent University,
Clifton Lane, Clifton, Nottingham NG11 8NS, UK
mufti.mahmud@ntu.ac.uk,muftimahmud@gmail.com

Abstract. Neurophysiological recordings, particularly neuronal signals recorded using multi-site neuronal probes or multielectrode arrays, are often contaminated with unwanted signals or artifacts from external or internal sources. Almost all types of neuronal signals including electroencephalogram (EEG), electrocorticogram (ECoG), local field potentials (LFP), and spikes very often suffer greatly from these artifacts and require extensive amount of processing to get rid of them. Despite considerable efforts in developing sophisticated methods to detect and remove these artifacts, it often appears a challenging task due to the inherent similar spatio-temporal properties of the artifacts and the recorded signals. In such cases, the incorporation of another modality can facilitate and improve the detection of these artifacts, and remove them. This paper focuses on the EEG signal and empirically analyses the role played by the addition of a new modality (e.g., cardiac signals, muscular signals, ocular signals, and motion signals) in detecting artifacts from EEG signals.

Keywords: Computational neuroscience · Neuroinformatics · Electroencephalogram · Neurophysiological signals

1 Introduction

Neuronal signals have been extensively used in a large range of applications including brain function decoding, brain-machine interfacing (BMI), rehabilitation, and so on. Among these signals there are invasive (electrocorticogram or ECoG, local field potentials or LFPs and neuronal spikes) and non-invasive (electroencephalogram or EEG) signals [25,46]. The EEG is a commonly used for monitoring brain activities non-invasively. It functions through the placements of conductive electrodes on the scalp, that record the electrical potentials that occur outside the head due to neuronal activity inside the brain [13]. One of its advantages is that it can be used in a variety of situations where other neuronal-activity acquiring systems can not, such as ambulatory neuromonitoring and

© Springer Nature Switzerland AG 2020
M. Mahmud et al. (Eds.): BI 2020, LNAI 12241, pp. 183–193, 2020.
https://doi.org/10.1007/978-3-030-59277-6_17

wearable BMI [19,21–23,36]. The downside lies in that it is susceptible to noise, and there is a limit to how much the improvement of electrodes and hardware can do to solve it. Not only EEG, all the neuronal signals when recorded are susceptible to external and internal noises [17,18,20]. Many times these signals and the noises have similar spatio-temporal characteristics which make them difficult to remove using conventional methods [24]. This means that a lot of processing must be done to the signal in order to obtain useful data.

There are many sources of noise, referred to as artifacts, which can be of physiological or environmental and methodological origin. In the first category we find ocular, cardiac, muscular, skin potentials or respiration sources. In the second one, transmission lines, cellphone signals,light stimulation, movement, electrode's poor contact, popping and lead movements. Each artifact has distinct amplitudes and frequency bands that overlap with the desired neuronal information [5].

A way to address this issue is incorporating another source of information to the system that allows to identify the abnormal activity. The combination of different formats of information is called multi-modality and is widely used in other neuroscience areas such as neuroimaging, where multi-modality provides clinicians with a metric of the relative health or dysfunction of the brain.

In this paper we evaluate the pros and cons of adding a second data source to detect artifacts. Specifically, those where the multi-modal data are a required input for the detection, not when it is only used to label data, train a model or adjust a filter. The remainder of the article is structured in the following manner: Sect. 2 reviews the approaches, Sect. 3 discusses the overall picture and Sect. 4 concludes the paper.

2   Multimodal Approaches

Each of the following sections first describes an artifact source (see Fig. 1), followed by the review of the multi-modal approaches to address it and finishes with an evaluation of the benefits of employing them.

2.1   Cardiac Artifacts

The electrical pulse from the heart has a strong signal intensity which can be picked up in various locations across the body. This electrical artefact appears as electrocardiogram (ECG) waveform recorded from scalp and forms the QRS complex. The majority of the cardiac artefact frequencies are 1 Hz and amplitude is in several millivolts. In addition, the expansion and contraction of the vessels produced by the beating of the heart generates voltage changes into the recordings. These are called ballistogardiogram (BCG) artifacts, and have a frequency range of around 0.5–40 Hz [43].

A reference channel of the ECG signal can be used to detect both QRS and BCG artifacts. Lanquart et al. [15] developed an QRS removal technique consisting of variance minimization, independent component analysis (ICA) and

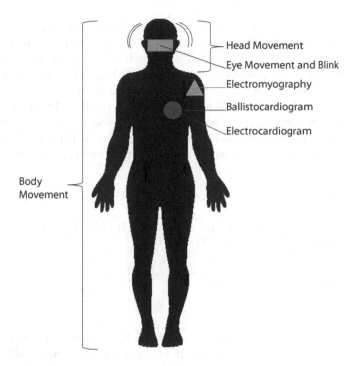

Fig. 1. Artifact sources.

morphological filters applied to the reference channel. Dora et al. [4] applied a Continuous Wavelet Transform to the ECG in order to detect the R peaks, and an estimated model of the QRS waves was generated with zero lines in between. Subsequently, A linear regression of the model and the contaminated EEG was applied to remove the artifacts.

Regarding BCG artifacts, Wang et al. [47] proposed using a clustering algorithm to the ECG channel to capture the BCG artifacts features and combining it with the constrained ICA algorithm to remove them from the EEG. McInstosh et al. [28] trained a recurrent neural network to create the nonlinear mappings between ECG and the BCG, which were later subtracted from the artifactual EEG for real-time analysis.

Modern computational methods have proven to be effectively remove both QRS [9] and BCG [14] artifacts, eliminating the need of an extra channel to monitor ECG activity. This is beneficial as fewer channels means lower expenses, shorter planning and simpler maintenance.

2.2 Muscular Artifacts

The frequency bandwidth of muscle contractions measured via electromyography (EMG), is of 20–300 Hz, with the majority of the power in the lower end of this range. When recorded in temporal EEG, the amplitude of muscle activity can be

$100\,\mu V$, compared to less than $1\,\mu V$ originating from high-frequency neuronal activity [29]. This calls for the need of an EMG artifact removal method.

Schwabedal et al. [40] utilized a CNN to predict the presence of artifacts in different states of consciousness (Wake, Non-REM, REM) in mice. Four-second-long sequences were sampled from signals extracted from the parieto-occipital lobes (EEG1), frontal lobe (EEG2) and neck muscles (EMG). The authors varied the number of recorded channels fed to the model, and the resulting F-1 score obtained in the respective validation sets are depicted in Table 1. The incorporation of the EMG channel noticeably improved the detection scores.

Table 1. Results obtained by different input channels of [40].

Condition	EEG1	EEG1+EEG2	EEG1+EEG2+EMG
Non-Rem	0.68	0.68	0.81
Rem	0.68	0.65	0.73
Wake	0.79	0.80	0.87

This suggests that the inclusion of additional EMG electrodes over key muscle groups may be useful. Nonetheless, it can prove to be too complicated due to the fact that the rich musculature of the head would need a large number of bipolar EMG electrodes. The effectiveness of computational techniques that don't depend on reference channels such as ICA, is debated in the literature as the processed data may still contain residual EMG [29].

2.3 Ocular Artifacts

Eye movement-related artifacts have the largest detrimental effect on EEG. As the eye alters position, the resting potential of the retina changes and can be measured using an electrooculogram (EOG). Blinking also causes involuntary movement of the retina as well as muscle movements of the eye lid. Due to the eyes' close proximity to the brain, as the signal propagates over the scalp, it can appear in the EEG as an artifact that can present serious complications in EEG analysis. The amplitude of these signals can be many times greater than the EEG signals of interest. This ocular signal can easily be measured using electrodes placed above and below the eye [43].

Instead, various authors have proposed the use of an eye tracker, in combination with processing algorithms to remove EOG artifacts. Mannan et al. [26] presented a system that utilized composite multi-scale entropy and eye tracker events to automatically identify blink and eye movement artifacts related independent components. Rivet et al. proposed [38] the estimation of EOG artifacts on EEG recordings by a coupled tensor factorization approach using an eye-tracker which was synchronously recorded. Maurandi et al.'s [27] contribution consists in de-noising the EEG data via the estimation of the common temporal structure between gaze signals and the EOG artifacts using Multiple Measurement Vectors.

In addition, Plochl et al. [34] developed an algorithm which classifies an independent component as an artifact if it displayed a higher activation during saccades than during fixation, using monocular pupil tracking. Samadi et al. [39] introduced an enhanced ICA algorithm that classifies an independent components as artifactual if, the cross-correlation of its first order derivative with the first order derivative of a boolean valued blink trigger, exceeds a threshold.

It is important to outline that these methods rely on high temporal resolution eye tracking devices, which in standard EEG experiments might not be available. In those situations, there are other single channel applications which do not require external sources, such as Ghosh et al.'s [6] which achieved a RMSE of 0.024 between the cleaned signal and the original noise free EEG, using a combination of an autoencoder and support vector machines.

2.4   Motion Artifacts

Motion can cause the position of the electrode on the skin to alter. This movement can cause a variation in the distance between the recording electrode and the skin, which results in a corresponding change in the electrical coupling, causing signal distortion [43]. The removal of these artifacts are of great importance as EEG is the only noninvasive brain imaging modality that uses sensors that are light enough to wear during mobility and possesses enough time resolution to record brain activity on the time scale of natural motor behavior. First we describe techniques that focus only on the movement of the head followed by those on the motion of the whole body.

Head Movement Artifacts. The main approaches to detect head movement artifacts is through the use of a sensor such as gyroscope or accelerometer. O'regan et al. extracted features from the signals of the former, and in conjunction with features of the EEG, trained the a linear discriminant analysis [32] and a support vector machine [33] classifier to detect artifactual segments.

Several authors approached it via the application of an accelerometer. Onikura et al. [31] and Daly et al. [3] removed the EEG's independent components whose Pearson's correlation coefficient between them and values of the accelerometer exceeded a threshold.

In a similar fashion, Tavildar et al. [44] used canonical correlation analysis to find the correlation between the orthogonal components of the EEG signal and of each of the accelerometer signals. Those above a threshold values were considered as artifacts and removed. Also, Sweeney et al.[42] used an empirically determined threshold to identify movement from accelerometer data, through a quality of signal metric.

Bang et al. [1] however utilized a motion capture camera instead of a movement sensor. Through the use of motion features captured by the frontal viewing camera and the frequency features of the EEG the best support vector machine classifier was obtained. They claim that their procedure is more flexible than the gyroscope-based and the accelerometer-based methods, because it can distinguish the many types of head movements. Having said that, the method discards the classified artifactual segments, generating a big loss of information.

Dynamic Motion Artifacts. Three distinct modalities to dynamic motion artifacts are found on the literature. First, Looney et al. [16] developed a sensor that records both electrical and mechanical activity, which allows to detect local skin-electrode motion. They used it in combination with the empirical mode decomposition algorithm to effectively remove motion artifacts.

Second, Kim et al. [11] employed an accelerometer and a gyroscope, to measure 3-axis acceleration and angular velocity, respectively. They removed the artifacts by separating motion-related independent components from EEG recordings based on the similarities with components from inertial measurement units. They were able to recover the contaminated EEG in motion comparably to the one obtained in a seated condition.

Lastly, Gwin et al. [8] incorporated the data from motion capture cameras and dual-belt in-ground force measuring treadmill to remove movement artifacts from EEG signals recorded during walking and running. In order for heel strike events to happen at the same adjusted latencies in each epoch, the signals were epoched, time-locked to single gait cycles and linearly time-warped. Subsequently, a channel-based artifact template regression procedure followed by spatial filtering was used to remove the artifacts.

The use of motion capture camera restricts the recording to laboratory settings, while the use of accelerometers and gyroscopes can be implemented in ambulatory scenarios, due to their ease of use. The latter's limitation lies in that the six degree of freedom motion of the head influences individual EEG channels differently, therefore head accelerometry is not correlated uniformly to all EEG channels [12]. As an alternative, Oliveira et al. [30] successfully presented a template correlation rejection of independent components for whole-body movement artifacts.

3   Discussion

Having commented the multi-modal approaches on the previous section, Table 2 shows the evaluation of the usefulness of each modality signal per artifact. We have dimmed that the use of small sensors do not interfere with the recording process and have a positive effect on the detection of artifacts. Other methodologies are able to aid detection but at the cost of expensive hardware or the use of more electrodes which maybe counterproductive outside laboratory settings. Overall, advanced computational techniques have diminished the need of multi-modal approaches in many artifacts. This is beneficial as they can be implemented through software, which is already a mandatory step in EEG usage.

Despite the fact that ICA has shown to be efficient to remove artifacts, it requires a large number of electrodes and the removed components may still contain some brain activities, leading thus to possibly misinterpretations of the brain waves. In this scenario, single channel techniques come in useful. A lot of progress has been done using machine learning techniques, which are able to learn the relationships between artifacts and neuronal recordings. As a negative, time must be spent labeling the recordings to train models or tune them to specific patients, which is still a time-consuming task.

Table 2. Multi-modal approaches evaluation

Artifact	Multi-modal Signal	Usefulness
QRS	ECG	Low: the data may not be available and fewer channels means lower expenses, shorter planning and simpler maintenance [9]
BCG	ECG	Low: the reference signals are not identical to the BCG, requires specialized hardware, and robust recording of reference signals [14]
EMG	EMG	Low: the extensive musculature of the head would need many bipolar EMG electrodes [29]
EOG	Eye tracker	Low: requires expensive hardware, not all are compatible with glasses or portable, which limits applications
Movement	Gyroscope	High: already integrated in some devices [3], no application restriction
	Accelerometer	
	Multi-modal sensor	
	Motion capture cameras	Situational: limits study to laboratory settings

As authors have used different metrics to report their results, comparing them is a difficult task. However it is clear that in present time, there is no universal method for artifact removal. Despite the fact that each discussed approach referrers mainly to specific artifacts, the combination of algorithms in sequence to improve the signal's quality through the use of multiple processing stages in which each step removes each artifact remains a possibility [45].

The recording complexity of multi-modal approaches lowers the availability of open datasets, as a bigger amount data of different formats need to be curated. In order to aid those looking for it, we would like to point towards the following datasets with reference data from: ECG [2], EMG [7], motion [41], EOG [35], and both EOG and EMG [10, 37].

4   Conclusion

We have described the individual artifacts which obstruct EEG analysis, reviewed the different multi modal approaches across the literature and evaluated their viability. In the majority of cases, incorporating an element to an already complicated set up is unrewarding, as modern algorithms have achieved successful results without them.

Many of these algorithms are machine learning applications, methods which are able to draw out the complex patterns in data. Despite their utility, they require big amounts of information, therefore a list of open datasets has been listed for readers looking to use multi-modality in artifact removal to benchmark a new algorithm or prove the effectiveness of them. In the future, we will develop a tool to help compare the results between artifact detection and removal methodologies.

References

1. Bang, J.W., Choi, J.S., Park, K.R.: Noise reduction in brainwaves by using both EEG signals and frontal viewing camera images. Sensors **13**(5), 6272–6294 (2013)
2. Barra, S., Fraschini, M., Casanova, A., Castiglione, A., Fenu, G.: Physiounicadb: a dataset of EEG and ECG simultaneously acquired. Pattern Recogn. Lett. **126**, 119–122 (2019)
3. Daly, I., Billinger, M., Scherer, R., Müller-Putz, G.: On the automated removal of artifacts related to head movement from the EEG. IEEE Trans. Neural Syst. Rehabil. Eng. **21**(3), 427–434 (2013)
4. Dora, C., Biswal, P.K.: Robust ECG artifact removal from EEG using continuous wavelet transformation and linear regression. In: 2016 International Conference on Signal Processing and Communications (SPCOM), pp. 1–5. IEEE (2016)
5. Fabietti, M., et al.: Neural network-based artifact detection in local field potentials recorded from chronically implanted neural probes. In: Proceedings of IJCNN, pp. 1–8 (2020)
6. Ghosh, R., Sinha, N., Biswas, S.K.: Automated eye blink artefact removal from EEG using support vector machine and autoencoder. IET Signal Proc. **13**(2), 141–148 (2018)
7. Grimaldi, G., Manto, M., Jdaoudi, Y.: Quality parameters for a multimodal EEG/EMG/kinematic brain-computer interface (BCI) aiming to suppress neurological tremor in upper limbs. F1000Research **2**, 282 (2013)
8. Gwin, J.T., Gramann, K., Makeig, S., Ferris, D.P.: Removal of movement artifact from high-density EEG recorded during walking and running. J. Neurophysiol. **103**(6), 3526–3534 (2010)
9. Issa, M.F., Tuboly, G., Kozmann, G., Juhasz, Z.: Automatic ECG artefact removal from EEG signals. Measur. Sci. Rev. **19**(3), 101–108 (2019)
10. Kemp, B.: The sleep-EDF database. World Wide Web. http://www.physionet.org/physiobank/database/sleep-edf/. Accessed August 2009
11. Kim, B.H., Chun, J., Jo, S.: Dynamic motion artifact removal using inertial sensors for mobile BCI. In: 2015 7th International IEEE/EMBS Conference on Neural Engineering (NER), pp. 37–40. IEEE (2015)
12. Kline, J.E., Huang, H.J., Snyder, K.L., Ferris, D.P.: Isolating gait-related movement artifacts in electroencephalography during human walking. J. Neural Eng. **12**(4), 046022 (2015)
13. Koessler, L., et al.: Automated cortical projection of EEG sensors: anatomical correlation via the international 10–10 system. Neuroimage **46**(1), 64–72 (2009)
14. Krishnaswamy, P., Bonmassar, G., Poulsen, C., Pierce, E.T., Purdon, P.L., Brown, E.N.: Reference-free removal of EEG-fMRI ballistocardiogram artifacts with harmonic regression. Neuroimage **128**, 398–412 (2016)
15. Lanquart, J.P., Dumont, M., Linkowski, P.: QRS artifact elimination on full night sleep EEG. Med. Eng. Phys. **28**(2), 156–165 (2006)

16. Looney, D., Goverdovsky, V., Kidmose, P., Mandic, D.P.: Subspace denoising of EEG artefacts via multivariate EMD. In: 2014 IEEE International Conference on Acoustics, Speech and Signal Processing (ICASSP), pp. 4688–4692. IEEE (2014)
17. Mahmud, M., Cecchetto, C., Vassanelli, S.: An automated method for characterization of evoked single-trial local field potentials recorded from rat barrel cortex under mechanical whisker stimulation. Cogn. Comput. **8**(5), 935–945 (2016). https://doi.org/10.1007/s12559-016-9399-3
18. Mahmud, M., Girardi, S., Maschietto, M., Vassanelli, S.: An automated method to remove artifacts induced by microstimulation in local field potentials recorded from rat somatosensory cortex. In: Proceedings BRC, pp. 1–4 (2012). https://doi.org/10.1109/BRC.2012.6222169
19. Mahmud, M., Bertoldo, A., Vassanelli, S.: EEG based brain-machine interfacing: Navigation of mobile robotic device. In: Bedkowski, J. (ed.) Mobile Robots-Control Architectures, Bio-Interfacing, Navigation, Multi Robot Motion Planning and Operator Training. IntechOpen (2011)
20. Mahmud, M., Girardi, S., Maschietto, M., Rahman, M.M., Bertoldo, A., Vassanelli, S.: Slow stimulus artifact removal through peak-valley detection of neuronal signals recorded from somatosensory cortex by high resolution brain-chip interface. In: Dossel, O., Schlegel, W.C. (eds.) World Congress on Medical Physics and Biomedical Engineering. IFMBE Proceedings, vol. 25/4. Springer, Berlin (2009). https://doi.org/10.1007/978-3-642-03882-2_547
21. Mahmud, M., Hawellek, D., Bertoldo, A.: EEG based brain-machine interface for navigation of robotic device. In: 2010 3rd IEEE RAS & EMBS International Conference on Biomedical Robotics and Biomechatronics, pp. 168–172. IEEE (2010)
22. Mahmud, M., Hawellek, D., Valjamae, A.: A brain-machine interface based on EEG: extracted alpha waves applied to mobile robot. In: 2009 Advanced Technologies for Enhanced Quality of Life, pp. 28–31. IEEE (2009)
23. Mahmud, M., Hussain, A.: Towards reduced EEG based brain-computer interfacing for mobile robot navigation. In: Castro, F., Gelbukh, A., González, M. (eds.) MICAI 2013. LNCS (LNAI), vol. 8266, pp. 413–422. Springer, Heidelberg (2013). https://doi.org/10.1007/978-3-642-45111-9_36
24. Mahmud, M., Travalin, D., Bertoldo, A., Girardi, S., Maschietto, M., Vassanelli, S.: An automated classification method for single sweep local field potentials recorded from rat barrel cortex under mechanical whisker stimulation. J. Med. Biol. Eng. **32**(6), 397–404 (2012)
25. Mahmud, M., Vassanelli, S.: Processing and analysis of multichannel extracellular neuronal signals: state-of-the-art and challenges. Front. Neurosci. **10**, 248 (2016)
26. Mannan, M.M.N., Kim, S., Jeong, M.Y., Kamran, M.A.: Hybrid EEG–eye tracker: automatic identification and removal of eye movement and blink artifacts from electroencephalographic signal. Sensors **16**(2), 241 (2016)
27. Maurandi, V., Rivet, B., Phlypo, R., Guérin–Dugué, A., Jutten, C.: Multimodal approach to remove ocular artifacts from EEG signals using multiple measurement vectors. In: Tichavský, P., Babaie-Zadeh, M., Michel, O.J.J., Thirion-Moreau, N. (eds.) LVA/ICA 2017. LNCS, vol. 10169, pp. 563–573. Springer, Cham (2017). https://doi.org/10.1007/978-3-319-53547-0_53
28. McIntosh, J.R., Yao, J., Hong, L., Faller, J., Sajda, P.: Ballistocardiogram artifact reduction in simultaneous EEG-FMRI using deep learning. arXiv preprint arXiv:1910.06659 (2019)
29. Muthukumaraswamy, S.: High-frequency brain activity and muscle artifacts in MEG/EEG: a review and recommendations. Front. Human Neurosci. **7**, 138 (2013)

30. Oliveira, A.S., Schlink, B.R., Hairston, W.D., König, P., Ferris, D.P.: A channel rejection method for attenuating motion-related artifacts in EEG recordings during walking. Front. Neurosci. **11**, 225 (2017)
31. Onikura, K., Iramina, K.: Evaluation of a head movement artifact removal method for EEG considering real-time processing. In: 2015 8th Biomedical Engineering International Conference (BMEiCON), pp. 1–4. IEEE (2015)
32. O'Regan, S., Faul, S., Marnane, W.: Automatic detection of EEG artefacts arising from head movements. In: 2010 Annual International Conference of the IEEE Engineering in Medicine and Biology, pp. 6353–6356. IEEE (2010)
33. O'Regan, S., Faul, S., Marnane, W.: Automatic detection of EEG artefacts arising from head movements using EEG and gyroscope signals. Med. Eng. Phys. **35**(7), 867–874 (2013)
34. Plöchl, M., Ossandón, J.P., König, P.: Combining EEG and eye tracking: identification, characterization, and correction of eye movement artifacts in electroencephalographic data. Front. Hum. Neurosci. **6**, 278 (2012)
35. Quax, S.C., Dijkstra, N., van Staveren, M.J., Bosch, S.E., van Gerven, M.A.: Eye movements explain decodability during perception and cued attention in MEG. Neuroimage **195**, 444–453 (2019)
36. Raif, P., Mahmud, M., Hussain, A., Klos-Witkowska, A., Suchanek, R.: A brain-computer interface test-bench based on EEG signals for research and student training. In: 2013 IEEE Symposium on Computational Intelligence in Healthcare and e-health (CICARE), pp. 46–50. IEEE (2013)
37. Rezaei, M., Mohammadi, H., Khazaie, H.: EEG/EOG/EMG data from a cross sectional study on psychophysiological insomnia and normal sleep subjects. Data in brief **15**, 314–319 (2017)
38. Rivet, B., Duda, M., Guérin-Dugué, A., Jutten, C., Comon, P.: Multimodal approach to estimate the ocular movements during EEG recordings: a coupled tensor factorization method. In: 2015 37th Annual International Conference of the IEEE Engineering in Medicine and Biology Society (EMBC), pp. 6983–6986. IEEE (2015)
39. Samadi, M.R.H., Zakeri, Z., Cooke, N.: VOG-enhanced ICA for removing blink and eye-movement artefacts from EEG. In: 2016 IEEE-EMBS International Conference on Biomedical and Health Informatics (BHI), pp. 603–606. IEEE (2016)
40. Schwabedal, J.T., Sippel, D., Brandt, M.D., Bialonski, S.: Automated classification of sleep stages and EEG artifacts in mice with deep learning. arXiv preprint arXiv:1809.08443 (2018)
41. Sweeney, K.T., Ayaz, H., Ward, T.E., Izzetoglu, M., McLoone, S.F., Onaral, B.: A methodology for validating artifact removal techniques for physiological signals. IEEE Trans. Inf Technol. Biomed. **16**(5), 918–926 (2012)
42. Sweeney, K.T., Leamy, D.J., Ward, T.E., McLoone, S.: Intelligent artifact classification for ambulatory physiological signals. In: 2010 Annual International Conference of the IEEE Engineering in Medicine and Biology, pp. 6349–6352. IEEE (2010)
43. Sweeney, K.T., Ward, T.E., McLoone, S.F.: Artifact removal in physiological signals–practices and possibilities. IEEE Trans. Inf Technol. Biomed. **16**(3), 488–500 (2012)
44. Tavildar, S., Ashrafi, A.: Application of multivariate empirical mode decomposition and canonical correlation analysis for EEG motion artifact removal. In: 2016 Conference on Advances in Signal Processing (CASP), pp. 150–154. IEEE (2016)
45. Urigüen, J.A., Garcia-Zapirain, B.: EEG artifact removal–state-of-the-art and guidelines. J. Neural Eng. **12**(3), 031001 (2015)

46. Vassanelli, S., Mahmud, M.: Trends and challenges in neuroengineering: toward "intelligent" neuroprostheses through brain-"brain inspired systems" communication. Front. Neurosci. **10**, 438 (2016)
47. Wang, K., Li, W., Dong, L., Zou, L., Wang, C.: Clustering-constrained ICA for ballistocardiogram artifacts removal in simultaneous EEG-FMRI. Front. Neurosci. **12**, 59 (2018)

A Machine Learning Based Fall Detection for Elderly People with Neurodegenerative Disorders

Nazmun Nahar[1] , Mohammad Shahadat Hossain[2(✉)] ,
and Karl Andersson[3]

[1] BGC Trust University Bangladesh Bidyanagar, Chandanaish, Bangladesh
nazmun@bgctub.ac.bd
[2] University of Chittagong, 4331 Chittagong, Bangladesh
hossain_ms@cu.ac.bd
[3] Lulea University of Technology, 931 87 Skellefteå, SE, Sweden
Karl.andersson@ltu.se

Abstract. Fall is one of the most serious clinical problems faced by the elderly people. Elder people with neurodegenerative disorders like Parkinson disease often fall. This leads to the damage of physical condition and also mental condition. Therefore, elderly people should be taken care of all the time. However, it is not possible to take care of them every moment. Therefore, an automatic fall detection system is required to track elderly at any time. An automated fall detection system will provide timely assistance and hence, it will reduce medical care costs significantly. The recent developments in motion- sensor technologies have allowed the efficient use of wearable sensors in the overall treatment of the elderly. The paper presents a machine learning framework consisting of data collection, preprocessing of data, feature extraction and machine learning classifiers. They comprise C4.5, Random Forest, RepTree, and LMT (Logistic Model Tree). Dataset used in this research has been collected by using 3-axis accelerometer sensors which are mounted on a person's waist. Features have been extracted from this dataset which are used by these classifiers. C4.5 gives the highest accuracy which is 97.36% in comparison to other classifiers.

Keywords: Neurodegenerative · Fall detection · Accelerometer sensor · Machine learning · Parkinson disease

1 Introduction

Regular natural processes sometimes place older people at an increased risk of falling [15]. Falls are a typical and often neglected reason for injuries in old age. Heart disease, hypotension, poor vision, muscle weakness etc. are the important reasons of the fall of elderly people. Beside these reasons, neurodegenerative diseases are another root cause of the fall of elder people which includes Parkinson's, Alzheimer's, and motor neuron disease. Progressive degeneration or death

© Springer Nature Switzerland AG 2020
M. Mahmud et al. (Eds.): BI 2020, LNAI 12241, pp. 194–203, 2020.
https://doi.org/10.1007/978-3-030-59277-6_18

of nerve cells of elderly people results in Neurodegenerative diseases which are almost incurable and makes the person in devastating health conditions. In a country especially in a developing nation, these diseases have a significant impact on the economy due to cost involved in treatment. Moreover, Neurodegenerative diseases have a distressing impact in our society. Ageing people who are affected by this disease face problems in movement, or mental functioning. One of the most important neurodegenerative diseases is Parkinson's disease that affects predominantly dopamine-producing ("dopaminergic") neurons in a specific area of the brain called substantia nigra. This disease is commonly known as older person's disease and is a combination of genetic and external factors. Tremor of the hands or legs, impaired balance, lack of coordination, sleep problem, changes of vision, increased sweating are main symptoms of the disease which are mainly seen at older age and these factors lead to fall that means make the chance of falling at surface. Therefore, a quick response from a concerned person is necessary when a fall of elderly people happens. But, the quick response is difficult when an ageing person lives alone or in remote zones. Taking into account the above reason, plenty of research interests have been seen to build up a fall detection framework. The fall identification frameworks can basically be separated into two groups: wearable device and context-aware device [8, 17]. Context-aware devices are working in the area appliance for example floor sensors, mouthpieces, pressure sensors, PIR sensors, and infrared sensors, cameras [8]. The main advantage of these devices is that an individual doesn't require putting on any equipment. Anyway, there are some limitations in camera-based frameworks. It can't ensure the clients' privacy and security, and it can't distinguish if clients fall where they do not introduce cameras or around dark areas. Moreover, dependent on 3D picture framework typically have certain delays. The limitation of a pressure sensor is that we can't recognize if pressure is from the client's weight, which might lead to the low accuracy. Approaches dependent on wearable devices rely upon clothing with embedded sensors to catch the direction and places of the subject's body. In view of wearable and cheap, the wearable-device based framework is the most generally utilized for fall identification. The wearable-device based framework is that clients wear a few devices with embedded sensors to get available data like acceleration, at that point the framework procedure information by algorithms to perceive the client if fall or not. In addition, the device is cheap, convenient to carry and operation of the device is easy to set up. This paper uses a tri-axial accelerometer sensor to detect fall of ageing people which is placed on a person's waist. The fall-features are calculated from a 3- axis accelerometer sensor followed by a supervised machine learning-based approach to capture fall events. This system is developed by training a learning algorithm of various kinds of fall and activities of daily living (ADL) patterns. After that an assessment algorithm marks various types of occurrence of fall or ADL. A classic fall identification framework is represented in Fig. 1. The fall recognition framework gathers information from the sensors and sends the information into the processing unit. Numerous attributes are separated from the sensor data by the processing unit. Fall is distinguished from the attributes by the suitable algorithms. At the point when the algorithms catch the occasions of fall, an alert is activated. The alert made an impression on the families or caring individuals or transmitting a sound admonition to pull in the consideration of concerned people. Such a framework is perfect for fall identification that can consequently recognize falls and give a warning mechanism. Using this system we can protect neurodegenerative diseases patient's from major loss by taking proper steps.   The distinguishing feature of this paper is that an assessment of

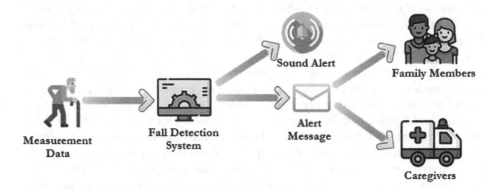

Fig. 1. A fall detection system.

the time-domain characteristics for the determination of the most discriminatory features of fall by using supervised machine learning methods. The remainder of the paper is categorized into different sections. Section two specified the literature review of the study and section three shows the methodology. Section four analyzes the experimental results while section five concludes and presents the future work.

2   Related Work

A variety of automated methods were recently introduced for fall detection. Automatic fall detection systems may be focused on the vision, sound, or the wearable device. Wearable fall detection sensors typically use the accelerometer, gyroscopes, or several modes of sensing devices. Srinivasan et al. [22] investigated the usual recognition of fall found on tri-axial accelerometer and Passive Infrared sensors (PIRs). The vestment of three-axis accelerometer was installed to capture falling events on the waist of the subject while PIRs were mounted to provide longitudinal information. PIR sensor has used motionless signals to validate fall events. Almeida et al. [4] introduced a walking cane with an integrated gyroscope founded to its base to detect falls and assess walking speed. Fall events were observed along sideward and forward axes depending on the amplitude of the resulting angular velocity. The speed was determined by the total angular velocity of two neighboring peaks, separated between the two peaks by the time interval. Warnings have been provided when a client is going quicker than his normal movement. Lin et al. [18] conducted an optical sensor-based fall detection, and nine micro-mercury switches were installed into a smart suit. In the left waist, the optical sensor was employed for detection of falls, while the fall features (i.e., backward and forward) and user's behaviors were detected with Micro mercury switches. Grassi et al. [9] have integrated a 3D time-of-flight, a wearable accelerometer (MEMS), and a microphone for fall detection. Three integrated sensors were processed and tested with the appropriate algorithms separately on a custom broad. For identification of fall detection floor image sensors is introduced by Rimminen et al. [21]. The fall classification has been carried out using a Markov two-state chain and Bayesian filtering approximation. Fall detection system using a three-axial accelerometer mounted on the waist of the subject along with a barometric pressure sensor is developed by Bianchi et al. [5]. They developed a fall detection system by using the concept of difference between the waist and the ground regarding ambient pressures. The experimental findings show that the sensor data are helpful for detecting fall events. In a study of fall detection Hou et al. [12] proposed a Smartphone device by using embedded acceleration sensors to record human motion. In their study they found that the accuracy of the SVM can reach 96.072%. Commodity based Smart watch sensor can reach 93.33% accuracy in a real world setting of fall detection by adjusting screaming data, sliding window and a Naïve machine learning method [20]. The smart watch sensor can give a competitive score than that of other expensive sensors. In this paper, we have used an accelerometer sensor for fall detection, which is mounted on a person's waist. Because the wearable sensor is the cheapest and it is also chosen for its high accuracy.

3   Methodology

For the detection of fall, a machine learning based methodology is proposed in this research. A publicly available dataset known as UR fall Detection dataset is used for the proposed algorithm. Proposed methodology consists of four major steps i.e. dataset collection, data preprocessing, feature extraction of the raw data and detection of fall using machine learning classifier, as shown in Fig. 2.

3.1   Data Collection

The first step of the methodology is the collection of data that will be used in further stages. In this research, a publicly available dataset is used for fall detection known as UR fall detection dataset. This dataset is developed by University of Rzeszow [16]. One IMU (Inertial Measurement Unit) with an accelerometer sensor was used for the data collection. The IMU device was connected by Bluetooth.

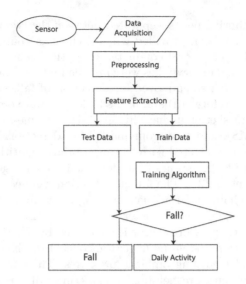

Fig. 2. Proposed methodology

This device was positioned at the waist of the volunteer's (near the pelvis). The data set includes 70 falls and ADL (Daily Livings Activities) sequences which were captured by six volunteers. There are two types of fall in the dataset: fall from standing and sitting on a chair. This dataset also comprises some normal activities, such as lying on the floor, lying on the couch, sitting down, walking and picking items from the ground. Each activity and trail has a single CSV file. Data set description is illustrated Table 1.

3.2   Feature Extraction

Feature extraction plays an important role in a classification system for fall detection, because the selected features can assess the system's accuracy. Five features are extracted from the sensor data. Each feature is extracted from the accelerometer sensor along with three x-axis, y-axis and z-axis. These features along with their mathematical expression are described in the below

The Magnitude of the Standard Deviation: The magnitude of the standard deviation (SDM) represents the change in the magnitude of the acceleration for each axis.

$$\alpha_{x_{y_z}} = \sqrt{\alpha_x^2 + \alpha_y^2 + \alpha_z^2} \tag{1}$$

This feature is sensitive to rotations without any change in magnitude, which enables abrupt tilt changes to be identified.

Table 1. Description of the dataset.

UR fall detection dataset	
Scenario of the environment	Office and home environment
Video clips	Yes
Spontaneity of the movements	Predefined
Number of types (ADLs/Fall)	5/4
Number of samples(ADLS/Fall)	70(40/30)
Duration of the sample	(2.11–13.57) s
Number of sensing point	1
Types of sensor	1 external IMU
Sensor position	Subjects Waist
Activities of daily livings	Lying on the floor
Falls	Forwards while seating

The Standard Deviation of Vector Magnitude. The standard deviation of vector magnitude can be calculated by using the following function.

$$\alpha_a = \alpha\sqrt{x^2 + y^2 + z^2} \tag{2}$$

This feature has been selected to track sudden acceleration change, which is not necessarily combined with body angle, for example, when someone falls on knees. This feature, therefore, recognizes sudden changes in signal amplitude (peaks), representing an impact resulting from a fall.

The Polar Angle Ratio: The polar angle is calculated with successive 20 samples. The polar angle is calculated using the following equations from raw accelerometer data.

$$arccos(z/\sqrt{x^2 + y^2 + z^2}) \tag{3}$$

This angle represents the body-angle and sudden change, which will indicate a fall has occurred. The angles apply to a sensor-associated coordinate system. Moreover, the ratio of its instant angle and its earlier values within a short time span represents a sudden change in the angle of inclination.

The Difference of Polar Angle: The difference between polar angles is also determined in successive windows $\delta\theta$. $\delta\theta$ also helps to cover large tilt angle variations.

The Difference of Polar Angle: Velocity can be calculated using the following equation:

$$V_2 = \sqrt{(\int a_x(t)^2) + (\int a_y(t)^2) + (\int a_z(t)^2)} \tag{4}$$

After the feature extraction, some machine learning algorithms were used for classifying the fall activities. The classification algorithm works on a selected feature.

3.3   Fall Detection

After the extraction of the feature, the next step is to determine whether it falls or not. The problem of fall detection is a binary classification problem. This means that we will classify it as fall or non-fall operation (i.e. ADL). Therefore, the entire dataset was divided into 2 classes. Class 1 on falling activities and class 2 on non-fall activities. All the feature vectors extracted from the data collected by the falling samples have been labeled Class 1. Feature vectors extracted from the ADL samples have been labeled as Class-2. After labeling the sample feature vector, we then used the 10-fold cross-validation technique to build better prediction models for the machine learning classifier and to minimize the bias. After that, four machine learning classifiers have been used to determine the efficiency of the proposed system. These classifiers include C4.5, Logistics Model Tree (LMT), RepTree and Random Tree. For evaluation and training, we split the dataset into two parts.70% of the data in the dataset are used for training and 30% for testing. Ten cross-validations have been conducted using various random sample partitions of each of the selected classification methods. Lastly, the test set, which the model never before saw, used to deter-mine the generalization of the model.

4   Result and Discussion

Once model training has been completed, the learned models are used to predict all classification problems. We have also demonstrated the results of 10 iterations of cross-validation throughout the training set so that the model did not overfit the training set. In this research, Weka [10] was used to evaluate classification algorithms' success rates. Our main aim is to identify the best model to distinguish accurately between fall and normal activities. For this purpose, we have used four well-known classifiers known as C4.5, LMT, RepTree and Random Tree. To evaluate the efficiency of the algorithm, we used accuracy, MAE and RMSE for the experiment. We have also measured the performance of the classification models using four metrics: sensitivity, specificity and F1-Measure. Table 2 shows the accuracy, MAE, and RMSE of the proposed classifier. From Table 2, it is evident that the C4.5 has the highest accuracy because it uses a random subspace method and using the bagging concept, the Multilayer Perceptron algorithm has the lowest accuracy. And also the C4.5agorithm has the

Table 2. Accuracy, MAE and RMSE of the Algorithm.

Classifier name	Accuracy (%)	MAE	RMSE
LMT	96.49%	0.118	0.216
C4.5	97.36%	0.039	0.162
RepTree	96.31%	0.052	0.182
Random Forest	95.61%	0.044	0.209

lowest MAE and RMSE value because the random forest algorithm has low bias and moderate variance. Random forest gives the result by averaging all trees which are present in the subspace. Figure 3 shows the graphical representation of the proposed classifier accuracy. Table 3 depicts the sensitivity, specificity, and F-measure of the proposed model. From Table 3, it can be shown that the C4.5

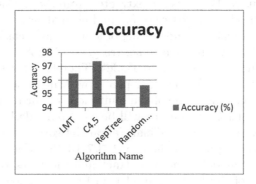

Fig. 3. Accuracy of the proposed classifier

Table 3. Performance metrics of the proposed classifier

Classifier name	Sensitivity	Specificity	F-measure
LMT	0.9677	0.9615	0.968
C4.5	0.9836	0.9622	0.976
RepTree	0.9578	0.9615	0.958
Random Forest	0.9521	0.9607	0.960

algorithm gives better precision, sensitivity, specificity, and F1-score, whereas Random Tree gives the lowest value of these performance matrices. The performance of the proposed C4.5-based scheme is also compared to the state-of-the-art techniques as shown in Table 4.

Table 4. Result comparison of the proposed algorithm with the State-of Art Techniques

Research study	Approach	Accuracy
A H Ngu [11]	SVM	93.8
A H Ngu [11]	Naïve Bayes	90
M Hoq [10]	SVM	92
The Proposed Approach	C4.5	97.36

5   Conclusion and Future Work

In this research, a very simple and computationally efficient machine learning based fall detection system has been proposed. For this purpose, publicly available UR fall detection dataset has been analyzed. The dataset comprises 70 types of fall and normal activities. One of the important aspects of this paper is the use of the statistical feature. Features are extracted from the raw accelerometer sensor which reflects the characteristics of fall and normal activities. The extracted feature is used for the training and testing of four machine classification. Among these classifier, C4.5 shows the highest accuracy, i.e., 97.36% which is better than the state-of-art techniques as shown in Table 4. Therefore, the C4.5 classifier can be effectively used to monitor the elder people with neurodegenerative diseases like Parkinson disease. This is one of the limitations of our research. In future, a dataset using an accelerometer sensor will be collected elderly people with neurodegenerative disease. A deep Artificial Neural Network can be implemented in advance of achieving better performance [1–3,7,13,19]. More data can be used to train the learning model. Finally, extract more features that will certainly help in the training of the learning model. In future, a knowledge-driven approach can be used to remove the uncertainty like belief rule based expert system [6,11,14].

References

1. Abedin, M.Z., Nath, A.C., Dhar, P., Deb, K., Hossain, M.S.: License plate recognition system based on contour properties and deep learning model. In: 2017 IEEE Region 10 Humanitarian Technology Conference (R10-HTC), pp. 590–593. IEEE (2017)
2. Ahmed, T.U., Hossain, M.S., Alam, M.J., Andersson, K.: An integrated CNN-RNN framework to assess road crack. In: 2019 22nd International Conference on Computer and Information Technology (ICCIT), pp. 1–6. IEEE (2019)
3. Ahmed, T.U., Hossain, S., Hossain, M.S., ul Islam, R., Andersson, K.: Facial expression recognition using convolutional neural network with data augmentation. In: 2019 Joint 8th International Conference on Informatics, Electronics, pp. 336–341. IEEE (2019)
4. Almeida, O., Zhang, M., Liu, J.C.: Dynamic fall detection and pace measurement in walking sticks. In: 2007 Joint Workshop on High Confidence Medical Devices, Software, and Systems and Medical Device Plug-and-Play Interoperability (HCMDSS-MDPnP 2007), pp. 204–206. IEEE (2007)
5. Bianchi, F., Redmond, S.J., Narayanan, M.R., Cerutti, S., Lovell, N.H.: Barometric pressure and triaxial accelerometry-based falls event detection. IEEE Trans. Neural Syst. Rehabil. Eng. 18(6), 619–627 (2010)
6. Biswas, M., Chowdhury, S.U., Nahar, N., Hossain, M.S., Andersson, K.: A belief rule base expert system for staging non-small cell lung cancer under uncertainty. In: 2019 IEEE International Conference on Biomedical Engineering, Computer and Information Technology for Health (BECITHCON), pp. 47–52. IEEE (2019)

7. Chowdhury, R.R., Hossain, M.S., ul Islam, R., Andersson, K., Hossain, S.: Bangla handwritten character recognition using convolutional neural network with data augmentation. In: 2019 Joint 8th International Conference on Informatics, Electronics & Vision (ICIEV), pp. 318–323. IEEE (2019)

8. Estudillo-Valderrama, M.Á., Roa, L.M., Reina-Tosina, J., Naranjo-Hernández, D.: Design and implementation of a distributed fall detection system-personal server. IEEE Trans. Inf Technol. Biomed. **13**(6), 874–881 (2009)

9. Grassi, M., et al.: A hardware-software framework for high-reliability people fall detection. In: SENSORS 2008, pp. 1328–1331. IEEE (2008)

10. Hall, M., Frank, E., Holmes, G., Pfahringer, B., Reutemann, P., Witten, I.H.: The WEKA data mining software: an update. ACM SIGKDD Explor. Newslett. **11**(1), 10–18 (2009)

11. Hossain, M.S., Habib, I.B., Andersson, K.: A belief rule based expert system to diagnose dengue fever under uncertainty. In: 2017 Computing Conference, pp. 179–186. IEEE (2017)

12. Hou, M., Wang, H., Xiao, Z., Zhang, G.: An SVM fall recognition algorithm based on a gravity acceleration sensor. Syst. Sci. Control Eng. **6**(3), 208–214 (2018)

13. Islam, M.Z., Hossain, M.S., ul Islam, R., Andersson, K.: Static hand gesture recognition using convolutional neural network with data augmentation. In: 2019 Joint 8th International Conference on Informatics, pp. 324–329. IEEE (2019)

14. Kabir, S., Islam, R.U., Hossain, M.S., Andersson, K.: An integrated approach of belief rule base and deep learning to predict air pollution. Sensors **20**(7), 1956 (2020)

15. Kannus, P., Khan, K.M.: Prevention of falls and subsequent injuries in elderly people: a long way to go in both research and practice. CMAJ **165**(5), 587–588 (2001)

16. Kwolek, B., Kepski, M.: Human fall detection on embedded platform using depth maps and wireless accelerometer. Comput. Methods Programs Biomed. **117**(3), 489–501 (2014)

17. Li, Y., Ho, K., Popescu, M.: A microphone array system for automatic fall detection. IEEE Trans. Biomed. Eng. **59**(5), 1291–1301 (2012)

18. Lin, C.S., Hsu, H.C., Lay, Y.L., Chiu, C.C., Chao, C.S.: Wearable device for real-time monitoring of human falls. Measurement **40**(9–10), 831–840 (2007)

19. Nahar, N., et al.: A comparative analysis of the ensemble method for liver disease prediction. In: International Conference on Innovation in Engineering and Technology (ICIET) (2019)

20. Ngu, A.H., Tseng, P.T., Paliwal, M., Carpenter, C., Stipe, W.: Smartwatch-based IoT fall detection application. Open J. IoT (OJIOT) **4**(1), 87–98 (2018)

21. Rimminen, H., Lindström, J., Linnavuo, M., Sepponen, R.: Detection of falls among the elderly by a floor sensor using the electric near field. IEEE Trans. Inf Technol. Biomed. **14**(6), 1475–1476 (2010)

22. Srinivasan, S., Han, J., Lal, D., Gacic, A.: Towards automatic detection of falls using wireless sensors. In: 2007 29th Annual International Conference of the IEEE Engineering in Medicine and Biology Society, pp. 1379–1382. IEEE (2007)

Machine Learning Based Early Fall Detection for Elderly People with Neurological Disorder Using Multimodal Data Fusion

Md. Nahiduzzaman[1] , Moumitu Tasnim[1]([✉]) , Nishat Tasnim Newaz[1] ,
M. Shamim Kaiser[1] , and Mufti Mahmud[2]

[1] Institute of Information Technology, Jahangirnagar University,
Savar, Dhaka 1342, Bangladesh
nahidsamrat2@gmail.com, anikatasnim118@gmail.com, tasnim0110@gmail.com,
mskaiser@juniv.edu
[2] Nottingham Trent University, Clifton Campus, Nottingham NG11 8NS, UK
mufti.mahmud@ntu.ac.uk

Abstract. Fall is deemed to be one of the critical problems for the elderly patient having neurological disorders as it may cause injury or death. It turns to be a public health concern and attracts researchers to detect fall using sensing devices wearable, portable, and imaging. With the availability of low cost pervasive sensing elements, advancement of ubiquitous computing and better understanding of machine learning approaches, researchers have employing various machine learning approaches in detecting fall from the sensor data. In this paper, we have proposed a recurrent neural network (RNN)-based framework for detecting fall/daily activity of a patient having a neurological disorder using Internet of things and then manage the patient by referring to doctor. If an anomaly is detected in the daily activity and notify caregiver/family member if fall is detected. The RNN based fall detection model fused knowledge from both the smartphone/wearable and camera installed on the wall and ceiling. The proposed RNN is trained with open-labeled and UR data-sets and is compared with the support vector machine and random forest for these two data-sets. The performance evaluation shows the proposed method is effecting and outperforms its counterparts.

Keywords: LSTM · Mobile phone

1 Introduction

Neurodegenerative disease (NDD) is a term which results in death of neurons by blocking of the nervous system which includes brain and spinal cord and this is often incurable as neurons do not reproduce [1], NDDs are the main cause

© Springer Nature Switzerland AG 2020
M. Mahmud et al. (Eds.): BI 2020, LNAI 12241, pp. 204–214, 2020.
https://doi.org/10.1007/978-3-030-59277-6_19

of the breakdown of communications among human brain cells. It can change balance, movement (called ataxias), speech, breathing, memory (called dementias), intelligence, and much more in human body [2,3]. Parkinson's, Alzheimer's, Huntington's, etc. are the most frequently diagnosed NDDs. NDDs are mostly considered incurable to disease progression without successful treatments, efficient therapies; patients could even die. A report generated by World Health Organization (WHO) represents that minimum 1 billion people across the world have been affected by neurological disorders such as multiple sclerosis, neuroinfections, headache, Parkinson diseases etc. [1]. It also shows that more than 50 million people are suffering form Alzheimer and other dementias which will be double in next 5 years. After the heart diseases it is the second leading cause of death with minimum 9 million deaths and 16.5% of global deaths [4]. A research show that 6% of total diseases are NDDs and these rate is high in developed and developing countries [5]. Due to the extensive popularity, Machine Learning (ML) methods have been used in biological data mining [6,7] image analysis [8], decision support system [9–13]. In the arena of management Of NDD, deep learning approaches are powerful tools that enable systems to learn from the measured data in order to develop ways of making smarter decisions that can lead to better management of these types of patients. It can help to process medical data with multi-layer neural networks which results in improved prediction capabilities for several specific applications in management of NDDs [6,7]. On the other hand, Internet of Things (IoT) devices are being used to monitor, manage and motivate a new generation of health care with the concept of smart home appliances for aged patients [14–16]. Recent IoT studies focus primarily on smart homes and communication technologies that support remote control of electrical, heating and lighting devices [17].

In this paper a RNN based fall detection framework for patient with NDD has been designed. The activity data from patient with NDD is collected using IoT sensor nodes (such as wearable, smartphone and camera), these information is pre-processed, and analysed in cloud and thereby differentiate fall and normal routine activities. The system can also be used for detecting an anomaly in the patient activity data and send the anomaly information to the doctor at the hospital and fall event to the caregiver/family member.

The rest of the paper is arranged as below: Sect. 2 outlined the related articles; Sect. 3 discussed system model, the methodology and results are explained in Sect. 4 and Sect. 5 respectively. Finally the paper concluded in Sect. 6.

2   Literature Review

This section discuss existing literature related to fall/activity detection and patient management. Sase et al. [18] proposed a method to detect fall using depth videos. By substracting background from extracted frames and doing some preprocessing like filter and analysis of connected components, Region of Interested (ROI) is calculated which helps to detect fall by comparing it to calculated threshold. Mostarac et al. [19] describes a system which can detect fall by using three axis accelerometric data. In this system at least two sensors are needed to collect personal data which contains information about treatment efficiency, mobility of patients which will be sent to the server by local receivers. System will alert the caregiver if fall is detected. Not only early detection of fall but also patient monitoring in real time will be served. Ali *et al.* [20] proposed a quick and precised system to detect fall by videos captured by surveillance camera. This system is represented on the basis of spatial based features and novel temporal which includes discriminatory prejudicial movement, individual location and geometric orientation. Doulamis *et al.* [21] proposed a system to detect fall by a single camera which is independent of direction of fall which using the background subtraction approach using hierarchical motion estimation and Gaussian Mixtures. The accuracy of this system to differentiate between fall and normal activities like sitting, bending is very high. Tzallas *et al.* [22] proposed a model called PERFORM for the real-times remote monitoring, assessment and management of patient's with PD which can be used for personalized treatment (such as therapeutic treatment) and motor status for PD based on recorded data. Pereira *et al.* [23] has developed a mobile application design for the assistance of people suffering from PD. The main focus of this application is to provide knowledge and professional support for both patients and care givers to improve healthcare assistance. Baga *et al.* [24] proposed a system which can minimize the wearable sensors for monitoring and develop quantification algorithm and detect symptoms to help the clinical and caregivers for taking decisions. Punin *et al.* [25] has developed non-invasive hardware-based wireless system to collect data from PD patients with FOG to induce progress of walking, avoid falling which will be collected by a processor and transferred to mobile through bluetooth and enhance the lifestyles of patients. Magariño *et al.* [26] has introduced a novel technology that could potentially support and monitor people with NDDs and focuses on the application of Fog computing to ease the bandwidth uses. LeMoyne *et al.* [27] aims to incorporate a Smartphone as a platform for wireless accelerometers Machine learning to identify deep brain characteristics Stimulator for the ultimate tremor. Three mature systems like a smartphone and machine learning has been successfully to improve the efficiency of deep brain stimulation treatment.

3   System Model

Figure 1 shows the proposed framework for the management of Neurodegenerative disease using machine learning and IoT. The NDD management is a vast process and due to the page limitation, we have considered the fall detection module and the pre/post-fall management using ML and IoT. The expected data can be collected via camera sensors and wearable devices such as mobile, portable devices, smartwatch etc. Accelerometer or Gyroscope is being used to collect data of action like shaking and spinning and camera sensor is being used for detecting the person's position. A smart home system is also connected to the mobile phone for giving immediate comfort such as turning on/off the light or fan etc for the patient's emergency. These acceleration, orientation data and

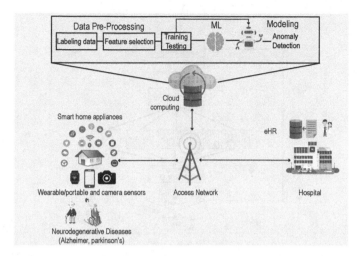

Fig. 1. A function model for Neurodegerative disease management using machine learning and IoT. The physiological, voice and video data collected from the patient using IoT system are sent the collected information to a cloud based platform. The ML algorithm in the cloud convert the data into actionable insight or detect anomaly from the data. The knowledge extracted from data can be sent to personal doctor, caregiver or even the family members.

the data from the camera sensor are being sent to the cloud and e-health records via wifi or cellular net or Ethernet for local access for the specified caretaker and doctors of the patients in the time of emergency. The data is being received and stored in the cloud. Due to page limit, we are not discussing about the processes how the computational cost will be managed in real time detection though cloud. The sent data is being pre-processed such as labeling the data set and feature selection. Then it trains and tests the data set as it expected and applies machine learning algorithms on the collected medical data for analyzing the data and processing patient's clinical assessment, assisting Decision support system and anomaly detection. By this, we can decide which data we should be stored and which not and make a decision. Here, repetitive data is not being saved. It helps to reduce storage size. Thus, the memory will be efficiently used. If an anomaly is detected that means the patient is fallen from chair or standing or any other way and it will automatically notify the caregiver/family member about patient's fall. The flow chart of the proposed fall detection process is illustrated in Fig. 2.

4 Methodology

In this section, we represent our ML framework which includes data collection, data preprocessing feature extraction and ML algorithm to detect a fall. We have used two dataset named UR dataset and Open labeled dataset. These datasets

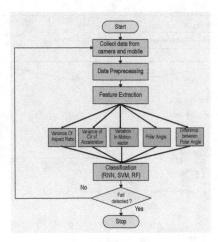

Fig. 2. Flowchart for proposed fall detection system.

have been preprocessed to extract features. From them test set and training set have been divided where train data have been classified by ML classifiers. Figure 3 shows Fall detection architecture and datasets used to train the model. We used two datasets named UR dataset and open labelled dataset in our model. Firstly batch normalization is applied in both datasets. Batch Normalization is a technique to improve the speed at which the network trains, allows higher learning rate by re-scaling and re-centering the input layer. Then RNN layer is applied on both datasets. Then Fully Connected layer applied on both dataset which converts RNN outputs to our desired shape. Softmax is implemented just before the output layer which assign decimal probabilities that must sum to 1. At last knowledge fusion from both datasets are used to detect the fall appropriately.

4.1   Dataset Description

Two datasets named UR dataset and Open labeled dataset have been used in our system (see Table 1). UR fall detection dataset are developed by kepski *et al.* [28] used seventy sequences where thirty are falls and fourty are activities of daily living (ADL). Two camera are used. One is front facing and other is from ceiling which provides the top views of the scene. Kinect cameras and corresponding accelerometric data are used to record fall and one device(camera 0) are used to record ADL. IMU and PS Move devices are used to collect sensor data. Two types of falls, one from standing and other while sitting on a chair are described here. Besides picking object from ground, lying on the sofa and floor, normal walking, sitting down are the ADL. Data needed to extract features of UR are

- **Height/Width**- Bounding box height to width ratio
- **l/w** - Major to minor axis ratio

- **H/Hmax** - A proportion expressing the height of the person's surrounding box in the current frame to the physical height of the person, projected onto the depth map and
- **Area** - A ratio expressing the person's area in the image to the area at assumed distance to the camera.

Wertner *et al.* [29] has created a labelled dataset which can be used for mobile phone with the data of accelerometer and gyroscope sensor. An orientation software based sensor is used to derive data from the accelerometer and geomagnetic field sensor which is attached to the mobile phone and the data is recorded by the mobile phone. Data needed to extract features of Open labelled are:

- **Acceleration of devices:** Acceleration is stored as 3D vector indicating acceleration along each device axis, not including gravity. It can be calculated as

$$a_{xyz} = \sqrt{x^2 + y^2 + z^2} \tag{1}$$

- **Orientation of devices:** Orientation is stored as 3D vector of angles azimuth, pitch and roll.

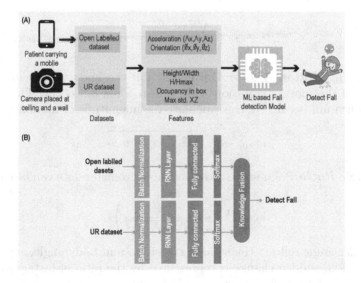

Fig. 3. Proposed Fall Detection Architecture and datasets used to train the model. (A) shows features used in the proposed RNN model and (B) illustrate the RNN architecture

Table 1. Information about the dataset used in this study.

Dataset	Sensor used	No of record	Training	Testing
Open Labelled	Smart phone	159300 records of acceleration and 159300 records of orientation	223020	95580
UR	Camera	70 (30 falls and 40 activities of daily living) sequences	49	21

4.2   Feature Extraction

A feature extraction module performs a significant role in the fall detection system. To enhance the fall detection rate, our focus was on the generation and selection of features. In this research we have extracted five features from UR and open labeled dataset.

It represents the variety of change of the magnitude of acceleration in x, y and z axis.

Variance of CV Acceleration:If we divide the standard deviation of acceleration by it's mean (μ) we can get the coefficient of variation.

$$\sigma_{xyz} = \frac{\sqrt{\sigma_x^2 + \sigma_y^2 + \sigma_z^2}}{\mu} \tag{2}$$

Variation in Motion Vector:During the fall the body is in a motion and magnitude of the motion variation will be high when fall occur. The variation will be 0 when fall occur. We can calculate the magnitude of motion by:

$$m_{xyz} = \sqrt{(m_x^2 + m_y^2 + m_z^2)} \tag{3}$$

Polar Angle Ratio:Polar angle ratio from accelerometer data can be calculated as follows:

$$\cos^{-1}\left(\frac{z}{\sqrt{x^2 + y^2 + z^2}}\right) \tag{4}$$

This polar angle reflects the sudden transition and body angle, suggesting a fall. In addition, sudden change is represented by the ratio of instant angle and it's previous values within a short period of time.

Difference Between Polar Angle: It is represented by $\Delta\theta$ which helps to cover large tilt angle variations.

4.3   ML Algorithm

Recurrent Neural Network (RNN): RNN mainly used for supervised time series analysis is a machine learning algorithm where outputs of the previous step are used for the inputs of next step. Hidden state are the most important feature of RNN. RNN with convolutionary layers are used to expand the successful neighborhood of pixels.

Random Forest (RF): Random forest is a supervised learning algorithm which is a combination of decision trees where the forest is build by an assemble of decision trees to increase the overall result by combining learning models. Here the input is evaluated by the decision tree forest and the output class is measured as the tree's response class.

Support Vector Machine (SVM): SVM which is mostly used for classification is a machine learning algorithm which helps to solve pattern recognition. Coordinates of individual observations are represented by support vector. It is a frontier that separates both classes at its best. Each data item is ploted in an n-dimensional space where n indicates the number of features we have and the value of each feature represent the value of a particular coordinates.

4.4   Model Training

For training purpose both the datasets are splitted into two parts: 70% data from each dataset is used for training and the remaining 30% is used for testing. For the 5-fold cross validation, we used random partition from the datasets.

5   Numerical Results

This section discussed the numerical results obtained using state-of-the-art classifiers. We have utilized Weka for evaluating the performance of the classification algorithms (RF, SVM, and RNN) which can be used to detect falls as well as the normal daily activities of the people with neurological diseases. For each classifier, we use precision, sensitivity, specificity, and F-1 score.

The proposed RNN based fall detection architecture contains two parallel structure, each consists of a batch normalization layer, an RNN layer and a fully-connected layer followed by softmax output layers. The model was trained using Adam optimizer and for 30 epochs with a learning rate of 0.001, batch size of 32 and RNN dropout of zero on the training dataset. After training, the model was tested using the separated test dataset.

Table 2 shows the classification performance of RF, SVM and RNN.

From the table (see Table 2), we can depicted that RNN and SVM have better accuracy, Precision, specificity and F1-Score than the RF. But the sensitivity is better in RF then the SVM and RNN. From overall analysis, we can see that the Fused algorithm gives better Accuracy, precision, sensitivity, specificity, and F1-score, whereas Open labelled gives the lowest value of these performance matrices.

Table 2. Performance comparison of RNN with RF and SVM

Dataset	Classifier	Accuracy	Precision	Sensitivity	Specificity	F1-Score
Open Labelled	RF	0.96801	0.95979	0.98411	0.94749	0.97179
	SVM	0.98101	0.9754	0.99139	0.96752	0.98333
	RNN	0.97226	0.96369	0.98711	0.95257	0.97555
URRF	RF	0.95652	0.96296	0.96296	0.94737	0.96296
	SVM	0.97778	0.96296	1	0.94737	0.98113
	RNN	0.95652	0.96428	0.96429	0.94444	0.96429
Fused	RF	0.9680	0.9598	0.9841	0.9475	0.9718
	SVM	0.9808	0.97506	0.9913	0.9675	0.9831
	RNN	0.9723	0.9637	0.9877	0.9526	0.9756

6   Conclusion

Management of neurodegenerative diseases is a vast and condemnatory process. As falls are the second leading cause of accidental or unintentional injury deaths worldwide among elderly people having a neurological disorder, in our proposed model, we have worked on designing a recurrent neural network-based framework which can detect any occurrence of fall/daily activity of a patient using IoT and then send this data to the specified doctor and also notify caregivers/family members about the fall events through the available communication line easily. In our RNN based fall detection Architecture, fused knowledge from wearable/portable and imaging devices (camera) has been used for the fall detection. Open-labeled and UR data-sets are used to train the preferred ML method, RNN and the performance is compared with two classifier like RF and SVM for these two data-sets. The comparison of the performance evaluation shows that the proposed RNN based fall detection framework is worthwhile and excels its counterparts. In future, we will integrate other management features with this model to extend the scope and enhance the quality of experiences.

References

1. Noor, M.B.T., Zenia, N.Z., Kaiser, M.S., Mahmud, M., Al Mamun, S.: Detecting neurodegenerative disease from MRI: a brief review on a deep learning perspective. In: Liang, P., Goel, V., Shan, C. (eds.) BI 2019. LNCS, vol. 11976, pp. 115–125. Springer, Cham (2019). https://doi.org/10.1007/978-3-030-37078-7_12
2. Bak, T.H., et al.: What wires together dies together. Cortex J. Devoted Study Nerv. Syst. Behav. **48**(7), 936–944 (2012)
3. Finkbeiner, S.: Huntington's disease. Cold Spring Harb. Perspect. Biol. **3**(6) (2011)
4. Carroll, W.M.: The global burden of neurological disorders. Lancet Neurol. **18**(5), 418–419 (2019)
5. Journal of National Institute of Neurosciences Bangladesh. Accessed 10 June 2020

6. Mahmud, M., et al.: Applications of deep learning and reinforcement learning to biological data. IEEE Trans. Neural Netw. Learn. Syst. **29**(6), 2063–2079 (2018)
7. Mahmud, M., Shamim Kaiser, M., Hussain, A.: Deep learning in mining biological data. arXiv:2003.00108 [cs, q-bio, stat], pp. 1–36, February 2020
8. Ali, H.M., Kaiser, M.S., Mahmud, M.: Application of convolutional neural network in segmenting brain regions from MRI data. In: Liang, P., Goel, V., Shan, C. (eds.) BI 2019. LNCS, vol. 11976, pp. 136–146. Springer, Cham (2019). https://doi.org/10.1007/978-3-030-37078-7_14
9. Kaiser, M.S., et al.: Advances in crowd analysis for urban applications through urban event detection. IEEE Trans. Intell. Transp. Syst. **19**(10), 3092–3112 (2018)
10. Zohora, M.F., et al. Forecasting the risk of type ii diabetes using reinforcement learning. In: Proceedings of the ICIEV, pp. 1–6 (2020)
11. Watkins, J., Fabietti, M., Mahmud, M.: Sense: a student performance quantifier using sentiment analysis. In: Proceedings of the IJCNN, pp. 1–6 (2020)
12. Mahmud, M., et al.: A brain-inspired trust management model to assure security in a cloud based iot framework for neuroscience applications. Cogn. Comput. **10**(5), 864–873 (2018). https://doi.org/10.1007/s12559-018-9543-3
13. Tania, M.H., et al.: Assay type detection using advanced machine learning algorithms. In: Proceedings of the SKIMA, pp. 1–8 (2019)
14. Lam, S., et al.: The future E-living for elderly. Int. J. Online Biomed. Eng. (iJOE) **6**(1), 4–11 (2010)
15. Afsana, F., Mamun, S.A., Kaiser, M.S., Ahmed, M.R.: Outage capacity analysis of cluster-based forwarding scheme for body area network using nano-electromagnetic communication. In: Proceedings of the EICT, pp. 383–388 (2015)
16. Asif-Ur-Rahman, Md, et al.: Toward a heterogeneous mist, fog, and cloud-based framework for the internet of healthcare things. IEEE Internet Things J. **6**(3), 4049–4062 (2018)
17. Arunvivek, J., et al.: Framework development in home automation to provide control and security for home automated devices. Indian J. Sci. Technol. **8** (2015)
18. Tsai, T.-H., et al.: Implementation of fall detection system based on 3D skeleton for deep learning technique. IEEE Access **7**, 153049–153059 (2019)
19. Automatic Fall Monitoring: A Review
20. Ali, S.F., et al.: Using temporal covariance of motion and geometric features via boosting for human fall detection. Sensors (Basel, Switzerland) **18**(6) (2018)
21. Doulamis, A., et al.: A real-time single-camera approach for automatic fall detection. ISPRS Comm. V Close Range Image meas. Tech. **38**, 207–212 (2010)
22. Tzallas, A.T., et al.: PERFORM: a system for monitoring, assessment and management of patients with Parkinson's disease. Sensors **14**(11), 21329–21357 (2014)
23. Pereira, C., Macedo, P., Madeira, R.N.: Mobile integrated assistance to empower people coping with Parkinson's disease. In: Proceedings of the ACM SIGACCESS, pp. 409–410. Association for Computing Machinery, New York (2015)
24. Baga, D., et al.: PERFORM: a platform for monitoring and management of chronic neurodegenerative diseases: the Parkinson and amyotrophic lateral sclerosis case. IEEE Conference Publication (2009)
25. Punin, C., Barzallo, B., Huerta, M., Bermeo, A., Bravo, M., Llumiguano, C.: Wireless devices to restart walking during an episode of FOG on patients with Parkinson's disease. IEEE Conference Publication (2017)
26. García-Magariño, I., Varela-Aldas, J., Palacios-Navarro, G., Lloret, J.: Fog computing for assisting and tracking elder patients with neurodegenerative diseases. Peer-to-Peer Netw. Appl. **12**(5), 1225–1235 (2019). https://doi.org/10.1007/s12083-019-00732-4

27. LeMoyne, R., Tomycz, N., Mastroianni, T., McCandless, C., Cozza, M., Peduto, D.: Implementation of a smartphone wireless accelerometer platform for establishing deep brain stimulation treatment efficacy of essential tremor with machine learning. IEEE Conference Publication (2015)
28. Kwolek, B., et al.: Human fall detection on embedded platform using depth maps and wireless accelerometer. Comput. Methods Programs Biomed. **117**(3), 489–501 (2014)
29. Wertner, A., et al.: An open labelled dataset for mobile phone sensing based fall detection. In: Proceedings of Computing, Networking and Services on 12th EAI International Conference on Mobile and Ubiquitous Systems, pages 277–278 (2015)

Informatics Paradigms for Brain and Mental Health Research

A Computational Model for Simultaneous Employment of Multiple Emotion Regulation Strategies

Bas Chatel⬤, Atke Visser⬤, and Nimat Ullah$^{(\boxtimes)}$⬤

Social AI Group, Vrije Universiteit Amsterdam, Amsterdam, The Netherlands
bastiaan.chatel@gmail.com, atke.visser@hotmail.com, nimatullah09@gmail.com

Abstract. Emotion regulation plays a major role in everyday life, as it enables individuals to modulate their emotions. Several strategies, for regulating emotions, can be used individually or simultaneously, such as suppression, rumination, acceptance, problem-solving, self-criticism, and experiential avoidance. This paper presents a temporal causal network model that simulates the employment of these seven emotion regulation strategies by a person experiencing varying intensity of anxiety. Simulation results are reported for both, the high and low, emotional intensity where the level of activation of these strategies vary with the intensity of negative emotions.

Keywords: Emotion regulation · Cognitive reappraisal · Expressive suppression · Rumination · Acceptance · Problem-solving · Self-criticism · Experiential avoidance · Temporal causal network modeling

1 Introduction

People continually deal with a large variety of stimuli that has to be processed in one way or another. The fact that their reactions to such stimuli are mostly tempered versus causing unceasing outbursts of emotional behavior suggests that some form of emotion regulation is employed [1]. These forms of emotion regulation can entail active and deliberate ways to override or redirect one's emotional response, however, it can also consist of relatively autonomous and effortless actions to divert the flow of emotions [2]. These attempts to manage one's emotional states, such as moods, stress and positive or negative affect are essential as individuals with poorly regulated emotions are exposed to, including but not limited to, higher risks of severe periods of distress that may, later on, evolve into diagnosable depression or anxiety [3]. Emotion regulation strategies such as suppression and avoidance are viewed as maladaptive responses to a plurality of stressors. Employing these strategies brings about not only risk factors such as the aforementioned depression and anxiety but also maladaptive behaviors such as substance abuse. Different theoretical models have disaggregated the set of

© Springer Nature Switzerland AG 2020
M. Mahmud et al. (Eds.): BI 2020, LNAI 12241, pp. 217–226, 2020.
https://doi.org/10.1007/978-3-030-59277-6_20

emotion regulation strategies into two types: adaptive and maladaptive strategies [3]. Maladaptive strategies are strategies that fail to modulate the intensity of an emotional experience, despite the individual's intention to achieve the contrary, whereas adaptive strategies succeed in this endeavor [4].

This paper considers the dynamical interplay between different emotion regulation strategies within a temporal-causal network. These strategies are either putatively adaptive (acceptance, cognitive reappraisal, problem-solving) or maladaptive (experiential avoidance, expressive suppression, self-criticism, rumination) and are adopted from [5]. A computational model has been proposed wherein all the aforementioned seven emotion regulation strategies are simultaneously employed to some degree as found out in [5]. The rest of the paper is organized as follows. Section 2 of the paper provides a general scenario for the model which has been explained by the background studies from social sciences. Section 3 presents the computational model. Section 4 provides simulation results and finally, Sect. 5 concludes this paper.

2   Background

To guide further endeavors we defined a scenario in which the simulation will operate. By defining the boundaries of our simulation, ambiguity is stripped away, and we can proceed with a clear common focus. We will then place each emotion regulation strategy within this scenario, explaining how it operates, and how it will intuitively function within a model. The scenario is as follows:

"At a company party, an employee has a conversation with the head of the HR department. After a few drinks, the employee starts talking about a colleague with whom he is friends, which, in retrospect, puts him in a bad light. The next day the employee wakes up with a feeling of anxiety, what if his colleague friend gets in trouble because of this?"

At this point in the scenario, the employee has a total of seven emotion regulation strategies in his repertoire to determine an action. Each regulation strategy will have a different effect on the employee's behavior if they obtained a dominant role in the narrative. The temporal aspect of emotion regulation is also of importance as they can be conscious or unconscious, automatic or controlled. The strategies employed in this research are categorized as antecedent-focused, these occur before an emotion has become completely active, and response-focused, taking place after the emotion is already activated [6]. In light of the above scenario, the courses of actions a person can opt for, form the given repertoire, are elaborated one by one. Starting from acceptance, the employee slowly accepts that there was a mistake, but that is now out of his hands. This reduces his anxiety, and he moves on with his day. Acceptance is an adaptive emotion regulation strategy where the person allows or accepts his/her feelings without attempts to alter or suppress the emotions. This entails a willingness to remain in contact with these experiences causing the emotion, even if they are unpleasant [5,7]. It alters the feeling state that one experiences [8]. In terms of timing, acceptance is categorized as a response focused strategy [9]. In problem-Solving, the employee decides to approach the head of the HR department and explains that he was just joking, therefore negating what he said the day before and defusing the situation. This strategy is adaptive and is a conscious attempt to alter stressful situations or contain its consequences and is, therefore, directly addressing the problem itself [10]. In terms of timing problem-solving is categorized as an antecedent focused strategy [11]. In self-criticism the employee blames and criticizes himself that he cannot do anything right. This strategy is said to be maladaptive and is tightly bound to feelings of shame [5]. The devaluation of self threatens the need to feel valued and queues additional negative affective states [12]. It is, therefore, not linked to decreasing emotion but is adding more layers on top of the already existing system. The regulation of this extra layer is, however, beyond the scope of this paper. In terms of timing, self-criticism is categorized as an antecedent focused strategy [13]. Moving on to the experiential avoidance, where the employee pinches himself every time he thinks about what had happened, to focus on other things. This strategy is also termed as maladaptive and is mediated by two emotion regulation strategies (i.e. suppression and reappraisal), it is an act of introducing another stimulus to avoid experiencing the initial stressor [14]. In terms of timing, experiential avoidance is categorized as an antecedent focused emotion regulation strategy [15].

Similarly, if the employee pretends like nothing has happened and tries to prevent others from seeing how bad he is feeling then it's called suppression. This strategy is response focused maladaptive strategy [15]. For how suppression can be modeled, please refer to [16,17]. Rumination is also referred to as worry and in the above scenario, if the employee keeps thinking about what had happened and keeps reiterating over what he has said, will be referred to as rumination. This is an antecedent focused maladaptive emotion regulation strategy [18]. For how to model rumination as a strategy, please refer to [19]. Reappraisal is when the employee convinces himself that it is for the good, as it was his colleague that made a mistake. This strategy is antecedent focused adaptive emotion regulation strategy [15]. Reappraisal has already been modeled by various studies, for instance [16,20,21]. These emotion-regulation strategies culminate into a dynamical model that is represented in the following section.

3   Conceptual Representation of the Model

This section gives an overview of the proposed computational model, which is designed using the Network-Oriented Modeling approach [22] see also [23]. This modeling approach is based on temporal-causal networks, in which each node represents a state or state variable, and each link represents a causal relation that defines how one state influences the other state over time. This paper presents a temporal causal network model that simulates the aforementioned seven emotion regulation over time. The conceptual representation of the introduced computational model is depicted in Fig. 1, and the states are explained in Table 1.

This model depicted in Fig. 1 models simultaneous employment of the seven emotion regulation strategies for coping with anxiety. Firstly, the emotion regulation strategy problem-solving modifies or eliminates stressors, which is depicted

Table 1. Nomenclature of the states in the model.

States	Description
X_1 ws$_p$	World state for the problem
X_2 ws$_s$	World state for the stimulus s
X_3 ss$_s$	Sensor state for the stimulus s
X_4 srs$_s$	Sensory representation state for the stimulus s
X_5 ps$_a$	Preparation state for action a
X_6 es$_a$	Execution state for action a
X_7 bs$_-$	Positive belief state about the stimulus s
X_8 bs$_+$	Negative belief state about the stimulus s
X_9 ps$_b$	Preparation state for body state b
X_{10} es$_b$	Execution state for body state b
X_{11} cs$_{rumin}$	Control state for rumination
X_{12} cs$_{pr.solv}$	Control state for problem-solving
X_{13} cs$_{self-cri}$	Control state for self-criticism
X_{14} cs$_{reapp}$	Control state for reappraisal
X_{15} cs$_{accep}$	Control state for acceptance
X_{16} cs$_{sup}$	Control state for suppression
X_{17} cs$_{exp.av}$	Control state for experiential avoidance
X_{18} ms$_{l.int}$	Monitoring state for low intensity
X_{19} ms$_{h.int}$	Monitoring state for high intensity
X_{20} ps$_{shame}$	Preparation state for shame
X_{21} es$_{shame}$	Execution state for shame
X_{22} ss$_{shame}$	Sensory state for shame
X_{23} srs$_{shame}$	Sensory representation state for shame
X_{24} fs$_{shame}$	Feeling state for shame
X_{25} ss$_b$	Sensory state for body state b
X_{26} srs$_b$	Sensory representation state for body state b
X_{27} fs$_b$	Feeling state for body state b
X_{28} ps$_{act}$	Preparation state for 'action' experiential avoidance
X_{29} es$_{act}$	Execution state for 'action' experiential avoidance
X_{30} ss$_{act}$	Sensory state for 'action' experiential avoidance
X_{31} srs$_{act}$	Sensory representation state for 'action' experiential avoidance
X_{32} fs$_{act}$	Feeling state for 'action' experiential avoidance

in the model as a negative connection from the control state for problem-solving cs$_{pr.sol}$ to the problem in the world ws$_p$. Secondly, in case of rumination, an individual worry about the situation and keeps thinking about it. This is represented in the model by a positive connection from the control state for rumination cs$_{rumin}$ to the sensory representation state of the stimulus srs$_s$. Thirdly, in self-criticism, no efforts are made to alter the emotions. Moreover, self-criticism relates to shame proneness, and therefore, the control state for self-criticism cs$_{self-cri}$ activates an entire loop which keeps increasing feeling of shame as the person criticizes him/herself. Fourthly, when employing reappraisal, the control state for reappraisal cs$_{reapp}$ diminishes the negative belief bs$_-$ about the stimulus, i.e. thinking differently about the stimuli.

The negative belief about the stimulus influences, in its turn, the body states b. At fifth comes acceptance, wherein the person accepts the consequences of the stimuli, i.e. not altering his emotions but this automatically reduces the intensity of negative emotions indicated by the negative connection to the feeling state of the body fs_b from the control state for acceptance cs_{accep}.

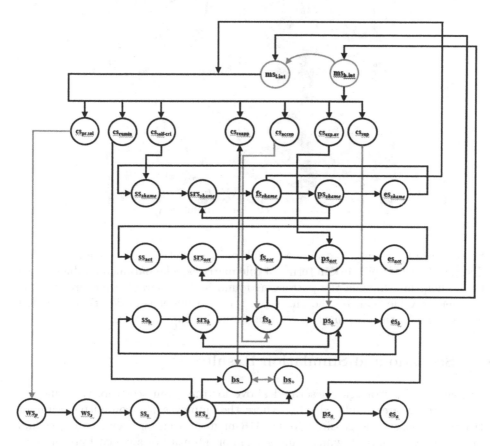

Fig. 1. Representation of the computational model.

As a penultimate strategy, if someone is employing experiential avoidance, the person performs some action, represented by the action states act in the model, to put the emotions out of his mind. The feeling state for this action fs_{act} suppresses the feeling state for the body fs_b. Finally, suppression, here the corresponding control state cs_{sup} suppresses the expression of emotions, indicated by the negative connection to preparation ps_b for body state b, while the negative belief of the stimulus remains unchanged.

The computational model presented above uses advanced logistic sum combination function for the aggregation of multiple incoming casual impacts. On contrary, [23] provides a library of over 36 combination functions which can also

mb connectivity: base connectivity		1	2	3	mcw connectivity: connection weights		1	2	3
X_1	ws_p	X_1	X_{12}		X_1	ws_p	0.8	-1	
X_2	ws_s	X_1			X_2	ws_s	1		
X_3	ss_s	X_2			X_3	ss_s	1		
X_4	srs_s	X_3	X_{11}		X_4	srs_s	1	0.1	
X_5	ps_a	X_4	X_{10}		X_5	ps_a	1	1	
X_6	es_a	X_5			X_6	es_a	1		
X_7	bs_-	X_4	X_8	X_{14}	X_7	bs_-	0.7	-0.4	-1
X_8	bs_+	X_4	X_7		X_8	bs_+	0.3	-0.4	
X_9	ps_b	X_7	X_{16}	X_{27}	X_9	ps_b	0.8	-0.8	0.8
X_{10}	es_b	X_9			X_{10}	es_b	1		
X_{11}	cs_{rumin}	X_{18}	X_{19}		X_{11}	cs_{rumin}	0.48	0.27	
X_{12}	$cs_{pr.solv}$	X_{18}	X_{19}		X_{12}	$cs_{pr.solv}$	0.18	0.39	
X_{13}	$cs_{self-cri}$	X_{18}	X_{19}		X_{13}	$cs_{self-cri}$	0.41	0.12	
X_{14}	cs_{reapp}	X_7	X_{18}	X_{19}	X_{14}	cs_{reapp}	0.1	0.1	0.35
X_{15}	cs_{accep}	X_{18}	X_{19}		X_{15}	cs_{accep}	0.15	0.25	
X_{16}	$cs_{s\,up}$	X_{18}	X_{19}		X_{16}	$cs_{s\,up}$	0.28	0.25	
X_{17}	$cs_{exp.av}$	X_{18}	X_{19}		X_{17}	$cs_{exp.av}$	0.4	0.25	
X_{18}	$ms_{l.int}$	X_{27}	X_{19}		X_{18}	$ms_{l.int}$	0.8	-1	
X_{19}	$ms_{h.int}$	X_{27}			X_{19}	$ms_{h.int}$	0.8		
X_{20}	ps_{shame}	X_{24}			X_{20}	ps_{shame}	0.8		
X_{21}	es_{shame}	X_{20}			X_{21}	es_{shame}	.06		
X_{22}	ss_{shame}	X_{21}	X_{13}		X_{22}	ss_{shame}	0.4	0.4	
X_{23}	srs_{shame}	X_{22}	X_{20}		X_{23}	srs_{shame}	0.4	0.6	
X_{24}	fs_{shame}	X_{23}			X_{24}	fs_{shame}	0.8		
X_{25}	ss_b	X_{10}			X_{25}	ss_b	0.8		
X_{26}	srs_b	X_9	X_{25}		X_{26}	srs_b	0.5	0.5	
X_{27}	fs_b	X_{15}	X_{26}	X_{32}	X_{27}	fs_b	-0.8	1	-1
X_{28}	ps_{act}	X_{17}	X_{32}		X_{28}	ps_{act}	0.4	0.2	
X_{29}	es_{act}	X_{28}			X_{29}	es_{act}	0.9		
X_{30}	ss_{act}	X_{29}			X_{30}	ss_{act}	0.8		
X_{31}	srs_{act}	X_{30}	X_{28}		X_{31}	srs_{act}	0.5	0.4	
X_{32}	fs_{act}	X_{31}			X_{32}	fs_{act}	0.6		

Box-1.   Role matrices for connectivity

be updated by adding own defined combination functions. **Box-1** and **2** below, display the whole network in terms of role matrices. The parameter values in the boxes help in achieving the pattern as found in the relevant literature. So, the parameter values can be chosen as per scenario under consideration. Detailed explanation of the role matrices can be found in [23].

4   Scenario and Simulation Results

Employing the strategies described above for the given scenario, two different sub-scenarios are simulated. One where the employee has committed a minor transgression, such as gossiping to the HR-manager that his friend/colleague had done something foolish which causes a minor intensity of anxiety. Furthermore, we will explore what would happen if the employee has committed something more serious (i.e. something that could get his friend fired), causing a higher intensity of anxiety. These strategies and the intensity of their activation has been adopted from [5] and a test subject has been selected who experienced different levels of anxiety to match that to the described scenario. Results of the simulations for low and high intensity of anxiety can be consulted below in Fig. 2 and Fig. 3, respectively.

The results for the emotion regulation strategies of the person experiencing anxiety at low emotional intensity are presented in Fig. 2. The figure represents only the most essential states out of the thirty-two states involved in the process. In the figure the world state for problem ws_p indicates that the problem i.e. stimulus has happened and therefore all the states on the casual path to feeling

| mcfw aggregation: | 2 | 21 | mcfp aggregation: | 2 | | 21 | ms timing: | |
combination func-tion weights	alog	id	combination func-tion parameters	σ	τ	id	speed factor	η
X_1 ws_p	1		X_1 ws_p	5	0.1		X_1 ws_p	0.08
X_2 ws_s		1	X_2 ws_s			1	X_2 ws_s	0.5
X_3 ss_s		1	X_3 ss_s			1	X_3 ss_s	0.5
X_4 srs_s		1	X_4 srs_s			1	X_4 srs_s	0.5
X_5 ps_a		1	X_5 ps_a			1	X_5 ps_a	0.5
X_6 es_a		1	X_6 es_a			1	X_6 es_a	0.5
X_7 bs_-	1		X_7 bs_-	5	0.2		X_7 bs_-	0.2
X_8 bs_+	1		X_8 bs_+	5	0.1		X_8 bs_+	0.2
X_9 ps_b	1		X_9 ps_b	5	0.2		X_9 ps_b	0.5
X_{10} es_b		1	X_{10} es_b			1	X_{10} es_b	0.5
X_{11} cs_{rumin}	1		X_{11} cs_{rumin}	5	0.2		X_{11} cs_{rumin}	0.1
X_{12} $cs_{pr.solv}$	1		X_{12} $cs_{pr.solv}$	5	0.2		X_{12} $cs_{pr.solv}$	0.1
X_{13} $cs_{self-cri}$	1		X_{13} $cs_{self-cri}$	5	0.1		X_{13} $cs_{self-cri}$	0.1
X_{14} cs_{reapp}	1		X_{14} cs_{reapp}	5	0.2		X_{14} cs_{reapp}	0.1
X_{15} cs_{accep}	1		X_{15} cs_{accep}	5	0.1		X_{15} cs_{accep}	0.05
X_{16} cs_{sup}	1		X_{16} cs_{sup}	7	0.1		X_{16} cs_{sup}	0.05
X_{17} $cs_{exp.av}$	1		X_{17} $cs_{exp.av}$	5	0.1		X_{17} $cs_{exp.av}$	0.05
X_{18} $ms_{l.int}$	1		X_{18} $ms_{l.int}$	5	0.1		X_{18} $ms_{l.int}$	0.4
X_{19} $ms_{h.int}$	1		X_{19} $ms_{h.int}$	60	0.3		X_{19} $ms_{h.int}$	0.4
X_{20} ps_{shame}	1		X_{20} ps_{shame}	5	0.3		X_{20} ps_{shame}	0.1
X_{21} es_{shame}	1		X_{21} es_{shame}	5	0.3		X_{21} es_{shame}	0.1
X_{22} ss_{shame}	1		X_{22} ss_{shame}	5	0.3		X_{22} ss_{shame}	0.1
X_{23} srs_{shame}	1		X_{23} srs_{shame}	5	0.3		X_{23} srs_{shame}	0.1
X_{24} fs_{shame}	1		X_{24} fs_{shame}	5	0.3		X_{24} fs_{shame}	0.1
X_{25} ss_b	1		X_{25} ss_b	5	0.3		X_{25} ss_b	0.5
X_{26} srs_b	1		X_{26} srs_b	5	0.3		X_{26} srs_b	0.5
X_{27} fs_b	1		X_{27} fs_b	5	0.25		X_{27} fs_b	0.5
X_{28} ps_{act}	1		X_{28} ps_{act}	5	0.3		X_{28} ps_{act}	0.1
X_{29} es_{act}	1		X_{29} es_{act}	5	0.3		X_{29} es_{act}	0.1
X_{30} ss_{act}	1		X_{30} ss_{act}	5	0.3		X_{30} ss_{act}	0.1
X_{31} srs_{act}	1		X_{31} srs_{act}	5	0.3		X_{31} srs_{act}	0.1
X_{32} fs_{act}	1		X_{32} fs_{act}	5	0.3		X_{32} fs_{act}	0.1

Box-2. Role matrices for aggregation and timing

state fs_b has gotten activated (not shown in the figure to make the figure readable except fs_b). The feeling state fs_b activates the respective monitoring state on the basis of the intensity of emotions i.e. monitoring state for low intensity $ms_{l.int}$, in this case. The monitoring state activates the control states for the emotion regulation strategies. The antecedent focused strategies (reappraisal, problem-solving, rumination, and self-criticism) are activated earlier than the response-focused strategies (suppression, acceptance, experiential avoidance).

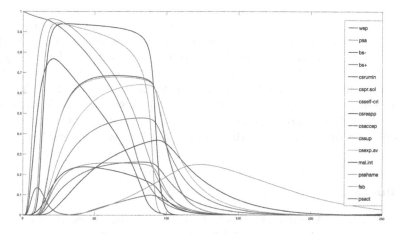

Fig. 2. Simulation results for a person experiencing anxiety with emotion regulation at low emotional intensity.

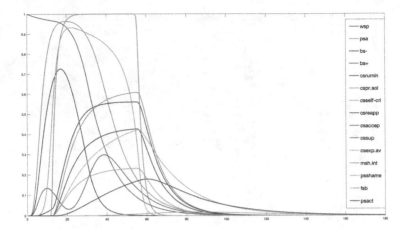

Fig. 3. Simulation results for a person experiencing anxiety with emotion regulation at high emotional intensity.

When the control states for the emotion regulation strategies are activated, first, problem in the world ws_p starts decreasing due to the control state for problem solving $cs_{pr.solv}$ which means the problem is tried to be solved. Similarly, all the other strategies try to influence their respective states either positively or negatively as indicated in the model in Fig. 1. When the individual experiences high emotional intensity, the activation level of the emotion regulation strategies is different from the activation level of the strategies when the person experiences emotions with relatively low intensity [5]. Figure 3 Shows the activation level of the various emotion regulation strategies in case of high intensity of negative emotions.

5   Conclusion

Several emotion regulation strategies can be used to manage emotions, such as suppression, rumination, acceptance, problem-solving, self-criticism, and experiential avoidance. The introduced model in this paper computes the employment of these emotion regulation strategies for an individual dealing with anxiety. In this paper, results are provided for high and low emotional intensity. The results for these scenarios correspond to literature. In future work, and adaptive model can be developed on top of the existing model for regulation of the shame developed as a result of self-criticism, thus adding another layer of complexity to the model.

References

1. Davidson, R.J.: Affective style and affective disorders: perspectives from affective neuroscience. Cogn. Emot. **12**(3), 307–330 (1998). https://doi.org/10.1080/026999398379628

2. Koole, S.L.: The psychology of emotion regulation: an integrative review. Cogn. Emot. **23**(1), 4–41 (2009). https://doi.org/10.1080/02699930802619031
3. Aldao, A., Nolen-Hoeksema, S., Schweizer, S.: Emotion-regulation strategies across psychopathology: a meta-analytic review. Clin. Psychol. Rev. **30**(2), 217–37 (2010). https://doi.org/10.1016/j.cpr.2009.11.004
4. Conklin, L.R., et al.: Relationships among adaptive and maladaptive emotion regulation strategies and psychopathology during the treatment of comorbid anxiety and alcohol use disorders. Behav. Res. Ther. **73**(2015), 124–130 (2015). https://doi.org/10.1016/j.brat.2015.08.001
5. Dixon-Gordon, K.L., Aldao, A., De Los Reyes, A.: Emotion regulation in context: examining the spontaneous use of strategies across emotional intensity and type of emotion. Personality Individ. Differ. **86**(2015), 271–276 (2015). https://doi.org/10.1016/j.paid.2015.06.011
6. Boss, A.D., Sims, H.P.: Everyone fails!. J. Manag. Psychol. **23**(2), 135–150 (2008). https://doi.org/10.1108/02683940810850781
7. Wolgast, M., Lundh, L., Viborg, G.: Cognitive reappraisal and acceptance: an experimental comparison of two emotion regulation strategies. Behav. Res. Ther. **49**(12), 858–866 (2011). https://doi.org/10.1016/j.brat.2011.09.011
8. Hofmann, S.G., Asmundson, G.J.G.: Acceptance and mindfulness-based therapy: new wave or old hat? Clin. Psychol. Rev. **28**(1), 1–16 (2008). https://doi.org/10.1016/j.cpr.2007.09.003
9. Wolgast, M., Lundh, L.-G., Viborg, G.: Cognitive restructuring and acceptance: an empirically grounded conceptual analysis. Cogn. Ther. Res. **37**(2), 340–351 (2013). https://doi.org/10.1007/s10608-012-9477-0
10. Billings, A.G., Moos, R.H.: The role of coping responses and social resources in attenuating the stress of life events. J. Behav. Med. **4**(2), 139–157 (1981). https://doi.org/10.1007/BF00844267
11. Compare, A., Zarbo, C., Shonin, E., Van Gordon, W., Marconi, C.: Emotional regulation and depression: a potential mediator between heart and mind. Cardiovasc. Psychiatry Neurol. **2014**(2014), 1–10 (2014). https://doi.org/10.1155/2014/324374
12. Gross, J.J.: Handbook of Emotion Regulation, 2nd edn. Guilford Press, New York (2014)
13. Thoma, C.N., McKay, D.: Working with Emotion in Cognitive-Behavioral Therapy: Techniques for Clinical Practice. The Guilford Press, New York (2015)
14. Kashdan, T.B., Barrios, V., Forsyth, J.P., Steger, M.F.: Experiential avoidance as a generalized psychological vulnerability: comparisons with coping and emotion regulation strategies. Behav. Res. Ther. **44**(9), 1301–1320 (2006). https://doi.org/10.1016/j.brat.2005.10.003
15. Appleton, A.A., Loucks, E.B., Buka, S.L., Kubzansky, L.D.: Divergent associations of antecedent- and response-focused emotion regulation strategies with midlife cardiovascular disease risk. Ann. Behav. Med. **48**(2), 246–255 (2014). https://doi.org/10.1007/s12160-014-9600-4
16. Gao, Z., Liu, R., Ullah, N.: A temporal-causal network model for age and gender difference in choice of emotion regulation strategies. In: Nguyen, N.T., Chbeir, R., Exposito, E., Aniorté, P., Trawiński, B. (eds.) ICCCI 2019. LNCS (LNAI), vol. 11683, pp. 106–117. Springer, Cham (2019). https://doi.org/10.1007/978-3-030-28377-3_9

17. Ullah, N., Treur, J., Koole, S.L.: A computational model for flexibility in emotion regulation. In: Samsonovich, A.V., Lebiere, C.J. (eds.) Post Proceedings of the 9th Annual International Conference on Biologically Inspired Cognitive Architectures, BICA 2018 (Ninth Annual Meeting of the BICA Society), held 22–24 August 2018 in Prague, Czech Republic, pp. 572–580. Elsevier B.V. (2018)

18. Peuters, C., Kalokerinos, E.K., Pe, M.L., Kuppens, P.: Sequential effects of reappraisal and rumination on anger during recall of an anger-provoking event. PLoS One **14**(1), 1–16 (2019). https://doi.org/10.1371/journal.pone.0209029

19. Ullah, N., Treur, J.: How motivated are you? A mental network model for dynamic goal driven emotion regulation. In: Proceeding of the 9th International Conference on Artificial Intelligence and Soft Computing. ICAISC 2020. Lecture Notes in Artificial Intelligence. Springer (2020, in press)

20. Ullah, N., Treur, J.: Better late than never: a multilayer network model using metaplasticity for emotion regulation strategies. In: Cherifi, H., Gaito, S., Mendes, J.F., Moro, E., Rocha, L.M. (eds.) COMPLEX NETWORKS 2019. SCI, vol. 882, pp. 697–708. Springer, Cham (2020). https://doi.org/10.1007/978-3-030-36683-4_56

21. Ullah, N., Gao, Z., Liu, R., Treur, J.: A second-order adaptive temporal-causal network model for age and gender differences in evolving choice of emotion regulation strategies. J. Inf. Telecommun. **1839**, 1–16 (2020). https://doi.org/10.1080/24751839.2020.1724738

22. Treur, J.: Network-Oriented Modeling: Addressing Complexity of Cognitive, Affective and Social Interactions. UCS. Springer, Cham (2016). https://doi.org/10.1007/978-3-319-45213-5

23. Treur, J.: Network-Oriented Modeling for Adaptive Networks: Designing Higher-Order Adaptive Biological, Mental and Social Network Models. SSDC, vol. 251. Springer, Cham (2020). https://doi.org/10.1007/978-3-030-31445-3

Deep LSTM Recurrent Neural Network for Anxiety Classification from EEG in Adolescents with Autism

Brian Penchina[1], Avirath Sundaresan[1], Sean Cheong[1], and Adrien Martel[2(✉)]

[1] The Nueva School, San Mateo, CA 94033, USA
{bripenc,avisund,seacheo}@nuevaschool.org
[2] Causal Brain Dynamics, Plasticity and Rehabilitation Team, Frontlab, Brain and Spine Institute, ICM, Paris, France
adrien.martel@icm-institute.org

Abstract. Anxiety is common in youth with autism spectrum disorder (ASD), causing unique lifelong challenges that severely limit everyday opportunities and reduce quality of life. Given the detrimental consequences and long-term effects of pervasive anxiety for childhood development and the covert nature of mental states, brain-computer interfaces (BCIs) represent a promising method to identify maladaptive states and allow for individualized and real-time mitigatory action to alleviate anxiety. Here we investigated the effects of slow paced breathing entrainment during stress induction on the perceived levels of anxiety in neurotypical adolescents and adolescents with autism, and propose a multi-class long short-term recurrent neural net (LSTM RNN) deep learning classifier capable of identifying anxious states from ongoing electroencephalography (EEG) signals. The deep learning classifier used was able to discriminate between anxious and non-anxious classes with an accuracy of 90.82% and yielded an average accuracy of 93.27% across all classes. Our study is the first to successfully apply an LSTM RNN classifier to identify anxious states from EEG. This LSTM RNN classifier holds promise for the development of neuroadaptive systems and individualized intervention methods capable of detecting and alleviating anxious states in both neurotypical adolescents and adolescents with autism.

Keywords: Anxiety · Autism · EEG · Deep learning · Breathing entrainment

1 Introduction

Anxiety, a common psychological and physiological state, is adaptive in response to danger and in the preparation of an appropriate coping strategy, but can also arise as, or develop into, serious mental health disorders. Anxiety-related disorders are especially prevalent amongst children and adolescents, accounting for a third of all mental health issues afflicting youth [1], and is found to be

© Springer Nature Switzerland AG 2020
M. Mahmud et al. (Eds.): BI 2020, LNAI 12241, pp. 227–238, 2020.
https://doi.org/10.1007/978-3-030-59277-6_21

comorbid with other neurological disorders such as autism spectrum disorder (ASD) [2], ADHD and depression as well as a predictor of substance abuse, suicide attempts, long-term use of psychiatric and medical services, and substantial functional impairment [3]. Amongst people on the spectrum, one in two are suffering from at least one form of co-occurring anxiety or depression [4–6]. A meta-analysis of studies involving anxiety in children and adolescents with autism found that as many as 40% of children and adolescents with autism meet the criteria for an anxiety disorder [7]. For individuals on the spectrum, comorbid issues such as anxiety confer unique impairments that have been associated with increased caregiver burden and reduced quality of life [8–10]. Importantly, anxiety has been identified as a significant hurdle in education for students [11], in particular for students with autism [12]. Moreover, anxiety and the design of appropriate intervention methods have been identified by the autism community and clinicians as a key priority [13]. Given the ubiquity of anxiety and its prevalence as a chronic mental disorder in children and adolescents with and without autism, it is of great importance to develop tools that can recognize anxious states and allow for tailored and targeted mitigation. As a first step to this end, we propose a deep learning-based classifier capable of identifying anxious states from ongoing electroencephalography (EEG) in youth with ASD and in neurotypical youth.

EEG is a noninvasive, mobile and low-cost method to measure brain activity that is widely used in neurological research and clinical diagnosis. Research has been conducted to assess EEG biomarkers of both transient anxiety and chronic anxiety disorders. Pavlenko et al. [14] demonstrated positive correlation between power spectral density of beta1 and beta2 EEG rhythms and state anxiety. Lewis et al. [15] observed a shift from greater left frontal activity to greater right frontal activity as test anxiety increased, and Blackhart et al. [16] showed that this right frontal asymmetry may predict future development of anxiety disorders. Oathes et al. [17] demonstrated that feelings of stress and worry induced gamma band activation in people with and without generalized anxiety disorder (GAD). However, as studies examining specific biomarkers of anxiety in EEG are few and far between [18] and often inconsistent [19], the analysis of particular biomarkers as proxies for anxiety is unreliable. This dilemma highlights the necessity of broader, data-driven approaches to detect anxiety within EEG data.

EEG analysis with machine learning has been shown to be a promising method to detect a wide range of covert cognitive and emotional states, including anxiety. One such machine learning algorithm, the support vector machine (SVM), has seen extensive use in EEG analysis [20] and has been shown to be effective to detect anxious states. Gaikwad and Pathane [21] designed a three-tier hierarchical SVM classifier that determined the stress level with 72.3% accuracy of 12 adults with no history of mental disorder or brain damage. Al-shargie et al. [22] developed a multilevel stress SVM classifier that was able to discriminate between anxious states induced by mental arithmetic with an accuracy of 94.7%.

Although SVM classifiers are conventional for EEG analysis and have been successfully applied to mental stress detection [22,23], a significant limitation lies in their inability to process many extracted features from EEG simultaneously. As a result, SVMs are constrained to a small number of features [24] and cannot consider a robust set of EEG timepoints, rendering them unable to examine the EEG time domain, a critical dimension for analysis. Deep learning methods have recently emerged as methods of analysis that can consider neurophysiological data in its entirety, including the time domain, and indeed these methods have been shown to be superior to classical methods, e.g. SVMs, in most areas of EEG analysis [25]. In addition, unlike SVMs, deep learning networks can automatically adjust and optimize their parameters, essentially alleviating the need for feature extraction and requiring far less processing and prior knowledge regarding the dataset [26, 27].

Convolutional neural networks are the most widely used deep learning algorithms in EEG analysis [27], and have been shown to be effective in emotion detection [28, 29] and anxiety classification [30, 31] in particular. Moreover, deep learning with convolutional neural networks (CNNs) have recently been shown to outperform the widely-used filter bank common spatial pattern algorithm by extracting increasingly more complex features of the data [32]. Accordingly, we applied EEGNet, a recently developed compact CNN for EEG-based BCIs [33], for the classification of different states of anxiety in ASD and neurotypical adolescents.

Long short-term memory recurrent neural networks (LSTM RNNs) are a type of neural net with the ability to "remember" long-term dependencies far better than traditional RNNs without the loss of short-term memory [34], enabling robust analysis of temporal trends in EEG data [35]. LSTM RNNs have also shown high accuracy in emotion detection [36], with RNN architectures performing better than the more conventional CNN and hybrid CNN-RNNs on DEAP, a major EEG emotion analysis dataset [27]. Building upon these recent advancements, we implemented a LSTM RNN to classify anxious states from EEG obtained from ASD and neurotypical adolescents. To our knowledge, ours is the first study to examine the efficacy of deep learning-based EEG anxiety classifiers for both adolescents with autism and neurotypical adolescents.

2   Methods

2.1   Participants and Data Acquisition

Eight students (1 female M: 15.13 SD: 1.45) with ASD from Learning Farm Educational Resources based in Menlo Park, (California), and five students (1 female M: 16.6 SD: 0.55) with no known mental or neurological disorders from The Nueva School in San Mateo, (California), voluntarily enrolled in the study. Participants and their parents or legal guardians were informed extensively about the experiment and all gave written consent. The study was approved by an Institutional Review Board composed of an educator from Learning Farm Educational Resources, an administrator from The Nueva School, and a licensed mental health professional at The Nueva School.

Participants were seated in an isolated and dimly lit room at a viewing distance of 70 cm of a 16" LCD monitor with a refresh rate of 60 Hz. 16-channel EEG data was acquired at 125 Hz using an OpenBCI system (Ag/AgCl coated electrodes + Cyton Board; https://openbci.com) placed according to the international 10–20 system (channels: 'Fp1', 'Fp2', 'C3', 'C4', 'P7', 'P8', 'O1', 'O2', 'F7', 'F8', 'F3', 'F4', 'T7', 'T8', 'P3', 'P4'). Participants were fitted with passive noise-canceling headphones to isolate them from ambient noise and to interact with the stress and breath modulating interface. The audio-visual stimuli was designed in close collaboration with Muvik Labs (https://muviklabs.io). The stimuli featured sequential trials of stressor, guided breathing, and unguided breathing sections (Fig. 1). The stimuli were procedurally generated by Muvik Labs' Augmented Sound^{TM} engine to ensure timing precision and effectiveness through evidence-backed breathing interventions driven by principles of psychoacoustics and behavioral psychology [37].

Prior to the main procedure, participants were asked to complete the trait anxiety component of Spielberger's State-Trait Anxiety Inventory for Children (STAI-C) [38], a well-validated state and trait anxiety screen used for typically developing youth that can also be accurately used to assess trait anxiety in children and adolescents with autism [39].

2.2 Stress Induction and Alleviation

Following an initial EEG baseline recording for 120 s, participants performed a 25-min session featuring stress induction and breath modulation tasks consisting of four main blocks. Each block began with a stressor featuring an augmented arithmetic number task, intensified by bright contrasting colors displaying numbers appearing sequentially, coupled with audible sonified timers mapped to rising pitches similar to Shepard tones (powered by Muvik Labs Augmented Sound^{TM}) [37], with a 90 s time constraint. Timed mental arithmetic has been widely used to induce stress [40,41]. The stress induction was followed by a period of breathing for 200 s. The first and third breathing periods had participants breathe at their own pace (unguided breathing) while the second and fourth breathing periods presented participants with a custom-generated breathing entrainment system, guiding breath airflow in and out of lungs at a relaxing pace of 6 breaths per minute [42] with both visual (i.e. growing/shrinking circle outlining the air flow volume of target respiration speed) and auditory guides (musical patterns featuring nature sounds that mimic the sound of inhalation and exhalation; Muvik Labs Augmented Sound^{TM}). Although the baseline, unguided breathing and guided breathing periods had participants in a similarly relaxed, non-anxious state, for the purposes of this study we assigned distinct labels to these three conditions, amounting to a total of four classes including the stress induction condition.

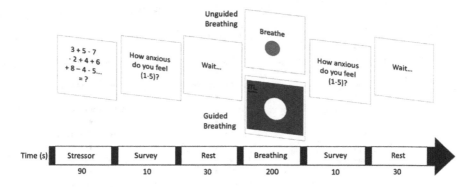

Fig. 1. Stress induction and alleviation procedure.

2.3   EEG Signal Processing and Training Data Selection

MNE [43], an open-source Python tool for EEG analysis, was employed to filter EEG data from all 16 channels. In preparation for classification analysis, EEG time-courses were high-pass filtered at 1 Hz to remove slow trends and subsequently low-pass filtered at 50 Hz to remove line noise. The routine clinical bandwidth for EEG is from 0.5 Hz to 50 Hz [44]. However, significant sinusoidal drift was observed on the 0.5 Hz–1 Hz interval and therefore the interval was excluded in the selected bandpass filter range. The data of two participants were rejected from all analyses due to unusually high impedances at the time of recording, which was confirmed offline by visual inspection: participant L1 from the ASD group, and participant T3 from the neurotypical group. Preprocessing of the EEG data was kept to a minimum in order to mimic online conditions found in a real-time BCI scenario.

For training sample preparation, a cropped training strategy was employed. A total of 243 samples with a length of 5s were extracted per participant from the EEG recorded during the 'Stressor', 'Guided Breathing', 'Unguided Breathing', and 'Baseline' periods of the procedure and were assigned corresponding labels. We may designate 'Stressor' samples as positive samples, and 'Guided Breathing', 'Unguided Breathing', and 'Baseline' samples as negative samples, as we have considered a participant to be in a relaxed state during the latter three periods.

2.4   Neural Signal Classification

We performed classification analysis on the selected EEG training samples using a two-layer LSTM RNN deep learning model, alongside a one-layer LSTM RNN architecture and the EEGNet CNN architecture [34] (Fig. 2). Wang et al. [45] found that LSTM RNN architectures with more than two LSTM layers did not significantly improve EEG classification accuracy over a two-layer LSTM RNN architecture, informing our decision to solely consider one-layer and two-layer LSTM models. We opted to avoid using calculated features as inputs in favor of

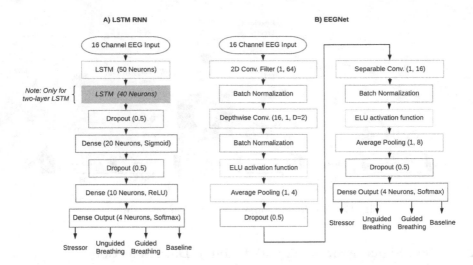

Fig. 2. A) One-layer and two-layer LSTM RNN classifier architectures. B) EEGNet CNN classifier architecture.

an end-to-end learning method with filtered EEG signal value inputs from all 16 channels. In addition, as different EEG channels represent neural signals from different areas of the brain, we elected not to combine channel data in order to preserve a spatial dimension of EEG analysis.

The EEGNet architecture is composed of 8 2D convolutional filters of size (1, 64), each with a temporal kernel length of 64, a Depthwise Convolution layer of size (16, 1) to learn multiple spatial filters for each temporal filter, a Separable Convolution layer of size (1, 16), and a 4 neuron dense layer with softmax activation to produce the output (for detail see Fig. 2A). The EEGNet model was trained over 1000 epochs with a batch size of 200.

The two-layer LSTM RNN model consists of two LSTM layers, two dense hidden layers, and a dense output layer. The first LSTM layer, containing 50 neurons, receives the input. The second LSTM layer contains 40 neurons. The number of neurons in both LSTM layers was informed by the amount used by Alhagry et al. [36] and adjusted to prevent underfitting and overfitting to our EEG data. Following the second LSTM layer, we include a dropout layer with a dropout rate of 0.5 to prevent overfitting. The first dense layer contains 20 neurons and uses a sigmoid activation function. Following the first dense layer, we include a dropout layer with a dropout rate of 0.5. The second dense layer consisted of 10 neurons and used a rectified linear unit (ReLU) as an activation function. The dense output layer of 4 neurons used softmax activation. While training, we implemented the Adam optimization algorithm [46] with a learning rate of 0.001 in place of the standard stochastic gradient descent (SGD) algorithm. The model was trained over 1000 epochs with a batch size of 200. The one-layer LSTM architecture is identical to the two-layer LSTM architecture excepting the 40 neuron LSTM layer (Fig. 2B).

We implemented Keras machine learning library in Python to build the classifiers. The models were trained on an Intel Core i9-9900X processor with 128 GB RAM supplemented by a 24 GB GDDR6 VRAM NVIDIA Titan RTX graphics processing unit (GPU) with 4608 CUDA cores and an auxiliary 8 GB GDDR6 VRAM NVIDIA GeForce RTX 2070 SUPER GPU with 2560 CUDA cores.

3   Results

During validation, samples were apportioned at a ratio of 70:30 to the train dataset and test dataset, respectively. The two-layer LSTM RNN classifier yielded an average accuracy of 93.27% on the test data across all four classes, outperforming the 70.12% average accuracy of the one-layer LSTM RNN and the 60.21% average accuracy of the EEGNet classifier. In addition, since we have designated the 'Stressor' class as our positive class, we may also note that the two-layer LSTM classifier was able to discriminate between anxious and non-anxious states with an accuracy of 90.82%, significantly higher than the 63.95% accuracy of the one-layer LSTM model and the 59.31% accuracy of the EEGNet (see Table 1).

Table 1. Class-wise and overall validation results.

Average accuracy	EEGNet	1-Layer LSTM	2-Layer LSTM
Stressor (%)	59.31	63.95	90.82
Unguided breathing (%)	60.38	62.89	91.19
Guided breathing (%)	59.99	80.09	94.57
Baseline (%)	61.18	73.53	96.50
Average (%)	60.21	70.12	93.27

Moreover, it is important to note that due to the longer length of the unguided and guided breathing periods compared to the stressor and the baseline periods, more samples were extracted from the unguided and guided breathing periods, creating an unbalanced dataset. Although this can lead to issues since an unbalanced dataset can artificially inflate the accuracy metric, the two-layer LSTM RNN model used here demonstrated high precision and class-wise sensitivity and specificity during validation (see Fig. 3), leading us to the conclusion that the unbalanced dataset was not a cause for concern.

3.1   LSTM RNN Performance with Individual Variation

We were interested in investigating the relationship between the two-layer LSTM model performance and preexisting mental conditions. First, we wished to see if there was a significant difference between model accuracy for participants with autism and neurotypical participants. On average, the two-layer LSTM model

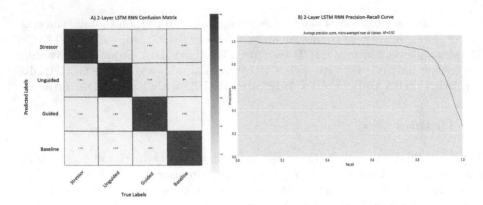

Fig. 3. A) Two-layer LSTM RNN model confusion matrix. B) Two-layer LSTM RNN model precision-recall curve.

Table 2. Classification accuracy and trait anxiety per participant.

Participant	Classification accuracy (%)	STAI-C trait anxiety score
L2	92.83	37
L3	92.83	32
L4	93.72	24
L5	93.69	30
L6	92.57	33
L7	93.72	32
L8	93.97	46
T1	92.83	25
T2	93.08	37
T4	93.47	42
T5	93.24	28

accuracy for a participant with autism was 93.33%, while the model accuracy for a neurotypical participant was 93.15%. A Mann-Whitney U test was conducted to compare model accuracy for the participants with autism and neurotypical participants and found no significant difference between model accuracy for the two groups ($p = 0.566$), indicating that the two-layer LSTM model performed similarly regardless of whether the participant had autism. We also wished to understand whether an individual's persistent (trait) anxiety can influence the performance of the two-layer LSTM RNN. We employed Spearman correlation to compare model accuracy and individual STAI-C trait anxiety scores (see Table 2); higher STAI-C scores indicate higher trait anxiety. The analysis yielded a Spearman's rho of 0.0393, indicating virtually no correlation between trait anxiety and the two-layer LSTM RNN performance.

4   Discussion

In this study, three different deep learning architectures were used to detect mental stress from the EEG of ASD and neurotypical adolescents performing a mental arithmetic task. The multiclass EEGNet CNN and LSTM deep learning models were employed to classify the EEG recorded from ASD and neurotypical adolescents into four distinct classes, three "relaxed" classes and one "anxious" class. The EEGNet CNN, one-layer LSTM and two-layer LSTM performed with an overall accuracy of 60.21%, 70.12% and 93.27%, respectively. Furthermore, we were able to train the latter LSTM RNN classifier to discriminate between anxious and non-anxious states with an accuracy of 90.82%, far higher than the one-layer LSTM accuracy of 63.95% and the EEGNet accuracy of 59.31%. To our knowledge, our study provides the first demonstration that an LSTM RNN architecture can be used to accurately assess stress-induced anxiety, a complex and covert mental state, from ongoing EEG data in adolescents with and without autism as well as in adolescents with varying levels of baseline anxiety.

There are some caveats to consider in the interpretation of our results. First, given that anxiety varies significantly with context and individual, and cannot therefore be induced reliably and equivalently across participants, we utilized mental stress induction via timed mental arithmetic as a proxy for anxiety. Second, our experiment was designed to minimize the time under stress to avoid any undue strain on the participants; conversely, more time was required for relaxation to set in and the breathing rate to normalize. As a result, the time for the mental arithmetic task and the guided or unguided breathing differed. Thus, the models were trained on an unbalanced dataset, with more unguided and guided breathing samples than stressor and baseline samples, with the potential for artificial inflation of model accuracy. However, this is unlikely to be a concern for the two-layer LSTM RNN model, which exhibited high sensitivity and specificity metrics across all classes. Lastly, it should be noted that a potential drawback of deep learning algorithms such as LSTM RNNs is over-reliance upon large datasets. For example, we performed the same classifications with smaller datasets including only 2 or 3 conditions, which lead to poor performance (data not shown).

To address this issue, we are currently setting up an extension of the current experiment that will include a much larger set of participants, both neurotypical and ASD, with the aim of refining and validating the two-layer LSTM RNN deep learning model for prospective implementation in an individualized neuroadaptive system. Such a system would be capable of detecting periods of mental stress and anxiety, opening new avenues of decoding covert mental states for BCI-based applications to benefit youth with autism. The ability for the model to discriminate between different breathing classes would allow for the implementation of a closed-loop breathing entrainment system that can detect anxious states in real-time, feedback this information to the user, and entrain an optimized breathing pattern to alleviate anxiety. A BCI-based neuroadaptive system would provide an effective and personalized intervention method to mitigate anxiety, with the potential of facilitating learning of adaptive behavioural strategies (e.g. slower breathing) in response to anxiety-inducing stimuli in daily life.

References

1. Bennett, K., et al.: Preventing child and adolescent anxiety disorders: overview of systematic reviews. Depress. Anxiety **32**, 909–918 (2015)
2. Zaboski, B.A., Storch, E.A.: Comorbid autism spectrum disorder and anxiety disorders: a brief review. Future Neurol. **13**, 31–37 (2018)
3. Kendall, P.C., et al.: Clinical characteristics of anxiety disordered youth. J. Anxiety Disord. **24**, 360–365 (2010)
4. Maddox, B.B., White, S.W.: Comorbid social anxiety disorder in adults with autism spectrum disorder. J. Autism Dev. Disord. **45**(12), 3949–3960 (2015). https://doi.org/10.1007/s10803-015-2531-5
5. Hofvander, B., et al.: Psychiatric and psychosocial problems in adults with normal-intelligence autism spectrum disorders. BMC Psychiatry **9**, 35 (2009)
6. Hepburn, S.L., Stern, J.A., Blakeley-Smith, A., Kimel, L.K., Reaven, J.A.: Complex psychiatric comorbidity of treatment-seeking youth with autism spectrum disorder and anxiety symptoms. J. Mental Health Res. Intellect. Disabil. **7**, 359–378 (2014)
7. van Steensel, F.J.A., Bögels, S.M., Perrin, S.: Anxiety disorders in children and adolescents with autistic spectrum disorders: a meta-analysis. Clin. Child Family Psychol. Rev. **14**, 302–317 (2011)
8. Kerns, C.M., Kendall, P.C., Zickgraf, H., Franklin, M.E., Miller, J., Herrington, J.: Not to be overshadowed or overlooked: functional impairments associated with comorbid anxiety disorders in youth with ASD. Behav. Ther. **46**, 29–39 (2015)
9. Antshel, K.M., et al.: Comorbid ADHD and anxiety affect social skills group intervention treatment efficacy in children with autism spectrum disorders. J. Dev. Behav. Pediatr. **32**, 439–446 (2011)
10. Ikeda, E., Hinckson, E., Krägeloh, C.: Assessment of quality of life in children and youth with autism spectrum disorder: a critical review. Qual. Life Res. **23**(4), 1069–1085 (2013). https://doi.org/10.1007/s11136-013-0591-6
11. Mazzone, L., Ducci, F., Scoto, M.C., Passaniti, E., D'Arrigo, V.G., Vitiello, B.: The role of anxiety symptoms in school performance in a community sample of children and adolescents. BMC Public Health 7 (2007)
12. Preece, D., Howley, M.: An approach to supporting young people with autism spectrum disorder and high anxiety to re-engage with formal education - the impact on young people and their families. Int. J. Adolesc. Youth **23**, 468–481 (2018)
13. Wallace, S.: One in a hundred: putting families at the heart of autism research. https://www.basw.co.uk/resources/one-hundred-putting-families-heart-autism-research
14. Pavlenko, V.B., Chernyi, S.V., Goubkina, D.G.: EEG correlates of anxiety and emotional stability in adult healthy subjects. Neurophysiology **41**, 337–345 (2009)
15. Lewis, R.S., Weekes, N.Y., Wang, T.H.: The effect of a naturalistic stressor on frontal EEG asymmetry, stress, and health. Biol. Psychol. **75**, 239–247 (2007)
16. Blackhart, G.C., Minnix, J.A., Kline, J.P.: Can EEG asymmetry patterns predict future development of anxiety and depression? A preliminary study. Biol. Psychol. **72**, 46–50 (2006)

17. Oathes, D.J., et al.: Worry, generalized anxiety disorder, and emotion: evidence from the EEG gamma band. Biol. Psychol. **79**, 165–170 (2008)
18. Newson, J.J., Thiagarajan, T.C.: EEG frequency bands in psychiatric disorders: a review of resting state studies. Front. Hum. Neurosci. **12**, 521 (2018)
19. Thibodeau, R., Jorgensen, R.S., Kim, S.: Depression, anxiety, and resting frontal EEG asymmetry: a meta-analytic review. J. Abnorm. Psychol. **115**, 715–729 (2006)
20. Lotte, F., et al.: A review of classification algorithms for EEG-based brain-computer interfaces: a 10 year update. J. Neural Eng. **15**, 031005 (2018)
21. Gaikwad, P., Paithane, A.N.: Novel approach for stress recognition using EEG signal by SVM classifier. In: 2017 International Conference on Computing Methodologies and Communication (ICCMC), pp. 967–971 (2017)
22. Al-shargie, F., Tang, T.B., Badruddin, N., Kiguchi, M.: Towards multilevel mental stress assessment using SVM with ECOC: an EEG approach. Med. Biol. Eng. Comput. **56**(1), 125–136 (2017). https://doi.org/10.1007/s11517-017-1733-8
23. Saeed, S.M.U., Anwar, S.M., Khalid, H., Majid, M., Bagci, A.U.: EEG based classification of long-term stress using psychological labeling. Sensors 20 (2020). https://doi.org/10.3390/s20071886
24. Faust, O., Hagiwara, Y., Hong, T.J., Lih, O.S., Acharya, U.R.: Deep learning for healthcare applications based on physiological signals: a review. Comput. Methods Programs Biomed. **161**, 1–13 (2018)
25. Roy, Y., Banville, H., Albuquerque, I., Gramfort, A., Falk, T.H., Faubert, J.: Deep learning-based electroencephalography analysis: a systematic review. J. Neural Eng. **16**, 051001 (2019)
26. Schmidhuber, J.: Deep learning in neural networks: an overview. Neural Netw. **61**, 85–117 (2015)
27. Craik, A., He, Y., Contreras-Vidal, J.L.: Deep learning for electroencephalogram (EEG) classification tasks: a review. J. Neural Eng. **16**, 031001 (2019)
28. Salama, E.S., El-Khoribi, R.A., Shoman, M.E., Wahby, M.A.: EEG-based emotion recognition using 3D Convolutional Neural Networks. IJACSA 9 (2018). https://doi.org/10.14569/IJACSA.2018.090843
29. Hwang, S., Hong, K., Son, G., Byun, H.: Learning CNN features from DE features for EEG-based emotion recognition. Pattern Anal. Appl. **23**(3), 1323–1335 (2019). https://doi.org/10.1007/s10044-019-00860-w
30. Wang, Y., McCane, B., McNaughton, N., Huang, Z., Shadli, H., Neo, P.: AnxietyDecoder: an EEG-based anxiety predictor using a 3-D convolutional neural network. In: 2019 International Joint Conference on Neural Networks (IJCNN), pp. 1–8 (2019)
31. Zeng, H., Yang, C., Dai, G., Qin, F., Zhang, J., Kong, W.: EEG classification of driver mental states by deep learning. Cogn. Neurodyn. **12**(6), 597–606 (2018). https://doi.org/10.1007/s11571-018-9496-y
32. Schirrmeister, R.T., et al.: Deep learning with convolutional neural networks for EEG decoding and visualization. Hum. Brain Mapp. **38**, 5391–5420 (2017)
33. Lawhern, V.J., Solon, A.J., Waytowich, N.R., Gordon, S.M., Hung, C.P., Lance, B.J.: EEGNet: a compact convolutional neural network for EEG-based brain-computer interfaces. J. Neural Eng. **15**, 056013 (2018)
34. Hochreiter, S., Schmidhuber, J.: Long short-term memory. Neural Comput. **9**, 1735–1780 (1997)
35. Xing, X., Li, Z., Xu, T., Shu, L., Hu, B., Xu, X.: SAE+LSTM: a new framework for emotion recognition from multi-channel EEG. Front. Neurorobot. **13**, 37 (2019)

36. Alhagry, S., Fahmy, A.A., El-Khoribi, R.A.: Emotion recognition based on EEG using LSTM recurrent neural network. IJACSA 8 (2017). https://doi.org/10.14569/IJACSA.2017.081046
37. Borthakur, D., Grace, V., Batchelor, P., Dubey, H., Mankodiya, K.: Fuzzy C-means clustering and sonification of HRV features. In: 2019 IEEE/ACM International Conference on Connected Health: Applications, Systems and Engineering Technologies (CHASE), pp. 53–57 (2019)
38. Spielberger, C.D.: Manual for the State-Trait Inventory for Children. Consulting Psychologists Press, Palo Alto (1973)
39. Simon, D.M., Corbett, B.A.: Examining associations between anxiety and cortisol in high functioning male children with autism. J. Neurodev. Disord. 5, 32 (2013)
40. Dedovic, K., Renwick, R., Mahani, N.K., Engert, V., Lupien, S.J., Pruessner, J.C.: The Montreal Imaging Stress Task: using functional imaging to investigate the effects of perceiving and processing psychosocial stress in the human brain. J. Psychiatry Neurosci. 30, 319–325 (2005)
41. Shilton, A.L., Laycock, R., Crewther, S.G.: The Maastricht Acute Stress Test (MAST): physiological and subjective responses in anticipation, and post-stress. Front. Psychol. 8, 567 (2017)
42. Szulczewski, M.T.: Training of paced breathing at 0.1 Hz improves $CO2$ homeostasis and relaxation during a paced breathing task. PLoS One 14, e0218550 (2019)
43. Gramfort, A., et al.: MNE software for processing MEG and EEG data. Neuroimage 86, 446–460 (2014)
44. Vanhatalo, S., Voipio, J., Kaila, K.: Full-band EEG (FbEEG): an emerging standard in electroencephalography. Clin. Neurophysiol. 116, 1–8 (2005)
45. Wang, P., Jiang, A., Liu, X., Shang, J., Zhang, L.: LSTM-based EEG classification in motor imagery tasks. IEEE Trans. Neural Syst. Rehabil. Eng. 26, 2086–2095 (2018)
46. Kingma, D.P., Ba, J.: Adam: a method for stochastic optimization (2014). http://arxiv.org/abs/1412.6980

Improving Alcoholism Diagnosis: Comparing Instance-Based Classifiers Against Neural Networks for Classifying EEG Signal

Shelia Rahman[1], Tanusree Sharma[2]([✉]), and Mufti Mahmud[3]

[1] Institute of Information Technology, Jahangirnagar University, Dhaka, Bangladesh
sheliatulyar@gmail.com
[2] University of Illinois at Urbana-Champaign, Champaign, IL, USA
tsharma6@illinois.edu
[3] Department of Computing and Technology, Nottingham Trent University,
Nottingham NG11 8NS, UK
mufti.mahmud@ntu.ac.uk, muftimahmud@gmail.com

Abstract. Alcoholism involves psychological and biological components where multiple risk factors come into play. Assessment of the psychiatric emergency is a challenging issue for clinicians working with alcohol-dependent patients. Identifying alcoholics from healthy controls from their EEG signals can be effective in this scenario. In this research, we have applied two instance-based classifiers and three neural network classifier to classify Electroencephalogram data of alcoholics and normal person. For data preprocessing, we have applied discrete wavelet transform, Principal component analysis and Independent component analysis. After successful implementation of the classifiers, an accuracy of 95% is received with Bidirectional Long Short-Term Memory. Finally, comparing the performance of the two categories of algorithms, we have found that neural networks have higher potentiality against instance-based classifiers in the classification of EEG signals of alcoholics.

Keywords: Alcoholism · EEG signal · Machine learning · Instance based classifier · Neural networks

1 Introduction

Alcoholism can be the cause of depression, anxiety, domestic violence, psychosis, and antisocial behavior and in extreme cases, psychiatric disorders. Brains are one of the commonly affected organs in alcoholism causing cognitive, emotional and behavioral disorders. Our brain is a complex system comprised of millions of interconnected neurons that controls our functional and cognitive activity by passing electrical signals among themselves. Alcoholism can damage brain cells consequently changing the electrical activity responsible for brain function. Electroencephalogram (EEG) is a popular medical test and can be used

© Springer Nature Switzerland AG 2020
M. Mahmud et al. (Eds.): BI 2020, LNAI 12241, pp. 239–250, 2020.
https://doi.org/10.1007/978-3-030-59277-6_22

to detect the abnormalities caused due to alcoholism by analyzing the electric signals recorded. EEG signals are very small non-stationary, nonlinear electrical signals measured only in micro-volts (μV) also tends to change from subject to subject. For a naked eye observation, EEG signals from both alcoholic and healthy control may look nothing different. The small variations are hard to detect for a physician just by looking at it. When a stimulus is presented to test subject, his/her brain might produce some neural responses against the stimulus. In EEG this neural response from a number of similar neurons are recorded in μV. These responses can differ from brain regions to regions. Machine learning (ML) algorithms can be useful for EEG processing to represent underlying frequency structure with its' mathematical models and classification models of neural response values. These models use neural response recordings as attributes to predict if a subject is different from another one. ML models uses mathematical and statistical approaches which enables classification procedure to be faster and more accurate to predict if a subject is alcoholic or not. This analysis can be helpful to build brain computer interface (BCI) for physicians for faster and accurate identification of alcoholic patients.

The aim of our research is two folds. In this research we will observe how well the ML algorithms can predict alcoholism. In addition, we compare the performance two different types of algorithms: Instance based learning and Neural Network. The reason for categorizing the algorithms is EEG signals are mainly time series data and we aim to observe if any particular category of ML has better performance than other one in analysing them. In most researches, new classification models have been proposed or used to predict alcoholism. However, in this study we observe the classification credibility of two different groups of algorithms as well as compare them in regards of time series EEG data. BCI is a great medium for building interpretive models to study behavior of our brains. Determining the best ML for designing a BCI is challenging. With the increase in alcohol consumption rate alcoholism is becoming a serious health and social issue. However, alcoholism is different from a typical drinking habit. Therefore, an early and accurate prediction is highly anticipated. Analysing EEG signals by ML algorithms, this work puts forward such prediction to facilitate the detection of minor abnormality in the brain signals which is nearly impossible for a physician just with naked eye observation.

The rest of the paper is organized as follows– Section 2 talks about the background of the work, and Sect. 3 discusses materials and methods. Section 4 provides experiment results including comparison among results of ML algorithms. Finally, concluding remarks and possible future works are depicted in Sect. 5.

2   Background

Alcoholism, also known as alcohol consumption disorder (AUD) refers to a condition of alcohol abuse where brain is one of the commonly affected organs. Alcoholics are reported to have less cortical grey, white matter volumes as well as reduced volumes of sulcal and ventricular CSF (cerebrospinal fluid) when compared to non-alcoholics [6]. The disturbance in the functional connectivity can be detected by recording the electrical signals in the brain. EEG records electrical activities in brain using electrodes. Contrast to the commonly questionnaire-based alcoholism identification methods, EEG represents changes of biophysical response in the cerebral cortex offering more accurate diagnosis of alcoholism. However, EEG signal itself is very random in nature and computation complex. ML algorithms provides mathematical models that automatically identifies the underlying structure in the EEG signal to identify the distinct frequency level responsible for different brain activity thus differentiating abnormal brain condition from healthy controls.

Numerous studies have been conducted regarding classification of abnormal subjects from healthy ones using ML on EEG data. ML provides an automated method with adaptability and generalization capability [11, 12] enabling analysis of complex EEG signals offering less human intervention. Some promising examples are CNN (convolutional neural network) for detection of Parkinson's disease from EEG data [14, 16]; experiment on emotion recognition [10] using K-nearest neighbor (KNN)classifier from EEG data. Automatic seizure detection from EEG data using ML has proven to be very successful in previous study [17]. Similar to these abnormal brain conditions, ML is tend to be used on EEG data for alcoholism detection. Utilization of perceptron-back propagation (MLP-BP) and probabilistic neural network (PNN) for alcoholic identification [19] suggest that though in a normal case the gamma band of EEG signal lies below 30 Hz, it can generate frequency between 30–50 Hz in case of an alcoholics. Support vector machine and neural networks were applied in [9] for alcoholism detection along with principal component analysis (PCA) for feature extraction. Recurrent neural network (RNN) is also reported to be used in EEG classification in numerous research [20, 21]. An automated diagnosis of alcoholics using numerous correlation function and support vector machine (SVM) was performed by [2]. The correlation functions identified the relation between different parts of the brain and if it changes in alcoholic condition. They have fond that certain parts of the brain communicate in normal decision-making process and in an alcoholic condition the communication reduces significantly.

In this research, we have considered an open source dataset [3] of EEG signals. In a previous study by Ruslan Klymentiev[1] on the same dataset showed that among all the electrodes the most significant correlation is seen between FPZ & FP1 and FP1 & FP2 around 90% [3]. Rather than finding the correlation, we have applied ML algorithms directly on the response value received from these electrodes and see if they are significant enough to distinguish between alcoholics and healthy control.

3   Materials and Methods

3.1   Overall System

In this experiment we have applied ML methods for prediction of alcoholism based on EEG signals. To classify alcoholics from healthy control and com-

---

[1] https://www.kaggle.com/ruslankl/eeg-data-analysis. Accessed on March 23th, 2020.

pare the performance of instance based learning and neural networks, we have designed a step by step system. A snapshot of the overall methodology of the system is provided in Fig. 1.

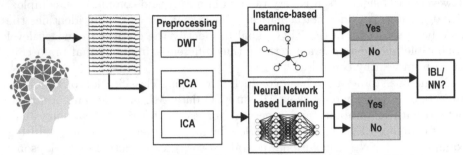

DWT: Discrete Wavelet Transform, **PCA**: Principal Component Analysis, **ICA**: Independent Component Analysis
IBL: Instance Based Learning, **NN**: Neural Network Based Learning

Fig. 1. Block diagram of the implemented pipeline showing different steps and execution sequence.

3.2 Dataset Description

For our experiment, we considered EEG dataset which was gathered to examine EEG correlates of genetic predisposition to alcoholism [3]. The characteristics of this dataset is multivariate, time series which has attributes with categorical, integer and real valued properties. The EEG was collected while the two groups of subjects were shown a set pictures from the 1980s Snodgrass and Vanderwart picture set [3]. The EEG were recorded from 64 electrode placement (10–20 standard EEG placement) on each subject. Each subject was exposed to either a single stimulus (S1) or to two stimuli (S1 and S2) and were asked to identify either a matched condition where S1and S2 were identical or in a non-matched condition where S1and S2 are different. The EEG recorded was sampled at 256 Hz (3.9 ms epoch) per second. The original dataset contains EEG of 20 subjects where each subject completed 120 trials for each stimulus. For our experiment we have randomly selected 5 alcoholics and 5 healthy controls among them. Then the response values of FPz, FP1 and FP2 are collected for all 120 trials of each given stimulus. The training and test data were prepared using stratified 10-fold cross validation.

3.3 Data Preprocessing

Data preprocessing is an important concepts in EEG data. In our case, EEG data shows high variance which required noise cleaning to get closer values. The high level idea is to enhance the likelihood for producing a cut above result. Our objective of research is to compare instance-based classifiers with NN to demonstrate variance of result in respect to alcoholism diagnosis. Hence cleaner data can potentially aid in experiment for making informed decision on model accuracy. Our inclusion criteria for choosing DWT, PCA and ICA were: first reviewing the evidence of efficacy from literature and the efficiency of their underlying mathematical model for computation. There are particular distribution based on different data source which are respectively Gaussian with different kurtosis. EEG data has a distribution of super-Gaussian which needs application of transformation that pass distribution of non-linearity to calculate entropy. ICA and PCA are quite similar based on their functionality. PCA is applied to the training data set to indicate transformation matrix which are used for measuring the final feature. For example, if transformation matrix is m with the dimension of $K \times N$, the outcome y will be: $y = m^T x$; where x is original vector by orthogonal basis where PCA help in feature reduction for our EEG dataset [7]. DWT offers a compressed approximation of the data that can be retained in a reduced representation of the original data. DWT can be also used for noise reduction by filtering out any particular order coefficients using a threshold.

DWT. Wavelet Transformation [18] is used for decomposition and summarizing a time-domain signal into a multidimensional representation comprised of a set of basis functions called wavelets. The wavelets are generated by scaling and shifting a mother wavelet. If transformation includes a discrete set of wavelets which are orthogonal to its translation and scaling, they are known as DWT. The DWT coefficient ($\Lambda\varphi[i, P]$) of a signal $x[n]$ is defined as:

$$\Lambda\varphi[i, P] = \frac{1}{\sqrt{k}} \sum_n (x[n]\Pi_{i,P}[n]) \tag{1}$$

Here, K is the number of samples and Λ is a wavelet function.

PCA. PCA [1] converts a set of observations of correlated variables into a set of values using an orthogonal transformation. The newly generated values are linearly uncorrelated and called principal components (PCs). Each PC must be orthogonal to its preceding components. If we have a matrix T of $p \times q$ then covariance matrix can be calculated as:

$$C_T = \frac{1}{n-1}(T - \overline{T})(T - \overline{T})^\gamma, \ T^\gamma \text{ is the transpose matrix of } T \tag{2}$$

From the covariance matrix C the eigenvalues and orthogonal eigenvector matrix P is calculated. Because the covariance matrix is positively semi-defined and symmetric in nature, the diagonal matrix Π is defined as $C_T = P\Pi P^\gamma$ The eigenvalues are contained in Π successively corresponds to the values contained in eigenvector P.

ICA. ICA [7] is a popular blind source separation method that finds a linear representation of non-Gaussian data in a signal statistically independent components (ICs). ICA can identify the original signal from noise at least to a certain

level if some information about the origin of the signal is known [7]. To understand the concept of ICA lets consider an observed signal $x_i(t)$ represents a
mixture of n signals. $x_i(t)$ can be modeled as:

$$x_i(t) = \sum_{j=1}^{m} \delta_{ij} S_j(t) \tag{3}$$

where, δ_{ij} is a constant parameter called mixing matrix $s_j(t)$ represents an IC at
time point t. s is the source signal to be separated from its mixed component δ_{ij}.
Denoting the elements δ_{ij} as T, it's inverse matrix W is calculated to obtained
the ICs as $s = Wx$. The ICs generated must have non-Gaussian distribution and
their number is equal to the number of observed sources.

3.4   Machine Learning Algorithms

Two types of ML models are used in this study: instance-based (IBL) and neural
networks (NN)-based. IBL algorithms do not create any learning model before
the actual classification process, thus, without separating the training and testing phases and creating a model local to certain test tuple or instance. This
study applies two IBL models: K-Nearest Neighbor (KNN) and Learning Vector
Quantization (LVQ). The reason to choose KNN and LVQ is that they are most
commonly used IBLs and have been reportedly used in time series data classification. On the other hand, NN is brain-inspired, where in each layer of the
network, the neurons learn from a training dataset. Later this model predicts
classes for given queries. Here three well known NNs will be applied Recurrent
Neural Network (RNN), Bidirectional Long-Short Term Memory (B-LSTM) and
Convolutional Neural Network (CNN).

Instance-Based Methods

KNN. KNN is one of the popular ML models. KNN does not necessarily create a
classifier model from the input space. When a query is fed into the classifier, KNN
algorithm chooses its k nearest neighbors by calculating the distance between the
query and other instances. From the number of methods for distance calculation,
commonly used distance metric calculation method is the Euclidean distance.
Euclidean distance is the rooted sum of squared distance between two values of
the same attribute. For two instances X and Y with I attribute the Euclidean
distance between them can be calculated as:

$$E = \sqrt{\sum_{i=1}^{n} (X_i - Y_i)^2} \tag{4}$$

After selecting the k nearest neighbor the class label of the instance with which
the query has the lowest distance will be assigned to the query.

LVQ. LVQ allows to determine exactly how many instances from the training set is needed to learn generating a more optimized classification model [8]. This particular set of instances is called the "window". The window is determined around the mid-plane of two variables m_x and m_y. m_x and m_y are two nearest neighbors of the query q such that if m_x and q belong to the same class, m_y and q will have different class label and vice-versa. The relation between m_x, m_y and q can be defined with the following equation:

$$m_x(i+1) = m_x(i) - \alpha(i)[q_i - m_x(i)] \tag{5}$$

$$m_y(i+1) = m_y(i) - \alpha(i)[q_i - m_y(i)] \tag{6}$$

Here, $\alpha(i)$ is individual learning rate factor. The value of m_x and m_y is updated at each step i until the closest instance m_x is found. Finally, the class label of m_x is assigned to the query q. In this experiment we have applied LVQ3 as it is more robust comparing to LVQ1 and LVQ2. It provides both binary and multi-modal classification.

Neural Network Based Methods

RNN. RNN is a modified feed-forward neural network which has an internal memory that contains information about previously learned data. At a certain hidden layer it makes decision from the current input and outputs from previous layer. Traditionally, the state of a hidden layer neuron of RNN is computed as:

$$\Lambda_i = A(\Lambda_{i-1}, x_t) = W_\Lambda \Lambda_{i-1} + W_x x_i + b \tag{7}$$

Here, W represents a weight parameter. At each hidden step Λ_t, the output is calculated using an activation function that is applied on input x_i of the current layer and output Λ_{i-1} of the previous layer. In this experiment we have used the modified version of RNN called long-short term memory (LSTM) [5] that can easily model time sequenced data such as EEG. RNN shows two long term dependency problem, the vanishing gradient problem and the exploding gradient problem. These problems can be handled by using LSTM. It uses designated hidden states called cell that stores information for long period of time so that particular information is accessible to both immediate subsequent steps and later nodes. It's special gates can control removing or adding information to a cell state. It has three specialized gates called the forget gate (F_i), input gate (I_i), and output gate (O_i). Each gate produces an output using similar equation to a RNN hidden gate. The final Output of an LSTM cell with these gates can be defined by:

$$\Lambda_i = O_i \otimes \tanh(L_i) \tag{8}$$

Here, L_i represents recurrent state of the LSTM node and has following form

$$L_t = L_{i-1} \otimes F_i \oplus \tilde{L}_i \otimes I_t \tag{9}$$

Our designed LSTM network The second layer uses activation function sigmoid that returns a number between 0 and 1 depending on the cell state.

B-LSTM. Bidirectional LSTM is an advanced LSTM that learns not only from the previous layer but also from the future elements. Therefore, instead of one recurrent network it trains two, respectively for previous and future outcomes. The input sequence is fed to one network in normal time order and the in-reversal time order for the other one. Both outputs are concatenated or summed at each time step to generate the current state. B-LSTM might use similar activation functions as LSTM.

CNN. CNN uses layers of convolution that convolve a filter also called window over an input dataset and generates a feature map where some activation function is applied. In convolution network, Convolution layer calculates the output of neurons, connected to local regions in the input by applying a dot product between their weights and values of the input volume in the local region. It is followed by a pooling layer that uses some aggregation function to create a pooled map along the spatial dimensions to reducing the size of the connected layer. Finally, the fully connected layer computes the classification score. In CNN multiple convolution and pooling layer is applied alternatively to create a more accurate classification model or network. In our study, we have applied 1-dimensional convolution layer where each instance acts as a input vector. A pooling layer of pooling size 2 is applied.

3.5   Evaluation Metrics

The classification result is evaluated using confusion matrix which represents the number of correct and wrong prediction for each ML algorithm. Based on the confusion matrix different performance metrics are calculated (Table 1).

Table 1. Performance evaluation metrics

Measurement	Formula
Accuracy	$\frac{TP+TN}{TP+TN+FP+FN}$
F-measure	$\frac{2TP}{2TP+FP+FN}$
G-mean	$\frac{TP}{\sqrt{(TP+FP)*(TP+FN)}}$
Sensitivity	$\frac{TP}{TP+FN}$
Specificity	$\frac{TN}{TN+FP}$
Type I Error	$1 - \frac{TN}{TN+FP}$
Type II Error	$1 - \frac{TP}{TP+FN}$

Table 2. Comparison of Instance-based and Neural Network Models

Type	Model	Acc	ROC	F-M	G-M	Sens	Spec	T1E	T2E
IBL	KNN	0.731	0.731	0.733	0.733	0.737	0.725	0.242	0.274
	LVQ	0.728	0.728	0.732	0.732	0.742	0.714	0.257	0.285
NN	LSTM	0.898	0.898	0.899	0.899	0.908	0.873	0.091	0.112
	B_LSTM	**0.950**	**0.950**	**0.950**	**0.950**	**0.945**	**0.955**	**0.054**	**0.044**
	CNN	0.850	0.850	0.855	0.855	0.882	0.819	0.117	0.180

Legend: Acc.: Accuracy; ROC: Receiver Operating Characteristics; F-M: F-Measure; G-M: Geometric Mean; Sens.: Sensitivity; Spec.: Specificity; T[1/2]E: Type [I/II] error; bold faced values denote the best performance.

4   Results and Discussion

The ML methods as well as the preprocessing techniques were implemented using the scikit library with Python. The evaluation metrics were measured separately for raw dataset and each preprocessing technique. The training and test dataset were prepared using stratified 10-fold cross validation.

4.1   Overall Comparison of the Algorithms

The performance of the considered algorithms against different evaluation metrics is shown in Table 2. We see that, in case of IBL, KNN achieved an accuracy of 73% and LVQ's accuracy was only 72%. On the other hand, in case of NN, LSTM, B-LSTM and CNN received accuracy of 89%, 95% and 85%, respectively. In terms of accuracy the NNs offer more accurate classification result than IBLs. Though both the IBL algorithms have moderate accuracy rate, they lag behind the NNs notably. In addition, if we observe the other performance metrics, LSTM and B-LSTM has the lowest error rate (both type I and type II error), around 9% and 5% of type I, and 11% and 4% of type II for LSTM and B-LSTM consecutively. The other NN algorithm CNN also has a low error rate of only 11% for type I and 18% for type II. However, both IBLs has higher error rate compared to all NNs applied. 24% of type I and 27% of type II error received for KNN and 25% of type I and 28% of type II error received for LVQ. The NNs shows better performance for other evaluation metrics as well (Table 2). Among the five algorithms from both IBL and NN, we can see that the best performance is received from B-LSTM which achieved an accuracy around 95% and highest result in other performance metrics. Between the two IBL methods the highest accuracy is obtained by KNN and it also shows better result in other metrics against LVQ.

4.2   Effect of Preprocessing on Model Performance

In this section, we take into account the best model from two type of models and discuss their performance after applying numerous data preprocessing techniques and also for the raw data. KNN is observed to be the best IBL classifier and B-LSTM is observed to be the best NN classifier (Table 3). In case of KNN the highest accuracy (88%) is received when the dataset is transformed using ICA. For DWT, PCA transformed data and raw data, accuracies obtained respectively are around 72%, 73%, 74%. As for B-LSTM, the highest accuracy achieved is for PCA transformed data (95%). DWT (accuracy 88%) and ICA (82%) did not necessarily improve the classification performance of B-LSTM, as the accuracy they achieved are lower than the accuracy received from B-LSTM when applied to raw data. The performance is similar for other evaluation metrics also.

B-LSTM outperforms KNN in case of raw data and other preprocessed data except for ICA (Table 3). When the dataset is preprocessed with ICA, KNN receives an accuracy of nearly 89% which is quite higher than B-LSTM who receives an accuracy of 82%. Based on the discussion above, we find that neural networks show better classification compared to instance based learning for alcoholism prediction with time series EEG data and B-LSTM is observed to be the best classifier in this experiment. However, there is one drawback observed of NNs which is each of them requires higher run-time than IBL algorithms.

4.3   Discussion

In this study we applied two groups of ML algorithms (KNN & LVQ for IBL and RNN, B-LSTM & CNN for NN) on EEG data to distinguish alcoholics from healthy controls. In addition, we compared the performance of these two groups using different performance metrics. There have been a number of previous studies analyzing EEG signals with ML for alcoholism detection. In this section we compare our study with some previous works regarding EEG analyzing with ML. In a study of automatic diagnosis of alcohol abuse [13] has shown significant difference between alcoholics and healthy controls in their EEG specially

Table 3. Effect of transformation on the performance of IBL and NN models

Model	PPM	Acc	AUC	F-M	G-M	Sens	Spec	T1E	T2E
IBL best model, KNN	DWT	0.720	0.720	0.721	0.721	0.724	0.715	0.275	0.284
	PCA	0.731	0.731	0.733	0.733	0.737	0.725	0.242	0.274
	ICA	**0.889**	**0.889**	**0.888**	**0.888**	**0.888**	**0.890**	**0.111**	**0.109**
	Raw	0.747	0.747	0.745	0.745	0.739	0.754	0.260	0.245
NN best model, B-LSTM	DWT	0.885	0.885	0.887	0.887	0.898	0.872	0.101	0.127
	PCA	**0.950**	**0.950**	**0.950**	**0.950**	**0.945**	**0.955**	**0.054**	**0.044**
	ICA	0.827	0.827	0.828	0.828	0.835	0.818	0.164	0.181
	Raw	0.920	0.920	0.919	0.919	0.910	0.930	0.089	0.069

Legend: PPM: Preprocessing Method; Acc.: Accuracy; ROC: Receiver Operating characteristics; F-M: F-Measure; G-M: Geometric Mean; Sens.: Sensitivity; Spec.: Specificity; T[1/2]E: Type [I/II] error; Bold are best performance.

in the left hemisphere. Besides discriminating EEG of alcoholics and healthy controls, they have also differentiated the EEG of alcoholics and alcohol abuser though there was no seemingly significant difference between the alcoholics and alcohol abusers. However, EEG of alcoholics and healthy controls have high difference in the delta and theta band. They have received an accuracy of 96% using SVM. In another study [15], wavelet transformation methods is applied to find non-linear correlation called correntrophy in EEG signals of alcoholics and normal. The correlation is then used with Squared SVM for classification which received an accuracy of 97%. However, their study does not provide any detail discussion on if EEG of any certain part of the brain carries any differentiating features between the alcoholics and the controls. In our study, We have considered response values of electrodes FPZ, FP1 and FP2 which collects neural activity in the prefrontal cortex of the brain. The prefrontal cortex is the part of the cortical region responsible for decision making as well as reasoning [4] based on past events. Therefore, we have considered the fact that neural response of alcoholics and the controls can have significant difference in their prefrontal cortex. In case of accuracy, both the papers [15] and [13] have marginally higher performance than ours where our best classifier B-LSTM have received an accuracy of 95%. However, the aim of this study was not only classify the EEG data, also compare the performance of IBL and NN algorithms. We have applied different preprocessing methods to both groups of methods and found that NN outperforms IBL in classifying non-linear EEG data, except when ICA is used.

5 Conclusion

Alcoholism is a psychological phenotype harmful to an individual as well as to society. The negative physical effects of its' can be transmitted genetically to the offspring. Therefore, identification of alcohol abusers from healthy people is becoming an important research topic to data scientists. Our experiment successfully implemented ML algorithms for classifying EEG data of alcoholics and healthy control. Neural networks outperformed instance based algorithms, however if the time-series EEG data is converted to linear data using ICA, the instance based networks significantly improve in classifying EEG of alcoholics, even outperform the neural networks. B-LSTM is proven to be the best classifier in this experiment receiving accuracy of at most 95%. Our experiment of comparing two different classifiers' performance with EEG signal suggest the best possible method for Alcoholism automated detection and therefore, reduce the diagnosis error. In the future we want to use the response values of all the patients that participated in the EEG data collection and see if the algorithms show scalability.

References

1. Abdi, H., Williams, L.J.: Principal component analysis. Wiley Interdiscip. Rev. Comput. Stat. **2**(4), 433–459 (2010)
2. Acharya, U.R., Sree, S.V., Chattopadhyay, S., Suri, J.S.: Automated diagnosis of normal and alcoholic EEG signals. Int. J. Neural Syst. **22**(03), 1250011 (2012)
3. Begleiter, H.: EEG database data set. Neurodynamics Laboratory, State University of New York Health Center Brooklyn, New York (1995). https://archive.ics.uci.edu/ml/datasets/EEG+Database
4. Fuster, J.: The Prefrontal Cortex. Academic Press, Cambridge (2015)
5. Hochreiter, S., Schmidhuber, J.: Long short-term memory. Neural Comput. **9**(8), 1735–1780 (1997)
6. Hommer, D.W., et al.: Evidence for a gender-related effect of alcoholism on brain volumes. Am. J. Psychiatry **158**(2), 198–204 (2001)
7. Hyvärinen, A., Oja, E.: Independent component analysis: algorithms and applications. Neural Netw. **13**(4–5), 411–430 (2000)
8. Kohonen, T.: Learning vector quantization. In: Kohonen, T. (ed.) Self-Organizing Maps. Springer Series in Information Sciences, vol. 30, pp. 175–189. Springer, Heidelberg (1995). https://doi.org/10.1007/978-3-642-97610-0_6
9. Kousarrizi, M.R.N., Ghanbari, A.A., Gharaviri, A., Teshnehlab, M., Aliyari, M.: Classification of alcoholics and non-alcoholics via EEG using SVM and neural networks. In: Proceedings of ICBBE, pp. 1–4. IEEE (2009)
10. Li, M., et al.: Emotion recognition from multichannel EEG signals using k-nearest neighbor classification. Technol. Health Care **26**(S1), 509–519 (2018)
11. Mahmud, M., Hawellek, D., Bertoldo, A.: EEG based brain-machine interface for navigation of robotic device. In: Proceedings of BioRob, pp. 168–172. IEEE (2010)
12. Mahmud, M., Kaiser, M.S., Hussain, A., Vassanelli, S.: Applications of deep learning and reinforcement learning to biological data. IEEE Trans. Neural Netw. Learn. Syst. **29**(6), 2063–2079 (2018)
13. Mumtaz, W., et al.: Automatic diagnosis of alcohol use disorder using EEG features. Knowl. Based Syst. **105**, 48–59 (2016)
14. Oh, S.L., et al.: A deep learning approach for Parkinson's disease diagnosis from EEG signals. Neural Comput. Appl. **32**, 1–7 (2018)
15. Patidar, S., Pachori, R.B., Upadhyay, A., Acharya, U.R.: An integrated alcoholic index using tunable-Q wavelet transform based features extracted from EEG signals for diagnosis of alcoholism. Appl. Soft Comput. **50**, 71–78 (2017)
16. Santa Maria Shithil, T.K.S., Sharma, T.: A dynamic data placement policy for heterogeneous hadoop cluster. 2017 4th International Conference on Advances in Electrical Engineering (ICAEE) (2017)
17. Shanir, P.M., Khan, K.A., Khan, Y.U., Farooq, O., Adeli, H.: Automatic seizure detection based on morphological features using one-dimensional local binary pattern on long-term EEG. Clin. EEG Neurosci. **49**(5), 351–362 (2018)
18. Shensa, M.J., et al.: The discrete wavelet transform: wedding the a Trous and Mallat algorithms. IEEE Trans. Sig. Process **40**(10), 2464–2482 (1992)
19. Sriraam, N., et al.: EEG based detection of alcoholics using spectral entropy with neural network classifiers. In: Proceedings of ICoBE, pp. 89–93. IEEE (2012)
20. Stoev, H.: Brain disease detection from EEGs: comparing spiking and recurrent neural networks for non-stationary time series classification. Masters dissertation. Technological University Dublin (2020). https://doi.org/10.21427/sv9j-t268
21. de Zambotti, M., et al.: 0141 effect of evening alcohol intake on polysomnographic sleep in healthy adults. Sleep **41**, A55 (2018)

A Monitoring System for Patients of Autism Spectrum Disorder Using Artificial Intelligence

Md. Hasan Al Banna[1] , Tapotosh Ghosh[1] , Kazi Abu Taher[1] ,
M. Shamim Kaiser[2(✉)] , and Mufti Mahmud[3]

[1] Bangladesh University of Professionals, Dhaka, Bangladesh
alifhasan39@gmail.com, 16511038@student.bup.edu.bd, kataher@bup.edu.bd
[2] Institute of Information Technology, Jahangirnagar University,
Savar, Dhaka 1342, Bangladesh
mskaiser@juniv.edu
[3] Nottingham Trent University, Clifton Campus, Nottingham NG11 8NS, UK
mufti.mahmud@ntu.ac.uk, mufti.mahmud@gmail.com

Abstract. When the world is suffering from the deadliest consequences of COVID-19, people with autism find themselves in the worst possible situation. The patients of autism lack social skills, and in many cases, show repetitive behavior. Many of them need outside support throughout their life. During the COVID-19 pandemic, as many of the places are in lockdown conditions, it is very tough for them to find help from their doctors and therapists. Suddenly, the caregivers and parents of the ASD patients find themselves in a strange situation. Therefore, we are proposing an artificial intelligence-based system that uses sensor data to monitor the patient's condition, and based on the emotion and facial expression of the patient, adjusts the learning method through exciting games and tasks. Whenever something goes wrong with the patient's behavior, the caregivers and the parents are alerted about it. We then presented how this AI-based system can help them during COVID-19 pandemic. This system can help the parents to adjust to the new situation and continue the mental growth of the patients.

Keywords: COVID-19 · Autism · Emotion Detection · Artificial intelligence

1 Introduction

The COVID-19 global pandemic is keeping its impact on every sector, taking away millions of lives. The world economy is collapsing, and healthcare providers face immense pressure to ensure health support to the help-seekers. People with

Md. H. A. Banna and T. Ghosh—These two authors contributed equally.

© Springer Nature Switzerland AG 2020
M. Mahmud et al. (Eds.): BI 2020, LNAI 12241, pp. 251–262, 2020.
https://doi.org/10.1007/978-3-030-59277-6_23

autism spectrum disorder (ASD) need more attention during a regular period than anyone else. They follow strict routines, which keep their health in stable condition. Due to the COVID-19 pandemic, these routines are violated. This disruption leaves ASD patients in a more vulnerable position. Since the institutional help is not available, a new support system is needed to meet the demand for help.

ASD refers to the condition, where the patients face difficulties in social interactions and communication, show repetitive behavior, lack language skills, and perform a limited range of activities. Some patients do not understand pain, and therefore, when they are angry, they get involved in self-destructive activities. Worldwide 0.625% of the children are affected with ASD [10]. This situation is much worse in developing and underdeveloped countries. They usually face more domination and violence in the domestic environment than a healthy person [14]. During a lockdown, this situation worsens with an increase in these incidents [34]. The health condition of an ASD patient can be improved by providing constant care and appropriate therapies. These therapies involve some reinforcements to the patient, which can be some praising words or some privileges. Unfortunately, during the COVID-19 pandemic, since most of the places are in lockdown conditions, help from the clinicians and the therapist are challenging to get. The educational institutions are also closed because of the pandemic. Therefore, an alternative way needs to be created to solve these problems.

Artificial Intelligence (AI) is a technology that mimics the functionality of the human brain and is used in many applications as biological data mining [19, 20], image analysis [5, 22, 23], anomaly detection [11, 36] and expert system [15, 21, 25, 31, 33, 39]. In the healthcare sector, AI is getting more popular and used for diagnosis purposes [6, 7]. During the global pandemic, as the number of clinicians is small, and they cannot personally interact with the patient directly, an AI monitoring and response system can help. This AI system should take environmental parameters, patient's current situation, and uncommon situations as input to provide responses analyzing the data. This will help the parents and caregivers as an assistant and take better care of the patient.

Courtenay et al. [8] investigated how COVID-19 pandemic can impact on people with intellectual disabilities. He mentioned that these people have a weak immune system, which makes them vulnerable to this disease. He also mentioned that if anyone with intellectual disabilities is affected by COVID-19, they can face serious consequences. Lima et al. [27] assessed the risk factors of ASD during COVID-19. They said that ASD patients have cytokine dysregulation abnormal factors, and the COVID patients who faced complications also showed raise in cytokine. Therefore, they proposed to take special care for the ASD patients during this pandemic. Yarımkaya and Esentürk [38] emphasized exercise for ASD patients during COVID-19 as they tend to get weights quickly and show signs of obesity. They also described the exercise set, time duration, and the frequency in their study.

There were some researches, where the emotion of the ASD patients was detected using sensors. Heni and Hamam [13] proposed a facial emotion detection system and an automatic speech recognition system for emotion detection of ASD patients. They followed the rapid object detection system proposed by Viola and Jones [32]. Krysko and Rutherford [17] experimented with the ability of ASD patients to detect angry behavior. They found that the patients can successfully detect angry and happy faces but show difficulty in understanding discrepant images. Smitha and Vinod [26] proposed a real-time emotion detection procedure using principal component analysis (PCA). They extracted the face from the background and detected happy, sad, surprise, neutral, and angry expressions with reasonable accuracy. Afrin [1] et al. proposed an AI-based approach to recognize facial expression recognition of autism individuals. They at first, took the image as an input and removed noise from the image using a median filter. They segmented the filtered image. Then a simple CNN was introduced to classify the image [4]. They simulated the whole architecture and found that the architecture was successful in classifying facial expression.

Sumi et al. [28] proposed an assistance system for caregivers of ASD patients in the form of a smart wearable device that can detect position, heartbeat, sound, and movement of the patient. These sensors use wireless interface to transmit data to the parents, caregivers, and in an external repository. GPS sensor was used for location, and an accelerometer sensor was used for finding repetitive patterns in the patients. [2,3,6,16] proposed an assistive system for caregivers dealing with ASD patients in the form of a playing element [23,37].

In this research, we have proposed a system that can work as a substitute for the caregivers of ASD patients. We have proposed a wearable sensor-based device along with a camera-based monitoring system. Then we introduced a transfer learning-based CNN model for emotion recognition, which will be used to interact with ASD patients. To the best of the author's knowledge, no research has been done, which detects emotion of ASD patient using transfer learning and use that to maintain and teach them. This system can monitor the ASD patients without any contact of the caregivers. Therefore, when some of the family member is affected with COVID-19, this monitoring system can help a lot. Finally, we have discussed how this model can help the patients and their caregivers during this pandemic. We hope that this research will help take care of the ASD patients in this pandemic and relief their parents.

In the next section, we will discuss the world health organization's (WHO) guidelines for maintaining ASD patients. In Sect. 3, we will discuss our methodology. Section 4 will cover the results of this research. Section 5 will cover the usage of the proposed model during COVID-19, and in Sect. 6, the conclusion and future works will be discussed.

2   WHO on Autism

The symptoms of ASD are visible within ages 1 to 5, which continues to adolescence and adulthood [35]. In most cases, ASD is accompanied by attention deficit hyperactivity disorder, anxiety, and depression, making the situation much worse. The number of ASD patients is ever on the rise, possibly because of more reliable diagnostic tools and people being more conscious about the diagnosis. Although, they say that 0.625% of the world's population is suffering from this disease, the numbers from underdeveloped and developing countries are not available. The causes of ASD are environmental and genetic. Though many think that childhood vaccination is a cause of ASD, there was no evidence supporting it. To overcome the problem of communication and social behavior, skill training can help a lot. In many cases, they need consistent help from others throughout their life which can be a burden for their family. Therefore, rehabilitation programs should be arranged for them, and social, employment, and educational discrimination should be eradicated. This is not a stigma, and during situations like a pandemic, they should not be deprived of the health services just because the caregivers do not know how to handle them.

3 Methodology

3.1 Proposed System

In this work, we are proposing a system consisting of a smart wrist band (SWB), an interactive monitor, and a camera device attached to the monitor for monitoring ASD patients. These devices will be connected to a mobile application to continuously monitor and keep them in a learning environment all day long without caregivers.

The SWB consists of accelerometer, gyroscope, magnetometer, GPS tracker, heart rate sensor, pedometer, and temperature sensor. Accelerometer senses vibration to detect acceleration. Gyroscope is used for measuring angular movement, and a magnetometer is used to locate the position about the north pole. GPS is widely used to track a person by providing geological coordinates.

These sensors will be attached with a microcontroller, esp8266, and a sim card module. When wi-fi is available, esp8266's built-in wi-fi module will send sensor data to the mobile server. In the case of non availability of wi-fi, the GSM module will be used to transfer data to the mobile application. This device collects data from its inbuilt heart rate sensor, pedometer, and temperature sensor and will send the patient's condition to the mobile server. An ambient temperature sensor will be set up in the corner of the room for continuous monitoring of the room. There will be some toys and counting objects in the room. RFID will be attached to them to detect its touching.

The output device will be a sound box and a computer screen, which will contain a camera to take the images of the patient for emotion analysis in every 5 min. All the devices described in this system will send data to the mobile server, and data will be stored for around 20 days. The processed data will be sent to the server from the mobile device. Our AI models will analyze the health condition of the autistic individual and operate through some visuals and sounds. Figure 1 depicts the proposed AI-based system for the ASD patients.

The children will have a routine for playing, learning, and sleeping. The AI-powered application will be installed on the mobile. It will produce some relaxation music during sleeping, show visuals during teaching, and help them

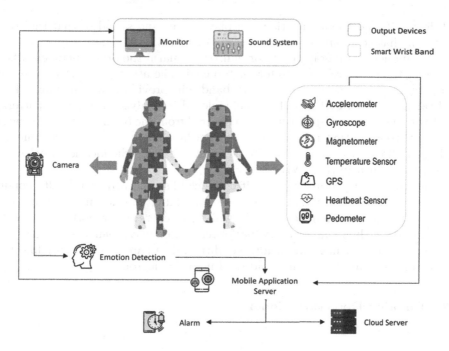

Fig. 1. An AI-based autism monitoring system. There are sensor elements such as accelerometer, gyroscope, magnetometer, temperature sensor, GPS, heartbeat sensor, pedometer, and a camera attached to the monitor, which shows visuals based on the mobile application decision. The camera output is used to detect the emotion of the ASD patient. When some unusual event happens, an alarm signal is sent to the caregivers. The mobile application takes the decision and sends it to the server.

play based on their emotion. We have proposed an Inception-ResNetV2 based model for emotion recognition from camera images. It can detect the positive, negative, and neutral state of a person.

If the child is in a positive mental state during the time of the study, the mobile application will show him some alphabets, pictures for teaching counting, or contents according to the school's guidelines on the screen. It will also provide sound to keep him attracted to this lesson. If his mindset becomes negative, the application will try to relax him by showing cartoons or some relaxation songs, which will make him ready to study again. The whole emotion state will be controlled through the proposed CNN model using images taken by attached camera in the monitor screen.

During playing, the software will give him the command to do something. If he is trying to play Lego, it will provide instruction in a language that the child can understand. RFID attached to the toys will detect the child's touch on it and will prompt the monitor to show the child a visual and a sound related to the visual. If he successfully does something, the application will praise him and take him to more laborious tasks. If the child is touching a dirty object, RFID will detect it, and the application will play visuals and sound so that the child can learn that he should not move the dirty objects.

The ambient temperature sensor will try to alarm the other members when the room temperature gets too hot or too cold. The attached heart rate sensor and temperature sensor in the smart band will provide a way of monitoring his health status. An AI model will be deployed to analyze his sleeping pattern, heart rate data, and temperature data collected from the band. It will then alarm parents through a text message and app notification. If the child goes outside without telling anyone, he can easily be found out using the location tracked by the GPS attached in the SWB.

The whole architecture will monitor the child's concentration, health condition, and activity continuously. If it finds something unusual, it will send messages to the parents immediately. It will also generate a report every week, including the child's daily activity, performance in games, mental state, activity log, progress in learning, and health condition. The parents can easily find the growth of their child through it and send it to the doctor.

3.2 Emotion Detection Model

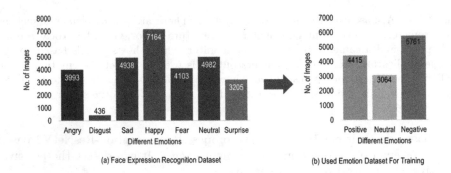

Fig. 2. (a) Distribution of images to seven different classes in the face recognition dataset. The class labeled "Happy" contains the highest number of images (7,164) and "Disgust" contains the least number of images (436) (b) Distribution of images after removing, shuffling, and re-labeling images from the face recognition dataset. Images of seven classes in the Face recognition dataset were distributed to three classes (Positive, Negative, Neutral). The negative class contains the highest number of images (5,761), and the neutral class contains the least number of images (3,064).

The emotion of ASD patient can be detected from real-time images. For training and testing the emotion recognition model, we have used a facial expression recognition dataset that is publicly available at Kaggle [24]. This dataset contains a total of 35,887 images divided into training and testing folders. This dataset contains images of 7 facial expressions: happy, sad, anger, disgust, surprise, sad, and neutral. The dimension of these images is 48 × 48 in grey-scaled form. In this work, we have divided the dataset into three classes: positive, neutral, and negative. We have considered the images labeled happy as positive, neutral labeled images were considered as neutral, and sad, disgust, and anger tagged images were labeled as the negative class. After removing, shuffling, and re-labeling images, we took 21,513 samples for training, testing, and validation. For training purposes, we have kept 13,240 samples, and 3,254 were used as a validation set. A set of 5,019 images were kept aside for testing the performance of the model.

We have also used a facial expression recognition dataset named CK+48 [18] for cross-validating the model. This dataset contained images of 7 facial expressions: happy, sad, anger, disgust, surprise, fear, and neutral. We converted it to 3 classes (positive, negative, neutral), where we did not consider the images of fear and surprise. The positive class contained images labeled as happy, the neutral class had the images labeled as neutral, and the negative class was a collection of images labeled as anger, disgust, and sad. Figure 2 presents how emotion recognition dataset was created from the Kaggle dataset. Figure 2(a) shows the number of samples in each class of the Kaggle dataset. Figure 2(b) shows the distribution of number samples in each class in the converted dataset.

Inception-ResNet [30] architecture is a state-of-the-art CNN architecture, a combination of InceptionNet [29] and ResNet [12]. These two architectures are capable of acquiring high precision in lower epochs in case of image classification. Inception-ResnetV2 combines the power of these two models. It contains 164 layers, which is trained with the ImageNet [9] dataset containing 1,000 classes. In this architecture, the Inception block is combined with a 1×1 convolution layer without activation for scaling up filter bank dimensionality. Convolution is done by multiplying filters with the image pixels to find new features. It is also necessary to match dimensionality with input block as it is mandatory to have the same dimension in input and output for residual operation. As the number of filters increases, residual networks tend to die. So, residual activation is scaled to in between 0.1 and 0.3 in Inception-ResNetV2. The total number of parameters in the Inception-ResnetV2 model is 55,873,736, and the size of the architecture is 215 MB.

The Inception-ResNetV2 model was trained and tested using the above mentioned facial expression recognition dataset. The model took images as input, converted it to a tensor of $299 \times 299 \times 3$, and was given input to the model's input layer. The model was trained using an adam optimizer, where the learning rate was set to 0.001. It was trained for 20 epochs. The model was then tested using a separated testing set of facial expression recognition. We have cross-validated the trained model using the CK+48 dataset. The images of this dataset were at first converted to $299 \times 299 \times 3$ as InceptionResNetV2 can take images of $299 \times 299 \times 3$ as input. Then they were given input to the trained model for predicting their class. We have removed the last layer from the original Inception-ResNetv2 and tried several combinations of fully connected layers and activation functions (Softmax, Sigmoid, Tanh). We have tried to improve the model's performance by changing learning rate (0.1, 0.01, 0.001, 0.0001). The best model is presented in this study (Fig. 3).

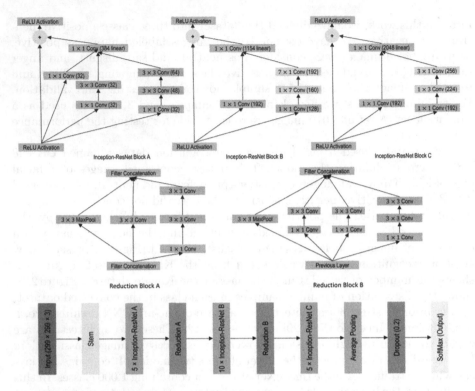

Fig. 3. The architecture of Inception-ResNetV2. There are three inception blocks where each of them has an additional 1×1 convolutional layer for scaling up the dimensionality. Reduction blocks are introduced to change tensor's height and width. The stem takes a $299 \times 299 \times 3$ image as input and performs some operations. After that, Inception blocks and reduction blocks extract significant features for classifying images.

4   Result Analysis

The Inception-ResNetV2 architecture achieved 78.56% accuracy in emotion recognition from facial images. It has classified 3961 out of 5019 images successfully into three different classes. Figure 4(a) shows the confusion matrix of the proposed model. This architecture was most successful in classifying positive emotions. It has successfully recognized emotion from 1,521 out of 1,978 samples in negative class, 884 out of 1,216 images from neutral class, and 1,556 out of 1,825 samples in positive class. Figure 4(b) shows the prediction ability of the model for classifying different emotions. The model was also cross-validated using a publicly available CK+48 dataset, where this model achieved an accuracy of 76.70%. The images of this dataset were not used for training purposes. So, it proves that the model is very much efficient in recognizing emotion from facial expression image. Figure 5(a) shows the comparison of the achieved testing accuracy of the model in the two different datasets.

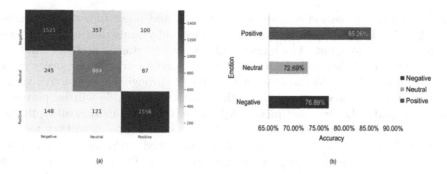

(a)   (b)

Fig. 4. (a) The confusion matrix of the emotion detection model. (b) Accuracy of the InceptionResNetV2 model to classify positive, negative, and neutral emotions.

Figure 5(b) shows the comparison between different ML algorithms and the Inception-ResNetV2 model for classifying emotions from a person's image. The ML models did not perform well with the data. Random forest (RF) and support vector machine (SVM) achieved accuracy around 57% mark, which is not very encouraging. On the other hand, our proposed transfer learning model achieved good accuracy for this job.

5 Utility of the Proposed Model During COVID-19 Pandemic

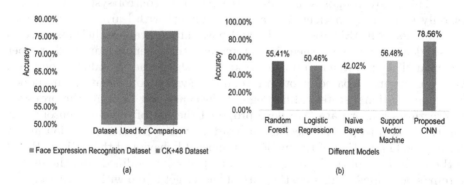

(a)   (b)

Fig. 5. (a) Comparison of testing accuracies for two different datasets for the proposed model. (c) Comparison of different ML models with the proposed CNN model. Among the ML algorithms, SVM performed better than the others, but the CNN model outperformed them.

Due to the Covid-19 pandemic, washing hands has become very important. Autistic children don't understand the importance of washing hands or putting on masks, and he cannot understand what he should do in this tough time.

The proposed application will show him visuals and make him washing hands every 2 h. It will also teach him through games and visuals that he should wear masks when he goes out. The games will have a few stages, and the child will be prompted to do some tasks in the virtual game for completing every steps. He will gather the understanding of COVID-19 through an interactive visual. If he is sitting for a very long time, the visuals and sounds will be played to make the child walk for sometimes. It will make them physically healthy, fit, and boost their immune system. If he is walking for a long time, it will try to make him rested for some time. The child will be prompted to do some easy physical activities such as hand raising, spreading, and so on. The system will keep the patient busy with engaging content and generate an alert in times of unusual behaviors. It will optimize the method of learning based on the patient's mood so that burden is not imposed on them. If the parents of the patient are affected by COVID-19, this system will help them maintain distance with the patient and maintain a healthy environment.

6 Conclusions

In recent years, technologies are offering considerable assistance to every sectors. AI has given some decision-making capabilities to electrical devices. Healthcare systems are adopting AI, so that they can assist the clinicians in monitoring and managing the patients. ASD patients need persistent assistance, which is tough to get during the COVID-19 pandemic. The availability of clinical help is limited, and emergency help is hard to get. A personalized monitoring and supporting system can help the ASD patients during this pandemic and afterward. This study proposes an automated AI-based control system which can not only monitor the patients but also give support with learning and therapy. The patients with ASD are mentally and physically unstable. Their response to any sudden event around them is extreme and this phenomenon needs proper attention. That is why environment near them should be as stable as possible. We are using an AI based emotion recognition system to evaluate their sudden change in emotional state and finding out the cause of it by using the proposed architecture's sensor data. We have proposed the use of different sensors that help the system to provide decisions accordingly. The emotion detection model offers a good indication of the mood and unusual behavior of the patient. Based on them, the level of the learning games and tasks are modified, and the reward system is developed. This way, the patients never get bored with the therapy. At last, we discussed how this proposed system could be used for maintaining the patients during COVID-19. This system can help the clueless parents in finding some space to get themselves sorted. In the future, more compact design and features like augmented reality will be incorporated with this proposed system. A human activity recognition model will be incorporated with this existing model as well.

References

1. Afrin, M., Freeda, S., Elakia, S., Kannan, P.: AI based facial expression recognition for autism children. IJETIE **5**(9), 7 (2019)
2. Afsana, F., Mamun, S., Kaiser, M., Ahmed, M.: Outage capacity analysis of cluster-based forwarding scheme for body area network using nano-electromagnetic communication. In: Proceedings of EICT, pp. 383–388 (2015)
3. Afsana, F., et al.: An energy conserving routing scheme for wireless body sensor nanonetwork communication. IEEE Access **6**, 9186–9200 (2018)
4. Al Banna, M.H., et al.: Camera model identification using deep CNN and transfer learning approach. In: Proceedings of ICREST, pp. 626–630 (2019)
5. Ali, H.M., Kaiser, M.S., Mahmud, M.: Application of convolutional neural network in segmenting brain regions from MRI data. In: Liang, P., Goel, V., Shan, C. (eds.) Brain Informatics, pp. 136–146. Cham (2019)
6. Asif-Ur-Rahman, M., et al.: Toward a heterogeneous mist, fog, and cloud-based framework for the internet of healthcare things. IEEE Internet Things J. **6**(3), 4049–4062 (2018)
7. Biswas, S., et al.: Cloud based healthcare application architecture and electronic medical record mining: an integrated approach to improve healthcare system. In: Proceedings of ICCIT, pp. 286–291 (2014)
8. Courtenay, K., Perera, B.: Covid-19 and people with intellectual disability: impacts of a pandemic. Irish J. Psychol. Med. 1–21 (2020)
9. Deng, J., Dong, W., Socher, R., Li, L.J., Li, K., Fei-Fei, L.: Imagenet: a large-scale hierarchical image database. In: Proceedings of CVPR, pp. 248–255 (2009)
10. Elsabbagh, M., et al.: Global prevalence of autism and other pervasive developmental disorders. Autism Res. **5**(3), 160–179 (2012)
11. Fabietti, M., et al.: Neural network-based artifact detection in LFP recorded from chronically implanted neural probes. In: Proceedings of IJCNN, pp. 1–8 (2020)
12. He, K., Zhang, X., Ren, S., Sun, J.: Deep residual learning for image recognition. In: Proceedings of CVPR, pp. 770–778 (2016)
13. Heni, N., Hamam, H.: Design of emotional educational system mobile games for autistic children. In: Proceedings of ATSIP, pp. 631–637 (2016)
14. James, W.: Domestic violence reports rise by a third in locked-down London, police say (2020). https://www.reuters.com/article/us-health-coronavirus-britain-violence/domestic-violence-reports-rise-by-a-third-in-locked-down-london-police-say-idUSKCN2262YI. Accessed 6 June 2020
15. Kaiser, M.S., et al.: Advances in crowd analysis for urban applications through urban event detection. IEEE Trans. Intell. Transp. Syst. **19**(10), 3092–3112 (2018)
16. Khullar, V., et al.: IoT based assistive companion for hypersensitive individuals (ACHI) with autism spectrum disorder. Asian J. Psychiat. **46**, 92–102 (2019)
17. Krysko, K.M., Rutherford, M.: A threat-detection advantage in those with autism spectrum disorders. Brain Cogn. **69**(3), 472–480 (2009)
18. Lucey, P., et al.: The extended Cohn-Kanade dataset (ck+): a complete dataset for action unit and emotion-specified expression. In: Proceedings of CVPR, pp. 94–101 (2010)
19. Mahmud, M., Kaiser, M.S., Hussain, A.: Deep learning in mining biological data. arXiv:2003.00108 [cs, q-bio, stat] abs/2003.00108, pp. 1–36 (2020)
20. Mahmud, M., Kaiser, M.S., Hussain, A., Vassanelli, S.: Applications of deep learning and reinforcement learning to biological data. IEEE Trans. Neural Netw. Learn. Syst. **29**(6), 2063–2079 (2018)

21. Mahmud, M., et al.: A brain-inspired TMM to assure security in a cloud based IoT framework for neuroscience applications. Cogn. Comput. **10**(5), 864–873 (2018)
22. Miah, Y., et al.: Performance comparison of ml techniques in identifying dementia from open access clinical datasets. In: Proceedings of ICACIn, pp. 69–78 (2020)
23. Noor, M.B.T., et al.: Detecting neurodegenerative disease from MRI: a brief review on a deep learning perspective. In: Liang, P., Goel, V., Shan, C. (eds.) Brain Informatics. LNCS, pp. 115–125. Springer, Heidelberg (2019). https://doi.org/10.1007/978-3-030-37078-7_12
24. Pierre Luc Carrier, A.C.: Challenges in representation learning: facial expression recognition challenge (2013). https://www.kaggle.com/jonathanoheix/face-expression-recognition-dataset. Accessed 11 June 2020
25. Rahman, S., Al Mamun, S., Ahmed, M.U., Kaiser, M.S.: PHY/MAC layer attack detection system using neuro-fuzzy algorithm for IoT network. In: Proceedings of ICEEOT, pp. 2531–2536 (2016)
26. Smitha, K.G., Vinod, A.P.: Facial emotion recognition system for autistic children: a feasible study based on FPGA implementation. Med. Biol. Eng. Comput. **53**(11), 1221–1229 (2015). https://doi.org/10.1007/s11517-015-1346-z
27. de Sousa Lima, et al.: Could autism spectrum disorders be a risk factor for COVID-19? Med. Hypotheses, **144**, 109899 (2020)
28. Sumi, A.I., et al.: fASSERT: a fuzzy assistive system for children with autism using internet of things. In: Brain Informatics, pp. 403–412 (2018)
29. Szegedy, C., et al.: Going deeper with convolutions. In: Proceedings of CVPR, pp. 1–9 (2015)
30. Szegedy, C., et al.: Inception-v4, inception-resnet and the impact of residual connections on learning. In: Proceedings of AAAI, pp. 4278–4284 (2017)
31. Tania, M.H., et al.: Assay type detection using advanced machine learning algorithms. In: Proceedings of SKIMA, pp. 1–8 (2019)
32. Viola, P., Jones, M.: Face detection. IJCV **57**, 2 (2004)
33. Watkins, J., Fabietti, M., Mahmud, M.: Sense: a student performance quantifier using sentiment analysis. In: Proceedings of IJCNN, pp. 1–6 (2020)
34. Weiss, J.A., Fardella, M.A.: Victimization and perpetration experiences of adults with autism. Front. Psychiat. **9**, 203 (2018)
35. WHO: Autism spectrum disorders (2019). https://www.kaggle.com/jonathanoheix/face-expression-recognition-dataset. Accessed 11 June 2020
36. Yahaya, S.W., Lotfi, A., Mahmud, M.: A consensus novelty detection ensemble approach for anomaly detection in activities of daily living. Appl. Soft Comput. **83**, 105613 (2019)
37. Yahaya, S.W., et al.: Gesture recognition intermediary robot for abnormality detection in human activities. In: Proceedings of SSCI, pp. 1415–1421 (2019)
38. Yarımkaya, E., Esentürk, O.K.: Promoting physical activity for children with autism spectrum disorders during coronavirus outbreak: benefits, strategies, and examples. Int. J. Dev. Disabil. 1–6 (2020)
39. Zohora, M.F., et al.: Forecasting the risk of type ii diabetes using reinforcement learning. In: Proceedings of ICIEV, pp. 1–6 (2020)

Artificial and Internet of Healthcare Things Based Alzheimer Care During COVID 19

Sabrina Jesmin[1] , M. Shamim Kaiser[1(⊠)] , and Mufti Mahmud[2]

[1] Jahangirnagar University, Savar, Dhaka 1342, Bangladesh
sabrina.jesmin.eee@gmail.com, mskaiser@juniv.edu
[2] School of Science and Technology, Nottingham Trent University, Nottingham, UK
mufti.mahmud@ntu.ac.uk

Abstract. Alzheimer patient's routine care at the onset of a catastrophe like coronavirus disease 2019 (COVID-19) pandemic is interrupted as healthcare is providing special attention to the patient having severe acute respiratory syndrome coronavirus 2 (SARS-COV-2) or COVID-19 infection. In order to decrease the spread of the disease, government has shut down regular services at the hospital, and advised all vulnerable people to stay at home and maintain social distance (of 3 fts) which hampered the routine care and rehabilitation therapy of elderly patient having a chronic disease like Alzheimer. On the other hand, the artificial intelligence (AI)-based internet of healthcare things allows clinicians to monitor physiological conditions of patients in real-time and machine learning models can able to detect any anomaly in the patient's condition. Besides, the advancement in Information and Communication Technology enable us to provide special distance care (such as medication and therapy) by dedicated medical teams or special therapists. This paper discusses the effect of COVID-19 on patient care of Alzheimer's Disease (AD) and how AI-based IoT can help special care of AD patients at home. Finally, we have outlined some recommendations for Family and Caregiver, Volunteer and Social Care which will help to develop the Government policy.

Keywords: IoT · Machine learning · SARS-COV-2 · Pandemic · Patient management

1 Introduction

Coronavirus disease 2019 (COVID-19), also called severe acute respiratory syndrome coronavirus 2 (SARS-CoV-2) disease, was first reported in Wuhan on December 2019 which was caused by positive sense single RNA virus named novel coronavirus. Due to its high transmissivity or spreading rate from human to human, World Health Organization (WHO) declared it to be a global emergency of public health concern [35]. For providing special attention to the patients

© Springer Nature Switzerland AG 2020
M. Mahmud et al. (Eds.): BI 2020, LNAI 12241, pp. 263–274, 2020.
https://doi.org/10.1007/978-3-030-59277-6_24

having COVID-19, the regular healthcare services at the hospital is interrupted and limited services are provided by the healthcare stuff to the patient suffering from chronic and lifestyle diseases such as stroke, heart disease, cancer, diabetes, Alzheimer's disease (AD), depression, HIV etc. as per WHO recommendation. [6,12].

The AD is an age-dependent chronic neurodegenerative disease that results in progressive memory impairment. More than 50 million people around the globe is suffering in AD right now [2]. Patient having AD may fail to maintain personal hygiene (such as washing hand) and WHO recommended safeguard for preventing COVID-19. Recent study found that AD gene has strong link for the high risk of severe COVID-19 [19]. Thus, a special care has to be taken while giving care to the AD patient. With no current cure to AD [23], we can only slow the worsening of dementia symptoms by regular care with existing researches. Due to the nature of the disease, an Alzheimer's patient needs continuous support such as caregiving, clinical assistancy etc. because they face difficulty in daily activities and eventually can lose response ability to their environment.

Chronic Disease management during COVID-19 pandemic is challenging. Taheri *et al.* [31] discussed management strategies for diabetic patients during COVID-19 by advising glucose control and routine self monitoring of glucose level along with text-messaging interventions. Authors stated that due to COVID-19, patients' normal routine care, physical activity, diet will be disrupted and they may suffer in mental stress more. Bornstein *et al.* [8] discussed a summary of expert recommendation in endocrinology and diabetic field about the relationship of COVID-19 and diabetes in their paper along with a few practical recommendations on management for diabetic patients during this pandemic. The European Society of Cardiology (ESC) [13] provided information about the risk factors and a guideline for diagnosis and management of cardiac patients during COVID-19. ESC also stated that heart and stroke patients are more likely to suffer critically due to COVID-19.

With the availability of low cost sensors, ultra high speed computing technology, and better understanding of deep learning (DL) algorithms, researchers and clinicians are collaboratively working in deploying data-driven DL models [20] on large scale healthcare data (also called electronic healthcare record or EHR) collected using ubiquitous Internet of Things (IoT) sensors. These models can be employed in predicting the incidence of diseases such as AD [25], developing drug, and assessing risk in different components (patient management and drug design, etc.) of healthcare system [16].

The role of community pharmacists can be remarkable to manage COVID-19. Kretchy *et al.* [18] discussed community pharmacists' role during COVID-19 outbreak in managing medication for patients having chronic diseases. The authors believed that the medication management by the community pharmacists is going to lessen the non-COVID disease burden from the healthcare system in countries having low and middle-income. Artificial Intelligence (AI) tools along with ML can be used to identify, to create awareness and to forecast the spread of COVID-19. ML and AI can make these tasks lot easier [21,22].

The contributions of this study are outlined below:

- we discussed the effect of COVID-19 on AD patient care and how AI based IoT can help special care of AD patients at home.
- we identified challenges and recommendations for family, caregiver and social care services in handling an AD patient at home/care-home, and
- we highlighted policies required for the management of AD patient at home during COVID-19 pandemic.

The rest of the paper is organized by the following: Sect. 2 introduced the basics of AD and its management plan; Sect. 3 reviewed effect of COVID-19 on AD care. The challenges and recommendation related to AD management during COVID-19 pandemic were discussed in Sect. 4. At the end, the work is concluded in Sect. 5.

2   AD and Its Management

AD is a form of dementia, a fatal neurological disorder, which gradually kills nerve cells of a person's brain causing a shrinkage in brain tissue which causes memory loss, confusion, difficulty in communication and dependency to others for daily activities. Unfortunately, no permanent cure has been reported till date but existing treatment may temporarily slow down the worsening of AD. Machine learning (ML) based AD prediction and its progression using EHR data has been proposed in [15,25].

The causes of AD is yet unknown. It might be caused by single or several factors. People having age more than 65; family history of AD; unhealthy lifestyle; physical/mental trauma; down syndrome (trisomy 21); Mild Cognitive Impairment (MCI) are more likely to suffer in AD [16].

When a person is diagnosed with AD at the hospital via imaging and laboratory test, they require proper AD education and support. Depending on their current level of dementia, they are prescribed with medicine and the doctor makes a treatment plan after taking consent from the patient and family member(s). Patients need to visit the doctor/therapist on a routine basis according to the care plan and any side effect arising may demand discontinuing medication and consultation with doctor (see Fig. 1(A)).

Usual management plans for AD patients may involve the following [2]:

- Having an attendant (caregiver/family member) to take care of AD patient and to help them in daily activities at home/carehome.
- Physical counselling service to cope with depression, apathy, wandering.
- Relaxation and meditation exercises for the well being of the patients.
- Maintaining a routine for AD patient.
- Sharing love, giving support to patients and paying attention to the tone while talking with them.
- Supporting them in complicated tasks that makes them confused.
- Educating caregivers so that they can take care of the patients well.
- Regular check up with the primary doctor according to care plan.

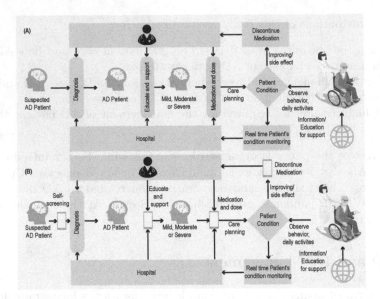

Fig. 1. A block diagrammatic representation of AD patient management. (A) Usual patient management (B) patient Management during COVID-19

AI has a number of applications such as biological data mining [20, 21], anomaly detection[24, 36, 37] and designing a clinical decision support system [17, 27, 28, 30, 32]. AI based smart diagnosis [14] and management [33] have been also developed for assisting clinicians, caregivers, and family members. AI can assist clinician, caregiver or family member to get a self-diagnostic report, predict any abnormality with AD patient while the physiological conditions (Blood pressure, pulse, oxygen saturation level, etc.) of patients are monitored remotely using Internet of Healthcare Things (IoHT) [1, 5]. Figure 1(B) represents patient management during COVID-19 which involves self screening of the patient to diagnose AD, educating and supporting with necessary instructions like medication and dose remotely [7, 26, 30].

Figure 2 shows an IoHT and AI for AD care where patient data can be collected using IoT sensors such as a smartphone/wearable device and camera(s) installed inside the room. These data can be processed using (micro)-processor of the smart/embedded devices. By employing AI based data-driven model we can detect any anomaly and can generate emergency alerts by real-time processing of the sensor data (Embedded Computing). For example, if an AD patient falls in a room, the gyroscope and accelerometer sensors in the smart device can track fall detection [34] and able to send notifications to emergency contact(s). The AI model in the fog computing system generates better insights from the data, and send it to the hospital. For example, an AI-based fall detection model can be developed using state-of-the-art fall detection dataset [34] to differentiate

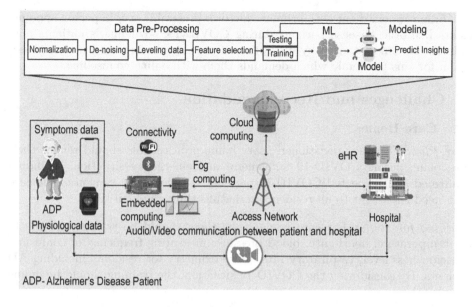

Fig. 2. AD care using AI and IoHT.

fall activities and non-fall activities. The data are stored in the cloud-based electronic health record (EHR). In the cloud, an advanced ML model can be applied in the patient care big data and generate brief knowledge visualization for the users via expensive processing and advanced ML algorithm. Finally, the visualized information can be sent to the [mobile]/[web]-application of the patient, caregiver, doctor, and family member. Such an app can also be used for tracking (but privacy is also a concern) the patient and help patient care via video conferencing (e.g. zoom call, google meet etc.) with the primary doctor or clinicians in the hospital during the situation like COVID-19 pandemic.

3   Effect of COVID-19 on Alzheimer Care

COVID-19 has affected the entire healthcare system during this ongoing pandemic. As long as COVID-19 is a communicable disease, COVID-19 makes it way difficult for patients to receive medical services from their primary doctors and clinical institutions in person but to depend on online servicing in most cases due to overburden in hospitals with COVID-19 patients. Lacking of PPE, ventilator, cleaning supplies, disinfectants is a common scenario in current condition. People are suffering economically which makes it difficult for them to bear the cost of their treatment. In some cases, supply chain problem has been occurred for medicine as well during this COVID-19 challenge.

AD patient care has been disrupted because of COVID-19 as well. During this pandemic caregiver/ family members should maintain at least 3 ft distance with AD patient during physical interaction [35].

Online appointment with primary doctor is preferable over in person appointments like other disease patients during COVID-19. Alzheimer's patients may suffer in loneliness caused by disruption of social gatherings and increased isolation for this pandemic which demands them with online counselling.

4   Challenges and Recommendation

4.1   Care Homes

Care Plan: General practitioners, care home professionals should review their care plans during COVID-19 for general and emergency situations including confirmed and suspected COVID-19 patients. An electronic version of the care plan need to be sent to all residents and stuffs through email [10].

Training for Stuffs: For care home stuffs there should be training for checking temperature, heart rate, blood pressure; measuring frequency of confusion, consciousness level, respiratory rate, pulse oximetry for residents including AD patients. By considering the COVID-19 situation, the training should be online based [11].

Emotional Health: COVID-19 is restricting social gathering which leads to isolation causing mental health problems to individuals including AD patients [9]. To eliminate isolation, by assessing individual risk, visitors might get allowed in care homes if there is no local emergency by following infection and PPE policy. If due to local emergency or other reason physical visit gets restricted, alternative communication should be provided like telephone calls, video chats etc. Online counselling need to be arranged for mental support of AD patients and family if needed. If the AD patient has exposed with COVID-19, care homes should not allow visitors physically until self-isolation period is over.

Urgent Medical Care: Care homes may have critical supportive treatments such as oxygen therapy, antibiotics and subcutaneous fluids. The policy when and how to use them needs to be reviewed carefully.

Admission Rule: New admissions need to undergo COVID-19 test and whether the result is positive or negative, they need to be isolated for 14 days. No new admission and returning of old residents should be accepted if there is shortage of resources in the care home.

4.2   Family, Caregiver and Volunteer

Educating and Checking COVID-19 Symptoms: Although a COVID-19 infected patient can be asymptomatic but most of them have reported to develop few common symptoms which may get exposed after 2 to 14 days of the infection including coughing, fever, nausea, vomiting, sore throat, diarrhea, runny nose, loss in appetite, smell dysfunction, headache, fatigue, difficulty breathing etc [12]. These symptoms need to be discussed with the family and caregivers along with the AD patients [9].

Educating Care-Givers: Care givers should be well-informed about the transmission risk of COVID-19 and should avoid unnecessary exposure. They need to follow appropriate protocols of hand washing for themselves and for AD patients. Covering coughs, disinfecting surfaces frequently, stocking medicines for 1–2 months if possible can be helpful. Telehealth appointments are recommended instead of getting in person appointment with primary doctor which is safer [9]. If the AD patient has exposed with COVID-19, caregiver should not serve AD patient physically until self-isolation period is over [3,11].

Organizing a Daily Routine and Activities: AD Patients need to be encouraged to establish a daily routine having a good balance of exercise, distant social contact and good sleep routine. According to individual's personal preference music, favourite TV show etc. can be included in their daily routine. As long as AD patients are forgetful, a written reminder post of washing hand can be kept in the bathroom and in other places. A healthy diet is also recommended by cutting down sugar level. Weight management, prioritizing fruits and vegetables by including lots of omega-3 fats is recommended. Strategy games, riddles and puzzle along with various memorization games can be helpful for their memory management [29].

Home-Based Medical Servicing: If AD patients receive home based medical servicing should keep these recommendations in mind:

- Contacting home health care providers to understand protocols that minimize spread of COVID-19.
- Health care provider should wear a mask.
- Asking health care professional if they have exposed to any COVID-19 positive patient. If so, they should not be allowed to enter the home.
- Checking body temperature of home health care provider. If their body temperature exceeds 100.4^0 F, then they should not be allowed to give service.
- Upon arrival health care provider should wash their hand.
- Even though all health care tips has been followed by CDC, entering any individual in a home always increases chance to COVID-19 infection.

Online Therapy: AD patients may suffer in mental disorders like depression causing apathy, isolation, impaired thinking, lack of interest in activities, difficulty in concentrations etc. To keep them away from mental disorders, online counselling should be given in a weekly basis. AD patients can participate in distant online meditation and relaxing activities for their stress management.

Online Socializing: For mental well-being of the AD patients social online gathering can be really helpful in weekly basis.

Maintain Social Distance and Going Out: Family/caregiver should maintain the social distance rule with patient and with other people due to COVID-19. Also, they should maintain good personal hygiene as per guideline of WHO or local authority. AD Patients need to be discouraged for public gatherings. They should not travel by public transportation as well during COVID-19 for ensuring safety [9].

AD Patient Tested Positive for COVID-19: If a AD patient gets tested positive with COVID-19, they should stay in their home preferably in a separate isolated room, only exception is to get medical service. They should avoid contact with pets and other animals and their sneezes and coughs should be covered with tissues with proper disposal. They need to sanitize their hand frequently with an alcohol based sanitizer and disinfect surfaces like phone, tables, toilets, keyboards etc. They should not share their personal belongings with others. They should also avoid public transportation/mass-gatherings. During going outside they need to wear masks maintaining all guidelines provided by WHO. Appointment in hospital should be taken by prior phone calls so that the authority can take proper precautions.

Fig. 3. Recommendation for AD care During COVID-19

Figure 3 shows some recommendations for AD patients during COVID-19. From the figure we can see, AD patient's should avoid gathering, public transportation and in person visits during this pandemic. Awareness should be created by convenient ways like phone calls, printed leaflet, TV, radio, religious organization, newspaper article etc. Patient care, social gathering, counselling and medication exercises should be done online. About the personal care we recommend ensuring patient care with proper care plan, mhealth etc.

4.3   Government Policy

Special Care Team: We need to build up a specialized team for Alzheimer patients' services including telephone hotline, electronic media, remote caregiving, online counselling etc. Due to COVID-19, telehealth is one of the way to expand benefit of medicare to seniors [2].

24/7 Helpline Services: Special 24/7 h telephone hotline servicing for AD patients should be available.

Awareness Programs: Arranging various awareness programs both online and offline through TV, local radio, electronic media, newspaper, telephone, websites etc. needs to be done. Government should Collect latest information from trusted organizations like WHO about COVID-19 and reach out those messages to people. Seeking medical advices by telephone from national and local authorities are very much recommended because family and caregivers will have latest information about COVID-19 from them. If someone is exposed to COVID-19 symptoms, they should seek medical attention by telephone to local authorities [35].

Mental Health Policy and Plan: A mental health plan should be developed by considering COVID-19 situation for AD patients [35].

Health Policy and Local Health Authority: A health policy should be developed to achieve COVID-19 free community, and local health authorities should be well informed about the latest COVID-19 information and detailed guideline [35].

AI Based Remote Monitoring: Providing remote monitoring services using AI for AD patients to track any risky movement and abnormality is essential.

Giving Financial Support to AD Patients: Alzheimer's patients may have limited or no ability to work thus many may get qualified for special benefits. Reducing and bearing medical costs of few AD patients with and without COVID-19 is necessary under special programs arranged by the Government or Non-Government organizations.

Weekly Online Consultation for Family and Caregiver: Institutions, e.g., Amwell [4], provides virtual care/telehealth solution for AD patient, caregivers and family members.

Figure 4 is the summarisation of challenges and recommendations of AD management discussed above.

Care homes:
1. A revised care plan for COVID-19 situation and reaching out the care plan to all residents and staffs.
2. Arranging necessary online training for stuffs.
3. Allowing visitors according to local COVID-19 situation by following infection and PPE policy.
4. Care homes should have critical supportive treatments.
5. No new admission is allowed if there is shortage of resources.

Family, caregiver and volunteer:
1. Proper explanation of COVID-19 to AD patient.
2. Educating COVID-19 symptoms to caregivers, family members and patient.
3. Organizing daily routine and activities.
4. Home based medical servicing should be allowed upon ensuring safety.
5. Online therapy for mental well-being of AD patients and their family.
6. Online socializing.
7. Social distance rule of at least 1 meter should be maintained during physical interaction.
8. AD patient tested positive for COVID-19 should be isolated from others until recovery.

Government Policy:
1. Specialized care team for AD patients during COVID-19.
2. 24/7 telephone helpline service for AD patients.
3. Awareness programs should be arranged.
4. Developing a mental health policy and plan for AD patients.
5. Developing a health policy to develop COVID free community.
6. Launching AI based remote monitoring.
7. Giving financial support to AD patients.
8. Weekly online consultation for family and caregiver.

Fig. 4. Summary of challenges and recommendations

5   Conclusion

This is obvious due to COVID-19 pandemic, the normal life has been disrupted to everyone including AD patients. Like other chronic disease patients, AD patients need frequent medical care and observation. Our AI- based internet of healthcare things (IoHT) can help in self-management/self diagnosis for AD patients and the caregivers and their family can monitor patients from distance by receiving required alert from the system. In addition, the ML model can detect any abnormality in patient's condition using real time physiological data collected from patient's smartphone and wearable device. In this paper, we tried to focus on how to change management plan for an AD patient during COVID-19 and the application of AI and ML which can help us to remotely track AD patients. This paper also provides some recommendations for care home, family members, caregivers which can be helpful for outlining Government policy.

References

1. Afsana, F., et al.: An energy conserving routing scheme for wireless body sensor nanonetwork communication. IEEE Access **6**, 9186–9200 (2018)
2. Alzheimer's Association: Alzheimer's and dementia (1980). https://alz.org/alzheimer_s_dementia. Accessed 10 June 2020
3. Alzheimers.net: what are the 7 stages of alzheimer's disease? (1996). https://www.alzheimers.net/stages-of-alzheimers-disease/. Accessed 10 June 2020

4. Amwell: About Amwell, September 2014. https://business.amwell.com/about-us/. Library Catalog: business.amwell.com
5. Asif-Ur-Rahman, M., et al.: Toward a heterogeneous mist, fog, and cloud-based framework for the internet of healthcare things. IEEE IoT J. **6**(3), 4049–4062 (2018)
6. Bernell, S., Howard, S.W.: Use your words carefully: what is a chronic disease? Front. Public Health **4**, 159 (2016)
7. Biswas, S., et al.: Cloud based healthcare application architecture and electronic medical record mining: an integrated approach to improve healthcare system. In: Proceedings of ICCIT, pp. 286–291 (2014)
8. Bornstein, S.R., et al.: Practical recommendations for the management of diabetes in patients with COVID-19. Lancet: Diabet. Endocrinol. **8**(6), 546–550 (2020)
9. Brightfocus: Coronavirus and alzheimer's disease (2020). https://www.brightfocus. org/alzheimers-disease/article/covid-19-and-alzheimers-disease. Library Catalog: www.brightfocus.org
10. British Geriatrics Society
11. CDC: What is alzheimer's disease?—CDC (1946). https://www.cdc.gov/aging/ aginginfo/alzheimers.htm. Accessed 14 June 2020
12. CDC: About chronic diseases—CDC (1947). https://www.cdc.gov/chronicdisease/ about/index.htm. Accessed 10 June 2020
13. ESC Press Office: New - ESC guidance for the diagnosis and management of heart disease during COVID-19 (2020). https://bit.ly/2XYh6U8. Accessed 10 June 2020
14. Farooq, A., Anwar, S., Awais, M., Alnowami, M.: Artificial intelligence based smart diagnosis of alzheimer's disease and mild cognitive impairment. In: 2017 ISC2, pp. 1–4. IEEE (2017)
15. Fisher, C.K., Smith, A.M., Walsh, J.R.: Machine learning for comprehensive forecasting of alzheimer's disease progression. Sci. Rep. **9**(1), 1–14 (2019)
16. Grassi, M., Perna, G., Caldirola, D., Schruers, K., Duara, R., Loewenstein, D.A.: A clinically-translatable machine learning algorithm for the prediction of alzheimer's disease conversion in individuals with mild and premild cognitive impairment. J. Alzheimers Dis. **61**(4), 1555–1573 (2018)
17. Kaiser, M.S., et al.: Advances in crowd analysis for urban applications through urban event detection. IEEE Trans. Intell. Transp. Syst. **19**(10), 3092–3112 (2018)
18. Kretchy, I.A., Asiedu-Danso, M., Kretchy, J.P.: Medication management and adherence during the COVID-19 pandemic: perspectives and experiences from low-and middle-income countries. Research in Social & Administrative Pharmacy (2020)
19. Kuo, C.L., et al.: APOE e4 Genotype Predicts Severe COVID-19 in the UK Biobank Community Cohort. J. Gerontol.: A (2020)
20. Mahmud, M., Kaiser, M.S., Hussain, A., Vassanelli, S.: Applications of deep learning and reinforcement learning to biological data. IEEE Trans. Neural Netw. Learn. Syst. **29**(6), 2063–2079 (2018)
21. Mahmud, M., Kaiser, M.S., Hussain, A.: Deep learning in mining biological data. arXiv:2003.00108 [cs, q-bio, stat] abs/2003.00108, pp. 1–36 (2020)
22. Mahmud, M., et al.: A brain-inspired trust management model to assure security in a cloud based IoT framework for neuroscience applications. Cogn. Comput. **10**(5), 864–873 (2018)
23. NHS: Is there a cure for dementia? (1948). https://www.nhs.uk/conditions/ dementia/cure/. Accessed 10 June 2020

24. Noor, M.B.T., et al.: Detecting neurodegenerative disease from MRI: a brief review on a deep learning perspective. In: Liang, P., Goel, V., Shan, C. (eds.) Brain Informatics, pp. 115–125 (2019)
25. Park, J.H., et al.: Machine learning prediction of incidence of alzheimer's disease using large-scale administrative health data. NPJ Digit. Med. 3(1), 1–7 (2020)
26. Paul, M.C., et al.: Low cost and portable patient monitoring system for e-health services in Bangladesh. In: Proceedings of ICCCI, pp. 1–4 (2016)
27. Rabby, G., et al.: TeKET: a tree-based unsupervised keyphrase extraction technique. Cogn. Comput. (2020). https://doi.org/10.1007/s12559-019-09706-3
28. Rahman, S., Al Mamun, S., Ahmed, M.U., Kaiser, M.S.: PHY/MAC layer attack detection system using neuro-fuzzy algorithm for IoT network. In: Proceedings of ICEEOT, pp. 2531–2536 (2016)
29. Selkoe, D.J.: Preventing alzheimer's disease. Science 337(6101), 1488–1492 (2012)
30. Sumi, A.I., Zohora, M.F., Mahjabeen, M., Faria, T.J., Mahmud, M., Kaiser, M.S.: ƒASSERT: a fuzzy assistive system for children with autism using Internet of Things. In: Wang, S., et al. (eds.) BI 2018. LNCS (LNAI), vol. 11309, pp. 403–412. Springer, Cham (2018). https://doi.org/10.1007/978-3-030-05587-5_38
31. Taheri, S., et al.: Managing diabetes in Qatar during the COVID-19 pandemic. Lancet: Diabet. Endocrinol. 6(6), 473–474 (2020)
32. Tania, M.H., et al.: Assay type detection using advanced machine learning algorithms. In: Proceedings of SKIMA, pp. 1–8 (2019)
33. Tapia, D.I., Corchado, J.M.: An ambient intelligence based multi-agent system for alzheimer health care. Int. J. Ambient Comput. Intell. 1(1), 15–26 (2009)
34. Wertner, A., Czech, P., Pammer-Schindler, V.: An open labelled dataset for mobile phone sensing based fall detection. In: EAI ICMUSCNS. ACM, August 2015
35. WHO: Coronavirus (1947). https://www.who.int/emergencies/diseases/novel-coronavirus-2019. Accessed 10 June 2020
36. Yahaya, S.W., Lotfi, A., Mahmud, M.: A consensus novelty detection ensemble approach for anomaly detection in activities of daily living. Appl. Soft Comput. 83, 105613 (2019)
37. Yahaya, S.W., et al.: Gesture recognition intermediary robot for abnormality detection in human activities. In: Proceedings of SSCI, pp. 1415–1421 (2019)

Towards Artificial Intelligence Driven Emotion Aware Fall Monitoring Framework Suitable for Elderly People with Neurological Disorder

M. Jaber Al Nahian[1]($\boxtimes$) iD, Tapotosh Ghosh[1] iD, Mohammed Nasir Uddin[1] iD, Md. Maynul Islam[1] iD, Mufti Mahmud[2] iD, and M. Shamim Kaiser[3] iD

[1] Bangladesh University of Professionals, Mirpur Cantonment, Dhaka, Bangladesh
nahianrism@gmail.com, 16511038@student.bup.edu.bd,
nasirbuet@gmail.com, maynul.mist@gmail.com
[2] Nottingham Trent University, Clifton Campus, Nottingham NG11 8NS, UK
mufti.mahmud@ntu.ac.uk, mufti.mahmud@gmail.com
[3] Institute of Information Technology, Jahangirnagar University,
Savar, Dhaka 1342, Bangladesh
mskaiser@juniv.edu

Abstract. The contemporary world's emerging issue is how the mental health and falling of a senior citizen with a neurological disorder can be maintained living at their homes as the number of aged people is increasing with the rising of life expectancy. With the advancement of the Internet of Things (IoT) and big data analytics, several works had been done on smart home health care systems that deal with in house monitoring for fall detection. Despite so much work, the challenges remain for not considering emotional care in the fall detection system for the old ones. As a remedy to the problems mentioned above, we propose an emotion aware fall monitoring framework using IoT, Artificial Intelligence (AI) Algorithms, and Big data analytics, which will deal with emotion recognition of the aged people, predictions about health conditions, and real-time fall monitoring. In the case of an emergency, the proposed framework alerts about a situation of urgency to the predefined caregiver. A smart ambulance or mobile clinic will reach the older adult's location at minimum time.

Keywords: Neurological disorder · Emotion recognition · Fall detection · IoT · Artificial Intelligence · Elderly

1 Introduction

The world population is increasing for different factors like more child mortality rate, the advancement of the medical sector. With the increase in the life

---

M. J. Al Nahian and T. Ghosh—Have contributed equally

© Springer Nature Switzerland AG 2020
M. Mahmud et al. (Eds.): BI 2020, LNAI 12241, pp. 275–286, 2020.
https://doi.org/10.1007/978-3-030-59277-6_25

expectancy rate, the number of older people has increased in recent years. There were 703 million people who matured 65 years or over on the planet in 2019. According to the United Nations, there is more than 30% growth of the elderly population anticipated by 2050 in 64 countries [16].

With age elderly people face various physical and mental health issues like neurological disorders [7], diabetes [34], hypertension, depression [1], heart problem, high pressure, and fall [14]. Fall is the leading cause of injury among the elderly. Older adults have fragile bones, less muscle strength, and poor eye vision for which they can lose balance and hurt themselves. In developed countries with elders living alone is rising the probability of deteriorating health problems as well as falling in the elderly as they are that time unable to alert anyone if they are unconscious. People aged 65 and 70 falls each year at a percentage of 28% and 32% respectively, according to the World Health Organization [9,15]. According to some mental health settings in Australia, most of the fall incidents were not reported [9]. Only 75.5% of fall events were reported, according to Hill et al. in [10]. People who have already faced a fall tend to face it again, which is more common among women than men [18,19,28].

The risk of falling is excessive among aged people who have neurological impairments. Elderly Patients with such disorders with indications of mild motor, nervous system deficit along with mental problems, and also someone who had a stroke or dementia are is at higher possibility of having a fall [11,26,31]. That risk is so high that even an elder with a very slight neurological disorder has thrice times more chance than an elder who doesn't have any neurological problem cues according to a study. Also, neurological patients fell thrice or more times higher every year, and that percentage is 13.2% contrast to the 3.6% in the same category of fit elderly peoples [11].

Falls not just effects physically but also mentally. Along with a neurologically disorder elder person's fragile bone getting injured, they were psychologically affected in many cases. Constant fear of falling can stick to their subconscious mind. Fear of falling is a significant health problem alongside the problem of falling itself and create various other cognitive disabilities [22]. It is an addition that an older person who had a fall or someone afraid of a fall even without having one in the past can lower that person's self-esteem and confidence in his day to day life. The incidents of falls can create anxiety in elder person emotions along with fear to fall again [27]. As anxiety is a result of fear of falls, their relationship is reciprocal. This anxiety can even create a depression and neurosis condition. Depression and Emotional stress can trigger more falls, which can create pelvic or hip fractures. Though there are several factors of fear of falling, these should be taken more seriously by proper involvement. It is now clear that falls and fear of falling are closely interrelated with mental health issues. It is high time to take the necessary steps to maintain the emotions and fall of aged people with a neurological disorder. With advancements, there have been many works conducted by researchers related to the detection of falls and emotion recognition separately. But no jobs have done before combining these two issues on how they are correlated. As we can see, their relationship is connected.

We are now addressing this research gap here and proposing an Artificial Intelligence (AI)-driven emotion aware fall monitoring framework suitable for elderly people with neurological disorder. With the help of this outcome acquired, we'll be able to detect emotions and eliminate the extra anxiety and depression among the elders and reduce the fall risks. We have arranged this research paper in the following way. In Sect. 2, we describe our cognitive framework scenario along with the architecture of the proposed framework, emotion recognition model, and fall detection model. In Sect. 3, we have presented the result of emotion recognition and fall detection modules. Some recommendations are highlighted in Sect. 4. Finally, Sect. 5 concludes the whole paper.

2   AI Driven Emotion Aware Fall Monitoring Framework for Elderly Peoples with Neurological Disorder

In this section, we describe our proposed emotion aware fall detection framework with a scenario.

2.1   Proposed Framework Scenario

To understand the framework of emotion aware cognitive elderly fall detection framework lets first consider a context, where an elderly person with neurological disorder who will consider as a client. The client lives in a smart house alone which has the provision of many IoT devices. The IoT devices with the help of a cloud server can capture and send signals. The cloud server will detect a fall by identifying those signals. Next, the client needs caregivers immediately sent by the service provider. To get the precise location of the client where he/she fell down, the caregivers will get that information by a general-purpose global positioning system (GPS). This will give the location of the client where he lives but still to be more accurate a definite indoor positioning system is needed. The caregivers can hurry to that definite spot once that is detected even without disturbing other people's privacy. The cognitive frameworks for emotion aware fall monitoring are designed in such a way that it can not only discover an elderly person's psychological health but can even find out electronic health background from any place no matter when by cloud and IoT automation. The aim of this framework is precise fall detection, emotion identification, the reasonable cost with trouble-free access, and these all can upgrade the quality of life. This new framework of advanced sensor devices will be a big benefit to elderly people, doctors, and stakeholders. The cognitive module records, examines and process data in real-time. The medical history is then stored on the cloud server and then can be obtainable by any medical specialist. This will create an advanced cognitive connection between elderly people and healthcare specialists after the registration procedure. At the same time, the registered stakeholders can use the cognitive module to access the health records of the elderly people living alone. Next, we need to implement this design, and to do so a camera device will be attached to the elderly home. That camera records their facial expression and can send it to the cloud server for identifying the elder person's emotion. Alongside the motions of the elder person being continuously monitored by wearable sensors such as accelerometer, gyroscope and magnetometer. The location of the elderly is persistently recorded at actual times. After collecting all the elderly movement data and their facial expression images, the sensor transmits the signal to the cloud server. The data are next processed by the AI-enabled system. The fall event and elderly emotion is detected by the AI-enabled module and prepares a result to be sent to the cognitive system. According to those results, the cognitive system creates a plan for further steps that need to be taken in the future. These health records are saved as data and any doctor can access them for analysis and examination. If the cognitive system alerts about a situation of emergency, a smart ambulance or mobile clinic will reach the elderly person's location at minimum time. That smart ambulance can take the shortest route to reach the elderly at least amount of time with the help of a smart traffic system. Along these lines, the cognitive elderly fall monitoring framework provides complete support to the elderly people with the neurological disorder in real time.

2.2   Proposed Framework Architecture

We have proposed an emotion aware elderly fall monitoring framework specially for the people of neurological disorder based on IoT and AI algorithms due to the popularity of AI methods in many diverse domains such as biological data mining [18], anomaly detection [6, 33], expert systems [13, 23, 24, 29, 30, 32] and cyber-security [25]. Elderly persons are monitored continuously in sensor integrated smart home environments. Different types of wearable and ambient sensors are employed to capture elderly movement information regularly and send it to a cloud server via a wireless sensor network for analyzing to detect falls and emotions. In a cloud server, an AI power cognitive engine is employed to take intelligence decision based on collected data. A theoretical architecture of our proposed framework has shown in Fig. 1.

The proposed framework consists of three layers. A smart home is the first layer where different IoT sensors are deployed to collect elderly health information continuously. There is a wide range of IoT sensors available for the smart home environment including camera, RFID, radar sensor. Some wearable IoT devices such as a smartwatch, wrist band, waistband containing accelerometer sensor, gyroscope, magnetometer, pedometer can be used to capture elderly movement information for detection of fall events. A wall-mounted camera can be employed to capture the elderly facial expression for emotion recognition. All IoT sensors captured data are transmitted to an edge cloud server which is the second layer of the proposed framework. The main objective of the edge cloud is to preprocess the huge amount of sensors data continuously and remove the redundant data for further processing. The edge cloud contains low computational power resources so that it cannot process high computational tasks. It is resided between IoT sensor-enabled smart home and cloud server and acts as an interface. The third layer is a cloud server where all intelligence decisions will be made.

After data are preprocessed in the edge cloud, important data are sent to the remote cloud server via 4G/5G technology for real-time processing. The cloud server comprises of cloud manager, cognitive engine, AI-enabled emotion recognition module, and elderly fall detection module. At first cloud manager verified the authorized elderly users' identity. Then accelerometer and gyroscope sensors data and captured facial expression images are sent to the AI-enabled fall detection module and emotion recognition module respectively. The emotion recognition module recognizes different emotional states of older people using facial expressions.

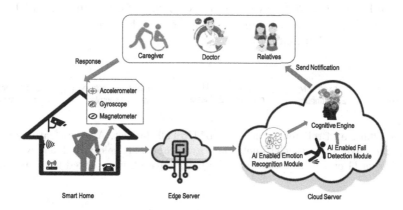

Fig. 1. Proposed emotion aware cognitive elderly fall monitoring framework. IoT sensors and camera device capture elderly movement data in smart home and transmit to a remote cloud server via an edge server. Cloud server contains a cognitive engine, AI enabled emotion and fall detection module. Whenever an emergency situation arise, the cognitive engine take decision and send notification to the caregiver, doctor and relatives.

On the other hand, the fall detection module utilized different machine learning algorithms to detect potential elderly falls using wearable sensors data. The outcome of the emotion detection module and fall detection module are sent to the cognitive engine to take intelligent decisions. The cognitive engine will then take real-time decisions about fall and emotional state information of elderly people with neurological disorder and take necessary steps. In case of emergency conditions, an emergency alert will send to the predefined contacts, respective health care professionals, and close relatives to take immediate response to the elderly people. All health, emotion, and fall-related information are recorded for further analysis to prevent fall risk and other health-related complexities.

2.3   Fall Detection Model

For fall detection, we are using the Up-Fall dataset [20]. This dataset contains values of a wide range of body-worn sensors and cameras. As we are only using a wearable accelerometer and gyroscope in the waist and ankle, we only considered related to these sensor data and removed all the remaining attributes. After removing attributes, there were 216 different attributes remaining which were then used. The dataset is labeled with 6 different daily activities and 5 different falls. We have converted this to two classes, where all the different daily activities are included in the daily activity section and all the falls are assigned as fall. We labeled activity of daily livings (ADL) class as 0 and fall class as 1. There were 32,294 total events, among them 31,339 events were ADL events and 955 were fall events. As it was imbalanced, we have reduced the number of ADLs to 2,669 and it converted the total event number to 3,624. Then we divided the dataset to train and test where 2965 events were considered for training and 659 events were kept aside for testing. Figure 2 illustrates the feature selection, relabeling and splitting of the Up Fall dataset.

Fig. 2. Shuffling and relabeling of events of Up Fall dataset. At first, features related to waist and ankle worn accelerometer and gyroscope were selected. Then events were relabeled from 11 classes to 2 classes. Finally, the dataset was splitted to train and test set.

We have used long short-term memory network (LSTM) [8] for fall detection. LSTM is very much efficient in sequential data classification. They can keep information and use it for a longer period. The proposed model consists of an LSTM layer and 3 dense layers. The events are given input to an LSTM layer which contains 216 nodes. Then the features are extracted and flattened. The features are then given input to a dense layer of 1075 nodes. Then it goes through another dense layer of 512 nodes. Then the final dense layer of 2 nodes representing two classes (ADL and fall) is classifying the event and providing the final output. All the layers except the final layer used ReLU activation function [4]. Figure 3 illustrates the whole training process and LSTM architecture.

Fig. 3. Proposed LSTM architecture. The events were at first given input to the LSTM layer and it goes through 3 dense layers. The final dense layer classified the event as fall or ADL.

The model was trained using Adam optimizer and for 30 epochs with a learning rate of 0.001 on the training dataset. After training, the model was tested using the separated test dataset.

2.4   Emotion Recognition Model

We have used kaggle face expression recognition dataset to classify the emotion of a person. This dataset contains images of 7 different emotions and among them, we selected 5 emotions to classify (angry, fear, happy, neutral, sad). The modified dataset was divided into train and test. The training set and the testing set contained 21514 and 5476 images consecutively. The training dataset was further divided into training (17214 images) and validation (4300 images) part. The testing dataset was kept aside for evaluating model performance. Figure 4 shows the class-wise distribution of images in train and test set.

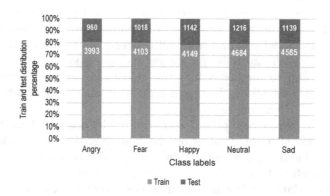

Fig. 4. Class wise distribution of emotion recognition dataset where splitting percentage between train and test set are delineated over the stacked bar chart

In this work, we have used a state-of-the-art CNN model 'MobileNetV1' for emotion recognition. The proposed MobileNetV1 based emotion recognition model is shown in Fig. 5.

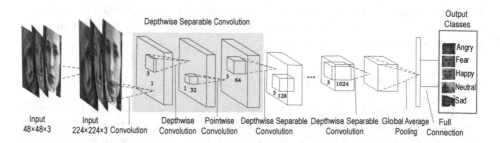

Fig. 5. Proposed MobileNetV1 based emotion recognition model. Input images are first converted to 224 by 224 from 48 by 48 original images. MobileNet architecture take the converted input image and perform depthwise and pointwise convolution. Last layer of the MobileNetV1 architecture changed for five emotion classes

MobileNetV1 architecture was first proposed in [12] based on one depthwise separable convolution [17,18,22]. It was first employed in ImageNet object detection competition and trained with a large ImageNet dataset [5] which contains a thousand classes. MobileNetV1 is different than standard CNN architecture. The Standard CNN model performs filtering and combining input in a single step whereas the MobileNetV1 model performs these two tasks in two separate stages. The MobileNetV1 performs depth wise convolution for filtering input channel and pointwise convolution is used to combine the depthwise convolution outputs. In the depthwise convolution stage, a single convolution is performed to each input channel separately. On the other hand, standard CNN performs convolution to all three channels at a time. After the depthwise convolution stage, 1 by 1 convolution performs to combine the output features of all three channels [3,21]. In this way, MobileNetV1 architecture is become highly efficient, reduce the model size and trade-off between latency and model accuracy. In addition, the width multiplier parameter and resolution multiplier parameter were also proposed to further reduce the model size and computational cost. This MobileNetV1 model can be used for different image classification tasks by adopting a transfer learning approach.

In this paper, we have employed a pre-trained MobileNetV1 model for emotion recognition which was trained on the ImageNet dataset. We keep all the parameters of the ImageNet dataset by freezing the base layer of pre-trained MobileNetV1 architecture. Only the top layers are trained by our Kaggle emotion recognition dataset. The last layer of the MobileNetV1 model which is a dense layer was changed to five neurons which are related to the number of classes (5 classes). It is predicting a class label among the selected classes (angry, fear, happy, neutral, sad). The model was trained using Adam optimizer, the learning rate was 0.001, and for 50 epochs. After training, the model was evaluated using the test set.

3 Results

In this section, we are presenting the outcome of our proposed fall detection model and emotion recognition model. The comparison among different machine learning algorithms are also described.

3.1 Fall Detection Result

The proposed model performed quite well in classifying fall events. It correctly classifies 614 events from 659 total events which were in the testing dataset. It achieved an accuracy of 93.17%. Out of 201 fall events that were in the testing set, it was successful in classifying 171 fall events. So the F1-score achieved by the proposed model in fall class was 85.07%.

We have used the same training and testing dataset in different machine learning classifiers such as logistic regression, SVM, SGD, Naïve Bayes, Random Forest, etc. to validate results. Logistic regression achieved the highest accuracy of 90.28% with an F1-score in the fall class of 83.42%. So, our proposed LSTM model outperformed these machine learning models in both accuracy and F1-score. Figure 6 (a) illustrates the comparison of the F1-score of fall class between proposed model and other machine learning models. Figure 6 (b) shows the confusing matrix of the test result and Fig. 6 (c) compares the performance of the proposed model and other machine learning models on the basis of accuracy.

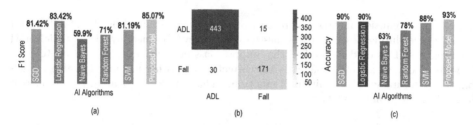

Fig. 6. (a) Comparison of F1-score of fall class between proposed model and other machine learning models. Proposed model performed better than other models in fall detection. (b) Confusion matrix that was generated from the test result by the proposed model. (c) Comparison of accuracy between proposed model and other machine learning models. The proposed model outperformed other models by achieving 93.17% accuracy.

3.2 Emotion Recognition Result

The MobileNetv1 model has achieved 61.11% accuracy in classifying emotion from images. It correctly classified 3346 images out of 5475 images. This model classified emotions that are labeled as 'happy' with around 81% accuracy. The model performed worst in classifying in sad images. The same training and testing set was used in different machine learning classifiers such as logistic regression, SVM, SGD, Naïve Bayes, Random Forest, etc. to validate results [2].

Random forest achieved the highest accuracy (46%) among the machine learning models which is way below the achieved accuracy by the proposed MobileNetV1. The proposed MobileNetV1 model provided the best accuracy in classifying emotion. Figure 7 (a) shows the confusion matrix obtained by the proposed MobileNetV1 architecture during testing. Figure 7 (b) shows the class wise accuracy obtained during testing and Fig. 7 (c) compares the performances showed by the MobileNetV1 and other machine learning models based on accuracy in classifying emotion from facial image.

4 Recommendations

Elderly people with the neurological disorder are very sensitive and they need constant support and monitoring. An automated decision support system can be

Fig. 7. (a) Confusion matrix generated from the result obtained by the MobileNetV1 architecture during testing. (b) Class-wise accuracy obtained by the MobileNetV1 architecture. This model classified the 'happy' class better than other classes. (c) Performance comparison of MobileNetV1 architecture and other machine learning models based on accuracy in recognition of emotions. The MobileNetV1 architecture outperformed all the other models.

developed for them. In this work, we have proposed installing accelerometer and gyroscope sensors. We can use smart bands for them. Smartband has an inbuilt pedometer, GPS, blood pressure monitoring sensor, heart rate monitoring sensor. These sensors can collect data and send it to the central processing system. Data collected by cameras, accelerometer, and gyroscope can also send data to this central processing system. These data can be analyzed using machine learning and find out significant insights related to their health condition which will ensure constant monitoring. Robots, screens, sound sensors can be installed to act according to the decision provided by the central processing system. Elderly people with a neurological disorder may fall anywhere in the house or building. So, to find them fast, an indoor positioning system can be built. GPS trackers can help in case they go outside of the house without telling anyone. In these ways, a complete intelligent decision support system can be created for monitoring and helping elderly people who are suffering from a neurological disorder.

5   Conclusion

We have proposed an AI driven emotion aware elderly fall monitoring framework using IoT sensors and different AI algorithms in this paper. We tried to make a bridge between elderly fall detection and their emotions as elderly people are very much prone to fall and getting emotionally distracted. We have presented a framework scenario where different intelligence wearable sensors and ambient sensors are employed to monitor elderly people continuously and send sensors data to the cloud server for further processing. In the cloud server, a cognitive engine is employed to take intelligence decision and send a notification to the respective caregivers. Two AI-enabled modules are implemented in the cloud server to detect elderly falls and recognize their emotion. We are proposing a popular state of the art CNN architecture, MobileNetV1 model for emotion recognition and validate the proposed model using a publicly available emotion recognition dataset. On the other hand, we also propose an LSTM based elderly fall detection model and utilize a publicly available fall detection dataset to evaluate the proposed fall detection model. A different state of the art machine learning algorithm is trained with the same dataset to compare the obtained result. In both cases, our proposed models outperform the other machine learning algorithms. In the future, we will implement the whole framework and deploy it in an actual elderly home environment. An indoor positioning module will also be included to locate elderly people without disturbing their neighbors.

Acknowledgement. This research received funding from ICT division of the Government of the People's Republic of Bangladesh.

References

1. Agüera-Ortiz, L., et al.: Depression in the elderly. Consensus statement of the Spanish psychogeriatric association. Front. Psychiatry **11**, 380 (2020)
2. Al Banna, M.H., Haider, M.A., Al Nahian, M.J., Islam, M.M., Taher, K.A., Kaiser, M.S.: Camera model identification using deep CNN and transfer learning approach. In: ICREST. IEEE (2019)
3. Ali, H.M., Kaiser, M.S., Mahmud, M.: Application of convolutional neural network in segmenting brain regions from MRI data. In: Liang, P., Goel, V., Shan, C. (eds.) BI 2019. LNCS, vol. 11976, pp. 136–146. Springer, Cham (2019). https://doi.org/10.1007/978-3-030-37078-7_14
4. Arora, R., Basu, A., Mianjy, P., Mukherjee, A.: Understanding deep neural networks with rectified linear units. arXiv preprint arXiv:1611.01491 (2016)
5. Deng, J., et al.: ImageNet: a large-scale hierarchical image database. In: Proceedings of IEEE CVPR, pp. 248–255 (2009)
6. Fabietti, M., et al.: Neural network-based artifact detection in LFP recorded from chronically implanted neural probes. In: Proceedings of IJCNN, pp. 1–8 (2020)
7. Ghaffar, A., Dehghani-Sanij, A.A., Xie, S.Q.: A review of gait disorders in the elderly and neurological patients for robot-assisted training. Disabil. Rehabil.: Assist. Technol. **15**(3), 256–270 (2020)
8. Greff, K., et al.: LSTM: a search space odyssey. IEEE Trans. Neural Netw. Learn. Syst. **28**(10), 2222–2232 (2017)
9. Heslop, K., et al.: Assessing falls risk in older adult mental health patients: a western Australian review. Int. J. Ment. Health Nurs. **21**(6), 567–575 (2012)
10. Hill, A.M., et al.: Measuring falls events in acute hospitals-a comparison of three reporting methods to identify missing data in the hospital reporting system. J. Am. Geriatr. Soc. **58**(7), 1347–1352 (2010)
11. Homann, B., et al.: The impact of neurological disorders on risk for falls in community dwelling elderly: a case-controlled study. BMJ Open **3**(11), e003367 (2013)
12. Howard, A.G., et al.: MobileNets: efficient convolutional neural networks for mobile vision applications. arXiv preprint arXiv:1704.04861 (2017)
13. Kaiser, M.S., et al.: Advances in crowd analysis for urban applications through urban event detection. IEEE Trans. Intell. Transp. Syst. **19**(10), 3092–3112 (2018)
14. Khraief, C., Benzarti, F., Amiri, H.: Elderly fall detection based on multi-stream deep convolutional networks. Multimed. Tools Appl. **79**, 19537–19560 (2020)
15. Lord, S., Sherrington, C., Menz, H., Close, J.: Falls in Older People: Risk Factors and Strategies for Prevention. Cambridge University Press, Cambridge (2001)

16. Luque, R., Casilari, E., Morón, M.J., Redondo, G.: Comparison and characterization of android-based fall detection systems. Sensors **14**(10), 18543–18574 (2014)
17. Mahmud, M., Kaiser, M.S., Hussain, A.: Deep learning in mining biological data. arXiv:2003.00108 [cs, q-bio, stat] abs/2003.00108, pp. 1–36 (2020)
18. Mahmud, M., Kaiser, M.S., Hussain, A., Vassanelli, S.: Applications of deep learning and reinforcement learning to biological data. IEEE Trans. Neural Netw. Learn. Syst. **29**(6), 2063–2079 (2018)
19. Mahmud, M., et al.: A brain-inspired TMM to assure security in a cloud based IoT framework for neuroscience applications. Cogn. Comput. **10**(5), 864–873 (2018)
20. Martínez-Villaseñor, L., et al.: Up-fall detection dataset: a multimodal approach. Sensors **19**(9), 1988 (2019)
21. Miah, Y., et al.: Performance comparison of ML techniques in identifying dementia from open access clinical datasets. In: Proceedings of ICACIn, pp. 69–78 (2020)
22. Noor, M.B.T., et al.: Detecting neurodegenerative disease from MRI: a brief review on a deep learning perspective. In: Liang, P., Goel, V., Shan, C. (eds.) BI 2019. LNCS, vol. 11976, pp. 115–125. Springer, Cham (2019). https://doi.org/10.1007/978-3-030-37078-7_12
23. Orojo, O., Tepper, J., McGinnity, T., Mahmud, M.: A multi-recurrent network for crude oil price prediction. In: Proceedings SSCI, pp. 2940–2945 (2019)
24. Rabby, G., et al.: TeKET: a tree-based unsupervised keyphrase extraction technique. Cogn. Comput. (2020). https://doi.org/10.1007/s12559-019-09706-3
25. Rahman, S., Al Mamun, S., Ahmed, M.U., Kaiser, M.S.: PHY/MAC layer attack detection system using neuro-fuzzy algorithm for IoT network. In: Proceedings of ICEEOT, pp. 2531–2536 (2016)
26. Ryu, Y.M., Roche, J.P., Brunton, M.: Patient and family education for fall prevention: involving patients and families in a fall prevention program on a neuroscience unit. J. Nurs. Care Qual. **24**(3), 243–249 (2009)
27. Scheffer, A.C., et al.: Fear of falling: measurement strategy, prevalence, risk factors and consequences among older persons. Age Ageing **37**(1), 19–24 (2008)
28. Stevens, J.A., Sogolow, E.D.: Gender differences for non-fatal unintentional fall related injuries among older adults. Injury Prev. **11**(2), 115–119 (2005)
29. Sumi, A.I., Zohora, M.F., Mahjabeen, M., Faria, T.J., Mahmud, M., Kaiser, M.S.: ƒASSERT: a fuzzy assistive system for children with autism using Internet of Things. In: Wang, S., et al. (eds.) BI 2018. LNCS (LNAI), vol. 11309, pp. 403–412. Springer, Cham (2018). https://doi.org/10.1007/978-3-030-05587-5_38
30. Tania, M.H., et al.: Assay type detection using advanced machine learning algorithms. In: Proceedings of SKIMA, pp. 1–8 (2019)
31. Thurman, D.J., Stevens, J.A., Rao, J.K.: Practice parameter: assessing patients in a neurology practice for risk of falls (an evidence-based review). Neurology **70**(6), 473–479 (2008)
32. Watkins, J., Fabietti, M., Mahmud, M.: Sense: a student performance quantifier using sentiment analysis. In: Proceedings of IJCNN, pp. 1–6 (2020)
33. Yahaya, S.W., Lotfi, A., Mahmud, M.: A consensus novelty detection ensemble approach for anomaly detection in activities of daily living. Appl. Soft Comput. **83**, 105613 (2019)
34. Zohora, M.F., et al.: Forecasting the risk of type ii diabetes using reinforcement learning. In: Proceedings of ICIEV. pp. 1–6 (2020)

Speech Emotion Recognition in Neurological Disorders Using Convolutional Neural Network

Sharif Noor Zisad[1]([✉]) [iD], Mohammad Shahadat Hossain[1]([✉]) [iD],
and Karl Andersson[2] [iD]

[1] Department of Computer Science and Engineering, University of Chittagong,
Chittagong, Bangladesh
mrzisad@gmail.com, hossain_ms@cu.ac.bd
[2] Department of Computer Science, Electrical and Space Engineering,
Luleå University of Technology, Skellefteå, Sweden
karl.andersson@ltu.se

Abstract. Detecting emotions from the speech is one of the emergent research fields in the area of human information processing. Expressing emotion is a very difficult task for a person with neurological disorder. Hence, a Speech Emotion Recognition (SER) system may solve this by ensuring a barrier-less communication. Various research has been carried out in the area of SER. Therefore, the main objective of this research is to develop a system that can recognize emotion from the speech of a neurologically disordered person. Since convolutional neural network (CNN) is an effective method, it has been considered to develop the system. The system uses tonal properties like MFCCs. RAVDESS audio speech and song databases for training and testing. In addition, a custom local dataset developed to support further training and testing. The performance of the proposed system compared with the traditional machine learning models as well as with the pre-trained CNN models including VGG16 and VGG19. The results demonstrate that the CNN model proposed in this research performed better than the mentioned machine learning techniques. This system enables one tohhhhhh classify eight emotions of neurologically disordered person including calm, angry, fearful, disgust, happy, surprise, neutral and sad.

Keywords: CNN · Speech emotion · RAVDESS · MFCC · Data augmentation

1 Introduction

Emotion is a mental state associated with the nervous system. It is what a person feels inside as the effects of the environment of his surrounding area. Emotions of a person can be detected in numerous ways. Some of them can be analyzed by tonal properties, facial expression and body gesture. The computing

© Springer Nature Switzerland AG 2020
M. Mahmud et al. (Eds.): BI 2020, LNAI 12241, pp. 287–296, 2020.
https://doi.org/10.1007/978-3-030-59277-6_26

or classification of emotion from speech or facial expression forms an important part of human information processing. We need to understand the emotions of a neurologically disordered person and react accordingly. This system can enable a neurologically disordered person to express their emotions and interact with us. The purpose of this research consists of developing a system capable of automatically recognizing eight different emotions from the speech of a neurologically disordered person. This purpose can be accomplished by training a neural network developed with deep learning methodology [1,7,14] by utilizing two databases, the RAVDESS dataset, and a custom local dataset. Finally, improving validation accuracy compared to other existing systems and maintaining a praiseworthy accuracy for each class had also been addressed. In the next section, some significantly related study on emotion recognition from the speech is presented.

2   Related Work

Emotion from speech recognition has become a popular area of research. Several researchers have analyzed various ways for better improvement of this field. R. Aloufi [3] extracted the F0 counter, spectral envelope, and aperiodic information in speech processing. They classified seven emotions including calm, angry, sad, happy, fearful, disgust, and surprised by using the RAVDESS dataset. Hence, they achieved an emotion recognition rate of 5%, speech recognition rate of 65%, and speaker recognition rate of 92%. M. Bojanić [4] has applied Linear Discriminant Classifiers(LDC) and k-Nearest Neighbor (kNN) in GEES corpus. The accuracy of anger was 88.8%, fear was 92.5%, joy was 84.2%, neutral was 97.1%, and sadness was 94.8% in LDC model. In kNN, anger became 86.8%, fear became 93.7%, joy became 83.6%, neutral became 95.9%, and sadness became 96.3%. M. Ghai [8] selected the frame samples of the sound signals at 16000 Hz and the selection duration 0.25 s of each frame for feature extraction. A. Iqbal [13] extracted 34 audio features from two datasets (RAVDESS and SAVEE) and selected frame size 0.05s and step size 0.025 s. They applied the Gradient Boosting method and classified four expressions. They achieved 33% accuracy for anger, 66% for happiness, 67% for sadness, and 50% for neutral in RAVDESS female dataset. In the RAVDESS male dataset, accuracy for anger became 87%, happiness became 87%, sadness became 67% and neutral became 66%. The accuracy was 56% for anger, 78% for happiness, 100% for sadness, and 78% for neutral after using the SAVEE dataset. S. Rovetta [20] selected final features using Analysis of variance (ANOVA) or mutual information (MI) test. They also classified seven emotions (anger, neutral, disgust, sadness, boredom, fear, and joy) by applying the EMO-DB dataset in the fuzzy clustering method. They achieved 35.157% accuracy for neutral, 60.757% for anger, 17.629% for boredom, 12.751% for disgust, 35.061% for fear, 18.743% for joy, and 25.485% for sadness. P. Tzirakis [22] resampled the RECOLA dataset at a frame rate of 40ms. They proposed a new Deep Neural Network (DNN) model by combining CNN and (Long ShortTerm Memory) LSTM network. The accuracy for arousal was 78.7% and valence was 44%.

N. Yang [23] applied EMO-DB dataset into BPNN, ELM, PNN and SVM model. They achieved 77.8% accuracy in BPNN, 78.4% accuracy in ELM, 81% accuracy in PNN, and 92.4% in SVM. Z. Zhao [25] used the Hamming Window function to generate spectrograms utilizing ShortTime Fourier Transform (STFT) with frame length 25ms at the rate of 10ms. They used the IEMOCAP dataset and applied the Attention-BLSTM-FCN model. The weighted accuracy was 68.1% and unweighted accuracy was 67% of this model. Different frame sizes of 10–20 ms [6,8], etc., were selected in different works. Entropy, spectral entropy, MFCC, ZCR (zero-crossing rate), pitch, energy, etc., were the common features for audio data. Most of the researchers used pitch and energy [6,19,24] for sound processing. Most of them calculated statistical features such as mean, standard deviation, etc., to improve performance. Previous researchers also developed different machine learning methods such as Gradient Boosting, Support Vector Machine (SVM), K-Nearest Neighbor (KNN), Neural Network, Random Forest, etc. to classify emotions from speech. They used multiple speeches emotional databases such as EMO-DB, BHUDES, RAVDESS, SUSAS, AIBO, SAVEE, etc. to build their systems.

3   Methodology

In this research, Convolution Neural Network (CNN) with data augmentation was used to develop the system. Figure 1 illustrates the flow chart of this system. According to the flow chart, the model takes audio data first from the dataset and starts preprocessing. After completion of preprocessing, it extracts the MFCC feature using the mfcc function offered by Librosa API. Then the features are normalized by changing shape. Noise is augmented by the NoiseAug function from Nlpaug Library. Finally, the augmented data is then fed into the proposed model for emotion prediction. There are four convolution layers in this model with 16, 32, 64, and 128 filters and the kernel size for each layer is 2*2. Rectified Linear Unit (ReLU) used as the activation function in each convolution layer as shown (1).

$$ReLU(y) = max(0, y) \tag{1}$$

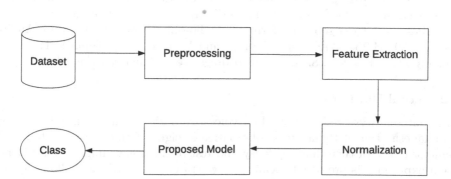

Fig. 1. System flow chart

The model has been provided with audio data of 16000 Hz as an input. Input shape of the RAVDESS dataset is (100, 196, 1), where 100 refers to the number of MFCC features extracted, 196 is the number of frames taking padding into account, and 1 signifying that the audio is mono. The model for the local dataset uses the input shape of (100, 3200, 1). After the convolution layer, there is a max-pooling layer where the pool size is 2*2. It selects the largest value from the rectified feature map and reduces the size of the data, so the number of parameters is decreased. Like the convolution layer, ReLU has been applied as an activation function in hidden layers. A dropout layer is also inserted with the dropout value of 0.2 which randomly deactivates 20% neurons to avoid over-fitting [21]. In the last hidden layer, one Global Average Pooling layer has been added which takes the average which is suitable for feeding into our dense output layer. The output layer of this model consists of eight nodes as it has eight classes. As an activation function, Softmax has been applied as shown (2) in this layer.

$$Softmax(y) = \frac{e^i}{\sum_j e^j} \tag{2}$$

As a model optimizer, Adam [5] has been used. Categorical Crossentropy has been used as a loss function. ModelCheckpoint and EarlyStopping are included as callbacks in the model. ModelCheckpoint will save the best model in the local storage while EarlyStopping will stop the training process if there is no improvement in minimizing loss value after 5 epochs. The overview of the CNN architecture that was designed for this model is illustrated in Table 1.

4   Databases

4.1   RAVDESS Database

The Ryerson Audio-Visual Database of Emotional Speech and Song (RAVDESS) is a validated database of emotional speech and song [18]. It contains 7356 files including 8 emotions such as anger, happiness, calm, neutral, surprise, sad, fear, and disgust. There were 24 professional actors where 12 were female and 12 were male actors vocalizing two statements, 'Kids are talking by the door' and 'Dogs are sitting by the door' in a neutral North American accent. It has speech and song files under three modality formats: Audio-only (16bit, 48kHz .wav), Audio-Video (720p H.264, AAC 48kHz, .mp4) and Video-only (no sound). There are no song files for Actor 18. All the recordings are in American English.

4.2   Local Dataset

This dataset is created by recording voices from 25 patients from Chittagong, Bangladesh. Ten of them are stroke patients, eight of them are affected with dementia, four of them have epilepsy and rest of them have migraine headache. Each expression is produced vocalizing two statements 'Kids are talking by the door' and 'Dogs are sitting by the door' in Bangladeshi accent. So there are 400 audio files in 8 emotions.

Table 1. System architecture

Content	Details
First Convolution Layer	16 filters of size 2×2, ReLU, input size 100*196*1 for RAVDESS and 100*3200*1 for local dataset
First Max Pooling Layer	Pooling size 2×2
Dropout Layer	Excludes 20% neurons randomly
Second Convolution Layer	32 filters of size 2×2, ReLU
Second Max Pooling Layer	Pooling size 2×2
Dropout Layer	Excludes 20% neurons randomly
Third Convolution Layer	64 filters of size 2×2, ReLU
Third Max Pooling Layer	Pooling size 2×2
Dropout Layer	Excludes 20% neurons randomly
Fourth Convolution Layer	128 filters of size 2×2, ReLU
Fourth Max Pooling Layer	Pooling size 2×2
Dropout Layer	Excludes 20% neurons randomly
Global Average Pooling Layer	N/A
Output Layer	8 nodes for 8 classes, SoftMax
Optimization Function	Adam
Callback	ModelCheckpoint

4.3   Preprocessing

There are only 2452 audio files in RAVDESS audio speech and song dataset. Hence, to increase our datasets and improve model performance, we also used Audio song samples. All files are used with a sampling rate of 16KHz using the parameter 'sr = 16000' in the load function of the Librosa library. For feature extraction, the Mfcc function of the Librosa library is used. The sample rate is 16KHz for each audio file. The number of MFCC extracted are 100. The shape of the extracted features would not be the same and the range would not be specific without normalization. The unstructured feature may reduce the accuracy and recognition rate. In this research, after extracting features from each file, we normalized them by subtracting each feature from the maximum one to make the shape the same. After normalization, these data are used to train and test the system. Augmentation in the audio database usually generates additional audio files by applying some special operation on the original database, such as injecting noise, adjusting pitch, changing vocal tract, adjusting speed, etc. In this work, all of the files are augmented with injecting noise by using the NoiseAug function from the nlpaug library.

5   Experiment

There are 1440 audio speech files and 1012 song files in the RAVDESS database. Each class has 192 files except neutral in audio speech files and the neutral class contains 96 files. On the other hand, angry, calm, fearful, happy, sad contains 184 files in each class in audio song files and the class Neutral contains 96 files. There are no song files for the class's disgust and surprise. To achieve the best performance from the model, it is necessary to enrich the database with relevant audio files. For this purpose, noise is injected into the existing database. After augmentation, the database becomes twice the size of the previous one. There are 4904 audio speech and song files after augmentation. Similarly, there are only 400 files in the local dataset where each class contains only 50 files. So each class can have 100 files after augmentation. The dataset was split into training set, validation set and testing set. Training set and validation set were used to train the model. Testing set was used to test the performance of the model. This model was trained using multiple split ratios (70:20:10, 75:15:10, 80:10:10), activation functions (relu, sigmoid, softmax, softplus), and optimizers (adadelta, adagrad, adamax, adam, nadam, sgd). During the learning process, the performance of this model was best when 75:15:10 split ratio, softmax activation function, and adam optimizer was used with five-fold cross validation.

6   Implementation

The system has been developed in Spyder IDE using Python as the programming language. The model was trained using google collaboratory. The required libraries for this experiment were: Keras, Tensorflow, NumPy, Librosa, sklearn, nlpaug, matplotlib, etc. Keras was used for developing the model by implementing some builtin functions such as layers, optimizers, activation functions, etc. Tensorflow supported in the backend of the system. Numpy library was used for numerical analysis. Loading audio files using a specific sampling rate was performed by the librosa library, where sklearn library generated confusion matrix, splitting train and test data, model checkpoint callback function, etc. Data was augmented by using nlpaug API where matplotlib library was used for graphical representation, such as confusion matrix, accuracy vs epochs graph, loss vs epochs graph, etc.

7   Result and Discussion

In the RAVDESS dataset, there are 2452 files (audio speech and song) before augmentation where 1839 files were used for training, 368 files were used for validation, and 245 files were used for testing the system. The best accuracy for training, testing, and validation was 0.857, 0.743, and 0.756 respectively. The average training, testing, and validation accuracy was 0.841, 0.740, and 0.744 respectively. After using data augmentation, the dataset becomes twice the previous size with a total of 4904 files in the dataset where 3679 files were used for

Table 2. Cross-Validation result of RAVDESS augmented dataset.

	Training accuracy	Validation accuracy	Testing accuracy
Fold-1	0.915	0.807	0.787
Fold-2	0.937	0.822	0.823
Fold-3	0.921	0.820	0.807
Fold-4	0.893	0.825	0.825
Fold-5	0.898	0.811	0.821
Average	0.913	0.817	0.813
Best	0.937	0.825	0.825

training, 736 files were used for validation, and 491 files were used for testing the system. The result of five-fold cross-validation for this augmented dataset is shown in Table 2. According to Table 2, the best testing accuracy was achieved in the fourth fold and it was 0.825. The best accuracy for training and validation was 0.937 and 0.825. The average testing accuracy became 0.813 where average training and validation accuracy became 0.913 and 0.817. Confusion matrix of RAVDESS augmented dataset with this best result is shown in Table 3. Some existing machine learning algorithms such as Support Vector Machine (SVM), Random Forest, Gradient Boosting, K Nearest Neighbor (KNN), Decision Tree Classifier, etc. and some CNN pre-trained model such as VGG16, VGG19, etc. were also trained using RAVDESS augmented dataset. A comparison between these models and our proposed model is shown in Table 4. From this table, it can be easily observed that the performance of our proposed model is better than other models because it achieved larger accuracy, precision, recall, and f1-score than others. Again in the Local dataset, there are 400 files before augmentation where 300 files were used for training, 60 files were used for validation, and 40 files were used for testing the system. The best testing accuracy was achieved in the third fold and it was 0.375. The best accuracy for training and validation

Table 3. Confusion matrix of RAVDESS augmented Dataset.

	Angry	Calm	Disgust	Fearful	Happy	Neutral	Sad	Surprised
Angry	65	0	2	0	1	3	2	1
Calm	3	67	0	2	1	0	2	2
Disgust	1	0	34	1	0	2	0	2
Fearful	3	2	2	60	3	4	2	4
Happy	4	2	3	2	52	2	4	2
Neutral	0	1	0	1	0	40	0	1
Sad	2	4	2	3	1	0	58	1
Surprised	1	1	2	0	1	0	1	29

Table 4. Model comparison using RAVDESS dataset

Model	Accuracy	Precision	Recall	F1-Score
SVM	0.791	0.796	0.791	0.792
Random Forest	0.634	0.656	0.634	0.630
Gradient Boosting	0.616	0.623	0.616	0.617
KNN	0.443	0.460	0.443	0.445
Decision Tree	0.342	0.346	0.342	0.342
VGG16	0.747	0.747	0.747	0.747
VGG19	0.763	0.768	0.763	0.768
Proposed model	0.825	0.831	0.825	0.828

was 0.477 and 0.375. The average testing accuracy became 0.372 where average training and validation accuracy became 0.470 and 0.371. After data augmentation, the number of files was 800 in the dataset where 600 files were used for training, 120 files were used for validation, and 80 files were used for testing the system. The result of five-fold cross-validation for this dataset is shown in Table 5. According to the table, the best testing accuracy was achieved in the third fold and it was 0.612. The best accuracy for training and validation was 0.685 and 0.625. The average testing accuracy became 0.610 where average training and validation accuracy became 0.680 and 0.619. The confusion matrix of the local augmented dataset with this best result is presented in Table 6.

Table 5. Cross-Validation result of local augmented dataset.

	Training accuracy	Validation accuracy	Testing accuracy
Fold-1	0.685	0.622	0.611
Fold-2	0.679	0.618	0.610
Fold-3	0.683	0.607	0.612
Fold-4	0.671	0.621	0.611
Fold-5	0.682	0.625	0.605
Average	0.680	0.619	0.610
Best	0.685	0.625	0.612

Table 6. Confusion matrix of local augmented Dataset.

	Angry	Calm	Disgust	Fearful	Happy	Neutral	Sad	Surprised
Angry	8	1	1	0	0	2	1	0
Calm	1	7	0	1	2	1	0	1
Disgust	1	1	6	0	1	0	1	1
Fearful	0	1	0	4	0	0	1	1
Happy	0	1	1	0	5	1	0	0
Neutral	1	0	1	1	0	7	1	0
Sad	0	1	0	0	1	0	3	0
Surprised	1	0	1	0	0	1	1	9

8   Conclusion

The goal of this research was to find the scope of improvement of the existing system of speech emotion recognition. Our proposed model, CNN with the data augmentation method has shown to be more effective compared to other existing models in this field. Although this model performed better, it needs a few improvements in some areas, such as: The dataset should increase. More data should be added in each class to get better performance. Noise reduction algorithm can be applied for model improvement. Real-time validation using this model should be improved. Finally, this system can be extended to an integrated framework with any sophisticated methodology like BRB [2, 9–12,15–17]. Moreover, researchers can attempt to improve this model more efficiently in the future so that a more standard speech emotion recognition system for neurologically disordered persons can be delivered.

References

1. Ahmed, T.U., Hossain, M.S., Alam, M.J., Andersson, K.: An integrated CNN-RNN framework to assess road crack. In: 2019 22nd International Conference on Computer and Information Technology (ICCIT), pp. 1–6. IEEE (2019)
2. Alharbi, S.T., Hossain, M.S., Monrat, A.A.: A belief rule based expert system to assess autism under uncertainty. In: Proceedings of the World Congress on Engineering and Computer Science, vol. 1 (2015)
3. Aloufi, R., Haddadi, H., Boyle, D.: Emotionless: privacy-preserving speech analysis for voice assistants. arXiv preprint arXiv:1908.03632 (2019)
4. Bojanić, M., Delić, V., Karpov, A.: Call redistribution for a call center based on speech emotion recognition. Appl. Sci. **10**(13), 4653 (2020)
5. Bottou, L.: Large-scale machine learning with stochastic gradient descent. In: Lechevallier, Y., Saporta, G. (eds.) Proceedings of COMPSTAT, pp. 177–186. Springer, Cham (2010). https://doi.org/10.1007/978-3-7908-2604-3_16
6. Chernykh, V., Prikhodko, P.: Emotion recognition from speech with recurrent neural networks. arXiv preprint arXiv:1701.08071 (2017)
7. Chowdhury, R.R., Hossain, M.S., ul Islam, R., Andersson, K., Hossain, S.: Bangla handwritten character recognition using convolutional neural network with data augmentation. In: 2019 Joint 8th International Conference on Informatics, Electronics and Vision (ICIEV), pp. 318–323. IEEE (2019)
8. Ghai, M., Lal, S., Duggal, S., Manik, S.: Emotion recognition on speech signals using machine learning. In: 2017 International Conference on Big Data Analytics and Computational Intelligence (ICBDAC), pp. 34–39. IEEE (2017)
9. Hossain, M.S., Habib, I.B., Andersson, K.: A belief rule based expert system to diagnose dengue fever under uncertainty. In: 2017 Computing Conference, pp. 179–186. IEEE (2017)
10. Hossain, M.S., Hossain, E., Khalid, S., Haque, M.A.: A belief rule based (BRB) decision support system to assess clinical asthma suspicion. In: Scandinavian Conference on Health Informatics, Grimstad, Norway, 22 August 2014, pp. 83–89. No. 102, Linköping University Electronic Press (2014)
11. Hossain, M.S., Rahaman, S., Kor, A.L., Andersson, K., Pattinson, C.: A belief rule based expert system for datacenter PUE prediction under uncertainty. IEEE Trans. Sustain. Comput. **2**(2), 140–153 (2017)

12. Hossain, M.S., Sultana, Z., Nahar, L., Andersson, K.: An intelligent system to diagnose chikungunya under uncertainty. J. Wirel. Mob. Netw. Ubiquit. Comput. Dependable Appl. **10**(2), 37–54 (2019)
13. Iqbal, A., Barua, K.: A real-time emotion recognition from speech using gradient boosting. In: 2019 International Conference on Electrical, Computer and Communication Engineering (ECCE), pp. 1–5. IEEE (2019)
14. Islam, M.Z., Hossain, M.S., ul Islam, R., Andersson, K.: Static hand gesture recognition using convolutional neural network with data augmentation. In: 2019 Joint 8th International Conference on Informatics, Electronics and Vision (ICIEV), pp. 324–329. IEEE (2019)
15. Islam, R.U., Ruci, X., Hossain, M.S., Andersson, K., Kor, A.L.: Capacity management of hyperscale data centers using predictive modelling. Energies **12**(18), 3438 (2019)
16. Kabir, S., Islam, R.U., Hossain, M.S., Andersson, K.: An integrated approach of belief rule base and deep learning to predict air pollution. Sensors **20**(7), 1956 (2020)
17. Karim, R., Andersson, K., Hossain, M.S., Uddin, M.J., Meah, M.P.: A belief rule based expert system to assess clinical bronchopneumonia suspicion. In: 2016 Future Technologies Conference (FTC), pp. 655–660. IEEE (2016)
18. Livingstone, S.R., Russo, F.A.: The Ryerson audio-visual database of emotional speech and song (RAVDESS): a dynamic, multimodal set of facial and vocal expressions in North American English. PloS One **13**(5), e0196391 (2018)
19. Martínez, B.E., Jacobo, J.C.: An improved characterization methodology to efficiently deal with the speech emotion recognition problem. In: 2017 IEEE International Autumn Meeting on Power, Electronics and Computing (ROPEC), pp. 1–6. IEEE (2017)
20. Rovetta, S., Mnasri, Z., Masulli, F., Cabri, A.: Emotion recognition from speech signal using fuzzy clustering. In: 2019 Conference of the International Fuzzy Systems Association and the European Society for Fuzzy Logic and Technology (EUSFLAT 2019). Atlantis Press (2019)
21. Srivastava, N., Hinton, G., Krizhevsky, A., Sutskever, I., Salakhutdinov, R.: Dropout: a simple way to prevent neural networks from overfitting. J. Mach. Learn. Res. **15**(1), 1929–1958 (2014)
22. Tzirakis, P., Zhang, J., Schuller, B.W.: End-to-end speech emotion recognition using deep neural networks. In: 2018 IEEE International Conference on Acoustics, Speech and Signal Processing (ICASSP), pp. 5089–5093. IEEE (2018)
23. Yang, N., Dey, N., Sherratt, R.S., Shi, F.: Recognize basic emotional statesin speech by machine learning techniques using mel-frequency cepstral coefficient features. J. Intell. Fuzzy Syst. (Preprint) 1–12 (2020)
24. Zhang, M., Liang, Y., Ma, H.: Context-aware affective graph reasoning for emotion recognition. In: 2019 IEEE International Conference on Multimedia and Expo (ICME), pp. 151–156. IEEE (2019)
25. Zhao, Z., Bao, Z., Zhao, Y., Zhang, Z., Cummins, N., Ren, Z., Schuller, B.: Exploring deep spectrum representations via attention-based recurrent and convolutional neural networks for speech emotion recognition. IEEE Access **7**, 97515–97525 (2019)

Towards Improved Detection of Cognitive Performance Using Bidirectional Multilayer Long-Short Term Memory Neural Network

Md. Shahriare Satu[1]([✉])[iD], Shelia Rahman[2][iD], Md. Imran Khan[3][iD], Mohammad Zoynul Abedin[4][iD], M. Shamim Kaiser[2][iD], and Mufti Mahmud[5][iD]

[1] Department of MIS, Noakhali Science and Technology University, Noakhali, Bangladesh
shahriarsetu.mis@nstu.edu.bd
[2] Institute of Information Technology, Jahangirnagar University, Dhaka, Bangladesh
[3] Department of CSE, Gono Bishwabidyalay, Dhaka, Bangladesh
[4] School of Maritime Economics and Management, Dalian Maritime University, Dalian, China
[5] Department of Computing and Technology, Nottingham Trent University, Clifton Campus, Clifton, Nottingham NG11 8NS, UK
mufti.mahmud@ntu.ac.uk, muftimahmud@gmail.com

Abstract. Cognitive performance dictates how an individual perceives, records, maintains, retrieves, manipulates, uses and expresses information and are provided in any task that the person is involved in, let it be from the simplest to the most complex. Therefore, it is imperative to identify how a person is cognitively engaging specially in tasks such as information acquisition and studying. Given the surge in online education system, this even becomes more important as the visual feedback of student engagement is missing from the loop. To address this issue, the current study proposes a pipeline to detect cognitive performance by analyzing electroencephalogram (EEG) signals using bidirectional multilayer long-short term memory (BML-LSTM). Tested on an EEG brainwave dataset from 10 students while they watched massive open online course video clips, the obtained results using BML-LSTM show an accuracy >95% in detecting cognitive performance which outperforms all previous methods applied on the same dataset.

Keywords: Cognitive performance · Machine learning · EEG signal · Confused students · Classifiers

1 Introduction

Cognitive performance is an important concept to realize the cognition level of individuals and implement different kind of tasks using their acquired knowledge.

© Springer Nature Switzerland AG 2020
M. Mahmud et al. (Eds.): BI 2020, LNAI 12241, pp. 297–306, 2020.
https://doi.org/10.1007/978-3-030-59277-6_27

Several ways are existing to estimate cognitive performance, including question-naire, physical and physiological based measures. Questionnaire based measures are the personal measures combines self-reported actions and observers. Then, physical measures include facial expression, gestures and postures detection and physiological measures specifies the assessment of internal features of individuals. Along with these approach, the analysis of brain signals, e.g., Electroencephalo-graph (EEG), functional Near Infrared (fNIR), and functional Magnetic Res-onance Imaging (fMRI) can provide useful information about human behavior and physiological abnormality to estimate cognitive performance of individuals. Among of them, EEG signal is easily acquirable and helps to identify relevant features of cognitive performance. So, these signals can lent a hand to process and extract features denoting brain states. Due to the non-stationary EEG sig-nals, the development of sophisticated analysis is challenging. In this process, machine learning (ML) has allowed dynamic analysis and extracted significant features from it. These EEG features can be analyzed and lead to the accurate detection of cognitive performance [7, 8].

According to the previous studies, many ML based classifiers are used to investigate cognitive performance through EEG signals and detected various neurological issues. For instance, linear discriminant analysis (LDA) was identi-fied a particular signal band that offers more distinct features in EEG signal [4]. Quadratic discriminant analysis (QDA) is closely related to LDA that manipu-lates a separate covariance matrix for each class and shows the excellent perfor-mance for classifying real time dataset. Multilayer perception (MLP) extracts the dominant features and decreases the complexity to identify abnormality in EEG signals like epileptic seizure analysis [10], academic emotions of students [3]. Naïve Bayes (NB) is a commonly used in medical and emotional data processing [2, 14] to classify EEG signals for detecting cyber-sickness [9]. Again, support vector machine (SVM) and k-nearest neighbour (KNN) were investigated EEG signals for different neurological problems as well as academic emotion analysis [2]. Therefore, RNN was also widely used for the EEG data analysis such as confused student's [11] and epilepsy detection [1].

The technical contribution of this work to assess cognitive performance more efficiently than previous approaches. Therefore, we proposed bidirectional multi-layer long-short term memory (BML-LSTM) neural network that can detect cog-nitive performance more accurately. It was implemented in an open source con-fused student EEG dataset and identified cognition of individuals. This work was conducted by various data transformation, machine and deep learning methods respectively. Several data transformation methods were employed into primary EEG dataset and generated several transformed datasets. Then, BML-LSTM was applied into the primary and transformed datasets and shows around 96% accuracy to identify confused students. In this case, baseline classifiers describes in previous portion were employed into these datasets. The prime motive of using these classifiers is to verify the performance of BML-LSTM and compare their results. But these classifiers are not exceeded the results of BML-LSTM. Hence, this proposed model shows the best performance than previous works who were investigated this confused students EEG dataset.

2   Proposed Method

To identify the cognitive performance from the EEG signals, a novel pipeline has been developed (see Fig. 1) which describes in the following subsections.

2.1   Data Transformation

Data transformation facilitates the conversion of instances from one to another format and represents values into more distinctive representation. In this work, to identify the appropriate composition of the pipeline, we employed distinct transformation methods such as discrete wavelet transform (DWT), fast fourier transform (FFT) and principal component analysis (PCA) into primary EEG dataset and generated several transformed datasets. In the previous literature [5], these methods were widely used to transform instances into suitable format and enhanced the diversity of classification results. For instances, DWT reduced noise by filtering particular coefficients and scrutinizing different non-stationary EEG signals [13]. Using FFT, confused students EEG signals can be converted from time to frequency domain and decreases noise [5]. Furthermore, EEG signals uses PCA to lessen dimensions, complexity and computational time and retain more variability [6]. According to this analysis, we implemented these methods into EEG dataset and get more diverse results along with raw dataset.

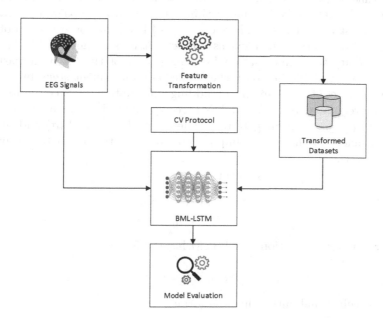

Fig. 1. Proposed pipeline for cognitive performance detection from EEG signals.

2.2   Bidirectional Multilayer LSTM (BML-LSTM)

To analyse the transformed EEG signals, we proposed a BML-LSTM to identify cognitive ability of the students. Recurrent Neural Network (RNN) consists of a recursive neural network where output from each layer is fed as input to the next layer. Nevertheless, the result of a processing node on a certain layer depends not only on the layer's correlation weight but also on a state vector of prior input or output. RNN remembers while learning and uses the same parameters in each calculation and performs on all the hidden layers at same task. Such computation reduces the parameter complexity contrast to other neural networks. Generally the hidden state S_t at step t of a RNN can be defined as follows:

$$S_t = A\left(S_{t-1}, x_t\right) \tag{1}$$

where, x_t is the input instance, S_{t-1} is the output from previous layer and A is called activation function. At every hidden layer, each hidden to hidden recurrent connection has a weight matrix W_s and the input to hidden recurrent connection has a weight matrix W_x. These weights are shared across time. The hidden state can be defined with all the weighted variables as:

$$S_t = W_s s_{t-1} + W_x x_t + b \tag{2}$$

where $W_s \in \mathbb{R}^{d_s \times d_s}$, $W_x \in \mathbb{R}^{d_x \times d_x}$, $b \in \mathbb{R}^{d_s}$ and d represents the size of the respective vector space.

The main drawback of RNN is vanishing gradient that explodes this problem. At each time step, this classifier contains some loss parameters and gradients carry this information from time to time. During back propagation, gradients travel from last to first layer. Therefore, LSTM is an improved version of RNN that handles long term dependencies problem. It uses designated hidden states called cell that stores information for long period of time so that particular information is available not only the immediate subsequent steps but also for later nodes. It control removing or adding information to a cell state which is carefully regulated by gates. It has three specialized gates called the forget (f_t), input (i_t) and output gate (o_t). Therefore, the sigmoid (σ) and *tanh* are activation function where *tanh* implies non-linearity to squash the activations between $[-1, 1]$.

$$f_t = \sigma\left(W_f \cdot [S_{t-1}, x_t]\right) \tag{3}$$

$$i_t = \sigma\left(W_i \cdot [S_{t-1}, x_t]\right) \tag{4}$$

$$o_t = \sigma\left(W_o \cdot [S_{t-1}, x_t]\right) \tag{5}$$

The recurrent connection in a LSTM has the form:

$$c_t = c_{t-1} \otimes f_t \oplus \tilde{c}_t \otimes i_t \tag{6}$$

and the cell's final output has the form:

$$s_t = o_t \otimes \tanh\left(c_t\right) \tag{7}$$

Here, $\tilde{c}_t$ is the output of the two fully connected layer defined as:

$$\tilde{c}_t = \sigma\left(W_o \cdot [S_{t-1}, x_t]\right) \tag{8}$$

BML-LSTM trains two RNN and generates the output based on the previous and future element. If all the time sequence is known, one network is trained the input sequence and the second network is trained the time reversal of the input sequence that significantly increase the accuracy. In the proposed model, three BML-LSTM layers have been implemented where first, second and third layers contained 5, 10 and 5 neural units, respectively. The *tanh* function is applied as the activation function for the hidden layer. This states are linked to the fully connected layer with *sigmoid* function and *adam* is used as the optimizer. Therefore, it produce the output 0 or 1 that indicates a robust and stable model to estimate cognitive performance respectively.

2.3 Baseline Classifiers

To justify the proposed BML-LSTM model performance, we used several baseline classifiers include LDA, QDA, MLP, NB, SVM, KNN and RNN were applied into confused student's EEG dataset.

2.4 Evaluation Metrics

Confusion matrix is described the performance of a classification model based on the test data where true values are known. It indicates the number of correct and incorrect predictions with count values and broken down each class. Based on positive and negative classes, this matrix is defined True Positive (TP), True Negative (TN), False Positive (FP) and False Negative (FN).

- Accuracy: It denoted the efficiency of the classifier in terms of probability of predicting true values.

$$\text{Accuracy} = \frac{TP + TN}{(TP + TN + FP + FN)} \tag{9}$$

- AUC: It explores how well positive classes are isolated from negative classes.

$$AUC = \frac{\text{TP rate} + \text{TN rate}}{2} \tag{10}$$

- F-measure: It measures the harmonic mean of the precision and recall.

$$F - \text{measure} = \frac{2 \times \text{precision} \times \text{recall}}{(\text{precision} + \text{recall})} = \frac{2\text{TP}}{2\text{TP} + \text{FP} + \text{FN}} \tag{11}$$

- G-mean: Geometric mean (G-mean) is the product root of class-specific sensitivity, creates a trade-off between the accuracy maximization on each of the classes and balancing accuracy.

$$\text{GMean} = \sqrt{(\text{TPrate} \times \text{TNrate})} \tag{12}$$

– Sensitivity: The proportion of correctly identified actual positives are measured by using following equation.

$$\text{Sensitivity} = \frac{TP}{(TP + FN)} \tag{13}$$

– Specificity: The proportion of correctly identified actual negatives are determined by using following equation.

$$\text{Specificity} = \frac{TN}{(TN + FP)} \tag{14}$$

– False Negative Rate: The ratio between correctly identified false negative and actual positive values are indicated as false Negative Rate / miss rate.

$$\text{False Negative Rate} = \frac{FN}{(FN + TP)} \tag{15}$$

– False positive rate: The ratio between correctly identified false positive and actual negative values are indicated as false positive rate / fall out.

$$\text{False Positive Rate} = \frac{FP}{(FP + TN)} \tag{16}$$

2.5   Dataset Description

The dataset was obtained from Wang et al. [14], who had collected 10 MOOC watching students' EEG signals. They prepared 20 online learning videos in two categories 10 of them contained normal conceptual videos and another 10 videos have different unusual or hard topics. In critical videos, 2 min clip was taken shortly from the middle of this videos that made more confusion to the students. They considered 10 sessions for a student where first lesson was given to refresh their mind for 30 s. In next lesson, students wore a wireless MindSet EEG device and tries to learn from these videos as possible where this activities around the frontal lobe have been captured by this device. The data points were sampled at every 0.5 s. Different features such as proprietary measure of mental focus (attention), proprietary measure of calmness (mediation), raw EEG signals, delta band (1–3 Hz), theta (4–7 Hz), alpha1 (lower 8–11 Hz), alpha2 (higher 8–11 Hz), beta1 (lower 12–29 Hz), beta2 (higher 12–29 Hz), gamma1 (lower 30–100 Hz) and gamma2 (higher 30–100 Hz) power spectrum were included respectively. After each session, each student graded his/her level on the scale of 1–7 where 1 indicated less confusing and 7 indicated more confusing. Moreover, three students observed student's attitude and graded them by following the same scale. Again, four observers witnessed each 1–8 students in that work. Therefore, these levels were quantized into two class that indicates whether the student is confused or not.

Table 1. Performance Comparison with Baseline Models

Classifier	Acc	AUC	F-M	G-M	Sen	Spe	ME	FO
KNN	0.5562	0.5557	0.5561	0.5557	0.5562	0.5552	0.4438	0.4448
LDA	0.5948	0.5951	0.5948	0.5951	0.5948	0.5954	0.4052	0.4046
MLP	0.5277	0.5265	0.5267	0.5265	0.5277	0.5253	0.4723	0.4747
NB	0.5414	0.5494	0.4914	0.5493	0.5414	0.5574	0.4586	0.4426
QDA	0.5526	0.5598	0.5128	0.5598	0.5526	0.5671	0.4474	0.4329
SVM	0.5126	0.5000	0.3474	0.4998	0.5126	0.4874	0.4874	0.5126
RNN	0.8725	0.8731	0.8725	0.8731	0.8725	0.8736	0.1275	0.1264
BML-LSTM	**0.9550**	**0.9551**	**0.9550**	**0.9551**	**0.9550**	**0.9552**	**0.0450**	**0.0448**

Legend: Acc: Accuracy; F-M: F-measure; G-M: G-Mean; Sen: Sensitivity; Spe: Specificity; ME: Miss Error; FO: Fall Out; bold values denote best performance.

3   Results and Discussion

In this work, we used scikit learn machine learning library [12] to transform and classify confused student's EEG dataset using 10-fold cross validation in Python. Then, the performance of each classifier is evaluated using different metrics respectively.

3.1   Overall Performance of the Model

When we implemented BML-LSTM along with baseline classifiers in the raw dataset. In this work, BML-LSTM represents the highest (96%) accuracy and the lowest miss rate (4.50%) and fall out (4.48%) respectively (see Table 1). In addition, it also represents similar results like accuracy for the other evaluation metrics respectively. RNN shows 87% accuracy and more metrics are generated same outcomes in this work. After RNN, LDA shows better results where it shows 59% accuracy, f-measure and sensitivity and 60% AUC, G-means and specificity respectively. However, KNN shows 56% all of its evaluation metrics except error rates. Later, another classifiers like QDA, NB, MLP and SVM also show their results for different evaluation metrics (see Table 1). Like other neural network performance e.g., BML-LSTM and RNN, MLP don't show more accuracy in this work. Therefore, SVM shows the lowest (51%) accuracy with other evaluation metrics except error rates. Besides, The AUC scores give some more insight about the outcomes to classify the EEG data of confused students in Fig. 2.

3.2   Effect of Preprocessing on Overall Model Performance

Therefore, the classification results of BML-LSTM for primary and transformed datasets are shown from Table 2. This analysis indicates how proprocessing steps such as data transformation methods can effect the results of proposed model. In the DWT transformed dataset, the performance of the classifiers are not more

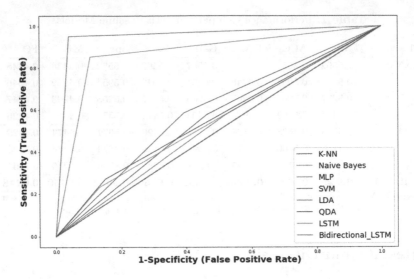

Fig. 2. ROC Curves of BML-LSTM and Different Classifiers for Raw Signals

satisfactory comparing to raw data analysis where BML-LSTM shows 70% accuracy and AUC respectively. In FFT transformed dataset, the proposed model represents 59% accuracy and AUC respectively. According to the Table 2, FFT models show the lowest results in this work. Alternatively, BML-LSTM shows better outcomes around 89% for the PCA transformed dataset. It performed well rather than DWT and FFT transformed datasets, but it is not exceeded the performance of BML-LSTM at raw EEG signals.

In this work, proposed BML-LSTM shows the best result than other baseline classifiers for the primary EEG dataset. Therefore, we also represented the effect of proposed model into transformed EEG datasets when the performance of BML-LSTM is represented in Table 2. In previous studies, several works had been happened to analyze bemused student's instances about watching educational video clips that makes them confusion in different levels. When we compared the outcomes of current study with previous works, most of them didn't justify their studies with preprocessing perspectives. In current study, we implemented

Table 2. Effect of Preprocessing in the Performance of the BML-LSTM model.

DT	Acc	AUC	F-M	G-M	Sen	Spe	ME	FO
DWT	0.6975	0.6975	0.6976	0.6975	0.6975	0.6974	0.3025	0.3026
FFT	0.5908	0.5904	0.5907	0.5904	0.5908	0.5900	0.4092	0.4100
PCA	0.8935	0.8932	0.8935	0.8932	0.8935	0.8928	0.1065	0.1072
Raw Signal	**0.9550**	**0.9551**	**0.9550**	**0.9551**	**0.9550**	**0.9552**	**0.0450**	**0.0448**

Legend: Acc: Accuracy; F-M: F-measure; G-M: G-Mean; Sen: Sensitivity; Spe: Specificity; ME: Miss Error; FO: Fall Out; bold values denote best performance.

most widely used data transformation methods to observe how these methods were worked in confused student's EEG dataset and generated significant results. Therefore, the classification results of transformed datasets are not shown better than raw EEG dataset. For only 11 features, feature selection methods are not worked as well. Therefore, our proposed BML-LSTM shows the best classification result comparing to previous studies. The comparison of current work with other studies are represented in Table 3. Though we use a few amount of EEG dataset, proposed model avoid overfitting and also increase the generalization ability using cross validation techniques.

Table 3. Comparative Study with Previous Works

Year	2013	2016	2019	2020
Author	Wang et al. [8]	Ni et al. [10]	Wang et al. [13]	Proposed Method
Classifier	Gaussain NB	B-LSTM	CF-B-LSTM	BML-LSTM
Neural Unit		50	50	5, 10, 5
Hidden Layer's Activation Function		tanh	tanh	tanh
Cross Validation		5	5	10
Output Layer's Activation Function		sigmoid	sigmoid	sigmoid
Accuracy		73.30%	75%	95%

4 Conclusion

Cognitive performance measures as a effective capabilities that can arise individual person at different circumstances. It can hamper for different reasons and needs to identify these risk factors about it. For instance, EEG signals can record the brain's electric activities during the learning process and identify confusion of students by scrutinizing extracted features in the signal sub-bands. ML methods are generated significant gain to classify EEG signals. Learning through MOOC videos, confusion occurs due to the lack of direct communication with the mentors. With its increasing popularity of MOOC providers, it required to look up individual methods and reduce such drawbacks. In this work, proposed BML-LSTM shows 96% accuracy to classify confused and non-confused students by analyzing their EEG signals. However, it represents the best result comparing to baseline classifiers as well as existing works. To categorize confused students, we used a open source EEG signal dataset which were not so much large for analysis. In future, we will gather more EEG data to explore various confusion related activities and generate numerous psychological outcomes.

References

1. Aliyu, I., Lim, Y.B., Lim, C.G.: Epilepsy detection in EEG signal using recurrent neural network. In: Proceedings of the 2019 3rd International Conference on Intelligent Systems, Metaheuristics and Swarm Intelligence, pp. 50–53 (2019)
2. AlZoubi, O., Calvo, R.A., Stevens, R.H.: Classification of EEG for affect recognition: an adaptive approach. In: Nicholson, A., Li, X. (eds.) AI 2009. LNCS (LNAI), vol. 5866, pp. 52–61. Springer, Heidelberg (2009). https://doi.org/10.1007/978-3-642-10439-8_6
3. Azcarraga, J., Marcos, N., Suarez, M.T.: Modelling EEG signals for the prediction of academic emotions. In: Workshop on Utilizing EEG Input in Intelligent Tutoring Systems (ITS2014 WSEEG), p. 1 (2014)
4. Fu, R., Tian, Y., Bao, T., Meng, Z., Shi, P.: Improvement motor imagery EEG classification based on regularized linear discriminant analysis. J. Med. Syst. **43**(6), 169 (2019)
5. Han, J., Pei, J., Kamber, M.: Data Mining: Concepts and Techniques. Elsevier, Amsterdam (2011)
6. Kottaimalai, R., Rajasekaran, M.P., Selvam, V., Kannapiran, B.: EEG signal classification using principal component analysis with neural network in brain computer interface applications. In: 2013 IEEE International Conference on Emerging Trends in Computing, Communication and Nanotechnology (ICECCN), pp. 227–231. IEEE (2013)
7. Mahmud, M., Kaiser, M.S., Hussain, A.: Deep learning in mining biological data. arXiv:2003.00108 [cs, q-bio, stat] abs/2003.00108, pp. 1–36 (2020)
8. Mahmud, M., Kaiser, M.S., Hussain, A., Vassanelli, S.: Applications of deep learning and reinforcement learning to biological data. IEEE Trans. Neural Netw. Learn. Syst. **29**(6), 2063–2079 (2018)
9. Mawalid, M.A., Khoirunnisa, A.Z., Purnomo, M.H., Wibawa, A.D.: Classification of EEG signal for detecting cybersickness through time domain feature extraction using Naïve bayes. In: 2018 International Conference on Computer Engineering, Network and Intelligent Multimedia (CENIM), pp. 29–34. IEEE (2018)
10. Narang, A., Batra, B., Ahuja, A., Yadav, J., Pachauri, N.: Classification of EEG signals for epileptic seizures using Levenberg-Marquardt algorithm based multilayer perceptron neural network. J. Intell. Fuzzy Syst. **34**(3), 1669–1677 (2018)
11. Ni, Z., Yuksel, A.C., Ni, X., Mandel, M.I., Xie, L.: Confused or not confused? Disentangling brain activity from EEG data using bidirectional LSTM recurrent neural networks. In: Proceedings of the 8th ACM International Conference on Bioinformatics, Computational Biology, and Health Informatics, pp. 241–246 (2017)
12. Pedregosa, F., et al.: Scikit-learn: machine learning in python. J. Mach. Learn. Res. **12**, 2825–2830 (2011)
13. Tzimourta, K.D., Tzallas, A.T., Giannakeas, N., Astrakas, L.G., Tsalikakis, D.G., Tsipouras, M.G.: Epileptic seizures classification based on long-term EEG signal wavelet analysis. In: Maglaveras, N., Chouvarda, I., de Carvalho, P. (eds.) Precision Medicine Powered by pHealth and Connected Health. IP, vol. 66, pp. 165–169. Springer, Singapore (2018). https://doi.org/10.1007/978-981-10-7419-6_28
14. Wang, H., Li, Y., Hu, X., Yang, Y., Meng, Z., Chang, K.M.: Using EEG to improve massive open online courses feedback interaction. In: Proceedings of the AIED Workshops, pp. 59–66 (2013)

Brain-Machine Intelligence
and Brain-Inspired Computing

Comparative Study of Wet and Dry Systems on EEG-Based Cognitive Tasks

Taweesak Emsawas[1]📧, Tsukasa Kimura[2](✉)📧, Ken-ichi Fukui[2]📧, and Masayuki Numao[2]📧

[1] Graduate School of Information Science and Technology,
Osaka University, Suita, Japan
taweesak@ai.sanken.osaka-u.ac.jp
[2] The Institute of Scientific and Industrial Research (ISIR),
Osaka University, Suita, Japan
{kimura,fukui}@ai.sanken.osaka-u.ac.jp, numao@sanken.osaka-u.ac.jp

Abstract. Brain-Computer Interface (BCI) has been a hot topic and an emerging technology in this decade. It is a communication tool between humans and systems using electroencephalography (EEG) to predicts certain aspects of cognitive state, such as attention or emotion. There are many types of sensors created to acquire the brain signal for different purposes. For example, the wet electrode is to obtain good quality, and the dry electrode is to achieve a wearable purpose. Hence, this paper investigates a comparative study of wet and dry systems using two cognitive tasks: attention experiment and music-emotion experiment. In attention experiments, a 3-back task is used as an assessment to measure attention and working memory. Comparatively, the music-emotion experiments are conducted to predict the emotion according to the user's questionnaires. The proposed model is constructed by combining a shallow convolutional neural network (Shallow ConvNet) and a long short-term memory (LSTM) network to perform the feature extraction and classification tasks, respectively. This study further proposes transfer learning that focuses on utilizing knowledge acquired for the wet system and applying it to the dry system.

Keywords: Brain-Computer Interface (BCI) ·
Electroencephalography (EEG) · Attention recognition ·
Music-emotion recognition · Transfer learning

1 Introduction

Brain-Computer Interface (BCI) is the concept of a communication tool between humans and systems by using a physiological signal, especially brain signals, to predict the cognitive state such as attention or emotion [1]. BCI is on the mainstream of emerging technologies from 2010 to 2018, according to the Gartner hype cycle[1], and possibly achieves the plateau reached in more than 10 years.

---

[1] https://www.gartner.com/.

© Springer Nature Switzerland AG 2020
M. Mahmud et al. (Eds.): BI 2020, LNAI 12241, pp. 309–318, 2020.
https://doi.org/10.1007/978-3-030-59277-6_28

For brain monitoring, the recording method of the electrical activity is an electroencephalography (EEG), which uses electrodes attached to the scalp and measures voltage fluctuations from ionic channels. There are many sensors built to record EEG signals and use in various disciplines, both medical and non-medical purposes.

A wet system means the EEG recording with placing electrodes on the scalp with a conductive gel. Many researchers typically use wet electrodes in expert disciplines, such as clinical neurology, neurobiology, and medical physics. The signal data, recording using wet electrodes, is highly reliable and can be used for medical purposes. However, the wet system is meticulous in using and considerably need both time and cost. Applying the concept of BCI, a wearable requirement is needed. The dry sensors are generally designed based on a wearable concept and use in practical application and non-medical tasks to investigate, entertain, or monitor brain activity.

In EEG-based cognitive recognition, the system needs several consequential steps to proceed from raw signals to cognitive labels, such as data preprocessing, data cleaning, feature extraction, and classification. Considering the feature extraction, we found that the frequency domain is the most popular technique according to [8] and [12] reviews. Meanwhile, a convolutional neural network (ConvNet) can efficiently perform deep feature learning by using advantage of the hierarchical pattern. For EEG signals or time series classification, there are various techniques and approaches. One of the effective techniques is a long short-term neural (LSTM) network [6]. LSTM architecture can preserve temporal dependencies using their memory blocks and gates. For the problem of data quantity, the concept of transfer learning is used as a learning paradigm to acquire knowledge from one system and apply it to solve the related system [10].

Accordingly, this study shows a comparative study of wet and dry systems by conducting two cognitive tasks: attention and music-emotion classification. Attention experiment assessed by using 3-back task and learned the sequence-to-sequence of EEG signals and attention sequence. Furthermore, we learned the sequence-to-label of EEG signals and emotion in the music-emotion experiment. To improve dry system performance and achieve the BCI concept, we further applied transfer learning by freezing the Shallow ConvNet [11] of the wet system and used it as feature extractor in the dry system.

2   Related Works

2.1   Frontal Brain Electrical Activity

Frontal brain electrical activity derives from a frontal lobe, which controls cognitive skills, such as emotional expression, working memory, and working memory capacity. Many studies attempt to achieve cognitive recognition with various stimuli by focusing on frontal brain activity. This research [13] found that the pattern of asymmetrical frontal EEG activity distinguished valence of the musical excerpts and higher relative left frontal EEG activity to joy and happy musical excerpts. Brain activity in the frontal region shows a significant relation with musical stimuli, consistent with many of the literature's findings. This study [5] not only deals with the emotional state but also the working memory. The frontal theta activity plays an active role in working memory. In particular, theta activity increases while doing the working memory task [7].

To investigate an association between brain activity and working memory, Wayne Kirchner introduced the n-back task [9]. It is a performance task that is commonly used as an assessment in cognitive research. In the n-back task, The subject is requested to memorize the sequence of a single character on the screen continuously. The task is to indicate if the current character is the same as the previous n-step before.

2.2 Segmentation and Classification Techniques

This study focuses on two different problems: sequence-to-sequence learning and window learning. The sequence-to-sequence learning proceeded by using an attention experiment (in Sect. 3.2), and the sequence-to-label proceeded by using a music-emotion experiment (in Sect. 3.3). The learning of comprehensive relation of physiological data over time is divided into two techniques: window recognition and sequence learning. Both techniques applied a sliding window for segmentation and then extracted the features from each segmented window. Window learning performs the classification on the individual window and accumulates the results into labeled class in case of sequence-to-labels learning. This learning is not able to transmit useful information from neighbors. In contrast, the sequence learning manifests the ability of dependencies learning. It properly performs sequence-to-sequence learning and able to learn sequence-to-label by using a model or network construction. This research of affect recognition in advertising [3], studied the comparison between window learning and sequence learning. The result indicates that sequence learning outperformed the accuracy through sequence-to-sequence learning and gain sequence emotional affect overtime.

2.3 Shallow ConvNet

The shallow convolutional neural networks (Shallow ConvNet) [11] is inspired by filter bank common spatial patterns (FBCSP). The main idea of FBCSP is transformations by combining the multi-filtering such as frequency filtering, spatial filtering, and feature selection. To imitate the same, Shallow ConvNet constructed band power feature extraction with 2 convolutional layers that perform temporal convolution and spatial filtering. Subsequently, the feature extractor layer is combined with the pooling and classification layers in the final step. This research [4] shows the study of attention using Shallow ConvNet and fully-connected neural network. Based on their overall result, they indicate that Shallow ConvNet is a promising classification technique, which outperforms other techniques. Besides, valuable knowledge is also successfully transferred to the new target domain even though the dataset has the corresponding environment.

3   Data Acquisition and Preprocessing

This study collected datasets from five healthy subjects, which are four males and one female. They are graduate students of Osaka University, between 20 and 30 years of age. The subjects were asked to finish two different cognitive tasks: attention experiments using the 3-back task and music-emotion experiments using the brAInMelody application. Meanwhile, the EEG signals were recorded while doing these cognitive tasks. The experiments were conducted twice in the corresponding task and setting but properly using different systems of dry and wet sensors.

3.1   Sensors

In this study, the experiments were conducted with two systems comparatively. The wet device is polymate AP1532 & EASYCAP GmbH with AP monitor cable connection, and the sampling rate is 1000 (Hz). On the other hand, the dry device is an imec sensor named EEG brAInMelody Gen-3 compatible[2] with brAInMelody application and Nyx software. The sampling rate of the sensor is 256 (Hz). EEG placement is in accordance with the international 10–20 system. Ten electrodes (Fz, Fpz, T3, F7, F3, Fp1, Fp2, F4, F8, and T4.) are placed in the frontal brain region. The Fpz and Fz set as ground and reference electrodes. The total signals gained are eight signals, consequently.

3.2   Attention Experiment Setting Using 3-Back Task

In the experiments, the subject performed the 33 repetitions of 3-back task, which is memorizing the 3-back character. Firstly, the subject was introduced instructions and then wore the sensor. Before doing the task, the '+' character appeared in the middle of the screen for 20 s. At the same time, the brain signals began to be recorded as a baseline. After that, the 33 repetitions of the 3-back task started sequentially. Each repetition consists of a 0.5-s character and a 2-s blank screen. Additionally, the experiment conducted in a closed room with minimal noise, and the subject was asked to minimize their movement to avoid the noises. To consider the comparison of two systems, all subjects performed the same task two times, with a different random set of characters, in both dry and wet setting.

This study classifies the recorded signals into two classes: attention and non-attention. The signal while doing the 3-back task is an attention class, and the baseline signal is a non-attention class.

3.3   Music-Emotion Experiment Setting

For the music-emotion experiment, the introductory and environment are the same as the previous attention experiment. Each subject was asked to listen to

---

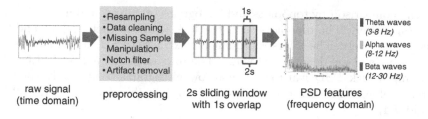

Fig. 1. Data preprocessing and feature extraction

five MIDI songs. Each song was added a 20-s baseline with no sound before the music started. After listening, the users immediately filled in the questionnaires, consisting of valence and arousal level between −1 to 1. They performed the same playlist for two times in a dry setting and a wet setting, respectively. The subjects also filled in the questionnaires for two times because their feelings might slightly change in the second round. Moreover, the subject is required to close the eyes while recording a baseline and listening to music.

In the music-emotion experiment, we study to investigate the emotional state from the EEG signals. The target labels or emotions obtained from the user's questionnaires are valence and arousal values from −1 to 1. For the reason that the emotion label is ambiguous, this study merely classifies two classes: positive and negative. The positive class represents positive valence and arousal, and the rest represents the negative class.

3.4   Preprocessing and Feature Extraction

In the recorded signals, there are missing values caused by the device connection. So, the signals were manipulated by duplicating the previous eight samples. Then, we applied a notch filter to remove 60 Hz power line noise and applied artifact removal using the EEGLAB [2] toolbox to avoid the severe contamination of EEG signals. In addition, the sampling rate of wet sensors was downsampled into 256, which equivalent to the dry sensors. To extract the features after preprocessing, we applied sliding window techniques with 2-s window size and 1-s overlapping for segmentation and sequential analysis. Then, the PSD features were extracted from each window sequentially. The process is shown in Fig. 1.

4   Statistical Analysis

This section shows the difference between dry and wet electrodes by calculating the statistical values and their tendencies. The reports investigated from range, mean, and standard deviation and noticed that there is a diversity among users and systems. Table 1 shows the statistical report of voltages and features each user data and each system.

After preprocessing and PSD feature extraction, we analyzed and found the different statistical values on both system and user dependency. Figure 2 and 3 show the comparison by topoplots and histograms on 3-back and music-listening tasks respectively. The topoplots show the PSD features: theta, alpha, and beta waves, respectively. The colors represent the extracted PSD values: red denotes high value, and blue denotes low value. The rows show the averages of baseline and doing-3-back PSD features. The below histograms sequentially show the difference of average PSD features from left to right (T3, F7, F3, Fp1, Fp2, F4, F8, and T4).

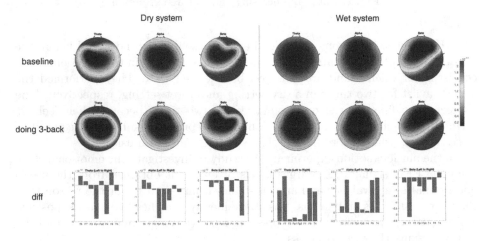

Fig. 2. The comparison between dry and wet systems on the 3-back task of user 4.

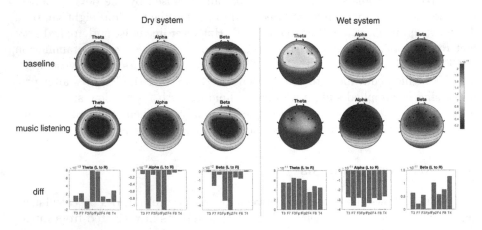

Fig. 3. The comparison between dry and wet systems on the music-listening task of user 2.

Table 1. The statistical report of voltages and PSD features in our 4 collected datasets

Task	Type	Raw data (μV)			PSD features ($\times 10^{-11}$)							
		Range	Mean	S.D	Theta		Alpha		Beta		Avg.	
					Mean	S.D	Mean	S.D	Mean	S.D	Mean	S.D
Emotion-Music	dry	21764.39	−34.65	68.65	9.65	6.21	5.22	3.48	5.61	2.32	6.83	4.00
	wet	1783.34	0.01	11.06	0.09	0.05	0.08	0.05	0.13	0.07	0.1	0.06
3-Back Task	dry	727.47	−26.25	39.07	8.64	3.46	4.51	1.4	5.54	1.21	6.23	2.02
	wet	486.42	−0.04	12.54	0.11	0.06	0.07	0.04	0.18	0.05	0.12	0.05

Fortunately, there are tendencies of the extracted features while doing tasks compared to baseline. For example, Fig. 2 shows the average PSD features. The different values between baseline and task seem to be the corresponding relatively. Notably, the theta of the left frontal brain (especially T3 and F7) identifies the increase while doing the 3-back task in both wet and dry systems. For the alpha and beta bands, they also have tendencies comparatively. These findings are consistent with other researchers in reviews.

On the other hand, in the example of the music-listening task which shows in Fig. 3, the PSD features of user two is plotted. We observe that theta and alpha bands have a similarity in increasing while the beta band is contrast. The high-frequency features might be sensitive and contaminated by the environment or unrelated noises. From this observation and investigation, we decided to classify these datasets by analyzing the extracted PSD features.

5   Proposed Method

The purposed model utilizes Shallow ConvNet and an LSTM network for sequence learning. In this case, 24 variables of three PSD channels and eight electrodes are used as the training features. This problem is a multivariate time series classification, which means each variable depends not only on its past values but also has some dependency on other variables. Besides, we utilized the z-score normalization to avoid the subject dependencies and focus on only the changes over time, according to the investigation in Sect. 4.

The network setting is shown in Fig. 4. It consists of two parts: the feature extractor and classification. In the first half, two 1D convolutional neural networks are built and then appended with the max-pooling layer with two of pool size to obtain the features. The filter size is 16, and the kernel size is three

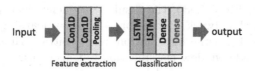

Fig. 4. The network structure of purposed model

according to three channels of PSD features. The activation function is a rectified linear unit (ReLU). In the second half, two LSTM layers are performed as the leaner of time dependencies. The hidden nodes are 100 for each layer with ReLU activation function. Lastly, the fully-connected layer is connected from LSTM layers to perform the classification. The number of nodes is equivalent to the number of window sequence with padding. For learning two classes, the activation function is sigmoid. Moreover, sequence-to-label learning adds one more fully-connected layer with a single node to classify the single label for each sequence.

For transfer learning, this study transferred the knowledge of feature extraction from the wet system to the dry system. The implementation is the freezing of feature extractor or the first half in the source domain and then apply it to the target domain. In transferring from wet to dry, we retrained only the second half layers and analyzed the result.

6   Experiments and Results

In the attention dataset, the data sequence individually consists of 84 pairs of input data and labels obtaining from 19 baseline windows and 65 doing-task windows. Each system entirely contains 420 pairs. When training and testing the models, we randomly chose the data as train and test samples without any user-dependencies or class-dependencies. While the music-emotion dataset, each system consists of 5 pairs of data and labels. Thus, there are 25 pairs of train and test samples for each system. In the case of window recognition, we trained the various size of windows, depending on the song duration, with the same labels and then accumulated the predicted label by the majority.

In both cognitive tasks, we compared two classifiers based on learning techniques. For window learning, support vector machine with radial basis function kernel (RBF-SVM) was implemented. While, the sequence learning perform the purposed method, sequence learning with Shallow ConvNet and LSTM network. The setting of both cognitive tasks are the same, but the difference in sequence-to-sequence learning and sequence-to-label learning. We implemented the leave-one-out (LOO) cross-validation for five users. The evaluation matrice is an F1-score to prevent the problem of an unbalanced dataset and prove the learning performance underlying the prediction.

6.1   Attention Classification (seq-to-seq)

From the graphs in Fig. 5 (left), the result of sequence learning, with Shallow ConvNet and LSTM network, outperforms window learning classification by using the ability to learn the information over arbitrary time intervals. It can process not only single window classification but also entire window sequences. Z-score normalization can help model generalization and support the learning of user independence. Especially, the dry system has more effect on improvement than the wet system. The best results are obtained by classifying PSD features

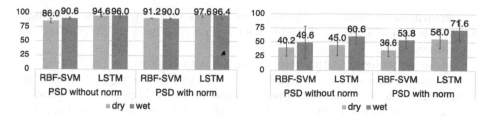

Fig. 5. (left) F1-score of attention/non-attention classification in 3-back task, and (right) F1-score of music-emotion classification (The error bars denote the standard deviation)

with normalization with the purposed method, which achieved 97.6% f1-score in the dry system and 96.4% f1-score in the wet system.

6.2   Music-Emotion Classification (seq-to-label)

These results resemble the previous experiment correspondingly. Whereas, the overall performance of emotion classification is lower than the attention classification explicitly. PSD features with normalization with the purposed method still outperformed window learning. It achieved 56.0% f1-score in the dry system and 71.6% f1-score in the wet system. Figure 5 (right) shows the music-emotion performance.

6.3   Transfer Learning

By using the modeling in Sect. 5, this experiment focused on the improvement of the dry system by using the proposed method with transfer learning. In the attention experiment, the new f1-scores of the purposed model with and without normalization using transferred feature extraction are 94.8% (+0.2% from 94.8%) and 97.6% (+0.0% from 97.6%), respectively. In the music-emotion experiment, the new f1-scores of the purposed model with and without normalization using transferred feature extraction are 56.8% (+11.8% from 45.0%) and 56.2% (+0.2% from 56.0%), respectively.

7   Discussion

In this study, we present a comparative study of wet and dry systems by performing 2 cognitive tasks: 3-back task and music-listening task. The result shows that the proposed method outperformed window learning, which is traditional techniques. The use of sequence learning also can obtain knowledge over time effectively. In the attention classification, we can distinguish the attention and non-attention from the observation of raw signals. So, the results are high performance relatively. In contrst to emotion classification, there is still an ambiguity between emotion expression, questionnaires, and emotion model, and It causes the performance of learning. However, we discovered the possibility of using a wearable sensor in a real-world application with transferring the knowledge from laboratory sensors.

The main problem of this research is the data limitation. This study conducted experiments on the small imbalanced-dataset. It directly causes sensitivity and variation of performance in concordance with the high values of standard deviation, especially the music-emotion results. In future work, we planned to scale up the number of subjects and tasks to verify the learning performance.

References

1. Al-Nafjan, A., Hosny, M., Al-Ohali, Y., Al-Wabil, A.: Review and classification of emotion recognition based on EEG brain-computer interface system research: a systematic review. Appl. Sci. (Switzerland) **7**(12) (2017). https://doi.org/10.3390/app7121239

2. Delorme, A., Makeig, S.: Eeglab_Jnm03.Pdf **134**, 9–21 (2004). https://doi.org/10.1016/j.techsoc.2013.07.004

3. Emsawas, T., Fukui, K., Numao, M.: Feasible affect recognition in advertising based on physiological responses from wearable sensors. In: Ohsawa, Y., et al. (eds.) JSAI 2019. AISC, vol. 1128, pp. 27–36. Springer, Cham (2020). https://doi.org/10.1007/978-3-030-39878-1_3

4. Fahimi, F., Zhang, Z., Goh, W., Lee, T.S., Ang, K., Guan, C.: Inter-subject transfer learning with end-to-end deep convolutional neural network for EEG-based BCI. J. Neural Eng. **16** (2018). https://doi.org/10.1088/1741-2552/aaf3f6

5. Gevins, A.S., et al.: Monitoring working memory load during computer-based tasks with EEG pattern recognition methods. Hum. Factors **40**(1), 79–91 (1998)

6. Hochreiter, S., Schmidhuber, J.: Long short-term memory. Neural Comput. **9**, 1735–1780 (1997). https://doi.org/10.1162/neco.1997.9.8.1735

7. Jensen, O., Tesche, C.: Frontal theta activity in humans increases with memory load in a working memory task. Eur. J. Neurosci. **15**, 1395–1399 (2002). https://doi.org/10.1046/j.1460-9568.2002.01975.x

8. Kim, M.K., Kim, M., Oh, E., Kim, S.P.: A review on the computational methods for emotional state estimation from the human EEG. Comput. Math. Methods Med. **2013** (2013). https://doi.org/10.1155/2013/573734

9. Kirchner, W.K.: Age differences in short-term retention of rapidly changing information. J. Exp. Psychol. **55**(4), 352 (1958). https://doi.org/10.1037/h0043688

10. Pan, S.J., Yang, Q.: A survey on transfer learning. IEEE Trans. Knowl. Data Eng. **22**(10), 1345–1359 (2010). https://doi.org/10.1109/TKDE.2009.191

11. Schirrmeister, R.T., et al.: Deep learning with convolutional neural networks for EEG decoding and visualization. Hum. Brain Mapp. **38**(11), 5391–5420 (2017). https://doi.org/10.1002/hbm.23730

12. Shu, L., et al.: A review of emotion recognition using physiological signals. Sensors (Switzerland) **18**(7) (2018). https://doi.org/10.3390/s18072074

13. Trainor, L.: Frontal brain electrical activity (EEG) distinguishes valence and intensity of musical emotions. Cogn. Emot. **15**, 487–500 (2001). https://doi.org/10.1080/02699930126048

Recall Performance Improvement in a Bio-Inspired Model of the Mammalian Hippocampus

Nikolaos Andreakos[1] , Shigang Yue[1] ,
and Vassilis Cutsuridis[1,2(✉)]

[1] School of Computer Science, University of Lincoln, Lincoln, UK
{nandreakos, syue, vcutsuridis}@lincoln.ac.uk
[2] Lincoln Sleep Research Center, University of Lincoln, Lincoln, UK

Abstract. Mammalian hippocampus is involved in short-term formation of declarative memories. We employed a bio-inspired neural model of hippocampal CA1 region consisting of a zoo of excitatory and inhibitory cells. Cells' firing was timed to a theta oscillation paced by two distinct neuronal populations exhibiting highly regular bursting activity, one tightly coupled to the trough and the other to the peak of theta. To systematically evaluate the model's recall performance against number of stored patterns, overlaps and 'active cells per pattern', its cells were driven by a non-specific excitatory input to their dendrites. This excitatory input to model excitatory cells provided context and timing information for retrieval of previously stored memory patterns. Inhibition to excitatory cells' dendrites acted as a non-specific global threshold machine that removed spurious activity during recall. Out of the three models tested, 'model 1' recall quality was excellent across all conditions. 'Model 2' recall was the worst. The number of 'active cells per pattern' had a massive effect on network recall quality regardless of how many patterns were stored in it. As 'active cells per pattern' decreased, network's memory capacity increased, interference effects between stored patterns decreased, and recall quality improved. Key finding was that increased firing rate of an inhibitory cell inhibiting a network of excitatory cells has a better success at removing spurious activity at the network level and improving recall quality than increasing the synaptic strength of the same inhibitory cell inhibiting the same network of excitatory cells, while keeping its firing rate fixed.

Keywords: Associative memories · Neural information processing · Brain · Inhibition

1 Introduction

Memory is our most precious faculty. The case of Henry Molaison (the infamous 'HM' patient) has taught us a lot about what happens when we cannot store memories. Without memory we are unable to remember our past experiences and our loved ones, while still being able to think about the future. Without memory we cannot learn

© Springer Nature Switzerland AG 2020
M. Mahmud et al. (Eds.): BI 2020, LNAI 12241, pp. 319–328, 2020.
https://doi.org/10.1007/978-3-030-59277-6_29

anything new. Associative memory is the ability to learn and remember the relationship between items, places, events, and/or objects which may be unrelated [1].

Hippocampus, the site of short-term storage of declarative memories [2], is one of the most studied brain areas yielding a wealth of knowledge of cell types and their anatomical, physiological, synaptic, and network properties [3]. Cells in various hippocampal regions have been hypothesized to compute information differently. Regions CA3 and CA1 have also been implicated in auto- and hetero-association (storage) of declarative memories, respectively [4].

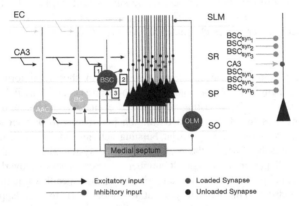

Fig. 1. Associative neural network model of region CA1 of the hippocampus and CA1-PC model with one excitatory (CA3) and six inhibitory (BSC) synaptic contacts on its SR dendrites. During retrieval only PC, BSC, and OLM cells are active. AAC and BC are inactive due to strong medial septum inhibition. BSC and PC are driven on their SR dendrites by a strong CA3 excitatory input, which presented the contextual information. Red circles on PC dendrites represent loaded synapses, whereas black circles on PC dendrites represent unloaded synapses. EC: Entorhinal cortical input; CA3: Schaffer collateral input; AAC: Axo-axonic cell; BC: basket cell; BSC: bistratified cell; OLM: oriens lacunosum-moleculare cell; SLM: stratum lacunosum moleculare; SR: stratum radiatum; SP: stratum pyramidale; SO: stratum oriens.

In 2010 a bio-inspired microcircuit model of region CA1 was introduced that controlled for itself the storage and recall of patterns of information arriving at high rates [5]. The model was based upon the biological details were then known about the hippocampal neural circuit [6, 7]. The model explored the functional roles of somatic, axonic and dendritic inhibition in the encoding and retrieval of memories. It showed how theta modulated inhibition separated encoding and retrieval of memories into two functionally independent processes. It showed how somatic inhibition allowed generation of dendritic calcium spikes that promoted synaptic long-term plasticity (LTP), while minimizing cell output. Proximal dendritic inhibition controlled both cell output and suppressed dendritic calcium spikes, thus preventing LTP, whereas distal dendritic inhibition removed interference from spurious memories during recall. The mean recall quality of the model was tested as function of memory patterns stored. Recall dropped as more patterns were encoded due to interference between previously stored memories.

Here, we systematically investigate the biophysical mechanisms of this bio-inspired neural network model of region CA1 of the hippocampus [5] to improve its memory capacity and recall performance. In particular, we examine how selective modulation of feedforward/feedback excitatory/inhibitory pathways targeting inhibitory and excitatory cells may influence the thresholding ability of dendritic inhibition to remove at the network level spurious activities, which may otherwise impair the recall performance of the network, and improve its mean recall quality as more and more overlapping memories are stored.

2 Materials and Methods

2.1 Neural Network Model

Figure 1 depicts the simulated neural network model of region CA1 of the hippocampus. The model consisted of 100 excitatory cells (pyramidal cells (PC)) and four types of inhibitory cells: 1 axo-axonic cell (AAC), 2 basket cells (BC), 1 bistriatified (BSC) and 1 oriens lacunosum-moleculare (OLM) cell. Simplified morphologies including the soma, apical and basal dendrites and a portion of the axon were used for each cell type. The biophysical properties of each cell were adapted from cell types reported in the literature, which were extensively validated against experimental data in [8–12]. Using known physical properties and effects of cell structures is a more efficient way to examine scientific hypothesis compare to blind computational optimization. The core of our research was biological properties and mechanisms because by we obtained a better understanding on how these mechanisms affected the whole circuit and gained some insightful intuitions. The complete mathematical formalism of the model has been described elsewhere [5]. Schematic representations of model cells can be found in [13]. The dimensions of the somatic, axonic and dendritic compartments of model cells, the parameters of all passive and active ionic conductances, synaptic waveforms and synaptic conductances can be found in [13]. All simulations were performed using NEURON [14] running on a PC with four CPUs under Windows 10.

2.2 Inputs

Network was driven by an excitatory CA3 input and an inhibitory medial septum (MS) input. The excitatory input was modelled as the firing of 20 out of 100 CA3 pyramidal cells at an average gamma frequency of 40 Hz (spike trains only modelled and not the explicit cells). PCs, BCs, AACs, BSCs in our network received excitatory input in their proximal-to-soma dendrites. The inhibitory input was modelled with the rhythmic firing of two opponent processing populations of 10 inhibitory cells each firing at opposite phases of a theta cycle (180° out of phase) [15]. Each such cell output was modelled as bursts of action potentials using a presynaptic spike generator. Each spike train consisted of bursts of action potentials at a mean frequency of 8 Hz for a half-theta cycle (125 ms) followed by a half-theta cycle of silence (125 ms).

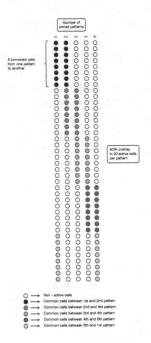

Fig. 2. Set of five memory patterns with 40% overlap between them.

Due to 8% noise in the inter-spike intervals, the 10 spike trains in each population were asynchronous. One inhibitory population input provided inhibition to BSCs and OLMs during the encoding cycle, whereas the other inhibitory population input provided inhibition to AACs and BCs during the retrieval cycle.

2.3   Network Training and Testing

The goal of this work is to test the recall performance of the model when the network had already stored memory patterns without examining the exact details of the learning process. To test the recall performance of the model the methodology described in [5] was adopted. Briefly, a memory pattern was stored by generating weight matrices based on a clipped Hebbian learning rule; these weight matrices were used to pre-specify the CA3 to CA1 PC connection weights. Without loss of generality, the input (CA3) and output (CA1) patterns were assumed to be the same, with each pattern consisting of N (N = 5 or 10 or 20) randomly chosen PCs (active cells per pattern) out of the population of 100. The 100 by 100 dimensional weight matrix was created by setting matrix entry (i, j), $w_{ij} = 1$ if input PC i and output PC j are both active in the same pattern pair; otherwise weights are 0. Any number of pattern pairs could be stored to create this binary weight matrix. The matrix was applied to our network model by connecting a CA3 input to a CA1 PC with a high AMPA conductance ($g_{AMPA} = 1.5$ nS) if their connection weight was 1, or with a low conductance ($g_{AMPA} = 0.5$ nS) if their connection was 0. This approach is in line with experimental evidence that such synapses are 2-state in nature [16].

2.4   Memory Patterns

We created sets of memory patterns at different sizes (1, 5, 10, 20), percent overlaps (0%, 10%, 20%, 40%) and number of active cells per pattern (5, 10, 20). For example, a 0% overlap between N patterns in a set meant no overlap between patterns 1 and 2, 1 and 3, 1 and 4, 1 and 5, 2 and 3, 2 and 4, 2 and 5, 3 and 4, 3 and 5, and 4 and 5. A 40% overlap between 5 patterns in a set meant that 0.4*N cells were shared between patterns 1 and 2, a different 0.4*N cells were shared between patterns 2 and 3, a different 0.4*N cells between patterns 3 and 4, a different 0.4*N cells between patterns 4 and 5 and a different 0.4*N cells between patterns 5 and 1 (see Fig. 2). For 20 active cells per pattern that meant that a maximum of 5 patterns could be stored by a network of 100 PCs. For 10 active cells per pattern, then a maximum of 10 patterns could be stored and for 5 active cells per pattern, a maximum of 20 patterns could be stored. Similar maximum number of patterns could be stored for 10%, 20% and 40% overlap and 5, 10 and 20 active cells per pattern, respectively. In the case of 10% overlap, 5 active cells per pattern, the maximum number of stored patterns was not an integer, so this case was excluded from our simulations.

2.5   Recall Performance Measure

The recall performance metric used for measuring the distance between the recalled output pattern, B, from the required output pattern, B*, was the correlation (i.e., degree of overlap) metric, calculated as the normalized dot product:

$$C = \frac{B \times B^*}{\left(\sum_{i=1}^{N_B} B_i \times \sum_{j=1}^{N_B} B_j^*\right)^{1/2}} \tag{1}$$

where N_B is the number of output units. The correlation takes a value between 0 (no correlation) and 1 (the vectors are identical). The higher the correlation, the better the recall performance.

2.6   Mean Recall Quality

Mean recall quality of our network model was defined as the mean value of all recall qualities estimated from each pattern presentation when an M number of patterns were already stored in the network. For example, when five patterns were initially stored in the network and pattern 1 was presented to the network during recall, then a recall quality value for pattern 1 was calculated. Repeating this process for each of the other patterns (pattern 2, pattern 3, pattern 4, and pattern 5) a recall quality value was calculated. The mean recall quality of the network was then the mean value of these individual recall qualities.

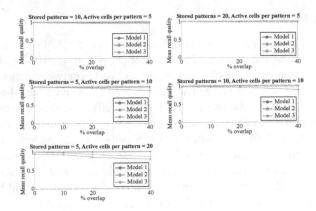

Fig. 3. Mean recall quality of 'model 1', 'model 2', and 'model 3' as a function of percent overlap (0%, 10%, 20%, 40%).

2.7 Model Selection

In [5], BSC inhibition to PC dendrites acted as a global non-specific threshold machine capable of removing spurious activity at the network level during recall. In [5] BSC inhibition was held constant as the number of stored patterns to PC dendrites increased. The recall quality of the model in [5] decreased as more and more memories were loaded onto the network (see Fig. 14 in [5]). To improve the recall performance of [5] we artificially modulated the synaptic strength of selective excitatory and inhibitory pathways to BSC and PC dendrites as more and more patterns were stored in the network (see Figs. 1 and 6):

1. Model 1: Increased CA3 feedforward excitation (weight) to BSC (Fig. 6A) increased the frequency of its firing rate. As a result, more IPSPs were generated in the PC dendrites producing a very strong inhibitory environment which eliminated all spurious activity.
2. Model 2: Increased BSC feedforward inhibition (weight) to PC dendrites (Fig. 6B) produced fewer IPSPs, but with greater amplitude, in the PC dendrites.
3. Model 3: Increased PC feedback excitation (weight) to BSC (Fig. 6C) had a similar effect as Model 1, but with less potency.

Comparative analysis of the above three models' recall performance is depicted in Figs. 3, 4 and 5.

3 Results and Discussion

A set of patterns (1, 5, 10, 20) at various percent overlaps (0%, 10%, 20%, 40%) were stored by different number of 'active cells per pattern' (5, 10, 20) without recourse to a learning rule by generating a weight matrix based on a clipped Hebbian learning rule, and using the weight matrix to prespecify the CA3 to CA1 PC connection weights. To test recall of a previously stored memory pattern in the model, the entire associated input pattern was applied as a cue in the form of spiking of active CA3 inputs (those belonging to the pattern) distributed within a gamma frequency time window. The cue pattern was repeated at gamma frequency (40 Hz). During the retrieval only the BSCs and OLM cells were switched on, whereas the AACs and BCs were switched off. The CA3 spiking drove the CA1 PCs plus the BSCs. The EC input, which excited the apical dendrites of PCs, AACs and BCs, was disconnected during the retrieval.

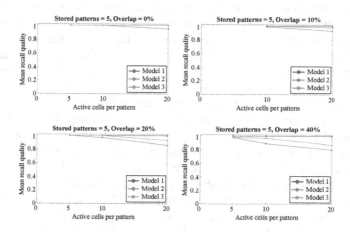

Fig. 4. Mean recall quality of 'model 1', 'model 2', and 'model 3' as a function of 'active cells per pattern'. Five patterns were stored in a network of 100 PCs at 0%, 10%, 20% and 40% overlap.

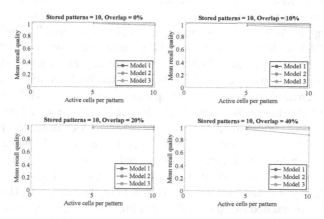

Fig. 5. Mean recall quality of 'model 1', 'model 2', and 'model 3' as a function of 'active cells per pattern'. Ten patterns were stored in a network of 100 PCs at 0%, 10%, 20% and 40% overlap.

It is evident from Fig. 3 that recall performance is best for all three models ('model 1', 'model 2', 'model 3) when there is no overlap between patterns or when the overlap is small (up to 10%) regardless of the number 'active cells per pattern' (i.e. the number of cells needed to represent a memory pattern) and patterns stored in the network. At overlaps larger than 10%, the recall performance depends solely on the number of 'active cells per pattern' and it is completely independent of how many patterns are stored in the network. When just 5 'active cells per pattern' are used to represent a memory, then the recall performance is best for all three models across all overlaps and irrespective of number of stored patterns. When 10 'active cells per pattern' are used to represent a memory, the performance of all three models are comparably similar when 5 or 10 patterns are stored and across overlap percentages. When 20 'active cells per pattern' are used to represent a memory, then even for just 5 patterns stored, the recall performance is consistently best for 'model 1' and consistently worst for 'model 2' across all overlaps. 'Model 3' performance is between 'model 1' and 'model 2'. The performances of 'model 2' and 'model 3' get worse as overlap increases (from 10% to 40%).

Figures 4 and 5 compare and contrast the recall performance of models 1, 2, and 3 against number of 'active cells per pattern' for various overlaps (0%, 10%, 20% and 40%) and stored patterns (5 or 10). When 5 or 10 'active cells per pattern' are used to represent a memory, then the recall performances of all three models when number of stored patterns were 5 or 10 was exactly the same at 0%, 10%, 20% and 40%, respectively. This means that the number of patterns stored in the network did not affect its recall quality. When 'active cells per pattern' were increased (from 10 to 20), then the recall qualities of models 2 and 3 progressively got worse as overlap between patterns increased (from 0% to 40%). 'Model 1' recall quality was consistently best (C = 1) across 'active cells per pattern', stored patterns, and overlap conditions.

Why was 'model 1' performance so consistently better than 'model 2' and 'model 3' across all conditions? Why the recall quality of 'model 1' was always perfect (C = 1) even when more patterns were stored in the network, more/less 'active cells per pattern' were used to represent a memory and greater percentages of overlap between patterns were used? As we stated in section "2.7 – Model selection", 'model 1' was the model where CA3 feedforward excitation to BSC was progressively increased as more and more patterns were stored, while the BSC inhibitory effect to PC dendrites was held fixed. 'Model 3' was the model where PC feedback excitation to BSC was progressively increased as more and more patterns were stored, while the BSC inhibitory effect to PC dendrites was held fixed. 'Model 2' was the model where the exact opposite took place: the inhibitory effect of BSC to PC dendrites progressively increased as more and more patterns were stored in the network, while keeping the BSC firing rate constant. In all simulations, 'model 1' outperformed 'model 3' across all conditions (overlaps and 'active pattern cells'). This was due to the fact that in 'model 1' BSC was excited by 100 CA3-PCs at high frequency (40 Hz), whereas in 'model 3' BSC was excited by 20 CA1-PCs that fired once or twice. Since in 'model 1' the BSC firing frequency response is higher than in 'model 3', then the postsynaptic effect of BSC on the PC dendrites in 'model 1' is higher in frequency and duration (but not in amplitude) than in 'model 3' (see Fig. 6A & 6C). Thus, 'model 1' has a better success at removing spurious activities and improving recall quality than 'model 3'. Since the BSC frequency response in 'model 2' was fixed, but its postsynaptic effect (weight) on PC dendrites increased, then the amplitude of the inhibitory postsynaptic potentials (IPSPs) on PC dendrites increased (compared to the IPSP amplitudes in

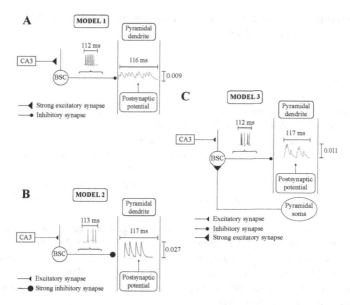

Fig. 6. Schematic drawing of presynaptic BSC firing response and inhibitory postsynaptic potentials (IPSPs) on PC dendrites in (A) 'model 1', (B) 'model 2' and (C) 'model 3'.

models 1 and 3), but their frequency response was low (lower than in models 1 and 3; see Fig. 6B). Each IPSP decayed to almost zero before another IPSP was generated post-synaptically on PC dendrites.

4 Conclusions

A bio-inspired neural model of mammalian hippocampal CA1 region [5] was employed to systematically evaluate its mean recall quality against number of stored patterns, percent overlaps and 'active cells per pattern'. We modulated the strength of selective excitatory and inhibitory pathways to BSC and PC dendrites as more and more patterns were stored in the network of 100 CA1-PCs and this resulted into three models, the performances of which were compared against each other. Model 1 recall performance was excellent (C = 1) across all conditions. Model 2 performance was the worst. A key finding of our study is that the number of 'active cells per pattern' has a massive effect on the recall quality of the network regardless of how many pattern are stored in it. As the number of dedicated cells representing a memory ('active cells per pattern') decrease, the memory capacity of the CA1-PC network increases, so interference effects between stored patterns decrease, and mean recall quality increases. Another key finding of our study is that increased firing frequency response of a presynaptic inhibitory cell (BSC) inhibiting a network of PCs has a better success at removing spurious activity at the network level and thus improving recall quality than an increased synaptic efficacy of a presynaptic inhibitory cell (BSC) on a postsynaptic PC while keeping its presynaptic firing rate fixed.

Acknowledgements. This work was supported in part by EU Horizon 2020 through Project ULTRACEPT under Grant 778062.

References

1. Suzuki, W.A.: Making new memories: the role of the hippocampus in new associative learning. Ann. N. Y. Acad. Sci. **1097**, 1–11 (2007)
2. Eichenbaum, H., Dunchenko, P., Wood, E., Shapiro, M., Tanila, H.: The hippocampus, memory and place cells: is it spatial memory or a memory of space? Neuron **23**, 209–226 (1999)
3. Cutsuridis, V., Graham, B.P., Cobb, S., Vida, I.: Hippocampal Microcircuits: A computational modeller's resource book, 2nd edn. Springer, Cham (2019). https://doi.org/10.1007/978-3-319-99103-0
4. Treves, A., Rolls, E.: Computational constraints suggest the need for two distinct input systems to the hippocampal CA3 network. Hippocampus **2**, 189–200 (1992)
5. Cutsuridis, V., Cobb, S., Graham, B.P.: Encoding and retrieval in a model of the hippocampal CA1 microcircuit. Hippocampus **20**, 423–446 (2010)
6. Klausberger, T., et al.: Brain-state- and cell-type-specific firing of hippocampal interneurons in vivo. Nature **421**, 844–848 (2003)
7. Klausberger, T., Marton, L.F., Baude, A., Roberts, J.D., Magill, P.J., Somogyi, P.: Spike timing of dendrite-targeting bistratified cells during hippocampal network oscillations in vivo. Nat. Neurosci. **7**, 41–47 (2004)
8. Poirazi, P., Brannon, T., Mel, B.W.: Arithmetic of subthreshold synaptic summation in a model of CA1 pyramidal cell. Neuron **37**, 977–987 (2003)
9. Poirazi, P., Brannon, T., Mel, B.W.: Pyramidal neuron as a 2-layer neural network. Neuron **37**, 989–999 (2003)
10. Santhakumar, V., Aradi, I., Soltetz, I.: Role of mossy fiber sprouting and mossy cell loss in hyperexcitability: a network model of the dentate gyrus incorporating cell types and axonal topography. J. Neurophysiol. **93**, 437–453 (2005)
11. Buhl, E.H., Szilágyi, T., Halasy, K., Somogyi, P.: Physiological properties of anatomically identified basket and bistratified cells in the CA1 area of the rat hippocampus in vitro. Hippocampus **6**(3), 294–305 (1996)
12. Buhl, E.H., Han, Z.S., Lorinczi, Z., Stezhka, V.V., Kapnup, S.V., Somogyi, P.: Physiological properties of anatomically identified axo-axonic cells in the rat hippocampus. J. Neurophysiol. **71**(4), 1289–1307 (1994)
13. Cutsuridis, V.: Improving the recall performance of a brain mimetic microcircuit model. Cogn. Comput. **11**, 644–655 (2019). https://doi.org/10.1007/s12559-019-09658-8
14. Hines, M.L., Carnevale, T.: The NEURON simulation environment. Neural Comput. **9**, 1179–1209 (1997)
15. Borhegyi, Z., Varga, V., Szilagyi, N., Fabo, D., Freund, T.F.: Phase segregation of medial septal GABAergic neurons during hippocampal theta activity. J. Neurosci. **24**, 8470–8479 (2004)
16. Petersen, C.C.H., Malenka, R.C., Nicoll, R.A., Hopfield, J.J.: All-or none potentiation at CA3-CA1 synapses. Proc. Natl. Acad. Sci. USA **95**, 4732–4737 (1998)

Canonical Retina-to-Cortex Vision Model Ready for Automatic Differentiation

Qiang Li$^{(\boxtimes)}$ (iD) and Jesus Malo (iD)

Image and Signal Processing Lab, University of Valencia, 46980 Valencia, Spain
{qiang.li,jesus.malo}@uv.es

Abstract. Canonical vision models of the retina-to-V1 cortex pathway consist of cascades of several Linear+Nonlinear layers. In this setting, parameter tuning is the key to obtain a sensible behavior when putting all these multiple layers to work together. Conventional tuning of these neural models very much depends on the explicit computation of the derivatives of the response with regard to the parameters. And, in general, this is not an easy task. Automatic differentiation is a tool developed by the deep learning community to solve similar problems without the need of explicit computation of the analytic derivatives. Therefore, implementations of canonical visual neuroscience models that are ready to be used in an automatic differentiation environment are extremely needed nowadays. In this work we introduce a Python implementation of a standard multi-layer model for the retina-to-V1 pathway. Results show that the proposed default parameters reproduce image distortion psychophysics. More interestingly, given the python implementation, the parameters of this visual model are ready to be optimized with automatic differentiation tools for alternative goals.

Keywords: Computational visual neuroscience · Retina · LGN · Primary Visual Cortex · Chromatic adaptation · Opponent channels · Contrast Sensitivity Functions · Deep linear+Nonlinear models · Python implementation · Automatic differentiation

1 Introduction

Current canonical vision models of the retina-to-V1 cortex include: light integration at the cones tuned to long, medium, and short (LMS) wavelengths [30], color adaptation mechanisms [8,29], transforms to chromatic opponent channels in cells of the Lateral Geniculate Nucleus (LGN) [5,27], different spatial bandwidth of achromatic and chromatic channels [3,4,22], and wavelet-like decompositions modelling achromatic and double opponent cells in the Primary Visual Cortex V1 [25,27]. In this pathway, the output of linear units is known to interact nonlinearly through recurrence [38] or divisive normalization [6,7,14,39]. These standard linear+nonlinear (L+NL) layers have been put to work together in image computable models [20,21,26]. These image computable models of the

© Springer Nature Switzerland AG 2020
M. Mahmud et al. (Eds.): BI 2020, LNAI 12241, pp. 329–337, 2020.
https://doi.org/10.1007/978-3-030-59277-6_30

visual pathway have obvious impact in engineering applications [15,17,18], but also in basic visual neuroscience because they allow to performing new psychophysical and physiological experiments [19,21,26,33]. However, the models in this standard family have *many* parameters, and parameter tuning is the key to obtain a sensible behavior given certain generic architecture. Minimalist architect Mies van der Rohe used to say that *god is in the details* [37]. In the conventional retina-to-cortex computational architectures, *the devil is in the parameters*.

Parameter tuning is very much dependent on the explicit computation of the derivatives of the response with regard to the parameters of the model. And, in general, this is not an easy task (see for instance [21]). Automatic differentiation is a tool developed by the deep learning community that solves similar problems without the need of explicit computation of the analytic derivatives [2]. Therefore, implementations of canonical models that are ready to be used in an automatic differentiation setting are extremely needed nowadays. When fitting complex models, initialization of parameters is extremely relevant [12]. Therefore, proper selection of a default state is of paramount relevance.

In this work, we introduce a python implementation of a canonical model for the retina-to-V1 pathway. Therefore, in this python setting, the parameters of the canonical visual model are ready to be optimized with the automatic differentiation tools for the goal function the user may design. The proposed image computable model comes with a set of default parameters taken from the large literature associated to each specific perceptual phenomenon addressed by each of the standard modules. In this work, we provide a proof of the psychophysical plausibility of this default model by showing that it reproduces human opinion in image distortion experiments with the default parameters. However, the advantage of the proposed python implementation is that these default parameters can be easily be optimized for other goals using the autodiff utilities of the pytorch/tensorflow environments.

The structure of the paper is as follows. Section 2 presents the structure of the model and its implementation. Section 3 shows experimental results that prove the psychophysical plausibility of the default parameters of the implementation. And finally, Sect. 4 discusses the differences of the proposed implementation with similar modelling efforts introduced since 2017 [1,11,15,17].

2   Model Structure and Implementation

The brain can be a perfect response (R) to certain stimuli (S), which is called encoding. Meanwhile, after the brain receives and decomposes external signals, it can be given feedback, this is defined as decoding. The encoding and decoding model which are the basic function of how the brain interacts with the outside world. It can be mathematically defined as:

$$\underbrace{\overbrace{\underbrace{S_n}_{\text{Stimuli}} = \underbrace{Retina(c) + \overbrace{Brain(\psi, \theta, w, l, i^2, d, e, v)}^{\text{Encoding } p(R-S)}}_{\text{Decomposition channels}}}_{\text{Decoding } p(S-R)}} \tag{1}$$

where $S_{n=1,2,\cdots,n}$, $n \in \mathbb{R}^\infty$ represent series of stimulus, r is neural response corresponding given stimuli, ψ is spatial frequency, θ is orientation, w is temporal frequency, l is adapting luminance, i^2 is stimulus size, d is view distance, e is eccentricity, c is chromatic information and v represents motion/speed. The brain is very sensitive to spatial frequency [9,23], spatial orientation, luminance, and local contrast and other very fine information of stimuli, and it can decompose the very complex natural world into very precise channel then drive the specific receptive field excitation or inhibition. The feed-forward pathway which encodes stimuli information in the brain, inverse, is called decoding which infers the stimuli from neural activity.

2.1 Multi-layer Linear Plus Nonlinear Model of V1

In the case of the visual information flow in the brain, we refer to the set of responses of a population of simple cells as the vectors. The considered models (linear+nonlinear) define a linear+nonlinear mapping (L+NL), that transforms the input vector (before the interaction among neurons) into the output cortex. The total structure of the model can be defined as bellows (Based on Eq. 1):

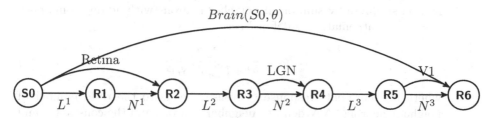

Where L denotes linear function and N refers to nonlinear transform. Finally, the model can be divided into three phases, which are the retina phase, LGN phase, and V1 cortex, respectively.

Retina Phase. The human retina mainly contributes to the physic optical function. The stimuli can randomly reflect light into the retina, then the size and density of the retina pupil can control how much spatial or optical information flows into the eyes. In the model, we implement a modulation transfer function (MTF) to simulate the retina physic optical function. The total function in the retina can be mathematically defined as:

$$R_1 = M * (S_0 + n(s_0)) + n_0(s_i) \tag{2}$$

Which the star denotes a linear convolution operation, M represents filter which considers both MTF and low-pass filtering which models by butter filter for remove input noise, $n(s_0)$ is input noise along with the image, the input noise created by man-made Gaussian white noise for better and optimization simulating our model, the details implement noise will explain below. $n_0(s_i), i = 1, 2, \cdots, n; n \in \mathbb{R}^\infty$ is intrinsic noise that models the neural self-noise. The total model in the retina can be divided by multiple LN stages.

1. **Linear stage**
   - Optical transform function with MTF filters for each chromatic channel.
   - Low-pass filters for removing Gaussian noise.
   - Chromatic channel summation then according to LMS sensitivity function transform from RGB2LMS and considered chromatic adaptation cognitive mechanisms with von-Kries Model.
   - After von-Kries Model, convert LMS to chromatic vision opponent(Achromatic, Tritanopic, Deuteranopic, ATD) which mainly represents white-black (WB), red-green (RG), yellow-blue (YB) channels that represent inhibitory and excitatory neuron in the ganglion cells.
2. **Nonlinear stage**
   - The half-squaring operation for avoiding negative response and correct response positive.
   - Non-linear divisive normalization of each chromatic channel. The divisive normalization model proposed by Heeger in the early 1990s which mainly used to simulate the primary visual cortex function [6,13,14,39]. The model defined neuron activity saturation phenomena when neuron processing tasks facing overload problem, in other words, the response of neuron suppress by sum of all neighbor neurons with adding some bias, it can be mathematically defined as:

$$R_2 = \frac{(R_2)^g}{b^g + (\sum_t NN_t)^g} \tag{3}$$

where R_2 represents response neurons, t refers to the total number of neighbor neurons. NN denotes neighbor neurons and the constant b and g prevents division by zero, it also controls the strength of normalization.

LGN Phase. The human brain is very sensitive to frequency bands change. Here, we implemented a band-pass filter with contrast sensitivity functional (CSF) and all responses happened in the Fourier domain then inverse for visualization [9,23,35].

V1 Phase. The wavelet transform approximately simulates primary visual cortex V1 multi-orientation and multi-scale properties. Multi-channel decomposition happened in the brain and via optimization parameters in the model which can reproduce the function of V1. The wavelet transform can capture frequency and space information both compared with Gabor function. Here, the steerable pyramid implemented in the model, it can decompose visual channel into the low, medium, and high-frequency channel, respectively.

1. **Linear stage**
   - Steerable pyramid transforms with 3 scales and 4 orientations. Steerable pyramid can efficient linear decomposition of an image into the scale and orientation subbands [28]. The basic principles of this function are high-order statistics of the directional derivative to calculate any desired order. Here, we instead Gabor functional with steerable pyramid transform to simulate the V1 multiscale and multiresolution psychophysiology properties.
2. **Nonlinear stage**
   - Non-linear saturation in the wavelet domain.

In summary, spatial interactions happen at different layers of the model: when including the convolutions associated with the MTF and CSFs, and in the convolutions with the receptive fields of the wavelet transforms. Nonlinearities are applied in the (color) Von-Kries adaptation and in the saturation of the ATD channels, and at the (contrast) saturation of the wavelet responses.

3   Results: Psychophysical Plausibility of the Default Mode

In this section, we experimentally show that the default parameters of the proposed implementation make psychophysical sense. This check is important because (as stated in the introduction) despite the architecture of the standard model is grounded in a large body of physiological, psychophysical, and statistical evidence, the key is in the parameter details. The specific behavior is determined by the specific value of the parameters, and the interested reader may find a detailed account of the parameters and the Python implementation can get here[1].

Here we illustrate the plausibility of the specific blocks (and parameters) considered in this work by predicting results in image distortion psychophysics. In image quality databases [24] human viewers assess the visibility of a range of distortions seen on top of natural images. A vision model is good if its predictions of visibility correlate with human opinion. The visibility of a distortion using a psychophysical response model is done by measuring the distance between the response vectors to the original and the distorted images [18,31]. In this context, we made a simple numerical experiment: we checked if the consideration of more and more standard blocks in the model leads to consistent improvements of the correlation with human opinion. Figure 1 confirms that the progressive consideration of the blocks leads to consistent improvements. Moreover, the resulting model is reasonable: the final correlation with human behavior in this non-trivial scenario is similar to state-of-the-art image quality metrics [15,18,21,34]. Note for instance that the acclaimed AlexNet [16] when trained to reproduce contrast thresholds [40] gets a Spearman correlation of 0.75 [15], and the widely used SSIM [31] gets 0.77 [32], while Fig. 1 shows that the proposed model with

---

[1] https://github.com/sinodanish/BioMulti-L-NL-Model.

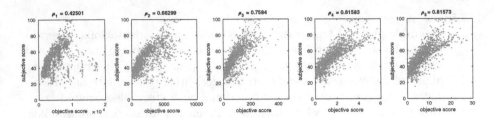

Fig. 1. Correlation with the human opinion as additional layers is added to the model. As different illuminations are not present in the considered database [24], we are not reporting the correlation after the Von-Kries adaptation since in this case is the identity. The first figure shows the prediction using the Euclidean distance. Then from left to right, we show the perceptual distance after the optical Modulation Transfer Function, the opponent channels, the Contrast Sensitivity Functions, and the Contrast Saturation, respectively. ρ refers to the Spearman correlation.

generic (non optimized) default parameters gets 0.82. These results illustrate the meaningfulness of the considered psychophysical blocks and its appropriate behavior when functioning together.

4   Discussion and Final Remarks

In this work, we presented an optics+retina+LGN+V1 model ready for automatic differentiation tuning given the Pytorch/Tensorflow nature of its implementation. Experimental results show that the default mode of the presented model reproduces image distortion psychophysics better than AlexNet tuned for contrast threshold prediction and classical SSIM.

This tunable model of early vision is in line with recent implementations of biologically plausible visual networks in automatic differentiation environments [1,11,15,17]. However, the implementation presented here has a number of differences in the architecture and considered phenomena. First, none of the above references includes a block to model the MTF of the eye. Second, Von-Kries chromatic adaptation as considered here is only considered in [15]. Third, references [1,15] learn the filters of the linear transforms with the corresponding possibility of overfitting. This is not the case in the presented implementation (which uses fixed center-surround and wavelet filters) nor in [17] which considers a pyramid of center-surround sensors and [11] which considers a steerable pyramid. Finally, regarding the nonlinearities, while [1,17] use restricted versions of the divisive normalization which do not consider spatial interactions, this is solved in [11,15] which do consider spatial interactions, either through divisive normalization [15], or through Wilson-Cowan recurrence [11]. Note that spatial interactions are strictly required for a proper account of masking [20,36].

Beyond the architecture differences mentioned above, it is worth mentioning that optimization for different goal functions (available through automatic differentiation) could lead to networks with substantially different behavior.

Possibilities include: (i) information maximization, as suggested in [11], (ii) rate-distortion performance, as done in [1], (iii) image quality, as done in [15,17,21], or (iv) texture synthesis, as done in [10]. Moreover, some of the cost functions mentioned above could have nontrivial behavior as for instance nonstationarity. In the current implementation, we rely on optimization based on a selected set of images (or batch). Therefore, strong dependence of the goal functions on the kind of images is a matter for further research. It is important to note that even when optimizing for sensible goal functions, one should always check that basic psychophysical behavior is still reproduced after the optimization. In this regard, biologically sensible architectures and economy of parameters (as in the implementation presented here) are highly desirable [20].

Acknowledgment. Thanks to all of the open-source contributors in the open-source community. We would like to thank the reviewers for their thoughtful comments and efforts towards improving our manuscript. Finally, we also want to thank all of the doctors in the world who keep all of us safe during the COVID 19 epidemic.

This work was partially funded by the Spanish Government through the grant MINECO DPI2017-89867 and by the Generalitat Valenciana through the grant Griso-liaP/2019/035.

References

1. Ballé, J., Laparra, V., Simoncelli, E.P.: End-to-end optimized image compression. In: 5th International Conference on Learning Representations, ICLR 2017 (2017)
2. Baydin, A., Pearlmutter, B., Radul, A., Siskind, J.: Automatic differentiation in machine learning: a survey. CoRR abs/1502.05767 (2015). http://arxiv.org/abs/1502.05767
3. Cai, D., DeAngelis, G., Freeman, R.: Spatiotemporal receptive field organization in the LGN of cats and kittens. J. Neurophysiol. **78**(2), 1045–1061 (1997)
4. Campbell, F., Robson, J.: Application of Fourier analysis to the visibility of gratings. J. Physiol. **197**, 551–566 (1968)
5. Capilla, P., Malo, J., Luque, M., Artigas, J.: Colour representation spaces at different physiological levels: a comparative analysis. J. Opt. **29**(5), 324 (1998)
6. Carandini, M., Heeger, D.: Summation and division by neurons in visual cortex. Science **264**(5163), 1333–1336 (1994)
7. Carandini, M., Heeger, D.J.: Normalization as a canonical neural computation. Nat. Rev. Neurosci. **13**(1), 51–62 (2012)
8. Fairchild, M.: Color Appearance Models. The Wiley-IS&T Series in Imaging Science and Technology, Wiley, Sussex, UK (2013)
9. Gardner, J., Sun, P., Waggoner, R., Ueno, K., Tanaka, K., Cheng, K.: Contrast adaptation and representation in human early visual cortex. Neuron **47**, 607–20 (2005). https://doi.org/10.1016/j.neuron.2005.07.016
10. Gatys, L.A., Ecker, A.S., Bethge, M.: A neural algorithm of artistic style (2015). http://arxiv.org/abs/1508.06576
11. Gomez-Villa, A., Bertalmio, M., Malo, J.: Visual information flow in Wilson-Cowan networks. J. Neurophysiol. (2020). https://doi.org/10.1152/jn.0487.2019
12. Goodfellow, I., Bengio, Y., Courville, A.: Deep Learning. MIT Press, Cambridge, MA (2016). http://www.deeplearningbook.org

13. Günthner, M.F., et al.: Learning divisive normalization in primary visual cortex. bioRxiv (2019). https://doi.org/10.1101/767285
14. Heeger, D.J.: Normalization of cell responses in cat striate cortex. Vis. Neurosci. **9**(2), 181–197 (1992)
15. Hepburn, A., Laparra, V., Malo, J., McConville, R., Santos, R.: PerceptNet: a human visual system inspired neural net for estimating perceptual distance. In: Proceedings of IEEE ICIP (2020). https://arxiv.org/abs/1910.12548
16. Krizhevsky, A., Sutskever, I., Hinton, G.: ImageNet classification with deep convolutional neural networks. In: 25th Neural Information Processing System, NIPS 2012, pp. 1097–1105, Curran Associates Inc., USA (2012)
17. Laparra, V., Berardino, A., Balle, J., Simoncelli, E.: Perceptually optimized image rendering. JOSA A **34**(9), 1511–1525 (2017)
18. Laparra, V., Muñoz-Marí, J., Malo, J.: Divisive normalization image quality metric revisited. JOSA A **27**(4), 852–864 (2010)
19. Malo, J., Simoncelli, E.: Geometrical and statistical properties of vision models obtained via maximum differentiation. In: SPIE Electronic Imaging, pp. 93940L–93940L. International Society for Optics and Photonics (2015)
20. Martinez, M., Bertalmío, M., Malo, J.: In praise of artifice reloaded: caution with natural image databases in modeling vision. Front. Neurosci. (2019). https://doi.org/10.3389/fnins.2019.00008
21. Martinez-Garcia, M., Cyriac, P., Batard, T., Bertalmío, M., Malo, J.: Derivatives and inverse of cascaded linear+nonlinear neural models. PLOS ONE **13**(10), 1–49 (2018). https://doi.org/10.1371/journal.pone.0201326
22. Mullen, K.T.: The CSF of human colour vision to red-green and yellow-blue chromatic gratings. J. Physiol. **359**, 381–400 (1985)
23. Pestilli, F., Carrasco, M., Heeger, D., Gardner, J.: Attentional enhancement via selection and pooling of early sensory responses in human visual cortex. Neuron **72**, 832–46 (2011). https://doi.org/10.1016/j.neuron.2011.09.025
24. Ponomarenko, N., Carli, M., Lukin, V., Egiazarian, K., Astola, J., Battisti, F.: Color image database for evaluation of image quality metrics. In: Proceedings of International Workshop on Multimedia Signal Processing, pp. 403–408 (2008)
25. Ringach, D.: Spatial structure and symmetry of simple-cell receptive fields in macaque primary visual cortex. J. Neurophysiol. **88**(1), 455–463 (2002)
26. Schutt, H.H., Wichmann, F.A.: An image-computable psychophysical spatial vision model. J. Vis. **17**(12), 12 (2017). https://doi.org/10.1167/17.12.12
27. Shapley, R., Hawken, M.: Color in the cortex: single- and double-opponent cells. Vis. Res. **51**(7), 701–717 (2011)
28. Simoncelli, E.P., Freeman, W.T., Adelson, E.H., Heeger, D.J.: Shiftable multiscale transforms. IEEE Trans. Inf. Theory **38**(2), 587–607 (1992). https://doi.org/10.1109/18.119725. Special Issue on Wavelets
29. Stockman, A., Brainard, D.: Color vision mechanisms. In: OSA Handbook of Optics, 3rd edn., pp. 147–152. McGraw-Hill, NY (2010)
30. Stockman, A., Sharpe, L.: The spectral sensitivities of the middle- and long-wavelength-sensitive cones derived from measurements in observers of known genotype. Vis. Res. **40**(13), 1711–1737 (2000)
31. Wang, Z., Bovik, A.C., Sheikh, H.R., Simoncelli, E.P.: Image quality assessment: from error visibility to structural similarity. IEEE Trans. Image Proc. **13**(4), 600–612 (2004)
32. Wang, Z., Simoncelli, E.: SSIM results in TID2008 (2011). http://cns.nyu.edu/lcv/ssim

33. Wang, Z., Simoncelli, E.P.: Maximum differentiation (MAD) competition: a methodology for comparing computational models of perceptual quantities. J. Vis. **8**(12), 8 (2008)
34. Watson, A.B., Malo, J.: Video quality measures based on the standard spatial observer. In: 2002 International Conference on Image Processing, Proceedings, vol. 3, pp. III-41. IEEE (2002)
35. Watson, A.B., Ramirez, C.: A standard observer for spatial vision based on modelfest dataset (1999)
36. Watson, A.B., Solomon, J.A.: Model of visual contrast gain control and pattern masking. JOSA A **14**(9), 2379–2391 (1997)
37. Whitman, A., Obituary, van der Rohe, M.: Leader of Modern Architecture. The New York Times (1969)
38. Wilson, H.R., Cowan, J.D.: A mathematical theory of the functional dynamics of cortical and thalamic nervous tissue. Kybernetik **13**(2), 55–80 (1973)
39. Zenger-Landolt, B., Heeger, D.: Response suppression in v1 agrees with psychophysics of surround masking. J. Neurosci. Off. J. Soc. Neurosci. **23**, 6884–6893 (2003). https://doi.org/10.1523/JNEUROSCI.23-17-06884.2003
40. Zhang, R., Isola, P., Efros, A., Shechtman, E., Wang, O.: The unreasonable effectiveness of deep features as a perceptual metric. In: Proceedings of IEEE CVPR, pp. 586–595 (2018)

An Optimized Self-adjusting Model for EEG Data Analysis in Online Education Processes

Hao Lan Zhang[1,2]([⊠]) [iD], Sanghyuk Lee[3] [iD], and Jing He[4] [iD]

[1] SCDM, Ningbo Institute of Technology, Zhejiang University, Ningbo, China
haolan.zhang@nit.zju.edu.cn
[2] Ningbo Research Institute, Zhejiang University, Ningbo, China
[3] Xi'an Jiaotong-Liverpool University, Suzhou, China
[4] Swinburne University, Melbourne, Australia

Abstract. Studying on EEG (Electroencephalography) data instances to discover potential recognizable patterns has been a emerging hot topic in recent years, particularly for cognitive analysis in online education areas. Machine learning techniques have been widely adopted in EEG analytical processes for non-invasive brain research. Existing work indicated that human brain can produce EEG signals under the stimulation of specific activities. This paper utilizes an optimized data analytical model to identify statuses of brain wave and further discover brain activity patterns. The proposed model, i.e. Segmented EEG Graph using PLA (SEGPA), that incorporates optimized data processing methods and EEG-based analytical for EEG data analysis. The data segmentation techniques are incorporated in SEGPA model. This research proposes a potentially efficient method for recognizing human brain activities that can be used for machinery control. The experimental results reveal the positive discovery in EEG data analysis based on the optimized sampling methods. The proposed model can be used for identifying students cognitive statuses and improve educational performance in COVID19 period.

Keywords: EEG pattern recognition · Online teaching · Brain informatics

1 Introduction

In this paper, we focus on analyzing EEG data sets that stimulated by EEG motion detection or environment change; and using the optimized methods to recognize the EEG data patterns. Environment change generally refers to the environment that EEG lab participants stay in has been changed, which results in EEG status change. Through conducting sensory stimulation, the cerebral cortex corresponding to cognitive center will generate corresponding electrical activities to create recognizable EEG patterns.

Electroencephalogram (EEG) is a graph obtained by continuously amplifying the spontaneous biological potential of the brain with the aid of precise electronic instruments and recording the rhythmic and spontaneous electrical activity of brain cell group by electric motor. EEG's most signification advantage is that it can record the change of brain wave during brain activity accurately, with a time resolution of 1 ms. The traditional EEG recognition adopts classification methods [1, 2].

© Springer Nature Switzerland AG 2020
M. Mahmud et al. (Eds.): BI 2020, LNAI 12241, pp. 338–348, 2020.
https://doi.org/10.1007/978-3-030-59277-6_31

Traditionally, EEG data analysis models have been utilized in studying the properties of cerebral and neural networks in neurosciences. In recent years, health informatics applications based on EEG have been successfully adopted in many fields, e.g. psychological research, physical recovery, robotic control, and so on [1–3].

The major disadvantages of EEG based methods can be briefly summarized as: (1) EEG analytical methods have poor spatial resolution, which cannot efficiently identify the location of the source of brain activity. (2) EEG signals are basically magnified signals, which normally can produce high noises. However, EEG-based models have the obvious advantages. The expanses of EEG equipment are much lower than MRI scanning and EEG is relatively tolerable to subject movements as compared to MRI. In addition, EEG caps can be flexibly applied to various applications. EEG based systems allow persons who are unable to make motor response to send signals. [1–3].

In this paper, we investigate motion actions induced EEG data. Our research indicates that motion actions can produce recognizable EEG patterns. In this research, EEG signals are acquired synchronously by EEG signal acquisition equipment; and the EEG signals are recorded. Relevant EEG signal characteristics are extracted and analyzed by corresponding signal analysis methods. This paper explores the research on the psychology and consciousness of users and their changing trend in different motion statues. Therefore, discovering consumers' brain activities through on EEG analysis based on motion change or cognitive environment change, such as background music, is this paper's major contribution and objective.

Existing EEG pattern recognition models are facing the challenging of dealing with time series data. In this paper, we propose an optimized model for EEG pattern recognition based on SEGPA [3]. The SEGPA model incorporates the clustering method, i.e. K-means, with logistic regression method for EEG pattern discovery.

Based on the above methods, the SEGPA model can dynamically adapt to the EEG recognition process, which can be more efficient than traditional classification methods. Currently, the SEGPA model is less efficient in dynamic adaptation and real time processing. The reminder of this paper is structured as follows. Section 2 reviews the existing research work on EEG-based classification and recognition. Section 3 proposes the optimized SEGPA model and the related methods used in the model. Section 4 provides the experimental design and analysis. The final section concludes the research findings.

2   Related Work

2.1   Classification Methods for EEG Analysis

Traditional classification methods for EEG recognition include linear discriminant analysis (LDA), regularized LDA and Support Vector Machines (SVMs), Neural networks (NN), Learning Vector Quantization (LVQ), Non-linear Bayesian classifiers, Bayes quadratic classifiers and hidden Markov models (HMMs), etc. However, the main challenges faced by classification methods for EEG recognition or BCI are the low signal-to-noise ratio of EEG signals and their nonstationarity over time among users [3–7], the limited amount of training data that is available to quantify the classifiers, and the overall low reliability and performance of current EEG pattern recognition and BCI data analysis [4, 8].

Bayesian classifier is a popular method for EEG analysis [4]. It is one of the classifiers with the least classification error probability or the least average risk at a given cost. Bayesian classifier is a statistical method. Its principle is to calculate the posterior probability of an object by using the Bayesian equation (as shown in Eq. 1); and select the category with the maximum posterior probability as the category of the object.

$$p(c|a) = \frac{p(a|c)P(c)}{P(a)} \tag{1}$$

Bayes rule is about the conditional probability and marginal probability of random events A and B. Which Eq. 1 can be further extended as below. Non-linear Bayesian classifiers model the probability distributions of each class and use Bayes' rule to select the class to assign to the current feature vector [3, 4].

$$p(y|x_1, \ldots, x_n) = \frac{p(x_1|y)p(x_2|y)\ldots p(x_n|y)p(y)}{p(x_1)p(x_2)\ldots p(x_n)}$$
$$= \frac{p(y)\prod_{i=1}^{n}p(x_i|y)}{p(x_1)p(x_2)\ldots p(x_n)} \tag{2}$$

where P(C|A) is the possibility of occurrence of A when B occurs. A_1, A_2, ...A_n is a complete event group. Pr(A|B) is the conditional probability of A after the occurrence of B, known as a posterior probability due to the value obtained from B.

Support vector machine (SVM) is a typical classifier for EEG classification, which classifies data according to supervised learning. Its decision boundary is the maximum margin hyperplane for learning samples. Least Square SVM (LS-SVM) is a variant of standard SVM. The difference between them is that LS-SVM does not use hinge loss function, but rewrites its optimization problem into a form similar to ridge regression. The optimization problems of soft margin SVM and LS-SVM are as follows.

$$\max_{w,b} \frac{1}{2}\|w\|^2 + C\sum_{i=1}^{N} e_i^2, e_i = y_i - (w^T X_i + b)$$
$$s.t. \quad y_i(w^T X_i + b) \geq 1 - e_i \tag{3}$$

where the hyper-plane normal vector w is the only optimization objective. Given the input data and learning objective: $x = \{x_1, \ldots, x_n\}$, $y = \{y_1, \ldots, y_n\}$. SVM is a fast and dependable classification algorithm that performs efficiently with a relatively small amount of data.

2.2 New EEG Classification Methods and Other Methods

The research on emerging and novel classification algorithms studied in past ten years focus on addressing the major EEG recognition challenges. Specifically, the adaptive classifiers and their parameters are incrementally updated and developed to deal with EEG non-stationarity in order to track changes [4].

The parameters of adaptive classifiers, e.g. the weights attributed to each feature in a linear discriminant hyperplane, are incrementally re-evaluated and renewed when new EEG data sets are collected [4, 9]. Unsupervised deployment of classifiers is more difficult, due to the class labels is unknown. Therefore, unsupervised methods have been proposed to estimate the class labels of new samples before adapting classifiers based on their estimation [4].

Some new classification methods are introduced recently, such as FAHT (Fairness-Aware Hoeffding Tree). FAHT is an extension of the well-known Hoeffding Tree algorithm for decision tree induction over streams, that also accounts for fairness. It is able to deal with discrimination in streaming environments, while maintaining a moderate performance over the stream [10]. The splitting criterion of FAHT to consider the fairness gain of a potential split is expressed as below.

$$fg(d, a) = |disc(d)| - \sum_{v \in dom(a)} \frac{|d_v|}{d} |disc(d_v)| \tag{4}$$

where d_v, $v \in dom(a)$ are the partitions induced by A.

Some researchers have been working on graph-based EEG pattern recognition methods in recent years. In [11], the EEG selection process adopts the graph-based method, which aims to search maximum weight cliques for EEG analysis.

3   An Optimized Pattern Recognition Model for Online Education

The optimized EEG pattern recognition model is proposed in this paper through combining clustering methods with association rule methods based on the SEGPA model. The major steps of this model can be summarized into six major steps. Each step has dependency to its previous process, which are introduced below.

The SEGPA model introduced in the previous work [12] consists of five major steps: (1) EEG data segmentation; (2) optimized Piecewise Linear Approximation (PLA) or granular computing; (3) processed EEG K-means clustering; (4) Logistic classification results generation; and (5) EEG pattern recognition based on classification and intelligent agents. The SEGPA model utilizes the clustering algorithm to generate EEG data clusters and takes time series data dependency analysis into consideration based on Savit and Green [17]. The SEGPA model generalizes the δ_j's that are sensitive to the assumption of j-dependence in k dimensions as below [17]:

$$\delta_j^{[k]} = \frac{C_k - (C_j/C_{j-1})^{k-j} C_j}{C_k} = 1 - \left(\frac{C_j}{C_{j-1}}\right)^{k-j} \frac{C_j}{C_k} \tag{5}$$

where δ_j denotes dependencies that are the result of averages over regions of a map.

The algorithm of the SEGPA pattern recognition is modified based on the previous graph-based EEG PR method; and the algorithm is listed as below:

Algorithm 1: Optimized SEGPA PR-tree Construction

Input: EEG time series data set C, Time elapsing t.

Output: EEG data pattern P(A).

1   Differentiate_List = Original(t_i) - Original(t_{i-1}).

2   **Calculate** distribution of C, PD(C) $\rightarrow$ F_i list (F_i list is in ascending order).

3   Perform K-means clustering based on distance.

4   **Calculate** $d(x, y) = \left(\sum_{i=1}^{n} |x_i - y_i|^p \right)^{\frac{1}{p}}$

5   Clusters_List = K-means(Differentiate_List)

6   Association_Rule_List = Apriori(Clusters_List)

7   P(A) = Sort(Association_Rule_List, i) #i is defined list size.

8   **Return** (P(A))

3.1   EEG Segmentation and PLA/Granular Method

In the previous work, we discovered that a segment of a large data set with proper size will inherit the original data set's characteristic [13]. EEG data sets follow Normal Distribution (ND) and Poisson Distribution (PD) in different statues. Based on this theory, splitting and extracting a smaller size of segment from a large EEG data set can still contain the crucial data information. In this way, the ND/PD based data splitting methods can be more efficient for dealing with large data sets [13].

The PDA/NDA segmentation procedures generate EEG data segments, which have been greatly minimized in size without much losing crucial information such as means, standard deviation, etc. A ND-based segmented EEG data example is shown as below (Table 1).

Table 1. Segmented EEG data based on ND model

Time	Amplified EEG (V)
0.01	−0.950942
0.02	1.701686
0.03	4.404364
0.04	1.301289
.....	....
13.33	2.50248
13.34	−4.504463

The ND/PD segmentation methods are combined and deployed in the first stage in order to accommodate EEG real-time analytical requirements. EEG caps normally consist of multi-channels for data collection. Therefore, EEG data is a multivariate distribution issue. The multivariate ND $f(z)$ is defined as follow.

$$f(z) = \frac{1}{(\sqrt{2\pi})^n \sigma_z} e^{-\frac{z^2}{2}}, \; z = \frac{x-\mu}{\sigma},$$
$$z^2 = \frac{(x_1-\mu_1)^2}{\sigma_1^2} + \frac{(x_2-\mu_2)^2}{\sigma_2^2} \cdots + \frac{(x_n-\mu_n)^2}{\sigma_n^2},$$
$$\sigma_z = \sigma_1 \sigma_2 \cdots \sigma_n \tag{6}$$

where μ is the mean or expectation of the distribution, σ is its standard deviation, $f(z)$ denotes multivariate distribution. The joint probability for a Multivariate Poisson distribution is a limiting distribution of binomial distribution $B(N, p_i)$ as $N \to \infty$ under the condition of N, $p_i = \lambda_t$ where λ_t is a non-negative fixed parameter.

The PD model in this paper adopts the Gamma function is employed for dealing with real and complex numbers, which is expressed as follows:

$$\Gamma(z) = \int_0^\infty \left[\ln\left(\frac{1}{t}\right) \right]^{z-1} dt \tag{7}$$

For a as integer n,

$$\Gamma(n, x) = (n - 1)! e^x \sum_{k=0}^{n-1} \frac{x^k}{k!} \tag{8}$$
$$= (n - 1)! e^{-x} e_{n-1}(x)$$

where $e_n(x)$ is the exponential sum function, which is implemented as Gamma[a, z] in the Wolfram Language.

The granular computing is an emerging concept and computing paradigm of information processing, covers all the theories, methods, technologies and tools related to granularity. It is mainly used for the intelligent processing of uncertain and incomplete fuzzy massive information. Some researchers have applied granular methods for data abstraction in order to reduce data volume. In this model, the optimal PLA method has been applied to reduce data volume and improve EEG recognition process for real-time processing. The optimal PLA computes $\underline{slp}[1, k]$ and $\overline{slp}[1, k]$ by using incremental and localization strategies, which can be expressed as follows[14]:

$$\begin{cases} \underline{slp}[1,k] = \max_{a \le i \le d} \left\{ \frac{(y_k - \delta) - (y_i + \delta)}{(x_k - x_i)}, \underline{slp}[1, k-1] \right\}, \\ \overline{slp}[1,k] = \min_{b \le i \le c} \left\{ \frac{(y_k + \delta) - (y_i - \delta)}{(x_k - x_i)}, \overline{slp}[1, k-1] \right\}. \end{cases} \tag{9}$$

where $slp[i, j]$ denotes the slope of a δ - representative line on time $slot[x_i, x_j]$. δ denotes the error bound for approximation (>0). (x_i, y_i) denotes at time slot x_i with value y_i.

The time complexity of Algorithm 1 is the sum of Aproiri time complexity and K-Means time complexity that is: $O(2^{|D|}) + O(n^2)$, where $|D|$ is the horizontal width (the total number of items) present in the data sets and n is the input data size. Equation 9 is the pre-processing phase for generating segmented EEG data sets for down stream processing, such as Algorithm 1 and other related procedures.

3.2   Combining K-means Clustering with Logistic Regression

The K-means clustering algorithm has been applied to the proposed model to generate the clusters that can distinguish the differences of various EEG instances. Table 2 shows the clustered EEG data instances based on K-means algorithm. The clustered instances are based on EEG data differentiation by time, i.e. the current EEG data point at time t minimizes the previous EEG data point at time $t - 0.01$.

The main goal of K-means clustering is to segment n observations into k ($\leq$ n) clusters. The distance within each cluster is minimized, which can expressed in the following Eq. (10) [15]. The K-means algorithm begins with initial K centroids, which can be randomly generated or selected from the data set.

$$\arg\min_{s} \sum_{i=1}^{k} \sum_{x \in S_i} \|x - \mu_i\|^2 = \arg\min_{s} \sum_{i=1}^{k} |S_i| VarS_i \tag{10}$$

where μ_i is the mean of points in S_i; S_i denotes a clustering set; x is a data item. The results are illustrated as below.

Table 2. Clustered EEG data based on K-means algorithm

Time	Amplified EEG (V)	Cluster
0.01	−6.506447	Cluster2
0.02	0.900892	Cluster0
0.03	6.806745	Cluster0
.....	....	....
14.09	−2.902877	Cluster3
14.10	2.001984	Cluster1

The clustering analysis can produce data sets according to centroids, which normally represents the average value of a cluster. We compare the EEG data sets collected from different EEG statuses using the clustering methods to distinguish the difference between different statuses. The clustering analysis is the initial step of EEG pattern analysis. The value distribution of centroids generates electrode recognizable and value bounded figures. The electrode recognizable figures meaning that independent electrodes have their recognizable electrode value change activities.

In order to further improve the SEGPA model efficiency; each node is assigned with pro-active and self-adaptive capability. We discovered that intelligent agents can efficiently fulfill the needs of the SEGPA model since multi-agent systems (MAS) promote the development of distributed applications in complex and dynamic environments to deal with complex problems [16]. The proposed new model aims combining MAS with SEGPA, which forms a multi-objective coordination model for brain research. Theoretically, the proposed model is efficient in terms of EEG data characteristic and brain activities.

4   Experimental Results

The experimental design and configuration are listed as follows. The collected EEG data instances are based on a 5–7 min online shopping simulation. The hardware and software configurations are: Windows 8 64-bit OS, Intel N3540 CPU, 4G RAM, C++ for ND segmentation software, Weka analytical software. The EEG recording time interval is 0.01 s for CONTEC KT88 used in this research. The lab environment and configurations are shown as below (Fig. 1).

Fig. 1. EEG lab settings and configuration.

Our online poll shows that 31.3% students would like to have some Artificial Intelligence (AI) related applications for assisting their studying. The poll further indicates that 65.4% students demand customized tutorials for their studies. The proposed EEG-based method could provide students with customized tutorials that can fulfill students' demands specially during the COVID19 period.

The LR classifier in the SEGPA model has a relatively high accuracy because of the efficient K-means clustering process. The clustering process actually replaces discretization process, which categorizes discrete EEG data in certain range. The clustering process in this paper generates simple cluster numbers as inputs for LR classifier, which improves the classification results and efficiency.

The prediction for electron 1 based on other electrons' EEG instances using LR classifier can achieve 97.3% accuracy. In this paper, we adopt one segment for experimental analysis. Mean absolute error is: 0.0174, total number of instances is: 1334. The classifier using 10 cross-validation mode can achieve 97.3% accuracy; the accuracy remains the same 97.3% accuracy through using training set mode.

Table 3 and 4 show the prediction for electron 1 and 5 based on electron 0–4 EEG instances using LR classifier can achieve 91.9% accuracy. Mean absolute error is: 0.0467, total number of instances is: 1334. The classifier using 10 cross-validation mode can achieve 91.9% accuracy; the accuracy can be improved to 92.12% through using training set mode.

Table 3. LR for electron 1 based on segmented EEG

TP rate	FP rate	Precision	Recall	MCC	Class
0.962	0.010	0.948	0.962	0.946	cluster0
0.925	0.003	0.984	0.925	0.947	cluster2
0.985	0.021	0.941	0.985	0.950	cluster1
0.979	0.001	0.997	0.979	0.984	cluster3
0.996	0.000	1.000	0.996	0.998	cluster4
0.973	0.008	0.974	0.973	0.966	Weighted Avg.

The segmentation software generated 15 segments for each electrode. The LR classifier for each segment require 0.5 s by using training set mode and 0.7 s by using cross-validation mode.

The results of PLA experiments are based on the full size of the original full driving simulation data since we are going to assess the overall PLA performance. In practice, this data sets can be replaced by ND/Poisson segmented data sets. The PLA compressed results are shown as below. Due to space limitation, we only illustrate the PLA results of 6 electrodes. The original driving simulation EEG data and full PLA compression and ND segmented results can be acquired upon requests.

Table 4. LR for electron 5 based on segmented EEG

TP rate	FP rate	Precision	Recall	MCC	Class
0.988	0.049	0.820	0.988	0.876	cluster0
0.549	0.005	0.949	0.549	0.689	cluster2
0.961	0.040	0.878	0.961	0.893	cluster1
0.997	0.007	0.979	0.997	0.984	cluster3
1.000	0.001	0.996	1.000	0.998	cluster4
0.919	0.021	0.925	0.919	0.901	Weighted Avg.

The optimized model based on the combination of ND/PD model and PLA process has achieved medium high accuracy performance and dramatic data reduction performance.

5 Conclusion

An optimized data analytical model has been introduced in this paper to identify statuses of brain activities and further discover potential patterns. The proposed model, the optimized SEGPA, incorporates optimized data processing methods and EEG-based analytical for EEG data analysis. In particular, the data segmentation techniques are incorporated in SEGPA model.

The experimental results show that EEG data sets can generate different results for 'meditation', 'meditating-left-hand-rise', 'meditating-right-hand-rise', 'left-hand-rise' and 'right-hand-rise'. Based on various results, we discovered some preliminary patterns for analysis. The future work will focus on delivering more efficient algorithm for EEG pattern generation and improve the EEG experimental data variety. The combination of the Association Rule algorithm with clustering K-Means algorithm has demonstrated the efficiency in reducing EEG data size by clustering and establishing connections among EEG electrons by association. The results evident the efficiency of the combination.

This research proposes a potentially efficient method for recognizing human brain activities that can be used for machinery control. The experimental results reveal the high classification accuracy that reflects the efficiency of the proposed model for EEG data analysis based on the optimized sampling methods. Our future work may seek the possibility of utilizing graph-based method in EEG pattern recognition.

Acknowledgement. This work is partially supported by Zhejiang Provincial Natural Science Fund (LY19 F030010), Zhejiang Provincial Social Science Fund (20NDJC216YB), Ningbo Natural Science Fund (No. 2019A610083), Ningbo Innovation Team (No.2016C11024) Ningbo Covid-19 and Education Special Fund (No.2020YQZX137), Zhejiang Provincial Education and Science Scheme 2020 (Post-COVID19 fund for education and recovery, special topic on AI and customized education in post-COVID19 education research) and National Natural Science Foundation of China Grant (No. 61872321).

References

1. Fiscon, G., et al.: Combining EEG signal processing with supervised methods for Alzheimer's patients classification. BMC Med. Inform. Decis. Mak. **18**, 35 (2018)
2. Amin, H.U., Mumtaz, W., Subhani, A.R., Saad, M., Malik, A.S.: Classification of EEG signals based on pattern recognition approach. Front. Comput. Neurosci. **11**, 103 (2017)
3. Zhang, H., Zhao, Q., Lee, S., Dowens, M.G.: EEG-based driver drowsiness detection using the dynamic time dependency method. In: Liang, P., Goel, V., Shan, C. (eds.) BI 2019. LNCS, vol. 11976. Springer, Cham (2019). https://doi.org/10.1007/978-3-030-37078-7_5
4. Lotte, F., et al.: A review of classification algorithms for EEG-based brain–computer interfaces: a 10 year update. J. Neural Eng. **15**(3), 1–28 (2018)
5. Grosse-Wentrup, M.: What are the causes of performance variation in brain–computer interfacing? Int. J. Bioelectromagn. **13**, 115–116 (2011)
6. Krusienski, D., et al.: Critical issues in state-of-the-art brain–computer interface signal processing. J. Neural Eng. **8**, 025002 (2011)

7. Mladenovic, J., Mattout, J., Lotte, F.: A generic framework for adaptive EEG-based BCI training. In: Nam, C., et al. (eds.) Operation Handbook of Brain-Computer Interfaces. Taylor & Francis, London (2017)

8. Lotte, F.: Signal processing approaches to minimize or suppress calibration time in oscillatory activity-based brain–computer interfaces. Proc. IEEE **103**, 871–890 (2015)

9. Schlögl, A., Vidaurre, C., Müller, K.R.: Adaptive methods in BCI research - an introductory tutorial. In: Graimann, B., Pfurtscheller, G., Allison, B. (eds.) Brain-Computer Interfaces. The Frontiers Collection. Springer, Heidelberg (2009). https://doi.org/10.1007/978-3-642-02091-9_18

10. Zhang, W., Ntoutsi, E.: FAHT: an adaptive fairness-aware decision tree classifier. In: Proceedings of IJCAI, pp. 1480–1486 (2019)

11. İşcan, Z., Nikulin, V.V.: Steady state visual evoked potential (SSVEP) based brain-computer interface (BCI) performance under different perturbations. PLOS ONE **13**(1), 0191673 (2018)

12. Zhang, H.L., Zhao, H., Cheung, Y., He, J.: Generating EEG graphs based on PLA for brain wave pattern recognition. In: IEEE Congress on Evolutionary Computation (CEC), pp. 1–7 (2018)

13. Zhang, H.L., Zhao, Y., Pang, C., He, J.: Splitting large medical data sets based on normal distribution in cloud environment. IEEE Trans. Cloud Comput. **8**(2), 518–531 (2020)

14. Xie, Q., Pang, C., Zhou, X., Zhang, X., Deng, K.: Maximum error-bounded piecewise linear representation for online stream approximation. VLDB J. **23**(6), 915–937 (2014)

15. Kriegel, H.-P., Schubert, E., Zimek, A.: The (black) art of runtime evaluation: are we comparing algorithms or implementations?. Knowl. Inf. Syst. **52**(2), 341–378 (2016)

16. Zhao, X., Chu, Y., Han, J., Zhang, Z.: SSVEP-based brain-computer interface controlled functional electrical simulation system for upper extremity rehabilitation. IEEE Trans. Syst. Man Cybern. Syst. **46**(7), 947–956 (2016)

17. Savit, R., Green, M.: Time series and dependent variables. Physica D **50**, 95–116 (1991)

Sequence Learning in Associative Neuronal-Astrocytic Networks

Leo Kozachkov and Konstantinos P. Michmizos[✉]

Computational Brain Lab, Department of Computer Science, Rutgers University,
New Brunswick, NJ 08544, USA
konstantinos.michmizos@cs.rutgers.edu
http://combra.cs.rutgers.edu

Abstract. The neuronal paradigm of studying the brain has left us with limitations in both our understanding of how neurons process information to achieve biological intelligence and how such knowledge may be translated into artificial intelligence and even its most brain-derived branch, neuromorphic computing. Overturning our assumptions of how the brain works, the recent exploration of astrocytes reveals how these long-neglected brain cells dynamically regulate learning by interacting with neuronal activity at the synaptic level. Following recent experimental studies, we designed an associative, Hopfield-type, neuronal-astrocytic network and analyzed the dynamics of the interaction between neurons and astrocytes. We show how astrocytes were sufficient to trigger transitions between learned memories in the network and derived the timing of these transitions based on the dynamics of the calcium-dependent slow-currents in the astrocytic processes. We further evaluated the proposed brain-morphic mechanism for sequence learning by emulating astrocytic atrophy. We show that memory recall became largely impaired after a critical point of affected astrocytes was reached. These results support our ongoing efforts to harness the computational power of non-neuronal elements for neuromorphic information processing.

Keywords: Associative networks · Astrocytes · Sequence learning

1 Introduction

Understanding intelligence is a fundamental goal in several disciplines. Translating the understanding of biological intelligence to machines is a fundamental problem in Computing [39]. The breadth of solutions now offered by deep learning has established the connectionist modeling of neural computation [22] as the most faithful representation of the brain's intelligence. Yet, despite their impressive performance, neural nets are challenged by their intrinsic limitations in real-world applications [25] related to their computational and energy efficiency and input variability [33,44]—tasks that brain networks are well-suited to execute by being radically different from the deep learning networks [30].

© Springer Nature Switzerland AG 2020
M. Mahmud et al. (Eds.): BI 2020, LNAI 12241, pp. 349–360, 2020.
https://doi.org/10.1007/978-3-030-59277-6_32

Neural connectionist algorithms are better fit for large-scale neuromorphic chips [9,13] that are designed to run spiking neural networks (SNN), where asynchronous computing units are emulated as spiking neurons and memory is distributed in the synapses [21]. Indeed, by following a more faithful representation of the brain's computational principles, we and others have used this non-Von Neumann architecture to introduce robustness to SNN [35,37], and SNN to robots [5] as energy-efficient [36] and highly accurate [34] controllers. The main criticism to neuromorphic solutions is that, in the absence of fundamental algorithmic contributions, these promising results do not currently share the same scaling abilities with the mainstream deep learning approaches. To address this point, one alternative is to further pursue their biological plausibility by introducing new brain principles currently under study at the forefront of neuroscience [31].

With neurons long-monopolizing brain research, many are surprised to learn that up to 90% of brain cells are not neurons, but are instead glial cells. The impressive empirical evidence of the importance of non-neuronal cells, particularly astrocytes, in all facets of cognitive processes [41], including learning and memory [1,16], is shaping a paradigm shift where brain function is now seen as a phenomenon emerging from the interaction between neurons and astrocytes [3]. This also opens prospects for establishing new connections between biological and artificial intelligence (AI) at the cellular, the most fundamental level of computing. Astrocytes receive input *from* neurons and also provide input *to* them. They do so by using their processes that extend from their somas and reach thousands nearby synapses [15,28], which are named *tripartite synapses* [2]. The main astrocytic signaling mechanism is the wave-like elevation of their Ca^{2+} concentration [4]. Astrocytes propagate these mysterious Ca^{2+} waves within themselves with individual astrocyte processes responding to pre-synaptic input with an elevation in their internal Ca^{2+} levels [4]. Interestingly, this neuronal-astrocytic interaction is dynamic and plastic, although little is known about the exact form of this plasticity [27,38]. Although the timescale of astrocyte Ca^{2+} excitability was believed to be on the order of seconds to hours, recent experiments have found a faster astrocytic response to synaptic activity—on the order of hundreds of milliseconds, taking place at the astrocytic process [20], reinforced by our computational speculations [29] on the role of these "fast" Ca^{2+} signals.

The leading hypothesis about learning is that memories are stored as modifiable connection strengths between neurons [17]. A computationally elegant model of memory, the Hopfield network, incorporates the above features to perform autoassociation: the tag to retrieve a network state is a corrupted version of the state itself [6]. Learning in a Hopfield network [18] means creating new attractors in the configuration space of the system, so that the system dynamically relaxes towards the nearest stored memory with respect to the current configuration, and stays there indefinitely. This model has been used to explain neuronal dynamics in several brain regions, including persistent activity in the cortex [8,43] and path integration in the hippocampus [23]. A challenge for Hopfield-type neural networks is explaining the origin of temporal sequences:

How can a network retrieve a given sequence of memories? Hopfield himself proposed a modification to his original model which allowed for the recall of temporal sequences by using an asymmetric synaptic weight matrix [18]. However, this method suffered from instabilities and was difficult to control. Sompolinsky et al. [32], independently and in parallel with Kleinfeld [19], showed that this scheme could be made robustly stable by the introduction of "slow-synapses" — synapses which compute a weighted average of the pre-synaptic neuron state.

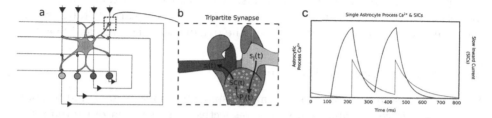

Fig. 1. a) An astrocyte ensheathing a fully-connected recurrent neuronal network with no self-connections (N = 4). Large colored circles: neurons; small colored circles: synapses, with the color corresponding to the color of the afferent neuron; b) The tripartite synapse, where a presynaptic activity $s_j(t)$ drove the astrocytic process state $P_j(t)$ which triggered the SC signal injected into the postsynaptic neuron; c) The dynamics of the local Ca^{2+} wave (blue) which rose in response to presynaptic activity and the related SIC (green) injected into postsynaptic neurons. The y-axes are in a.u. (Color figure online)

Here, we present a theoretical abstraction of the astrocytic response to neuronal activity, analyze the associated dynamics of the neuron-astrocyte interaction, and derive a neuromorphic framework for sequence learning. Specifically, we propose a Hopfield-type recurrent neuronal-astrocytic network (NAN), where each synapse is enseathed by an astrocytic process (Fig. 1a, b). The network used its neuronal component to learn distinct memories and its astrocytic component to transition between the stored memories. We also suggest a Hebbian-type astrocytic mechanism to learn the transition between stored memories, upon triggering the network state changes. We validated our model by studying its performance as a function of astrocytic atrophy, following studies on cognition-impairing diseases [40]. Interestingly, we found a strong correlation between the level of atrophy and the error in the network's ability to recall a sequence, in agreement with studies on cognitive impairment.

2 Methods

2.1 Neurophysiological Background

Astrocytes share the same mechanisms with neurons as they, too, modulate the flux of ions into and out of the neurons. The current injected into the neurons can be positive or negative–denoted slow-inward current (SIC) and slow-outward current (SOC), respectively [26]. SICs appear to be released into postsynaptic neurons when the Ca^{2+} level inside the astrocyte reaches a certain threshold from below [42]. SOCs seem to follow a similar time-course to SICs [24]. Here, we present a biophysically plausible model of how astrocytes may employ the SICs and SOCs to enable the transition between memories in a network. We also propose a Hebbian-type learning rule between the astrocyte and the post-synaptic neuron, which formalizes the notion of astrocyte-neuron plasticity [38]. Incorporating the recently discovered "fast" Ca^{2+} astrocytic signals, our memory model used astrocytes to trigger the transitions between learned states, where the transitions' timing was governed by the dynamics of the SICs and SOCs.

2.2   Deriving Network Dynamics

We modeled neurons as zero-temperature, spin-glass units, with 1 and 0 representing the active and quiescent states, respectively. The output of neuron i was aligned with the local field, h_i:

$$s_i(t+1) = sgn(h_i(t)). \tag{1}$$

We expanded h_i to include the effects of astrocyte-mediated post-synaptic SICs and SOCs:

$$h_i(t) = h_i(t)^{neural} + h_i(t)^{astro}, \tag{2}$$

$$h_i(t)^{neural} = \sum_{j=1}^{N} J_{ij}s_j(t), \tag{3}$$

$$h_i(t)^{astro} = \sum_{j=1}^{N} T_{ij}SC_j(t), \tag{4}$$

where N was the number of neurons, J_{ij} was the stabilizing, symmetric matrix, and T_{ij} was the matrix of amplitudes for the astrocyte-mediated slow-currents (SCs), either a SIC or a SOC. All N^2 synapses were tripartite synapses. Since all the processes that take neuron i as its input were synchronized, the vector of SCs was of size N^2/N. Let ξ_i^{μ} denote the activity of neuron i during memory μ, and m denote the number of memories stored in the network. Then

$$J_{ij} = \frac{1}{N} \sum_{\mu}^{m} (2\xi_i^{\mu} - 1)(2\xi_j^{\mu} - 1), i \neq j, \tag{5}$$

$$T_{ij} = \frac{\lambda}{N} \sum_{\mu}^{q} (2\xi_i^{\mu+1} - 1)(2\xi_j^{\mu} - 1), i \neq j, \tag{6}$$

where $q < m$, the $\xi_i^{\mu+1}\xi_j^{\mu}$ terms define the sequence of memories, and λ controls the relative strength between the two matrices. We set al.l diagonal elements of both matrices to zero, not allowing self-connections. Following experimental evidence [24], the SCs exponentially decayed after a rapid rise time (Fig. 1c):

$$SC = e^{\frac{t-\delta_{cal}}{\tau_{SC}}},\tag{7}$$

where δ_{cal} is the time at which the astrocyte Ca^{2+} reached the SC-release threshold, c_{thresh}. We propose a minimal model for Ca^{2+} level in the process, P_j, where the time evolution of P_j depended linearly on the activity of the presynaptic neuron s_j and the previous state. Dropping the j subscript, an astrocyte process activity at time $t+1$ is given by:

$$P_{t+1} = \alpha P_t + \beta s_t, \text{ where } 0 \leq \alpha < 1.\tag{8}$$

2.3   Modeling the Effects of Astrocytic Atrophy to Memory Recall

To evaluate our model, we randomly selected a percentage (from 0 to 100%) of astrocytic processes that were atrophied and for each selected process, we introduced a gain (from 0 to 1, representing high and no atrophy, respectively). We validated the network performance as follows: for an ordered sequence of q memories, the performance error was the number of times a memory did not appear in its appropriate spot, divided by the number of possible errors (to ensure the error is between 0 and 1). We excluded the first memory from the evaluation, as it did not depend on the astrocyte dynamics.

3   Results

3.1   Deriving Transition Times and Stability

Equation 8 is solved in terms of s_t, α and β by defining the operator $\hat{L}$ such that

$$\hat{L}P_t \equiv P_{t-1}$$

$$\hat{L}^2 P_t \equiv P_{t-2}$$

We can then arrive at an expression for P_t:

$$P_t = \frac{\beta s_t}{1 - \alpha \hat{L}} = \beta \sum_{t'=0}^{\infty} (\alpha \hat{L})^{t'} s_t = \beta \sum_{t'=0}^{\infty} \alpha^{t'} s_{t-t'}$$

We can now derive the time it takes for the Ca^{2+} to reach the SC-release threshold, which in turn determines the duration a network spends in a quasi-attractor (τ) (Fig. 2). The analysis is simplified in the continuous limit:

$$\frac{c_{thresh}}{\beta} = \int_0^{\tau} \alpha^{\tau-'t}dt',\tag{9}$$

which has the general solution:

$$\tau = \frac{ln(\frac{c_{thresh}}{\beta}ln(\alpha) + 1)}{ln(\alpha)}. \tag{10}$$

Though the choice of β and c_{thresh} are arbitrary (for $\tau > 0$ and $0 < c_{thresh} < 1$), if we assume that $\beta\alpha^t$ is normalized to unity, the expression becomes:

$$\tau = \frac{ln(1 - c_{thresh})}{ln(\alpha)}. \tag{11}$$

The biological interpretation of the normalization $\beta = ln(\frac{1}{\alpha})$ is that the more the astrocyte process depends on its own Ca^{2+} level, the less it depends on the presynaptic neuronal activity.

We can now examine the dynamics of the network in detail. The analysis is simplified by switching to the $s_i = \pm 1$ neuronal representation, which is related to the $s_i = 0, 1$ representation by the transformation $2s_i - 1$. Let at time $t = 0$ the network enter into the attractor for memory ξ^1. The Ca^{2+} thresholds have not been hit (i.e. $SC_j(t) = 0$ for all j). The total field felt by neuron i is:

$$h_i(t) = \sum_{j=1}^{N} J_{ij}\xi_i^1 = \xi_i^1 + noise. \tag{12}$$

If we assume low loading ($p \ll N$), the noise term vanishes. This field persists until $t = \tau$, the time at which c_{thresh} is reached by the active astrocyte processes. Now the field becomes:

$$h_i(t) = \frac{1}{N}\sum_{\mu=1}^{m}\xi_i^\mu\xi_j^\mu\xi_j^1 + \frac{\lambda}{N}\sum_{\mu=1}^{q}\xi_i^{\mu+1}\xi_j^\mu SC_j(t). \tag{13}$$

Since the SCs are only released from an astrocyte process if the neuron has been in the active state for $0 < t < \tau$, the vector of SCs at $t = \tau$ is equal to the vector of neuron states when $0 < t < \tau$. In other words, we identify $SC_j(t) = \xi_j^1$, which permits the simplification

$$h_i(t) = \xi_i^1 + \lambda\xi_i^2. \tag{14}$$

In the zero noise limit, the neurons will align with memory ξ^2. The field persists until $t = 2\tau$, when the next transition is precipitated by the astrocyte (Fig. 2).

3.2   Model Generality

The results are insensitive to the choice of response function for Ca^{2+}, so long as the Ca^{2+} crosses the threshold periodically. It is interesting to consider cases when τ is time-dependent, since simulations of biophysically-detailed Ca^{2+} response [14] suggest that astrocytes can perform frequency modulation (FM)

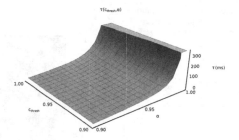

Fig. 2. The derived time the network spends in each quasi-attractor τ, as a function of α and c_{thresh}.

and amplitude modulation (AFM) encoding of synaptic information. Let us consider the case of a frequency modulated sinusoid:

$$y(t) = cos(\omega(t)t)$$

and its first time derivative

$$\frac{dy}{dt} = [\frac{d\omega}{dt}t + \omega(t)]sin(\omega(t)t).$$

To solve for τ, we attempt to solve for t such that: $y(t_{thresh}) = 0$ and $\frac{dy}{dt}|_{t_{thresh}} > 0$. We assume that SC-threshold equals zero without loss of generality and that the SC-threshold must be reached for glio-transmission. For example, if $\omega(t) = w_0 t$, then the time between the nth SC-threshold crossings can be written as:

$$\tau_n = \sqrt{\frac{\pi}{2\omega_0}}(\sqrt{4n+1} - \sqrt{4n-3})$$

which, for large n, approximately equals $\sqrt{\frac{\pi}{2\omega_0 n}}$. Note that τ_n tends to zero for large n, as expected when the frequency tends to infinity.

3.3 Astrocytic Learning

For learning, we propose a Hebbian-type mechanism by which the NAN could arrive at the correct form of the matrix T. Assume that at $t = 0$ the network is presented a pattern, ξ^μ, until some later time $t = t_{switch}$ when the network is presented $\xi^{\mu+1}$. If $t_{switch} \gg 0$, the astrocyte process which takes neuron i as its input will be very nearly equal to ξ^μ. At $t = t_{switch}$, the astrocyte process correlates its current state with the state of the post-synaptic neuron and adjusts the levels of future gliotransmitter release accordingly—changing the sign and amplitude of future SC release (Fig. 3a). This can be expressed as

$$\Delta T_{ij} = \eta s_i(t_{switch})P_j(t_{switch}) = \eta s_i(t_{switch})s_j(0) = \eta \xi_i^{\mu+1}\xi_i^\mu, \qquad (15)$$

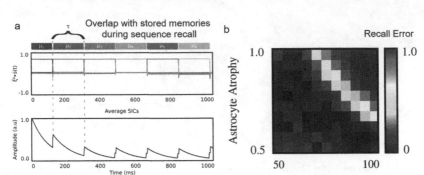

Fig. 3. a) (Up) Overlap of the neuronal network state with the stored memories (N = 500, p = 7, q = 6). (Down) Average SCs injected into the post-synaptic neurons; b) Network performance as a function of increasing astrocytic atrophy. As the fraction of affected astrocytes (x-axis) and the degree of atrophy (y-axis) increase, the sequence recall error increases. The recall errors are averaged over 50 trials per (x, y) point.

which yields the T-matrix above (assuming $\eta = 1$ and the sequence is presented to the network exactly one time), in the $s_i = \pm 1$ representation. Notably, this mechanism requires retrograde signaling between the post-synaptic neuron and astrocyte process, which is known to occur through endocannabinoid mediated pathways [11].

3.4   Memory Retrieval Robustness to Astrocytic Impairment

The degree of a cognitive impairment depended strongly on the degree of astrocytic atrophy (Fig. 3b), in agreement with experimental data [3, 7, 40]. This result can be understood on the basis of stability arguments. Atrophying the astrocyte SC signal is equivalent to decreasing λ. Thereby, increasing the effective λ below 1 at a given neuron will make that neuron unstable. After a critical point of unstable neurons was reached, the network error rapidly increased to 1.

4   Discussion

Here, we presented a Hopfield-type NAN and derived the dynamics of the interactions between neurons and astrocytes to effectively transition between memories. Building from the bottom-up, our model was inspired by the last decade of memory-related glial research and the studies on the fast signaling taking place between astrocytes and neurons; it was also qualitatively evaluated by studies on memory impairment. We demonstrated how astrocytes were sufficient to trigger transitions between stored memories. By injecting a "fast" Ca^{2+} triggered current in the postsynaptic neuron, astrocytes modulated the neuronal activity into predictable patterns across time, sharpening a particular input and, thereby, recalling a learned memory sequence. This ability of astrocytes to modulate neuronal excitability and synaptic strength can have several implications, both theoretical and practical, for neuromorphic algorithms.

On the theory side, Sompolinsky et al. showed mathematically that the introduction of "slow-synapses"—synapses that perform a running average of presynaptic input using a weighting function $w(t - \tau)$ would stabilize the sequence of memories [32]. The authors were able to show this quite generally, placing only a few requirements on the choice of $w(t - \tau)$. Here, we showed how the time delay, τ, could emerge naturally out of the reported dynamics of Ca^{2+} dependent gliotransmission. Formally, the dynamics of our biomimetic approach are mathematically equivalent to the case where: $w(t - \tau) = \delta(t - \tau)$, where $\delta(t)$ is the delta function. Interestingly, these results demonstrate how biologically plausible models of recently identified cellular processes may provide a mechanistic explanation for theoretical analyses conducted at the network scale, decades ago. Previous astrocyte modelling efforts have focused primarily on reproducing the Ca^{2+} response of astrocytes by numerically solving systems of coupled differential equations, where each equation determines the time evolution of an organelle believed to be important for the mechanism of Ca^{2+} oscillation, such as ATP or IP3. While crucial for our understanding of astrocytic Ca2+, these studies typically shy away from proposing and modelling actual computational roles for astrocytic function. A notable exception is from Wade et al. [42], who showed that astrocyte oscillations can induce synchrony in unconnected neurons, using the same mechanism of Ca2+ dependent gliotransmission as our study. De Pittà et al. [10] also explored the role of astrocyte Ca^{2+} oscillations in long term potentiation (LTP) and long term depression (LTD), two phenomena known to play a key role in brain computation and learning. While previous efforts on fleshing out mechanisms known to be involved in brain computation, our work presents an end-to-end solution, an associative network that uses astrocytic mechanisms to perform a function, sequence memory recall.

On the applications side, by enabling the most faithful representation of neurons, networks and brain systems, neuromorphic computing allows for studies that not necessarily follow a mainstream machine learning direction [35]. NAN on neuromorphic chips may be used to study hypotheses on astrocytes failing to perform their critical synaptic functions, as we did here. For instance, mounting evidence suggests that astrocytes change the strength of their connections in learning [12]. We speculate that the astrocytic training does not only encompass learning the correct sequence of memories, but also the time spent in each memory for a given sequence. This is biologically faithful, as the amount of time spent in each memory (e.g. the duration of a note when humming a melody) is crucial for correctly recalling a learned sequence. In the framework of our model, this can be achieved by dynamically modifying τ–which in turn is controlled by the SC-release threshold and the astrocytic sensitivity to pre-synaptic activity. Learning is at the core of neuromorphic computing. By reproducing the functional organization of NAN, as well as the dynamics of astrocytic Ca^{2+} activity and astrocyte-neuron interactions, we suggest a learning role for astrocytes operating on temporal and spatial scales that are larger than the ones of neurons. The underlying mechanisms of having parallel processing on different temporal and spatial scales is an open question in brain science, but it is already considered as a computational method that increases the processing efficiency of a system: Our work tackles this problem by combining millisecond-scale neuronal activity with the comparatively slow Ca^{2+} activity of astrocytes.

Most of the neuroscience knowledge accumulated over the past couple decades has yet to be funnelled in AI. Being shadowed by the wide applications of neural nets, we might not appreciate that the mounting knowledge on the biological principles of intelligence is partially harnessed on the computational side. Can we establish new push-pull dynamics between newly identified biological principles of intelligence and the computational primitives used to build our artificial models of brain computation? To explore this fascinating possibility, our work couples computational modeling and neuromorphic computing to introduce to neurocomputing a long-neglected non-neuronal cell, astrocytes, which are now placed alongside neurons, as key cells for learning. The further scaling of the astrocytic roles will support real-world neuromorphic applications, where astrocytes will be able to mine intrinsically noisy data, by virtue of their low spatial and temporal resolution. Drawing from newly identified primitives of biological intelligence, the results presented here suggest that the addition of astrocytes as a second processing unit to neuromorphic chips is a direction worth pursuing.

References

1. Adamsky, A., Kol, A., Kreisel, T., et al.: Astrocytic activation generates de novo neuronal potentiation and memory enhancement. Cell **174**(1), 59–71 (2018)
2. Araque, A., Parpura, V., Sanzgiri, R.P., Haydon, P.G.: Tripartite synapses: glia, the unacknowledged partner. Trends Neurosci. **22**(5), 208–215 (1999)
3. Barres, B.A.: The mystery and magic of glia: a perspective on their roles in health and disease. Neuron **60**(3), 430–440 (2008)
4. Bazargani, N., Attwell, D.: Astrocyte calcium signaling: the third wave. Nat. Neurosci. **19**(2), 182–189 (2016)
5. Blum, H., Dietmüller, A., et al.: A neuromorphic controller for a robotic vehicle equipped with a dynamic vision sensor. In: Robotics: Science and Systems (2018)
6. Chaudhuri, R., Fiete, I.: Computational principles of memory. Nat. Neurosci. **19**(3), 394–403 (2016)
7. Chung, W.S., Welsh, C.A., Barres, B.A., Stevens, B.: Do glia drive synaptic and cognitive impairment in disease? Nat. Neurosci. **18**(11), 1539–1545 (2015)
8. Cossart, R., Aronov, D., Yuste, R.: Attractor dynamics of network up states in the neocortex. Nature **423**(6937), 283–288 (2003)
9. Davies, M., Srinivasa, N., Lin, T.H., Chinya, G., et al.: Loihi: a neuromorphic manycore processor with on-chip learning. IEEE Micro **38**(1), 82–99 (2018)
10. De Pittà, M., Brunel, N., Volterra, A.: Astrocytes: orchestrating synaptic plasticity? Neuroscience **323**, 43–61 (2016)
11. Fellin, T., Pascual, O., et al.: Neuronal synchrony mediated by astrocytic glutamate through activation of extrasynaptic NMDA receptors. Neuron **43**(5), 729–743 (2004)
12. Fields, R.D., Araque, A., Johansen-Berg, H., Lim, S.S., Lynch, G., et al.: Glial biology in learning and cognition. Neuroscientist **20**(5), 426–431 (2014)

13. Furber, S.B., Galluppi, F., Temple, S., Plana, L.A.: The spinnaker project. Proc. IEEE **102**(5), 652–665 (2014)
14. Goldberg, M., De Pittà, M., et al.: Nonlinear gap junctions enable long-distance propagation of pulsating calcium waves in astrocyte networks. PLoS Comput. Biol. **6**(8), e1000909 (2010)
15. Halassa, M.M., Fellin, T., Takano, H., et al.: Synaptic Islands defined by the territory of a single astrocyte. J. Neurosci. **27**(24), 6473–6477 (2007)
16. Han, X., et al.: Forebrain engraftment by human glial progenitor cells enhances synaptic plasticity and learning in adult mice. Cell Stem Cell **12**(3), 342–353 (2013)
17. Hebb, D.O.: The Organization of Behavior: A Neuropsychological Theory. Psychology Press (2005)
18. Hopfield, J.J.: Neural networks and physical systems with emergent collective computational abilities. PNAS **79**(8), 2554–2558 (1982)
19. Kleinfeld, D., Sompolinsky, H.: Associative neural network model for the generation of temporal patterns. Theory and application to central pattern generators. Biophys. J. **54**(6), 1039–1051 (1988)
20. Lind, B.L., et al.: Rapid stimulus-evoked astrocyte Ca2+ elevations and hemodynamic responses in mouse somatosensory cortex in vivo. PNAS **110**(48), E4678–E4687 (2013)
21. Maass, W.: Networks of spiking neurons: the third generation of neural network models. Neural Netw. **10**(9), 1659–1671 (1997)
22. McCulloch, W.S., Pitts, W.: A logical calculus of the ideas immanent in nervous activity. Bull. Math. Biophys. **5**(4), 115–133 (1943). https://doi.org/10.1007/BF02478259
23. McNaughton, B.L., Battaglia, F.P., et al.: Path integration and the neural basis of the 'cognitive map'. Nat. Rev. Neurosci. **7**(8), 663–678 (2006)
24. Pál, B.: Astrocytic actions on extrasynaptic neuronal currents. Front. Cell. Neurosci. **9**, 474 (2015)
25. Papernot, N., McDaniel, P., Jha, S., et al.: The limitations of deep learning in adversarial settings. In: IEEE EuroS&P, pp. 372–387. IEEE (2016)
26. Parpura, V., Haydon, P.G.: Physiological astrocytic calcium levels stimulate glutamate release to modulate adjacent neurons. PNAS **97**(15), 8629–8634 (2000)
27. Polykretis, I., Ivanov, V., Michmizos, K.P.: The astrocytic microdomain as a generative mechanism for local plasticity. In: Wang, S., et al. (eds.) BI 2018. LNCS (LNAI), vol. 11309, pp. 153–162. Springer, Cham (2018). https://doi.org/10.1007/978-3-030-05587-5_15
28. Polykretis, I., Ivanov, V., Michmizos, K.P.: A neural-astrocytic network architecture: astrocytic calcium waves modulate synchronous neuronal activity. In: ACM Proceedings of 2018 ICONS, pp. 1–8 (2018)
29. Polykretis, I.E., Ivanov, V.A., Michmizos, K.P.: Computational astrocyence: astrocytes encode inhibitory activity into the frequency and spatial extent of their calcium elevations. In: 2019 IEEE EMBS BHI, pp. 1–4. IEEE (2019)
30. Rosenfeld, A., Zemel, R., Tsotsos, J.K.: The elephant in the room. arXiv preprint arXiv:1808.03305 (2018)
31. Sejnowski, T.J., Churchland, P.S., Movshon, J.A.: Putting big data to good use in neuroscience. Nat. Neurosci. **17**(11), 1440 (2014)
32. Sompolinsky, H., Kanter, I.: Temporal association in asymmetric neural networks. Phys. Rev. Lett. **57**(22), 2861 (1986)
33. Su, J., Vargas, D.V., Sakurai, K.: One pixel attack for fooling deep neural networks. IEEE Trans. Evol. Comput. **23**(5), 828–841 (2019)

34. Tang, G., Kumar, N., Michmizos, K.P.: Reinforcement co-learning of deep and spiking neural networks for energy-efficient mapless navigation with neuromorphic hardware. In: IEEE/RSJ International Conference on Intelligent Robots and Systems (IROS), pp. 1–8 (2020)
35. Tang, G., Polykretis, I.E., Ivanov, V.A., Shah, A., Michmizos, K.P.: Introducing astrocytes on a neuromorphic processor: synchronization, local plasticity and edge of chaos. In: ACM Proceedings of 2019 NICE, vol. 1, no. 1, pp. 1–10 (2019)
36. Tang, G., Shah, A., Michmizos, K.P.: Spiking neural network on neuromorphic hardware for energy-efficient unidimensional slam. In: IEEE/RSJ International Conference on Intelligent Robots and Systems (IROS), pp. 4176–81 (2019)
37. Tavanaei, A., Ghodrati, M., Kheradpisheh, S.R., Masquelier, T., Maida, A.: Deep learning in spiking neural networks. Neural Netw. **111**, 47–63 (2018)
38. Theodosis, D.T., et al.: Activity-dependent structural and functional plasticity of astrocyte-neuron interactions. Physiol. Rev. **88**(3), 983–1008 (2008)
39. Turing, A.M.: Intelligent machinery, a heretical theory. In: The Turing Test: Verbal Behavior as the Hallmark of Intelligence, vol. 105 (1948)
40. Verkhratsky, A., Olabarria, M., Noristani, H.N., Yeh, C.Y., Rodriguez, J.J.: Astrocytes in Alzheimer's disease. Neurotherapeutics **7**(4), 399–412 (2010)
41. Volterra, A., Meldolesi, J.: Astrocytes, from brain glue to communication elements: the revolution continues. Nat. Rev. Neurosci. **6**(8), 626 (2005)
42. Wade, J.J., McDaid, L.J., Harkin, J., Crunelli, V., Kelso, J.S.: Bidirectional coupling between astrocytes and neurons mediates learning and dynamic coordination in the brain: a multiple modeling approach. PLoS ONE **6**(12), e29445 (2011)
43. Wimmer, K., Nykamp, D.Q., Constantinidis, C., Compte, A.: Bump attractor dynamics in prefrontal cortex explains behavioral precision in spatial working memory. Nat. Neurosci. **17**(3), 431–439 (2014)
44. Zhang, C., Bengio, S., Hardt, M., Recht, B., Vinyals, O.: Understanding deep learning requires rethinking generalization. arXiv preprint arXiv:1611.03530 (2016)

EEG Based Sleep-Wake Classification Using JOPS Algorithm

Abdullah Al-Mamun Bulbul[1,2] , Md. Abdul Awal[2(✉)] ,
and Kumar Debjit[3]

[1] Department of Electronics and Telecommunication Engineering (ETE),
Bangabandhu Sheikh Mujibur Rahman Science and Technology University,
Gopalganj 8100, Bangladesh
bulbulmamun@yahoo.com
[2] Electronics and Communication Engineering Discipline, Khulna University,
Khulna 9208, Bangladesh
m.awal@ece.ku.ac.bd
[3] Faculty of Health, Engineering and Sciences, University of Southern
Queensland, Toowoomba, Australia
debjit_l@live.com

Abstract. Classification of sleep-wake is necessary for the diagnosis and treatment of sleep disorders, and EEG is normally used to assess sleep quality. Manual scoring is time-consuming and requires a sleep expert. Therefore, automatic sleep classification is essential. To accomplish this, features are extracted from the time domain, frequency domain, wavelet domain, and also from non-linear dynamics. In this study, a novel Jaya Optimization based hyper-Parameter and feature Selection (JOPS) algorithm is proposed to select optimal feature subset as well as hyper-parameters of the classifier such as KNN and SVM, simultaneously. JOPS is self-adaptive that automatically adapts to the population size. The proposed JPOS yielded the accuracy of 94.99% and 94.85% using KNN and SVM, respectively. JPOS algorithm is compared with genetic algorithm and differential evaluation-based feature selection algorithm. Finally, a decision support system is created to graphically visualize the sleep-wake state which will be beneficial to clinical staffs. Furthermore, the proposed JOPS can not only be used in sleep-wake classification but could be applied in other classification problems.

Keywords: Sleep-Wake cycle · Hyper-parameter tuning · Feature Selection · JOPS algorithm · Classification · Decision Support System

1 Introduction

Sleep is considered one of the vigorous physiological activities as it is responsible for the optimum functioning of the human body. Sleep helps the brain to string preceding experiences, zenith individuals' memories, and cause the relief of hormones controlling

---

A. A.-M. Bulbul and M. Abdul Awal—Equal Contributions.

M. Mahmud et al. (Eds.): BI 2020, LNAI 12241, pp. 361–371, 2020.
https://doi.org/10.1007/978-3-030-59277-6_33

spirit, attitude, and mental sharpness and temper. Besides, sleep assists in alleviating, soothing, and overhauling blood veins, the artery, and the heart of the human body. These types of assistance indirectly reduce the chance of kidney failure, diabetes, intensive blood-pressure, heart attack, and other diseases. Healthy sleep plays a vital role in reducing the possibility of obesity as it controls the ghrelin and leptin hormone regulating the appetite or full, respectively [1]. The deficiency of sleep causes a high level of ghrelin that makes individuals feel more appetite. Sound sleep advantages the individuals with the equilibrium in the regulation and generation of hormones to sustain a healthy life. To cope with the technological growth of modern life, people have to live a hectic life which causes acute disturbance in normal sleep structure. As a consequence, numerous neural, psychological, and behavioral ailments are widely present among people [2]. A number of 84 distinct sleep disorders (SDs) are present among people [3]. These are the prime cause for both short term and long-term effects on daily life including hypertension, difficulty concentrating, amnesia, etc. [4]. According to a study on more than six thousand people, impoliteness, degraded performance, and rudeness are present among people suffering from SD [5]. Hence sleep staging and analysis carry a high level of significance.

Conventional polysomnography (PSG) signals are used to analyze the sleep stage. Though this method is termed as the '*gold standard*', it is a complicated method as it requires multiple biomedical signals namely EEG, EMG, EOG, blood oxygenation, etc. [6]. Experts visualize these signals to diagnose sleep structure. This type of manual evaluation is tiresome, time prolonging, laborious, and highly susceptible to error [7]. It takes higher critical form in developing countries such as Bangladesh since these countries suffer from the crisis of expert diagnosticians and analysts. Contrariwise, automatic evaluation of the sleep stage will not only reduce the workload of the physician but also reduce time consumption maintaining a higher accuracy level. In cooperation with signal processing and artificial intelligence, machine learning algorithms may be practiced to carry out an automatic evaluation of sleep scoring and staging simultaneously. Both single-channel (SC) and multi-channel (MC) EEGs can be used in this respect. While providing exclusive results, MC-EEGs create diverse complexities. In addition, MC-EEGs are very expensive. On the other hand, SC-EEG is not only simpler and fast but also inexpensive compared to MC-EEGs.

Numerous researches have been carried out using SC-EEG signals to achieve automatic sleep scoring and staging. In [7], an automatic sleep staging has been proposed that used the Complete Ensemble Empirical Mode Decomposition with Adaptive Noise (CEEMDAN) on SC-EEG signals which is followed by multiple probabilistically features computation using modes functions. Extracting numerous features, namely linear statistical error energy, mean, variance, kurtosis, and skewness, the method achieved 86.89% accuracy in 6-class sleep staging using partial least squares (PLS) algorithm and Adaptive Boosting (Ada-Boost). A similar type of method has been proposed in [8] where Empirical Mode Decomposition (EMD) has been practiced to extract features. These extracted features are then fed to eleven different classifiers i.e., Naive Bayes, random forest (RF), support vector machine (SVM), neural network (NN), discriminant analysis (DA), SV-DA, least-square-SVM (LSSVM), etc., to carry out automatic sleep staging. The proposed method exhibited 90.38% accuracy in 6-class sleep staging. In [9], another automatic sleep staging method has been proposed using the entropy-based features. The method attained about 80% accuracy. An SC-EEG based sleep staging model has been proposed in [10], where features are extracted using multi-scale convolutional-NN (CNN). After feature extraction, recurrent NN (RNN) and conditional RF (CRF) are introduced to attain the contextual information among consecutive epochs. This contextual information takes part in concluding the type of sleep stage and thereby the method achieved about 81 to 88% accuracy on different sleep data. In [11], an automatic SC-EEG based sleep staging method has been presented which captures features using relevance and redundancy-based feature selection (FS) method. Then RF classifier has been applied to the features which is followed by the application of Hidden Markov Model (HMM) to minimize false positives via the integration of the information of the temporal formation of shifts among different sleep stages. The proposed method attained about 79.4 to 87.4% accuracy for 6-class sleep staging.

Stirred from the above studies, the SC-EEG signal is taken for the analysis and automatic classification of sleep staging in this paper. We have extracted numerous features, namely the time domain (TD), frequency domain (FD), and time-frequency domain (wavelet) features as well as the entropy-based features. Then the highly discriminant features are selected as well as the values of classifier hyper-parameters are evaluated at the same time by applying the proposed Jaya Optimization based hyper-Parameter and feature Selection (JOPS) algorithm. The JOPS algorithm is not only easier to understand than nature-inspired algorithms such as genetic algorithm. Moreover, nature-inspired algorithms have algorithm-specific parameters that need to be tuned for better performance other than the common parameters like population size and maximum iterations. For example, genetic algorithm (GA) tunes the cross-over probability, mutation probability, selection operator for optimization [12]. Thereby, the JOPS algorithm avoids the necessity of separate classifier hyper-parameter selection step and saves computational time. The algorithm is based on an intelligent version of the Jaya algorithm, namely the self-adaptive Jaya algorithm (SAJA). In addition, we have designed a decision support system to analyze the sleep quality of any individual as well as perform automatic sleep staging.

2   Materials and Methods

A schematic diagram of the proposed automatic sleep staging method is shown in Fig. 1. First, we have collected data from the open database of Harvard-MIT, physionet.org, where the sleep staging of data is already leveled using the R&K method. The collected data is cleaned applying pre-processing. After that, the feature extraction is performed on the clean data which is followed by the application of an JOPS algorithm. Features are extracted from time domain (TD), frequency domain (FD), wavelet domain, and also from non-linear dynamics. JOPS will not only select the distinguishing features but also evaluate the value of hyper parameters of the classifiers, simultaneously. Then, the state-of-the-art classifiers will perform the classification on the optimized feature subsets to define the six-class sleep stages. These processes will result in an optimized sleep staging model. Finally, the performance of the optimized sleep staging model on the testing the dataset will be evaluated through different classification performance indexes i.e., accuracy, sensitivity, etc.

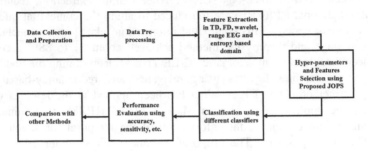

Fig. 1. Schematic diagram for the work flow of this study.

2.1 Data Collection and Preparation

Since sleep EDF is an open-source database, it has gained popularity among researchers working on sleep scoring. We have extracted the Harvard-MIT open source sleep EDF database available at https://physionet.org/ [13]. We have taken data for eight participants whose age ranges from twenty-one to thirty-five years. The participants were forbidden to have medicine. As shown in Table 1, the database is classified into two categories namely the sleep cassette indicated by '*SC*' and sleep telemetry indicated by '*ST*'. A dataset with *ST* as the prefix was collected in a hospital during the night using a mini-telemetry scheme [7] (Fig. 2).

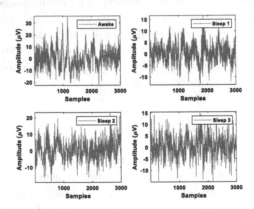

Fig. 2. Sample sleep wave classes found from MIT-BIH sleep EDF database.

Table 1. The three cases categorized in this paper.

Category	No. of class	Sleep stages	Dataset identity
Case-S	Two	AW, Sleep (RM, N1, N2, N3, N4)	sc4112e0, sc4102e0, sc4012e0, sc4002e0, st7132j0, st7121j0, st7052j0, st7022j0

The database is comprised of EEG signals taken via both Pz-Oz and Fpz-Cz channels. Between them, the Pz-Oz channel shows superior performance in automatic sleep scoring as per the earlier researches [7]. This motivates us to use the Pz-Oz channel-based EEG data. The sampling interval for this dataset is 0.01 s. In this paper, we have molded a particular sleep case (Case-S) by forming two special sleep classes considering AW, RM, N1, N2, N3, and N4, where N denotes the sleep stage; see Table 1. After forming the sleep class, the segmentation of the data is performed and thereby the epoch length (Awake epoch = 1726 and Sleep epoch = 14906) is set to be thirty seconds or, three thousand samples.

2.2 Data Pre-processing

The segmented data are then fed to 3rd order Butterworth filter in the frequency band ranging from 0.5 to 30 Hz since the significant sleep information exists in this region. The filtering process results in a clean, noise-free EEG signal more suitable for the automatic sleep staging model of this study.

2.3 Feature Extraction

We have extracted a total of 125 features, see [14] for details. These features are useful and have been used in other sleep studies [14].

2.4 Feature Selection: Using Proposed JOPS

A novel and intelligent FS method is proposed in this study for the optimum selection of features and hyper-parameters values at the same time. This would avoid the use of a separate optimization technique to evaluate the usefulness of hyper-parameters. The proposed JOPS algorithm is based on a smart version of Jaya algorithm i.e., SAJA. The proposed JOPS algorithm is described in the following subsection.

Proposed JOPS Algorithm. JOPS aims to perform the task of hyper-parameters and features selection simultaneously. FS is performed based on SAJA which is a variant of Jaya algorithm. Jaya algorithm introduced by Rao does not involve the regulation of any algorithm dependent variables [15]. The algorithm acts in a loop manner where each iteration shifts the value of the object function closer to the optimum solution. In this manner, this method attempts to achieve victory in attaining the optimum solution. This implies the name of this algorithm as 'Jaya' which means victory in Sanskrit. In this algorithm, N preliminary solutions are initiated following the maximum and minimum limits of processing variables. A probabilistic modification is accomplished for each processing variable in the solutions using the following equation.

$$B(x+1,y,z) = B(x,y,z) + R(x,y,1)\{B(x,y,s) - |B(x,y,z)|\} \\ - R(x,y,2)\{B(x,y,i) - |B(x,y,z)|\} \tag{1}$$

Here, x, y, and z denote the iteration number, variable number and probable solutions number.

SAJA is a smart version of Jaya. Similar to other population-oriented algorithms, the conventional Jaya involves the choice of the ordinary controlling variables of population volume and number of generations by the user. But, the selection of an optimum value for the population volume in diverse cases is quite problematic [16]. SAJA avoids this user-specific choice of population size, rather it automatically evaluates the population volume [17, 18]. SAJA starts by setting an original population size, $U = 10 \times c$, where c is the no. of design variables. In each iteration until the stopping condition of the algorithm fulfilled, the population size is updated as follows [17, 18]:

$$U_{updated} = round(U_{previous} + c \times U_{previous}) \tag{2}$$

Here, the value of c ranges from -0.5 to $+0.5$ and it acts as a tuning parameter by either increasing or decreasing the population size. A flowchart of the proposed JOPS algorithm is shown in Fig. 3.

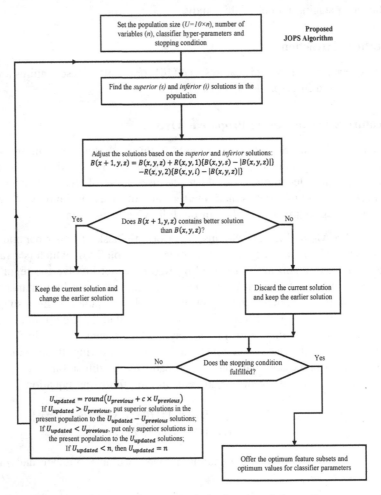

Fig. 3. Flowchart for the proposed Jaya Optimization based hyper-Parameter and feature Selection (JOPS) algorithm.

Hyper-parameters are tunable variables of classifiers which require proper tuning to get optimum performance from any machine learning model. These parameters are classifier specific. We have used KNN and linear SVM as they have used in other studies for feature selection [19]. The controlling parameters of KNN are no. of neighbors (K), distance function (e.g. Euclidean or Manhattan), distance weight (e.g., equal, inverse, squared inverse) and for linear SVM the controlling parameters Cost (C) parameters that regularize the classifiers.

2.5 Performance Evaluation

Multiple performance indices are assessed for the performance evaluation of the classifiers in this study. These indices include accuracy, error, sensitivity, specificity, and F1-score.

3 Results and Discussion

This study proposed JOPS algorithm for feature and hyper-parameter selection and used this algorithm for sleep-wake classification by following the methodology presented above. To accomplish this, 70% of the total data was used for training and validation purposes and 30% of the data is used for testing purposes. Table 2 shows the performance of JOPS algorithm on training, validation, and testing dataset. It can be seen that, in the case of KNN, both sensitivity and F1 Score on training dataset are 100% whereas on validation dataset and test dataset these values are 98.15%, 97.23%, and 98.17%, 97.23%, respectively. On the other hand, in the case of SVM, sensitivity and F1 Score on training dataset are 98.47% and 97.31% whereas on the validation dataset and test dataset these values are 98.30%, 97.30%, and 98.61%, 97.17%, respectively.

Table 2. Performance analysis of KNN and SVM using JOPS algorithm.

	Training results		Validation results		Test results	
Classifiers	KNN	SVM	KNN	SVM	KNN	SVM
Accuracy (%)	100	95.13	94.99	95.10	94.99	94.85
Error (%)	0	4.871	5.01	4.92	5.012	5.152
Sensitivity (%)	100	98.47	98.15	98.30	98.17	98.61
Specificity (%)	100	66.31	67.77	67.20	67.5	62.28
F1_score (%)	100	97.31	97.23	97.30	97.23	97.17

As the dataset was collected on the only 8 subjects, the 10-fold cross validation[1] was also performed. The accuracy of the 10-fold cross-validation has been used for box-plotting and the statistically significant test has been performed by t-test and finally, p value is reported in this study. It can be seen from the boxplot presented in Fig. 4 that the classification accuracy of SVM is higher than KNN which is statistically significant as the p value is 0.0009.

The proposed JOPS algorithm is compared with other state-of-the-art optimization algorithm used in the feature selection such as genetic algorithm (GA) [20, 21] and differential evaluation [19]. It can be seen from Table 3 that the training accuracy using our proposed JOPS was 100% and 95.13% for KNN and SVM classifiers, respectively. On the other hand, GA based feature selection provides 96.87% and 95.20% accuracy for KNN and SVM classifiers, respectively. The DE based feature selection yielded 96.95% and 95.00% accuracy. Moreover, compared to GA and DE based feature selection our proposed algorithm sleeted a moderate number of features. The classification performance without FS yielded lower accuracy using KNN and provided similar accuracy using SVM.

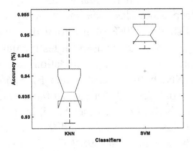

Fig. 4. Box plot for sleep wake classification for KNN and SVM classifiers.

Table 3. Comparison with other optimization algorithms and without feature selection (FS).

	JOPS optimization		GA based [20, 21]		DE based [19]		Without FS	
Classifiers	KNN	SVM	KNN	SVM	KNN	SVM	KNN	SVM
Accuracy	100	95.13	96.87	95.20	96.95	95.00	94.41	95.45
Error	0.00	4.87	3.13	4.80	3.05	5.00	5.59	4.51
No. of selected features	27	55	48	62	20	20	125	125

---

[1] In 10-fold cross validation, one-fold is used for testing and nine other folds are used for training and repeated ten times so that each fold i.e. whole dataset is tested.

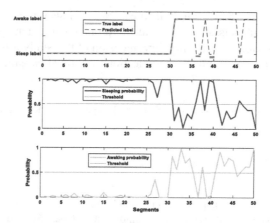

Fig. 5. A DSS for sleep-wake classification. (Color figure online)

Regarding the comparison with other studies relevant to sleep-wake classification, the fuzzy logic-based iterative method provided 95.4%, statistical features and bagging provided 95.04%, and PSD of single-channel EEG and ANN-based method 96.90%. Our approach is very similar to their works. The intention of this study is the simultaneous selection of classifier hyper parameter and feature subset.

We have provided a decision support system using our proposed algorithm. A decision support system (DSS) can be built to support clinical staffs. We have created a program that visually presents the probable patient state, in terms of posterior probabilities. An example of hypnograms consisting of 50 epochs generated by the machine (i.e., the proposed method) and a sleep expert is shown in Fig. 5. The misclassification is marked as red color. In addition, the probability of sleep and awake have also been shown. The 2nd subplot shows the sleeping probability. The sleeping probability ≥ 0.5 indicates that the subject is in sleep stage and sleeping probability <0.5 indicates the subject has less chance to stay sleep stage. The 3rd subplot can be interpreted in the similar way for awaking stage. In this way, the intensity of sleeping e.g., deep sleep, mild sleep etc. can be measured from this DSS.

4 Conclusion

This paper presents a novel algorithm for simultaneously select the optimal classifier hyper-parameter and optimal features namely, the JOPS algorithm from the high dimensional feature set. It is then applied to the EEG based sleep-wake classification. The KNN and SVM were applied in this study. The 10-fold cross-validation results provide the average accuracy for KNN and SVM of 93.77% and 95% with a standard deviation of ±0.0065 and ±0.0041, respectively. Only two classifiers have been used in this study. The DSS created by this study is also useful to sleep expert and needs further experiment to apply in clinical settings. Unlike GA and DE based feature selection, JOPS is very simple and adaptive and therefore, could be useful for non-specialist user. It is necessary to assess the JOPS performance with other classifiers such as XGboost, kernel KNN, random forest, etc. It is also necessary to use a larger database with more subjects and other real-life problems to examine the efficiency of the JOPS algorithm. However, the primary intension of this study is to provide a simple but adaptive algorithm for simultaneous selection of optimal classifier hyper-parameter and optimal features.

Acknowledgements. This work is a part of the work supported by Khulna University Research Cell (KURC).

References

1. Littman, A.J., et al.: Sleep, ghrelin, leptin and changes in body weight during a 1-year moderate-intensity physical activity intervention. Int. J. Obes. **31**, 466–475 (2007)
2. Park, H.-J., Oh, J.-S., Jeong, D.-U., Park, K.-S.: Automated sleep stage scoring using hybrid rule- and case-based reasoning. Comput. Biomed. Res. **33**, 330–349 (2000)
3. Yeh, Z.-T., Chiang, R.P.-Y., Kang, S.-C., Chiang, C.-H.: Development of the insomnia screening scale based on ICSD-II. Int. J. Psychiatry Clin. Pract. **16**, 259–267 (2012)
4. Leger, D., Pandi-Perumal, S., Healthcare, I.: Review of sleep disorders: their impact on public health. Public Health **30**, 92161 (2007)
5. Ram, S., Seirawan, H., Kumar, S.K.S., Clark, G.T.: Prevalence and impact of sleep disorders and sleep habits in the United States. Sleep Breath. **14**, 63–70 (2010). https://doi.org/10.1007/s11325-009-0281-3
6. Vaughn, B.V., Giallanza, P.: Technical review of polysomnography. Chest **134**, 1310–1319 (2008)
7. Hassan, A.R., Bhuiyan, M.I.H.: Automatic sleep stage classification. In: 2nd International Conference on Electrical Information and Communication Technologies (EICT), pp. 211–216 (2015)
8. Hassan, A.R., Bhuiyan, M.I.H.: A decision support system for automatic sleep staging from EEG signals using tunable Q-factor wavelet transform and spectral features. J. Neurosci. Methods **271**, 107–118 (2016)
9. Rodríguez-Sotelo, J.L., Osorio-Forero, A., Jiménez-Rodríguez, A., Cuesta-Frau, D., Cirugeda-Roldán, E., Peluffo, D.: Automatic sleep stages classification using EEG entropy features and unsupervised pattern analysis techniques. Entropy **16**, 6573–6589 (2014)
10. Chen, K., Zhang, C., Ma, J., Wang, G., Zhang, J.: Sleep staging from single-channel EEG with multi-scale feature and contextual information. Sleep Breath. **23**(4), 1159–1167 (2019). https://doi.org/10.1007/s11325-019-01789-4
11. Ghimatgar, H., Kazemi, K., Helfroush, M.S., Aarabi, A.: An automatic single-channel EEG-based sleep stage scoring method based on hidden Markov Model. J. Neurosci. Methods **324**, 108320 (2019)
12. Tiwari, V., Jain, S.C.: An optimal feature selection method for histopathology tissue image classification using adaptive jaya algorithm. Evol. Intel. 1–14 (2019). https://doi.org/10.1007/s12065-019-00205-w
13. Hassan, A.R., Bhuiyan, M.I.H.: Automated identification of sleep states from EEG signals by means of ensemble empirical mode decomposition and random under sampling boosting. Comput. Methods Programs Biomed. **140**, 201–210 (2017)

14. Rahman, M.A., Hossain, M.A., Kabir, M.R., Sani, M.H., Abdullah Al, M., Awal, M.A.: Optimization of sleep stage classification using single-channel EEG signals. In: 2019 4th International Conference on Electrical Information and Communication Technology (EICT), pp. 1–6 (2019)
15. Rao, R.: Jaya: a simple and new optimization algorithm for solving constrained and unconstrained optimization problems. Int. J. Ind. Eng. Comput. 7, 19–34 (2016)
16. Teo, J.: Exploring dynamic self-adaptive populations in differential evolution. Soft. Comput. 10, 673–686 (2006). https://doi.org/10.1007/s00500-005-0537-1
17. Rao, R.V., Rai, D.P., Balic, J.: A multi-objective algorithm for optimization of modern machining processes. Eng. Appl. Artif. Intell. 61, 103–125 (2017)
18. Venkata Rao, R., Saroj, A.: A self-adaptive multi-population based Jaya algorithm for engineering optimization. Swarm Evol. Comput. 37, 1–26 (2017)
19. Khushaba, R.N., Al-Ani, A., Al-Jumaily, A.: Feature subset selection using differential evolution and a statistical repair mechanism. Expert Syst. Appl. 38, 11515–11526 (2011)
20. Siddiqi, U.F., Sait, S.M., Kaynak, O.: Genetic algorithm for the mutual information-based feature selection in univariate time series data. IEEE Access 8, 9597–9609 (2020)
21. Babatunde, O.H., Armstrong, L.: A genetic Algorithm-Based feature selection. Br. J. Math. Comput. Sci. 5, 889–905 (2014)

Peer-Reviewed Abstracts Presented at the 13th International Conference on Brain Informatics (BI2020), September 19, 2020, Held Virtually

Neurosymbolic Expert System for Disorders of Consciousness

Paola Di Maio ⓘD

Center for Systems, Knowledge Representation and Neuroscience,
Taitung, 950001, Taiwan
paola.dimaio@gmail.com

Abstract. Thanks to the increased availability of neuroscience technologies and data, it is now possible to study a wide range of brain and mind states using available images and data analysis tools. Disorders of Consciousness (DOC) are observed mainly in patients suffering from brain injury or other head trauma. Equivalent or similar symptoms, however, are also present in a range of other disorders, including schizophrenia autism and locked-in syndrome. There is a need to widen the applicability of diagnoses to broader classes of patients, including individuals affected by emotional traumas, and to widen the diagnosing modality include broader sets of parameters by leveraging the convergence of multiple approaches, from neurology to psychiatry to behaviour and cognitive from multiple cases. As the knowledge required for extensive and complex navigation of diagnostic rules is incremental, an expert system is conceived to support both the integration, navigation and reasoning of relevant knowledge sets.

This work introduces the rationale, motivation and outline of a modular web based expert system (ES) that facilitates the integration of multiple clinical perspectives (e.g., cognitive, behavioural and neurological) using neurosymbolic knowledge integration and neurules, a hybrid logical construct aimed at leveraging symbolic and neurosymbolic representation. This expert system can be used in support of remote consultations and diagnostics.

Keywords: Disorder of consciousness · Awareness · Expert system · Neurosymbolic knowledge integration

The Resolution Matrix for Visualizing Functional Network Connectivity

Keith Dillon

University of New Haven, 300 Boston Post Rd, West Haven, CT 06516, USA
kdillon@newhaven.edu

Abstract. The resolution matrix is a mathematical tool for analyzing inverse problems such as computational imaging systems. When treating network connectivity estimation as an inverse problem, the resolution matrix describes the degree to which network nodes and edges can be resolved. This is useful both for quantifying robustness of the network estimate, as well as identifying correlated activity. Theoretically, there is a close relationship between the resolution matrix and the partial correlation estimates defining Gaussian graphical models. Univariate correlation describes the similarity between signals collected from different points, which would conceptually be similar to a resolution cell describing the blurring of points together. However, the act of computationally reconstructing the image unmixes this blurring to the degree possible, hence resolution (and partial correlation) provide a kind of sharpened estimate as compared to univariate correlation. While the goal of resolution estimation in imaging is to identify which regions are unresolvable due to physical limitations of the imaging system, partial correlation is used to suggest network relations such as causality. In application to networks, therefore, resolution provides a combination of both kinds of information. We analyzed the resolution matrix for functional MRI data from the Human Connectome project. We find that common metrics of the resolution metric can be used to identify networked activity, yielding patterns reminiscent of well-known networks such as the default-mode and frontoparietal networks. These two networks in particular were originally defined as being positively correlated, while being negatively correlated between each other. Further, Independent component analysis generally separated the frontoparietal network into a unilateral pair. However, from the perspective of resolution cells, we find a different combination of regions and asymmetry, with a symmetric network of lateral regions, and an asymmetric network with symmetric medial regions and asymmetric lateral regions.

Keywords: Resolution · Brain networks · Functional MRI

Knowledge Representation for Neuroscience

Paola Di Maio ⓘD

Center for Systems, Knowledge Representation and Neuroscience, Taitung,
950001, Taiwan
paola.dimaio@gmail.com

Abstract. As artificial intelligence is increasingly used to perform analysis of vast amounts of brain data, the relationship between KR (Knowledge Representation) and Neuroscience is becoming stronger and can be mapped across several dimensions. Following up on past developments (e.g., Brain Informatics conference 2019, held at Haikou, China), it is important to continue to characterize aspects of the complex but necessary relationship between KR (as in Artificial Intelligence) and Neuroscience. The research published in the past evaluated a broad range of state-of-the-art Artificial Neural Network (ANN) models on the match of their internal representations to 84 neural datasets from three humans spanned all major classes of existing language models and included embedding models. It concluded that a key missing piece in scholarly literature in the mechanistic modeling of human language processing is a more detailed mapping from model components onto brain anatomy. In particular, aside from the general targeting of the fronto-temporal language network, it is unclear which parts of a model map onto which components of the brain's language processing mechanisms. In models of vision, for instance, attempts are made to map ANN layers and neurons onto cortical regions and sub-regions. However, a similar mapping is not yet established in language beyond the broad distinction between perceptual processing and higher-level linguistic interpretation. It is therefore important to seek to explore paths and obstacles to the brain-to-model mapping taking a systems neuroscience view. The correspondence between KR and various aspects of Neuroscience needs to be explored in particular with respect to the importance of higher brain functions such as consciousness, free will and metacognition. Similarly, illustration of the challenges of identifying appropriate levels of abstraction and functional/systemic knowledge boundaries (network view vs. systems view), overview of data standards/model integration conceptual/ontological mapping considerations are also important.

Keywords: Knowledge representation · Neuroscience · Brain to model

Epileptic Seizures Could Be Abated in Advance by Changing the Synchronicity and Directionality of Onset Propagation with Stimulation

Denggui Fan (ID)

University of Science and Technology Beijing, Haidian District, Beijing 100083,
China
worldfandenggui@163.com

Abstract. Many neurological and psychiatric diseases are associated with clinically detectable, altered brain dynamics. To better understand seizure onset and propagation, as well as propose an effective seizure interfering strategy, we need to identify the coherence and transferring process of the dynamic information evolutions within the epileptogenic network. In this paper, we employ a simple methodology to successively estimate the synchronicity and directionality over time between signals from different brain areas. First, the reliability of this method is numerically assessed with a coupled mass neural model, which shows that this estimating method is effective for expressing the causality characteristics of the simulated epileptic signals. Then this method is applied to investigate the foci localization and its synchronous evolution based on the intracranial human EEG recordings. It is shown that the dominant, recessive and extended seizure foci as well as their propagation paths could be detected and traced through this estimation method for synchronicity and directionality. In addition, the aberrant brain activity, in principle, can be restored through electrical stimulation. It is verified that the synchronicity and directionality can be changed with the deep brain stimulation (DBS) applied on the dominant foci using the spatiotemporally extended neural model network. In particular, the dominant and extended seizure foci vanish when the recessive focus is removed or destroyed by DBS. These results suggest that the coherence and transferring process of brain information evolutions can be dynamically identified, and also computationally evidence the effect of DBS on the seizure control, and also provide new insights into the seizure prediction and detection and DBS therapy.

Keywords: Epileptic seizures · Mean-field model · Synchronicity and directionality · Deep brain stimulation (DBS) · Seizure abatement

Author Index

Printed in the United States
By Bookmasters